RETHINKING ECONOMIC EVOLUTION

Wherever possible, the articles in these volumes have been reproduced as originally published using facsimile reproduction, inclusive of footnotes and pagination to facilitate ease of reference.

For a full list of all Edward Elgar published titles visit our website at
www.e-elgar.com

Rethinking Economic Evolution

Essays on Economic Change and its Theory

Ulrich Witt

Director Emeritus of the Evolutionary Economics Research Group, Max Planck Institute of Economics, Germany and Adjunct Professor, Griffith Business School, Griffith University, Australia

EE Edward Elgar
PUBLISHING

Cheltenham, UK • Northampton, MA, USA

Published by
Edward Elgar Publishing Limited
The Lypiatts
15 Lansdown Road
Cheltenham
Glos GL50 2JA
UK

Edward Elgar Publishing, Inc.
William Pratt House
9 Dewey Court
Northampton
Massachusetts 01060
USA

A catalogue record for this book
is available from the British Library

Library of Congress Control Number: 2016931513

This book is available electronically in the **Elgar**online
Economics subject collection
DOI 10.337/9781785365072

ISBN 978 1 84844 304 4 (cased)
ISBN 978 1 78536 507 2 (eBook)

Contents

PART I   THE ROAD MAP FOR EVOLUTIONARY ECONOMICS

PART II   THE ROLE OF NOVELTY FOR EVOLUTION AND EVOLUTIONARY METHODOLOGY

PART III   EVOLUTIONARY THINKING AT WORK

Acknowledgements

The editor and publishers wish to thank the authors and the following publishers who have kindly given permission for the use of copyright material.

Cambridge University Press for excerpt: Ulrich Witt (2008), 'Evolutionary Economics and Psychology', in Alan Lewis (ed.), *The Cambridge Handbook of Psychology and Economic Behaviour*, Chapter 20, 493–511.

Cambridge University Press via the Copyright Clearance Center's RightsLink service for article: Ulrich Witt (2008), 'Observational Learning, Group Selection, and Societal Evolution', *Journal of Institutional Economics*, **4** (1), April, 1–24.

Elsevier Ltd via the Copyright Clearance Center for articles: Ulrich Witt (2005), '"Production" in Nature and Production in the Economy—Second Thoughts about Some Basic Economic Concepts', *Structural Change and Economic Dynamics*, **16** (2), June, 165–79; Ulrich Witt (2009), 'Propositions about Novelty', *Journal of Economic Behavior and Organization*, **70** (1/2), May, 311–20; Ulrich Witt (2011), 'The Dynamics of Consumer Behavior and the Transition to Sustainable Consumption Patterns', *Environmental Innovation and Societal Transitions*, **1** (1), June, 109–14.

Max Planck Institute of Economics for article: Ulrich Witt (1996), 'A "Darwinian Revolution" in Economics?', *Journal of Institutional and Theoretical Economics*, **152** (4), December, 707–15.

Palgrave Macmillan for excerpt: Ulrich Witt (2008), 'Evolutionary Economics', in Steven N. Durlauf and Lawrence E. Blume (eds), *The New Palgrave Dictionary of Economics, Second Edition*, 67–73.

Springer Science and Business Media B.V. via the Copyright Clearance Center's RightsLink service for article: Ulrich Witt (2003), 'Economic Policy Making in Evolutionary Perspective', *Journal of Evolutionary Economics*, **13** (2), April, 77–94; Ulrich Witt and Thomas Brenner (2008), 'Output Dynamics, Flow Equilibria and Structural Change—A Prolegomenon to Evolutionary Macroeconomics', *Journal of Evolutionary Economics*, **18** (2), April, 249–60; Ulrich Witt (2008), 'What is Specific about Evolutionary Economics?', *Journal of Evolutionary Economics*, **18** (5), October, 547–75.

Taylor & Francis Ltd (www.tandf.co.uk) via the Copyright Clearance Center's RightsLink service for articles: Ulrich Witt (2002), 'How Evolutionary is Schumpeter's Theory of Economic Development?', *Industry and Innovation*, **9** (1/2), April/August, 7–22; Ulrich Witt (2004), 'On the Proper Interpretation of "Evolution" in Economics and Its Implications for

Production Theory', *Journal of Economic Methodology*, **11** (2), June, 125–46; Ulrich Witt (2009), 'Novelty and the Bounds of Unknowledge in Economics', *Journal of Economic Methodology*, **16** (4) December, 361–75.

Ulrich Witt for his own work: (2003), 'Generic Features of Evolution and Its Continuity: A Transdisciplinary Perspective', *Theoria*, **18** (3), 273–88.

Introduction: The Evolutionary Way of Thinking in Economics[1]

Ulrich Witt

Can we gain new insights about the human economy, its long term development, and its future by putting on the looking glasses of the theory of evolution? More than a century ago, when the Darwinian theory of natural selection began to thrive, Thorsten Veblen (1898) suggested to do just this. In the study of the life sciences in general and the study of human behavior in particular, the Darwinian theory indeed provides a fruitful and by now generally accepted, overarching frame of reference for research (see Brown and Richerson 2014). Not so in economics. Canonical economic theory is committed instead to the rational actor model and the theory of general equilibrium (see, for example, Mas-Colell et al. 1995). Both notions are rooted in classical, Newtonian mechanics (Mirowski 1989) which pre-dated the Darwinian revolution in the sciences. Not surprisingly, in the canonical economic perspective, the economy is usually seen as a sphere of reality for which the theory of evolution has little, if any, significance. Can such a perspective do justice to the observable unfolding of the economy, its growth and incessant transformations?

As a matter of fact, ever new products, technologies, organizations, institutions are thought up and tried out. They fuel an endless competitive struggle in which earlier vintages are outcompeted and the extant natural and social environment is transformed. New firms, industries, and markets emerge and grow while others stagnate or decline. In a relentless collective adaptation, institutions are designed and redesigned under economic and political pressures and made new. All this looks like a process of evolutionary change, albeit one that has a genuine new quality: it is *cultural* evolution. Under the influence of human creativity and deliberation it transforms the economy at a much higher pace than natural selection could do. Indeed, in cultural evolution, reproductive success under natural selection is only a long term shaping force or – in the language of multi-level selection theory – selection criterion (see Wilson 2015). In the short run, other, human-made forces shape the unfolding of the economy.

Several questions thus arise when an attempt is made to use the looking glasses of an evolutionary theory for gaining new insights on the economy. What are the principles governing economic change? What relevance does the Darwinian theory have for these principles? How can these principles help to improve economic theory? The chapters in the present volume seek to provide answers to these and other questions, which an evolutionary approach to economics faces. To pave the ground for the discussion, Part I of the book (*Chapters 1 to 4*) addresses three challenges confronting the application of evolutionary thinking in the economic context. First we need to come to grips with the fact that, in the literature, a variety of sometimes incommensurable interpretations of an evolutionary approach to economics exist. A second, albeit related, challenge is to identify what particular conditions characterize economic evolution. Do these conditions imply that the overarching evolutionary theory in the sciences is irrelevant for evolutionary theorizing in economics? The third challenge is to establish where and how evolutionary theorizing deviates from canonical (textbook) economics. Sections 1, 2, and 3 of this introductory chapter take up each of these three challenges in turn.

Sections 4 and 5 offer a preview of Part II of the book (*Chapters 5 to 8*). Center stage in this part is the role of novelty as a cause of evolutionary change. Section 4 outlines the epistemological and methodological problems, which the emergence of novelty implies for evolutionary theorizing. In the economic context, novelty comes in the form of discoveries, inventions, and innovations. Is their emergence to be treated as an exogenous shock or is it endogenous to the process of economic change? Accordingly the question is whether explaining the emergence is part of the task of economic theory. If so, what do we know about discoveries, inventions, and innovations and about how they come about?

Section 5 extends the perspective beyond the domain of economics. As argued later in the book, if novelty is a universal driver of evolution, its emergence and diffusion are abstract concepts – in fact, in a wider sense, Schumpeterian principles – by which the unfolding processes can be logically structured. However, especially the emergence of novelty plays a pivotal role also in the theory of self-organization. The point to be discussed then is how the emergence and diffusion of novelty relate to the principles of variation, selection, and replication which are often suggested for characterizing evolution in abstract terms. Put differently, given their shared interest in the emergence of novelty, it can be asked how self-organization and evolution – and the corresponding two paradigmatic interpretative frames in the sciences – relate to each other.

The subsequent Section 6 in this Introduction offers an outlook on Part III of the book (*Chapters 9 to 14*). This part sets out to show in an exemplary fashion what new insights an evolutionary way of thinking in economics can contribute. The cases to be discussed are taken from diverse research fields. Consumer behavior and the historical growth of consumption expenditures are discussed, as are the institutional conditions of cooperation and exchange. Further topics are the evolution of production technology, macroeconomic dynamics, and, last but not least, the theory of economic policymaking. Some conclusions are finally offered in Section 7.

1. Evolutionary economics – coping with the patchwork of concepts and theories

Evolutionary thought has been gaining more attention in economics in recent years (Silva and Teixeira 2009; Hodgson et al. 2014). However, the interpretation of the attribute 'evolutionary' and, correspondingly, the concepts and models that are used vary substantially. While canonical economics presents itself as a coherent paradigmatic theory of optimization and general equilibrium, the contributions to evolutionary thinking in economics take the form of a patchwork of different ideas diversely pursued by different authors. Many of them agree, though, in their rejection of exactly the notions of optimization and general equilibrium as unsuitable for evolutionary theorizing.[2] Agreeing on what needs to be rejected is, of course, no effective substitute for developing a coherent alternative. In this respect not much has changed since Veblen's (1898) initial plea for 'evolutionary economics' which he supposed to be the alternative to the neoclassical economic theory of his time.

Today 'evolutionary economics' is frequently associated with the Neo-Schumpeterian interpretation which is outlined in *Chapter 1* of this volume. The Neo-Schumpeterians belong to those authors who oppose the rational choice framework and its focus on equilibrium states. Starting with Nelson and Winter (1982), they use a loose analogy to natural selection theory to instead describe the economy as being subject to an incessant transformation process. This process is argued not to be under rational control in any strict sense (see Nelson and Winter 2002; Metcalfe 2008; Winter 2014). The analogy to natural selection theory is based on a synthesis of two separate strands of thought. The first gives the school its name: it is Schumpeter's (1942) theory of innovative capitalism. Its thematic focus is on innovation competition, technical progress, and the growth of firms and industries.

The second strand of thought is the behavioral theory of the firm. This theory goes back to March and Simon (1958) and Cyert and March (1963) and draws on their concept of bounded rationality. According to that theory, firms heavily rely on the use of rules-of-thumb and organizational routines in their daily operations rather than systematic, discretionary rational decision-making. Nelson and Winter start from the assumption that the routines which the firms use are organizational inertia. If so, the profits of the firms can be argued to depend on how well-adapted the routines are to the competitive conditions under which the firms operate. Moreover, if profit differences between firms translate into corresponding differences in the firms' growth rates, the better adapted routines can be expected to become more prevalent within the industry. This means that firms using the right routines also grow in market share. In contrast, firms using less well-adapted routines lose in market share and eventually exit the market – and with them their routines. What matters for explaining economic change is thus the population level rather than the individual level.

The connection to Schumpeter's theory of innovative capitalism is made by interpreting the innovative economic process as a process of variation of firm routines. This is in noteworthy contrast to Schumpeter's (2002[1912]) explicit rejection of any biological analogies. Nelson and Winter and their Neo-Schumpeterian followers conceptualize the innovative transformation process in terms of an analogy to the theory of natural selection. They submit that innovations change the composition of routines in the industry's overall 'routine pool' much like mutations in the gene code of an individual organism change the distribution in the gene pool of a species. Over time, the forces of market competition then discriminate against firms with less well adapted routines. These routines tend to be driven out of the 'routine pool' like natural selection winnows out less fit genes.[3] Changes in the composition of an industry's 'routine pool' are thus seen as adaptions not taking place at the firm level but at the industry level.

The loose analogy to natural selection models and algorithms and the corresponding 'population thinking' are the distinctive features of Neo-Schumpeterian approach (Metcalfe 2008). Whether, and, if so, how economic evolution relates to evolution on this planet more generally and cultural evolution in particular is not considered. The economic sphere of reality is treated as if it were a sphere of its own, distinct from the one for which the Darwinian theory of natural selection is directly relevant. Accordingly, no attempt is made to clarify what relevance the overarching interpretative frame of evolutionary research in the sciences might have for economics. Therefore, meaning which the attribute 'evolutionary' economics has for the Neo-Schumpeterians differs from, for example, that in evolutionary psychology and evolutionary anthropology.

As is argued in *Chapters 2* and *3* of this volume, it can of course be asked why the Darwinian theory of evolution – properly extended in order to reflect the significant influence of culture – should not be considered relevant for the economic domain. Humans as economic agents are an outcome of evolution, after all. Why then not adopt the 'naturalistic' perspective on economic activities which the theory of evolution suggests?[4]

While not on the Neo-Schumpeterian agenda, this question was center stage in Veblen's (1898) version of 'evolutionary economics'. Veblen had been as critical of the rational choice assumption underlying the neoclassical theory of his time as Neo-Schumpeterians are of its present-day variants. But he drew different conclusions from his critique. The Neo-Schumpeterians seek to solve the problem at a rather formal level. Making metaphorical use of, or constructing analogies to, the Darwinian theory, they substitute population-based selection algorithms for the discarded individual optimization algorithm. In contrast, Veblen thought of directly bringing to bear the substance of the Darwinian theory to develop a new way of thinking about the human economy. More specifically, Veblen (1899, 1914) traced the determinants of economic behavior back to instinct (genetic influences) and habit (the influence of cultural learning) and explored their role in the evolution of economic institutions.[5]

Once a naturalistic approach has been adopted, long term economic evolution can be re-cast as a history of the creative struggle of a unique species trying to expand its natural niche. The roots of such behavior can accordingly be identified in innate survival strategies that emerged under natural selection pressure when the ancestors of modern humans had to adapt to the ancestral environment. Seeing evolutionary economic change in such a long term perspective, further contributions to evolutionary thinking in economics come to mind. Among them, for example, are Hayek's (1988) theory of societal evolution by group selection (see *Chapter 11* in this volume), North's (1997) particular brand of evolutionary institutionalism, and Georgescu-Roegen's (1971) work on the ecological constraints of economic evolution (see Gowdy 1994 for a discussion).

Chapter 4 in the present volume is devoted to drawing up a road map for an encompassing conception of evolutionary economics in which all these contributions have a place. For navigating purposes two criteria are introduced. The first concerns, what is called in the philosophy of science, the *heuristic* that an author uses. This refers to the interpretative frame that an author has in mind when she reflects on 'evolution'. This frame shapes the often tacit way in which she derives her 'evolutionary' hypotheses. As far as the heuristic is concerned, it turns out that one group of authors makes use of an abstract reduction of the Darwinian theory to three general principles: variation, selection, and replication. These principles provide a heuristic scheme originally suggested by Campbell (1965) for structuring evolutionary processes of whatever kind.

There is room for interpretation of this scheme, of course. Neo-Schumpeterians apply the three principles as inspiration for constructing their analogies between natural and economic selection (see Nelson 2006). For the proponents of Generalized Darwinism the three principles represent the analytical core of any evolutionary theory whatsoever (Hodgson and Knudsen 2010). In contrast to the group of adherents of Campbell's scheme, other authors like Schumpeter (2002[1912]) deny the Darwinian theory any relevance for understanding economic development. Schumpeter instead draws upon a heuristic frame originally developed in the 19th-century diffusionism (see Section 4 below). This frame focuses on the interplay of two other principles, namely the emergence and diffusion of novelty, in the evolution of human societies.

The second aspect dealt with in *Chapter 4* relates to the *ontological* assumptions often only implicitly made by the various authors. These assumptions determine how reality is represented in a theory either by way of a monistic or a dualistic ontology. Roughly speaking, a dualistic ontology separates the sphere of nature from the sphere of cultural phenomena. The latter is given a distinct status: it is considered uniquely dependent on the exercise of the human mind. In contrast, a monistic ontology rejects the assumption of two separate spheres of reality. Schumpeter and the Neo-Schumpeterians make no statement of their ontological position. But by explicitly denying the Darwinian theory any relevance for the economic sphere (as Schumpeter does) or completely ignoring it (as the Neo-Schumpeterians do) they act as if they were ontological dualists. In contrast, authors like Veblen, Georgescu-Roegen, and, in his late works, Hayek take an explicit monistic position. For them, evolution in nature and the corresponding theory are relevant for understanding the evolution of the economy. Since ontology and heuristics are two independent features of evolutionary theories of economic change, the different combinations of these features are used in *Chapter 4* for developing a typology of these theories.[6]

2. Explaining economic evolution – how relevant is the Darwinian theory?

As discussed in the preceding section, whether and, if so, how evolution in nature and evolution in the economy relate to each other is a matter of controversy. So, too, is the question of whether or not the Darwinian theory applies to explaining evolution in the economy as the overarching scientific framework. If evolution in nature and evolution in the economy are two entirely different pairs of shoes, the Darwinian theory can at best be relevant for the economic domain as an inspiration for constructing analogies. (This is the Neo-Schumpeterian position.) However, analogies of this kind are not without problems. This has been pinpointed by Winter (1964) with his – rhetorical – question regarding the economic analogue: 'what are the genes?'[7] Of course, there is neither anything in the economy that is comparable to the genes of natural organisms. Nor do products, technologies, industries, or institutions 'reproduce' in the sense understood by biology. Evolution operates via very different transformation mechanisms in the biological and the economic domain. The question therefore arises how far one can expect to get in explaining economic evolution by constructing analogies to the theory of natural selection.

If, alternatively, evolution in nature and in the economy is understood as representing interconnected processes, a different perspective emerges. Its focus is not on seeking analogies but on recognizing the continuity of the evolutionary adaptation process on this planet. The process started with the evolution of living nature and continues with the co-evolution of nature and human culture. Even though cultural evolution seems to unfold and shape the human economy according to its own rules and adaptation criteria, this process is embedded in, and continues to be constrained by, the evolution of nature. Such a 'continuity hypothesis', discussed in more detail in *Chapter 3*, obviously implies a monistic ontology.

The reason why cultural or, for that matter, economic evolution seems to follow its own rules is the pervasive role played in these forms of evolution by human creativity, learning, deliberation, symbolic communication, and knowledge accumulation.[8] In the span of just one generation, multitudes of new products, technologies, industries, and institutions can now be purposefully created. Both creativity and knowledge that is being accumulated and broadly accessible are the basis of the human capacity to adapt to changing physical and social constraints in ever shorter periods of time. As a consequence, cultural/economic evolution has a much faster pace than evolution guided by natural selection. It is also characterized by a much higher rate of variation.

Differences between the two forms of evolution also concern the criteria that govern their adaptation processes. In evolutionary biology, the adaption criterion is the value of the heritable characteristics of an organism or a population for enhancing survival and having offspring, in short called their 'adaptive value'. It is measurable in terms of reproductive fitness of the organism or population carrying those characteristics. In theories of cultural evolution, including evolutionary economics, the concept of adaption and, hence, the corresponding criterion is much less clear. What is being improved here in the process of evolution?

Consider human societies living in an environment that implies a relatively high selection pressure on their members. Under such conditions, the adaptation criterion also governing the cultural evolution of these societies is likely to be reproductive fitness, that is, whether and how culturally acquired characteristics of human behavior enhance survival and having offspring. However, owing to the accomplishments of their cultural and economic evolution, many societies have gained control over their environment to such an extent that selection pressure on their members has slackened. Once this happens, reproductive fitness can be expected to lose its predominant role as adaptation criterion. In its stead, room seems to open up for a multitude of domain-specific adaptation criteria of which many may themselves be culturally contingent.

What can be said more specifically about the criterion governing the adaptation processes in economic evolution? Is it possible at all that there is one unique criterion, given that these adaptation processes represent the multitude of individually pursued attempts to accomplish one's goals – whatever these goals are? An answer to the question confronts the same challenge that economic theory faces with the task of substantiating the notion of welfare as a single criterion for economic progress. To derive more specific information we can take recourse to the continuity hypothesis and explore some aspects of human behavior that evolved in human phylogeny and now shape and constrain the paths that cultural and economic evolution can take.

The point of departure thus is the hypothesis that the human genetic endowment includes some motivational dispositions, that is, inclinations to act (drives, needs, emotions, see *Chapter 9*), that have emerged in ancestral times under selection pressure. These innate motivational dispositions are likely to have had adaptive value, in those times, in the sense of reproductive fitness.[9] The motivational dispositions are still present, and widely shared (with the usual genetic variance), within the human population today. They can be expected to influence the goals that are pursued in the individual adaptation strategies in economic evolution even where reproductive fitness itself is no longer of overriding importance.

From an economic point of view, these innate motivations to act seem to have a significant consequence in common. More or less, the actions they induce come down to a striving for command over resources. This striving was clearly instrumental for enhancing survival and reproduction chances of the human species in times of severe resource shortage. As a consequence of cultural/economic evolution, living conditions in the highly developed modern economies with their relative resource abundance are now much different. Yet, the motivational dispositions and striving for raising income or wealth, which they imply, are still present and seem to establish an independent adaptation criterion for economic evolution. Where behavior generating greater resource command once meant being able to better adapt to the environment and have more offspring, behavior generating greater resource command now seems to have become a goal in its own right.[10]

However, under the present condition, motivational dispositions that were once functional may now not only have lost their functional status. They may become dysfunctional. The result then is what biologists call 'evolutionary mismatch'. Indications of such mismatch can indeed be found in the economic domain in recent times precisely because the implied striving for greater command over resources can increasingly better be satisfied. Examples are innate consumption motivations and time discounting attitudes that tend to favor excessive resource consumption behavior wherever it becomes feasible. Such behavior was functionally advantageous for reproductive success under the ancestral scarcity conditions. With the present relative resource abundance it creates problems such as, for instance, obesity at the individual level and resource depletion and environmental degradation at the collective level (see *Chapters 9* and *10*).

Economic evolution can thus be claimed to unfold according to its own rules and adaptation criteria. This hypothesis is neither meant to imply that the unfolding is disconnected (in the sense of an ontological dualism) from the evolutionary process that continues to transform nature. Nor should the hypothesis be misinterpreted to postulate an end of co-evolutionary interactions between the human economy and nature. To the contrary, the evolving economy remains subject to the fundamental constraints of the co-evolving ecosystem in which it is embedded (see van den Bergh 2007 for an illuminating discussion). In the long run, the presence of these constraints means that human societies, if not the human kind in total, and the ways in which they run the economy are not exempted from the process of natural selection. This may only go unnoticed because, measured in human time scales, the pace of the latter process is extremely slow.

3. Why deviate from the canonical economic paradigm?

The notions of optimization and general economic equilibrium are core elements of the canonical economic paradigm (see, for example, Mas-Colell et al. 1995). As already mentioned, they are frequently criticized by the advocates of an evolutionary approach to economics. As far as the critique of the optimization hypothesis is concerned, it is neither new nor based on genuinely evolutionary arguments. In the form of the rational actor model, the optimization hypothesis is a heuristic that devises a template for explaining the actors' empirically observed behavior. The behavior is reconstructed – or rationalized – by means of 'situational logic' (Popper 1960, Chapter 31) as an instance of optimal decision-making. The underlying assumption is that choices are made rationally. This assumption, in turn, means: (1) the actors' choices are made deliberately; (2) the alternatives are represented sufficiently well by the subjective perceptions of the actors; and (3) their preferences are transitive and cover the complete set of alternatives.

The critics – among them many Neo-Schumpeterians – have argued long since that all these assumptions are a far cry from how, and on what basis, choices are actually made. More recent research in behavioral economics is now able to support the critique experimentally. Regarding (1) the deliberation assumption, it has been found that many choices are made on the basis of an automated decision system and, hence, without deliberation (Kahneman 2003; Loewenstein 2004). In the case of choices that are deliberately made, such deliberation can be biased by intervening emotions and wishful thinking. Decision-making then falls short of the standard of well-structured, logically-consistent thinking.[11]

Turning to (2) the subjective perceptions, the following finding is relevant. Due to constraints on time and cognitive resources, at any point in time, spontaneous individual information processing can cover only a limited number of alternatives potentially available. The individuals' perceptions therefore tend to represent more complex choice situations with a greater degree of imperfection. In response to this finding, Simon (1955) proposed the notion of *bounded* rationality more than half a century ago. More recently it has been noted that these constraints may be the reason for why intuitive thinking uses a set of 'fast and frugal' decision heuristics (Gigerenzer and Goldstein 1996). They obviously do not match the standard of full rationality.

Further evidence for distortions in subjective perceptions relative to the standard of full rationality is provided by the fact that the representation of the choice set is always context-dependent (see, for example, Glimcher 2015). Finally, regarding (3) the decision-makers' preferences, it is far from proven that the completeness and transitivity assumptions are satisfied. Especially when the set of potentially available alternatives is large and complex their complete and consistent representation in preference orders is doubtful. Yet, when the representation of the alternatives during the decision process is volatile, this can undermine the transitivity condition.

What consequences are to be drawn from this critique for the evolutionary approach to economics? As it seems, two alternative strategies can be chosen. One corresponds to the Neo-Schumpeterian recipe of creating an evolutionary economic theory by means of analogies to natural selection theory. The strategy is to react to the critique by doing away not only with the particular rational actor heuristic, but also with methodological individualism in its entirety. Both are replaced by the methodology of selection models founded on population thinking (Nelson and Winter 1982; Metcalfe 2008). Accordingly, the focus shifts from explaining why individuals adapt their behavior to changing circumstances to instead explaining how selection mechanisms winnow out some variants of inert behavior ('routines') rather than others.

However, shifting focus from the individual level to that of the population means that, by the same token, evolutionary economic theorizing loses touch with the behavioral foundations of economics. This may appear as no great loss if, as in the Neo-Schumpeterian approach, the Darwinian theory is considered relevant for the economic domain only as a source of inspiration for analogy constructions. But if, in the spirit of the continuity hypothesis and its monistic ontology, the Darwinian theory represents the overarching scientific frame of reference, it is precisely in the behavioral foundations that insights derived from the Darwinian theory are most important. The neglect by evolutionary economic theorizing of the individual level would therefore come at a high cost. For this reason, the consequence to be drawn from the critique of the canonical optimization paradigm should be a strategy that maintains the individualistic perspective for evolutionary economic theorizing. Accordingly, the second strategy requires going beyond the rational actor heuristic and adopting a 'naturalistic' explanatory approach to economic behavior. More specifically, this means to elaborate an *evolutionary* behavioral economics as outlined by Burnham et al. (2015).[12]

The other core element of the canonical economic paradigm, the notion of general equilibrium, is tied to the following condition. The economy is said to be in a state of general equilibrium if, at a certain point in time, neither excess demand nor excess supply exists in any of its constituent markets. It is assumed that, in making their demand or supply decisions, the market participants have optimally accounted for their respective constraints. The general equilibrium condition then implies that *all* agents in the economy are not only able, but also have no reason to seek something better than, to realize their plans. However, as an empirical hypothesis such a claim is difficult to accept at least for modern economies. In these economies it can be observed that, at all times, at least some agents in the economy do seek to do better by pursuing innovations that would change their constraints. How can the general equilibrium hypothesis be defended against the implications of this observation? Is it at all possible to verify whether or not an economy is presently in a state of general equilibrium?

In view of these questions, a brief look at the history of the notion of general economic equilibrium is informative. In the works of classical writers like Adam Smith (1976[1776], Book I, Chapter 7), the notion of general equilibrium represented a logical construct. It described the fictitious end state of a process that would occur if all market participants had enough information and time to complete their coordination efforts. Owing to its fictitious status, this end state was not characterized with any great accuracy. It was recognized that, whether by market entry or exit, investment or disinvestment, variations in demand or supply, and so on, the actions of some market participants would always disrupt the coordination process before it reaches the end state.

The neoclassical revolution in economics at the end of the 19th century discarded this somewhat elusive classical conception of general equilibrium. Guided by the ideal of Newtonian physics, an attempt was made to replace it by what was considered a more exact interpretation. The latter was based on the calculus used in classical mechanics for physical systems such as the planetary system. By means of that calculus, a state of equilibrium can be determined as a state in which all free energy is dissipated. The calculus was analogously applied in economics to determine the general equilibrium in the markets as a state in which all excess demand and/or supply has vanished (Mirowski 1989). In contrast to the classical understanding of general economic equilibrium as a fictitious end point of the coordination process in the markets, the neoclassical interpretation holds that the general equilibrium state is reality. Modern canonical economic theory seems to subscribe to that claim (see, for example, Mas-Colell et al. 1995).

It is not clear, though, how to prove the claim. Except for highly-organized trading places it is very difficult, if not impossible, to empirically observe whether at a certain point in time all excess demand/supply has vanished and, hence, whether the markets are in a state of equilibrium or disequilibrium. In fact, it is usually simply assumed without further proof that the economy is in a state of general equilibrium – an assumption that is invoked not least for reasons of mathematical convenience. The unproven assumption is hard to accept for the adherents of an evolutionary approach. Instead, they consider Schumpeter's (1942) 'perennial gale of creative destruction' the adequate description of modern economies. Innovative as these economies are, they experience permanent structural change. This implies that, at any point in time, there are disequilibrium states at least in some of the markets.[13]

The theory of general economic equilibrium is often thought necessary for demonstrating the coordinating power of the price mechanism. However, as explained elsewhere (Witt 1985), general equilibrium theory represents the state of coordination in a highly idealized way as one with a *perfect* degree of coordination. The actual conditions under which the coordinating power of the price mechanism would have to be demonstrated are quite different. They are characterized by the presence of some excess supply or demand in the market system, for example, as a consequence of false expectations or the disruptive impact of innovative activity. As a consequence, the actual degree of coordination is not perfect.

Instead, the price mechanism is able to generate a *viable* degree of coordination in the sense that it suffices for most of the market participants to be able to get along in their economic affairs. Most firms will remain profitable. Most of existing labor supply will remain employed. Consumers will be able to obtain most of the goods and services which they demand. Very likely, though, the frustration of the plans of some agents by the market process may motivate those agents to pursue opportunities for innovative change on their part. Thus, the fact that some of the individual plans must remain unfulfilled if the degree of coordination is only 'viable' may disappoint some theoretical expectations. At the same time, however, it appears to be a constitutive element in keeping the market system innovative.

While in an evolutionary perspective the theory of a *general* economic equilibrium does not make sense, there is certainly room for a different notion of equilibrium in an evolutionary approach. Theories inquiring into evolutionary dynamics can, for example, be confronted with situations in which several processes of change interact in such a way that they produce a (temporary) stalemate between them. In that case, it is possible to conceptualize the ensuing situation using the equilibrium notion.

Equilibria of this kind obviously represent a rather special, transitory, state of affairs. In multi-layered, complex adaptive systems, such equilibria can typically be attained at one layer while the continuing developments at other layers prevent their adjustment dynamics from reaching equilibria simultaneously. As a result, the evolutionary way of thinking expects a stalemate situation at some layer to be disrupted sooner or later by the uneven pace of adjustments at other layers. For the complex adaptive system as a whole the disruption of equilibrium states is thus endogenously caused. The observation of an equilibrium at some layer of a complex adaptive evolutionary system – some part of the economy, say – should therefore alert the observer of processes at different layers which may already develop the potential for disrupting the equilibrium state.

4. Schumpeter's 'diffusionism' as an incomplete approach to economic evolution

In modern capitalism, products, production technologies, firms, markets, and other institutions are at all times in the process of being transformed more or less rapidly. The transformations ultimately result from the incessant pursuit and creation of novelty. The merit of having placed this insight on the agenda of economics belongs to Schumpeter and his theory of economic development (1934[1912]). He introduced the novel analytical concepts of innovation and imitation and elaborated the role that entrepreneurship plays for them. He argued that it is through the imaginative power and ability of pioneering entrepreneurs that major, sometimes even path-breaking, innovations come into existence.

The activities of these entrepreneurs involve establishing major new product lines, revolutionizing technologies and the structure of entire industries, mobilizing means to tap into and utilize new types of resources, and opening up the potential of new markets. When successful in their efforts, innovators can earn huge fortunes. For the transformation of the economy to be completed, it is necessary, though, that the success of the pioneering entrepreneurs encourages subsequent imitation processes. They require growing numbers of 'ordinary' business people whose imitate activities allow for the innovations to be diffused throughout the economy with more or less delay.

The exalted view of entrepreneurial leadership promoted by Schumpeter was not unusual in the intellectual circles of early 20th-century Vienna to which he belonged (Streissler 1982). Also his interpretation of economic development as driven by the emergence and diffusion of novelty used a theoretical template then enjoying certain popularity. It figured prominently in the diffusionism school in social and cultural anthropology founded by the German geographer Friedrich Ratzel and in the 'Kulturkreis' doctrine of ethnologists Frobenius and Graebner.

The diffusionism school focused on how the development of homogenous cultural areas – a notion boosted, inter alia, by the discovery of language families – followed the patterns of regional emergence and diffusion of novelty. The school was understood as opposition to 19th-century stage-evolutionism and its tenet that all human societies develop along the same lines, namely progressing from lower to ever higher stages. An influential branch of the school was associated with the research of Vienna social anthropologists Wilhelm Koppers and Wilhelm Schmidt. Although there is no record of a personal encounter between Schumpeter and these social scientists, his familiarity with their approach is evident.[14] As Kobayashi (2014) has argued, it therefore seems plausible that Schumpeter's innovation-cum-imitation conceptual framework of economic development may have been inspired by the diffusionism school.

However, as is explained in *Chapter 5* of the present volume, Schumpeter's grasp of the emergence and diffusion of novelty is in one respect incomplete. He argued that innovations spring 'from within' the economy, but failed to inquire into how their origin depends on inventive activities and their contingencies. Where Schumpeter (1934[1912]) did mention inventions this was just to distinguish them from innovations and to claim that, since inventions are always abundantly available, no further explanation of them is required. By making this claim, it became possible for Schumpeter to portray the economic transformation process exclusively as interplay of innovation and imitation.[15]

However, successful innovations do not only elicit imitative activities. The innovator's success also puts increasing competitive pressure on established businesses. This creates incentives for these businesses to explore possibilities for their own inventions in order to escape the rising competitive pressures. Because of his neglect of inventive activities, Schumpeter did not recognize the feedback loop between innovations and inventions that keeps the economic transformation process going. Instead, he simply postulated that ever new 'swarms of innovations' will occur. In effect, Schumpeter thus treated newly invented products, techniques, and practices as 'falling from heaven'. Their occurrence is tantamount to an exogenous shock.

Such an interpretation of emerging novelty is, of course, more congenial to the conceptual frame of canonical economics than many Neo-Schumpeterians would be prepared to admit. When the occurrence of newly invented products, techniques, and practices is treated as an exogenous shock and their characteristics are assumed to be immediately known to the decision-makers, the way is paved for the use of optimization and equilibrium analysis. It is not surprising, therefore, that a variety of 'Schumpeterian' models were eventually developed in canonical economics exactly along these lines. They suggested optimal strategies for 'innovation' races, optimal investments in 'innovations', and the determination of market equilibria or even equilibrium growth paths arising from exogenous 'innovation' shocks (Reinganum 1985; Aghion and Howitt 1992). Aside from their Schumpeterian diction there is not much difference between these models and models of conventional investment calculus and comparative-statics game-theory.

Returning to the connection between Schumpeter's theory of economic development and the diffusionism school in anthropology that opposed 19th-century stage-evolutionism, a more general question can be raised. That school had promoted a theory of cultural change that was independent of the contemporary Darwinian interpretations of cultural development. Schumpeter had a similar attitude and consequently denied that the principle of natural selection had any relevance for explaining economic development (Schumpeter 2002[1912]). It may therefore be asked how diffusionist principles for characterizing historical change at the most abstract level are comparable to selectionist principles. This topic is the subject matter of *Chapter 6* in the present volume.

Since Campbell (1965) it is frequent practice to refer to variation, selection, and retention or replication as the abstract principles of the Darwinian theory. Whether or not the abstract representation makes sense for the Darwinian theory is controversial (see Levit et al. 2011). Nonetheless, the very same principles figure prominently in many attempts to formulate a generally applicable theory of evolutionary change. In Universal Darwinism (for example, Dawkins 1983, Hull 2001) and Generalized Darwinism (Hodgson and Knudsen 2010) these principles are claimed to properly account for all evolutionary processes, whether occurring in natural or cultural contexts. However, these principles have been attained through abstract reduction of the domain-specific elements of evolutionary biology. It is not evident that they would similarly result, if it would really be tried to distill abstract principles from observing evolutionary change in domains other than biology. How do the core concepts of diffusionism, that is, the principles of emergence and diffusion of novelty, by comparison fare. Are they able to characterize evolution (broadly understood as systematic historical change) in abstract terms in a manner that is not specific to any particular domain?

A reason for answering the question in the affirmative is that the principles of emergence and diffusion of novelty appear to be very general indeed. While not derived from the Darwinian theory, these principles are compatible with that theory, because variation, selection, and replication can be shown to be special cases. Variation of already existing elements is a particular, but not the only possible, way of generating novelty. Likewise, selective replication is the result of particular, but not the only possible, diffusion processes in which several variants compete for diffusion success. Further, the principles of emergence and diffusion of novelty are also compatible with constitutive properties of self-organization. Self-organization theory makes a distinction between two types of processes. These are (temporarily) self-amplifying processes which foster the emergence of new structures and self-stabilizing processes (Jantsch 1980) including the diffusion of new types or structures stabilizing their (co-)existence. Via the principles of emergence and diffusion of novelty, the two scientific paradigms of natural selection and self-organization can thus be connected in an advantageous way.

5. Novelty and the epistemological bounds of economic theorizing

Important as the process of emergence of novelty is for both evolution and self-organization, what happens in this process is poorly understood. As far as the economy is concerned, the emergence of novelty, coming in the form of new technologies, new products and services, or new organizations and institutions, is the mainspring of development and growth. Yet, economic theory usually treats their occurrence as exogenous shock which amounts to admitting that no explanation can be offered. It seems worthwhile therefore to more generally explore the reasons for the difficulties which the emergence of novelty poses. Such an exploration may also help clarify what, in spite of the difficulties, can positively be stated about the emergence. *Chapter 7* in the present volume is devoted to this task.

The obvious epistemological limitation in dealing with novelty follows from the trivial fact that the meaning of novelty cannot, by its very nature, be anticipated. The specific content needs to be recognized or experienced which is possible only once novelty has occurred. Where novelty arises from recombining pre-existing elements, the epistemological problem can be determined more precisely by noting that two logically distinct operations are involved in the emergence of novelty. The first is a generative operation producing new (re-)combinations of pre-existing elements. The second is an interpretative operation identifying the meaning which the new combinations have in the context in which they occur.

The generative operation can be emulated mechanically or by a computer program and in simple cases even be described by a mathematical algorithm. This means that the generative operation does not pose any particular epistemological problem. Its results can often be characterized in generic form *ex ante*, for example, by means of a probability distribution. This is different in the case of the interpretative operation. It can neither be emulated by any means nor is it possible to characterize its outcome (that is, the meaning, if any, of the newly generated combinations) *ex ante*.[16] The epistemological constraint is binding. In the case of novelty mentally created by recombining pre-existing content, the reason is the complexity of the associative act of attributing meaning to the new combination (the core of the interpretative operation). This associative act is achieved in the brain in a way in which the complexity is far greater than presently understood.

It may of course be asked whether the epistemological constraint on the interpretative operation is equally binding for all kinds of mentally created novelty. One newly created action may mean a radical break with everything that was previously known or expected, while another novel action may just mean a minor deviation from what preceded it. For example, the creation of computerized book keeping does not seem comparable in this respect with the creation of just a new book keeping rule. Are the epistemic limitations equally binding *ex ante* no matter how 'radical' the emerging novelty is, or at least appears, when looked upon *ex post*?

In order to be able to distinguish between those instances of novelty that appear to be more radical than others, an *ex ante* measure for degrees of novelty is needed. *Chapter 7* discusses such a measure and its prerequisites. The distinction between the generative and the interpretative operations is again a good starting point for the inquiry. Considering the generative operation in isolation, it is often possible to construct a probabilistic measure regarding its outcome. Because of the binding epistemological limitation this is not possible for the outcome of the interpretative operation. The simple reason is that the state space on which the probability measure would have to be defined cannot be pre-specified. It is for the interpretative operation therefore that a measure for degrees of novelty is relevant. Once established, a comparison of this measure with the probabilistic measure, that is, between degrees of likelihood and degrees of novelty, is straightforward. As will turn out, the epistemological difference between degrees of probability and degrees of novelty translates into a continuous measure of uncertainty for the former and a basically dyadic measure of uncertainty for the latter.

Two further problems arising from the 'bound of unknowledge' implied by the emergence of novelty are outlined in *Chapter 8* of the present volume. The first revolves around the question of whether the principle of causation has to be given up whenever within the explanatory domain of a theory it is possible that novelty emerges. This is sometimes argued to be necessary (see Hodgson 1995; Koppl et al. 2015). In discussing this claim it is useful to distinguish between two different problems relating to causation. The first problem is associated with the explanation of why novelty occurs: is there a cause for why economic agents create novelty? The second problem is related to the content of novelty that is being created: is there a cause for why it has the particular meaning that is recognized *ex post*?

In the first case, it is not difficult to find out that there is a cause. It is the reason that motivates economic agents to search for, and arrive at, novel ideas, artefacts, or actions. In the second case, however, the associative act that is mentally carried out in the process of identifying meaning is so complex that a detailed attribution of specific causes is not possible. Yet this does not mean that there are no causes. The attempts presently under way to improve our understanding of the 'conceptual integration' that happens in the associative act are all designed to develop causal explanations (see Fauconnier and Turner 2002). The fact that a binding epistemological constraint exists is not sufficient to support the claim that, with respect to novelty, the principle of causation and the scientific ideal of causal explanations must be renounced.

The existence of epistemological constraints does present some difficulties, though, for devising theories about the development over time of systems in which novelty emerges. This is the second problem to be discussed in *Chapter 8*. Where the occurrence of novelty cannot be ruled out *ex ante*, the epistemological constraint impedes the ability to positively predict future developments. The problem is relevant, in particular, for explaining and predicting economic time series by means of difference or differential equations as, for example, in theories of the business cycle or of economic growth. By these equations the future development over time is predetermined once the initial conditions are specified. In the sciences such equations can be used to explain the development over time if at least one of two provisions is satisfied. Either the emergence of novelty is not to be expected (such as in the movements of the planetary system) or it has no effect on the trajectories (such as in the case of natural laws that remain valid whatever novelty will emerge).[17]

Neither of the two stipulations is, however, satisfied in the economic domain. The possibility of novel products, techniques, policies, regulations, and so on occurring in the future cannot be excluded. Nor can the possibility be excluded that, as a consequence of their occurrence, changes in the previously observed regularities occur – in economics there are no natural laws, after all. As explained, the concept of probability is inadequate for characterizing the unknown effect of such changes. Therefore, the practice of adding a randomly distributed error term in economic models is no option to solve the problem of the unknown effects. Changes in the very structure of the economic models can be neither excluded nor anticipated. For that reason, it is highly misleading when the impression is created that the prevalent use of differential and difference equations in economic theory and time series analysis can effectively predict the development of an innovative economy except for some random 'noise' The truth is that the reliability of predictions of time series models for innovative economies is poor and that this should not be unexpected.

6. Elements of an evolutionary economic theory

Conceptual, methodological, and historical reflections about an evolutionary paradigm in economics are important. But ultimately the test of the paradigm will be what theories it inspires and what new insights on the economy these theories can provide. Part III of the present volume is therefore devoted to presenting selected elements of economic theory that are informed by evolutionary thinking. *Chapter 9* starts with an important part of what has so far been widely neglected in evolutionary economics, namely a properly founded evolutionary theory of economic behavior.

On the one hand, there is ample evidence for the influence of genetic dispositions on economic behavior that change very slowly, if at all (first and foremost among them innate motivations such as instincts, drives, needs). On the other hand, history teaches that economic behavior is extremely malleable. The human genetic endowment must therefore comprise mechanisms that make the malleability, that is, rapidly adapting behavior, possible. One of these adaptive mechanisms is represented by reinforcement and conditioning learning shared by all humans and other animals as well. The other adaptive mechanism is that of cognitive and observational learning. Given the unique human capacity of memorizing and communicating, both mechanisms allow the accumulation of an ever more extended and differentiated cultural knowledge.[18]

Chapter 9 sets out to demonstrate the relevance of the approach for the case of consumption behavior and its evolution. A key role has to be attributed in this context to the motivational aspects of individual behavior. While they figure prominently in psychology,[19] in economics questions about individual motivation are subsumed within the *terra incognito* of individual preferences. Unlike time preferences, risk preferences, and other-regarding (altruistic) preferences, which have recently gained attention in behavioral economics, consumption preferences proper continue to be a neglected research topic. It is not surprising, therefore, that little progress has been made with the explanation of the enormous changes that have occurred and are going to continue on the demand side of modern economies, that is, in consumer behavior.

In order to make progress it is necessary to understand the motivations that are expressed in the consumers' preferences and the effects of the mentioned adaptive mechanisms on changes in these motivations. In a rough sketch one can refer first to the category of innate motivations such as the need for food, clothing, and shelter, which affect consumer preferences. They are likely to have been shaped in ancestral times because of their contribution to survival and reproductive success. Since humans have always been social animals involved in social competition for reproduction, the same holds for the motivation to seek social status and social recognition. Another important motivation for consumption behavior that seems to be hardwired into our genetic endowment is that for seeking 'arousal', that is, cognitive and emotional stimulation.

A feature of innate motivations that is significant in the context of consumption is their satiability. If a need such as that for food is completely satiated, the motivation to consume – in this case to eat – vanishes (except when there are also other motivations for eating that are not yet satiated). The question then is how quickly satiation occurs in terms of pro rata consumption when the ability to spend increases as a consequence of rising levels of per capita income. Differences in the patterns of satiability are apparent in the shape of Engel curves based on aggregate household expenditure data on consumption categories serving the corresponding needs.

For example, where data on long term expenditures are available, it can be seen that the share of food expenditures relative to all household expenditures consistently decreases over time as well as across income percentiles. In contrast, the relative expenditure share of the consumption category of housing has steeply increased. The expenditure category can be associated with the status-seeking motivation (Frank 2010) that is not easily satiable when income rises. The reason is a tendency toward an unstable expenditure race. It is caused by the positional character of social status and how, as a result, relative positions remain unaffected by similar increases in the spending within a comparison group (Frank 2012). Also strongly increasing are the relative expenditures shares of entertainment and tourism.[20] A major motivation for spending on these two categories can be conjectured to be seeking a certain level of 'arousal'. This motivation is not easily satiable either. However, in this case, the reason is a stupefaction effect (Scitovsky 1981) or hedonic adaptation process which arousal is subject to. In order to uphold a comparable level of arousal, consumption of new and stronger stimuli is continually required which tend to be more expensive.

Besides the innate motivations that drive individual consumption behavior there are culturally conditioned motivations as well. They emerge from the two adaptive mechanisms of conditioning learning, that is, learning of reinforcers (Leslie 1996, Chapter 2.14) and cognitive learning. Formed over a lifetime history of individual learning, this class of motivational forces explains a substantial part of the huge variety of, and idiosyncrasies in, individual consumption expenditures. If the ability to spend increases, the motivation to consume items that serve these culturally conditioned motivations does not seem to vanish. To the contrary, higher expenditures seem to induce a more intense learning. As a result consumers develop increasingly differentiated tastes and a corresponding willingness to pay for differentiated goods and services. Due to constraints on the opportunity and time for learning, the differentiation process cannot cover the entire range of possible, culturally conditioned motivations. It is rather a selective process during which consumers learn to specialize in what they favor and consume (Witt 2001).

Chapter 10 extends the inquiry into consumer behavior and its historical evolution to considerations of possible normative aspects. The focus of this chapter is on the consequences of a growing material consumption of the human species. It impacts on a natural environment that can ultimately offer this species only a finite niche to meet its needs for survival. Unfortunately, despite all its achievements, cultural evolution has not been able so far to generate practices that bring the social costs of the global growth of consumption under control. How should the omnipresent quest for further growth of income and consumption be assessed in this light?

In less developed economies, calls for economic growth and more consumption are motivated by the fact that many consumers are deprived even with respect to more easily satiable needs such as food and shelter. In their miserable situation, raising per capita income and consumption has high priority even if can only be accomplished at the cost of severe damages to the natural environment. In wealthier, more developed economies such deprivation is no longer present. Nonetheless, the striving for additional material growth does not vanish. The quest for more consumption is only motivated differently, namely by the less easily satiable needs and by culturally conditioned and cognitively constructed motives, standards, and norms of consumption (such as those of signaling status, see Witt 2010). However, expanding consumption means no less more material consumption that increases environmental stress and degradation and resource depletion.

In view of the detrimental environmental effects of further growth of material consumption, the question arises whether the motivations that drive the process and the significant differences between them in rich and poor economies, respectively, are ethically relevant. Is the quest for further consumption growth equally legitimate independently of whether it is articulated in rich or poor economies? More specifically, if global consumption growth needs to be constrained, what weight should be given to issues of fairness and justice regarding the question where to curtail the expansion first? These issues have a long history.[21] They can now be discussed on the basis of a more detailed understanding of consumer behavior provided by an evolutionary behavioral theory of consumption.

The problem of the social costs of material consumption and the prior production processes can neither be solved by private negotiations (as considered by Coase 1960) nor to political bodies hampered in their decision-making by interest groups. What seems to be needed instead is a more enlightened attitude of the consumers regarding the ethical relevance of their consumption motivations particularly in the wealthier economies. Consumers need to be invited to reflect on the innate dispositions and learned motivations that guide their consumption behavior, especially in light of the fact that marketing and advertising efforts often try to prevent this from occurring (Scitovsky 1962).

Such reflections can presumably only be hoped to be triggered by a broad public discourse on the moral legitimacy of the various motivations underlying consumption which consumers can assess for themselves. Consumer sovereignty represents a significant ideal in a free society, but it should not be mistaken for prohibiting a discourse of this kind. Accepting responsibility for the consequences of one's own action is an equally significant ideal in a free society and a fundamental ethical postulate. It demands reflection of what motivations are driving one's action – in this case striving to expand consumption – and the decision of whether or not the motives are worth the consequences that ensue.

Chapter 11 turns from consumer behavior to an evolutionary perspective on behavior in situations of social and economic exchange. Social exchange behavior is a characteristic of all social animals, but particularly of humans. A key problem of human sociality is keeping defection and free-riding under control. It is likely that the problem has been solved already in the life of the small bands of the early humans by the evolution of partly inheritable, partly socially conditioned cooperative social exchange behavior and moral aggression against offenders (Boehm 2012). In the course of history, human sociality of course outgrew the conditions of small bands and their solution of the problem. Living in larger social formations and the corresponding changes in the division of labor required further adaptations not least to make economic exchange and trade possible. These are much more recent, cultural adaptations. Nonetheless, the genetic dispositions that had originally evolved in relation to social exchange behavior seem to have intuitively been extended to situations of economic exchange within and between much larger groups.

Such an 'exaptation' (Gould 1991) of inherited social attitudes explains why norms of reciprocity and fairness – originating from the realm of social exchange in small groups – can also have affective value for the broader economic exchange behavior. There is one proviso, however: the economic exchange partners need to be seen the same way as social exchange partners are seen, namely as being equals or peers and close to oneself. If that proviso is not met, particularly in anonymous interactions, norms of reciprocity and fairness are unlikely to be felt as binding in economic exchange behavior. In that case, economic exchange will only be possible, if other ways of preventing or sanctioning defective behavior in trade can be developed. They face the problem that an individual contribution to enforcing cooperation amounts to the provision of a public good. While the group as a whole would benefit from the existence of credible enforcement, individual group members may incur substantial costs from having to engage in enforcement activities and may therefore be tempted to free-ride.[22]

Chapter 11 examines a cultural adaption process that can be imagined to solve the problem without presuming that formal institutions capable of credibly sanctioning defection already exist. The framework chosen for the discussion is the theory of cultural evolution suggested by Hayek (1988). In this framework it is essential for group behavior – and, hence, the conditions for group selection – to be able to change as a result of within-group imitation and between-group migration (see also Richerson and Boyd 2005). Accordingly, the specific form which group behavior takes becomes dependent on observational learning as a way of determining one's behavior. The decision between free-riding or instead contributing to costly punishment activities hinges on what other group members are observed to do. The relative advantage of the one behavior over the other is determined by the relative frequencies with which the respective behavior has been adopted in the group. Owing to the corresponding balance between individual fitness and the group's fitness, it is possible that groups with a high frequency of punishing behavior can enforce the conditions required for economic exchange and can thus become more prevalent.

Keeping the threat of defective behavior under control is also necessary to protect investment in production capital and the deepening of the division of labor. However, besides a favorable institutional context, improvements in the capital stock and its production technology also depend on the development of productive knowledge, that is, knowledge necessary to exploit natural resources better and more widely. This is the topic of *Chapter 12* in the present volume. From the evolutionary perspective, the interaction between the growth of productive knowledge and the expanding anthropogenic utilization of nature should be seen as the constitutive element of an economic theory of production.

In economic theory, production is traditionally interpreted as being constrained by the availability of capital, labor, and land. These factors of production have been conceived by the classical economists of the proto-industrialization period to represent the proper analytical concepts for one particular reason. These economists were interested in elaborating on (and often also castigating) the manner in which the social product was distributed. Since this time, few economists have found it necessary to reconsider and ultimately challenge the classical conception of the factors of production. One important exception in this regard is Nicholas Georgescu-Roegen (1971). In his view, the traditional approach does not adequately reflect the true constraints on human economic activity, namely those imposed by the laws of nature and the laws of thermodynamics in particular.

In a similar vein, *Chapter 12* takes up the question of how the conceptual underpinnings of production theory can be improved by adopting a naturalistic perspective. More specifically, to induce such a perspective, a comparison between non-anthropogenic productive processes in the biosphere and human production processes is suggested. The results of the comparison are, first, a critical reappraisal of the conventional understanding of 'productive' factors and why capital, labor, and land have been chosen to represent them. These factors are appropriate for an analysis of how economic surplus is distributed once it has been generated. They are of less help for explaining how this surplus is generated in the first place. For this reason, the traditional attempt to simultaneously explain both the generation and distribution of economic surplus appears less convincing than usually assumed.

Second, in exploring non-anthropogenic productive processes in the biosphere it becomes apparent that the analytical concept of productive factors can be used there as well, albeit for knowledge, energy, and matter as factors of production. If anthropogenic production processes are analyzed in terms of these factors, a different explanation for the generation of surplus results. Third, the role of the factors knowledge, energy, and matter seems to condition, but not to replace, the role of the traditional factors capital and labor when it comes to explaining the historical growth of human production. To clarify the relationships between the different sets of productive factors is therefore a major task for an evolutionary theory of production. An inherent advantage of such a theory is the integrative view of economic surplus generation and its environmental and resource effects.

Nothing has so far been said in relation to how the evolutionary way of thinking can be brought to bear on macroeconomic theory. In Neo-Schumpeterian evolutionary economics the question has no high priority as most of the work focuses on economic processes at the 'meso'-level (Dopfer et al. 2004). When macroeconomic topics are addressed, this happens for the most part in data-driven international comparisons of technology-driven growth and catching up processes (see Fagerberg 2003 for a survey). One characteristic of canonical macroeconomics is its strong reliance on the concept of market equilibria when analyzing the aggregated markets for goods, and services, labor, and money. This concept is the equivalent to the already criticized notion of general equilibrium in microeconomics. From an evolutionary point of view, it is straightforward therefore to start with a discussion of the role of equilibrium concepts in macroeconomic contexts.

Opposition to the corset imposed by the equilibrium condition on macroeconomic processes has traditionally been voiced in the Keynesian and post-Keynesian literature. However, this literature has little in common with the evolutionary way of thinking (see Foster 2011). *Chapter 13* therefore approaches the problem in a different, namely Hayekian (rather than Keynesian), spirit. Hayek had earned much of his academic reputation with his writings in the 1930s on capital theory, monetary theory, and business cycle theory (nowadays considered macroeconomic topics see, for example, Hayek 1941). In the 1950s he turned his back on these topics (McCormick 1992) and started to work instead on social philosophy and his theory of societal evolution (see Hayek 1979 and 1988). With the new orientation of his research he also abandoned the notion of general market equilibrium on which he had heavily relied in his earlier work on macroeconomics. The new, and much weaker, notion which he developed in his social philosophy was that of a spontaneous order of the markets. Can this notion also be applied to macroeconomic contexts and, if so, what would it imply? In a little-regarded paper Hayek (1981) presented an answer in terms of a flow metaphor.

In the markets countless individual decisions are made with respect to businesses that are set to materialize at some time in the future. These decisions reflect the information about future states of the economy available to the agents when their choices have to be made. Yet, the states of the economy frequently change in between the time of making decisions and the time at which the planned transactions are set to occur. It is likely therefore that the flow of goods and services supplied or demanded in any point in time does not match the market conditions that actually prevail. As a consequence, the originally planned businesses are often likely not to materialize as planned.

Nonetheless, the flow itself may be in equilibrium if the stream of goods and services entering and leaving the market is just balanced. This means that the notion of '*flow* equilibrium' at the macro level is compatible with a situation of market *disequilibrium* in many or most markets at the micro level, provided the markets are cleared. The prices prevailing at a given point in time may clear the market, but do not perfectly coordinate the individual plans. There will instead be surprises, excess supply or demand, corresponding losses and misallocations. They negatively impact many agents involved, although not to the extent that would force more than a minority out of business. This is the case of a viable rather than perfect state of coordination as it was called in Section 3 above.

Accordingly, *Chapter 13* elaborates on the notion of macroeconomic flow equilibrium as an alternative to the concept of general equilibrium and its macroeconomic equivalent. It is explained how a flow equilibrium can be used as a benchmark for assessing fluctuations in aggregate economic activity. These fluctuations are commonly associated with the business cycle. In canonical macroeconomics they are interpreted as a result of exogenous shocks that disrupt the existing equilibrium states of the markets. In contrast, the notion of flow equilibrium suggests that deviations from the flow equilibrium build up endogenously from earlier ('up-stream') decision-making in the markets leading to excess demand or supply of a size that cannot instantaneously be cleared by the price mechanism. A macroeconomic model is presented in which some variables appear that are not usually considered in the macroeconomics context, but are helpful for capturing important aspects of the flow concept. The role which these new variables perform is highlighted by means of an empirical investigation utilizing data for the period from the time of the German unification until 1994.

Finally, *Chapter 14* in the present volume turns to economic policymaking from an evolutionary point of view. If economic evolution is the process by which the economy *self-transforms*, then policymaking obviously represents an integral part of this process. A first consequence to be drawn from an evolutionary perspective therefore is that the activities of policymakers need to be made an endogenous factor in explaining economic change. This is far from being the standard approach.[23] In many contributions in the literature, 'policy implications' of the presented work are discussed in the following way. The author(s) ascribe some set of goals to a fictitious (and usually benevolent) policymaker and assume that the advice which the presented work can give on how to reach these goals is needed (see Tinbergen 1967 for the classical statement of such an instrumental approach to economic policymaking). Another variant of the works on economic policymaking is couched in normative or prescriptive terms. These contributions discuss the policy goals and their legitimacy in relation to a (hypothetical) set of normative criteria in the form of an applied ethics.

The evolutionary way of thinking is compatible with any of the approaches to economic policymaking. Its characteristic is, however, to extend the approaches so as to account for the pervasive role of learning and innovation – the constitutive features of cultural/economic evolution. Although this extension may appear trivial, its consequences are all too often underrated. In an explicative approach to policymaking, the upshot is that the policymaker's understanding of what a certain policy mix involves is subject to systematic changes which are contingent on the experiences to be made. Politicians no less run down a learning curve in this respect than technicians or managers do with respect to their tasks. For that reason, the process guiding how policymakers learn and the effect of different institutional conditions on their learning deserve attention. This is all the more true as the learning process can also involve changes in the interests which policymakers pursued. Constellations of interests and power can therefore not simply be taken as given as is typically done in public choice theory.

For an instrumental approach to policymaking, acknowledging the significance of learning and cognitive deliberation means to recognize that also the addressees of policy measures are likely to learn. Specifically, those agents detrimentally affected by some particular measure have incentives to engage in an active search for remedies. As a consequence, they often respond to the policy measure in innovative ways. Policymakers may then be forced to over and again readjust their policy design in order to reach their goals. The assessment of the suitability and effectiveness of policy measures should therefore include reflections on what incentives a measure creates for innovative responses and what likely directions the search for remedies may take. Moreover, since innovative responses cannot be anticipated, the design of policy measures should already account for the fact that future readjustment will be required. One possible solution is to implement an adaptive or 'rolling' policymaking design from the beginning (Metcalfe 1994; van den Bergh and Kallis 2013).

Concerning the normative side of economic policymaking and its goals, the evolutionary way of thinking does not coincide with any one specific norm or set of norms. An attempt to drive any particular normative foundation from a positive theory of evolution would constitute a naturalistic fallacy. As a matter of fact, cultural evolution has produced a multiplicity of often incompatible norms and value judgments at different times and places. This is a result of learning taking place also with respect to normative judgments (so long as emotional barriers do not forestall such learning). Individual norm preferences and the value judgments that constitute them are malleable. They may change as a result of factual experience and/or under the influence of social conformity pressure and operant conditioning. While the influence of experience tends to undermine claims to the supremacy and absolute validity of particular norms (as found in many totalitarian ideologies), this is not necessarily true for the other influences. At the experiential level, the culturally contingent diversity of norms and value judgments may be interpreted to imply a certain norm-relativism. Awareness of this implication may prove helpful in protecting against totalitarian norm preferences.

7. Conclusions

Modern economies are in a permanent process of being transformed. How can these transformations be explained? What modifications are required to the existing concepts and methods in economics in order to be able to account for evolution in the economy? Some preliminary answers to these questions have been provided in this Introduction. In previewing and putting in perspective the chapters in the present volume, a wide range of topics has been covered. The aim was to give an idea of what is implied by the evolutionary way of thinking about the economy. Unsurprisingly, the complexity of economic evolution allows for many different, and sometimes perhaps incommensurable, interpretations of 'evolutionary economics'. Some of these interpretations have been discussed here, along with their specific reasons for why all of them deviate from the optimization-cum-equilibrium core of canonical economics.

The particular approach to evolutionary economics pursued in this volume can be called a naturalistic one, given that it is founded on the continuity hypothesis briefly explicated above. In such an approach there is room for co-evolutionary interpretations (Richerson and Boyd 2005) and multi-level selection theory (Wilson 2015). The particular focus is on the pervasive role of learning and innovation as the characteristic features of economic evolution. It is on account of these features that economic evolution is ultimately the consequence of the ceaseless human quest to not only adapt to, but overcome the constraints of the natural and social environment. A central element of the explanatory framework of evolutionary economics understood this way is therefore the emergence of novelty and its often ambiguous character. On epistemological grounds, the emergence of novelty implies bounds of unknowledge for any form of economic theorizing. However, it should have become apparent that, despite the epistemological limitations, the evolutionary way of thinking has to offer fruitful new research perspectives on classical economic topics such as consumption, exchange, production, macroeconomic dynamics, and economic policymaking.

Notes

1. Thanks go to Chad Baum for helpful comments on an earlier draft of this Introduction.
2. There is no general consensus on this point, however. Evolutionary thought often takes the form of algorithms and models that are borrowed from evolutionary biology. Reliance on such methods can also be interpreted as an enrichment of, rather than an alternative to, canonical economics. This holds in particular for evolutionary game theory, see, for instance, Weibull (1995), Samuelson (2002), as well as the critique of Hodgson and Huang (2012).
3. Assume that a firm's innovation allows reducing the unit production costs. Then the average unit cost in the industry is also falling and, so too, is the industry's price level under competitive conditions. Non-innovative firms with higher unit costs will sooner or later be driven out of the market. Formally, the competitive process can be modeled as a variant of the replicator dynamics (Metcalfe 2002).
4. In such a perspective, a core issue that needs to be clarified is the deeper reason for why the transformations of the economy are relentlessly driven forward. An answer to this question demands a deeper appreciation of the motivational aspects of human nature than has so far been attained in economics (see Witt 2011). For a more general discussion of a naturalistic economic philosophy see Herrmann-Pillath (2013).
5. For a survey of Veblen's approach and its further fate in the 20th century see Hodgson (2004).
6. For a critique of the suggested typology see Rice and Smart (2011). Their critique is misled in so far as they interpret the two features, heuristic and ontology, as necessary conditions for, rather than just characteristics of, evolutionary economic theories. However, they rightly argue that classifying authors with respect to whether or not their heuristic stance involves the principles of variation, selection, and replication – as done in *Chapter 4* – can be problematic. There is much room for interpretation indeed when the authors' publications precede the formulation of these principles in Campbell (1965).
7. The question referred to the early controversy about natural selection analogies in economics between Alchian (1950), Penrose (1952), and Friedman (1953). Remarkably, at that time, Winter discussed the controversy with a quite critical attitude toward such analogies.
8. See Witt (2015) for a discussion. Although learning necessarily takes place at the level of the individual agents, it is nevertheless strongly shaped by the social interactions in which they take part. In groups of individuals who continually interact with each other, socially contingent learning can thus generate shared knowledge in the form of mental habits, values, and norms. When knowledge can be encoded in symbolic form, it becomes present outside the individual mind and can be accumulated and transmitted between individuals and between generations independent of face to face interactions.
9. They do not differ in this respect from other innate mental traits for which this argument has been made in evolutionary psychology, see Buss (2003).
10. In his theory of societal evolution, Hayek (1988) argues in a similar vein that it is economic fitness rather than reproductive fitness that matters for societies. Those of them with a culture and with instititions – customs, rules of conduct, and economic order – that are better adapted according to this criterion enjoy comparative prosperity. It is their prosperity that then allows these societies to expand and their culture and institutions to spread. Such societies may have higher population growth due to higher birth rates or due to immigration. Or they may impose their characteristics on populations in foreign territories which they are able to conquer or dominate; see Gray (1998) and Beck (2015) for a discussion.
11. See Loewenstein (2000). Logical calculus is, after all, nothing humans are naturally endowed with. It is a cultural achievement that required millennia of human reflection to be developed and contrasts with what, in the light of the logical ideal, are perceived to represent the shortcomings of the intuitive mode of human thinking.
12. In its present form, behavioral economics is not rooted in evolutionary theory, see Witt (2011) for a discussion.
13. Permanent structural change is endogenous to the modern 'capitalist engine' (Metcalfe 1998). It results from the ceaseless efforts of market participants to improve their competitive position. It is worth noting that such a view

is difficult to align with the mechanical analogies introduced by the neoclassical writers. In a system of physical forces that is in an equilibrium state, change can only occur as a result of an impulse from outside the system. If what happens in a system of markets is modeled analogously to what happens in a system subject to physical forces, the consequence is that the causes of economic change have to be attributed to exogenous shocks.

14. Schumpeter (1955, Part IV, Chapter 3, Sec. 2b) devotes a whole subsection to discussing the tenets of Graebner, Koppers, and Ratzel.

15. In terms of the epistemological boundary separating the conditions of emergence of novelty from those of its diffusion, innovations as conceived by Schumpeter do not belong to the process of emergence (as inventions and discoveries do), but rather denote the beginning of a process of diffusion of novelty.

16. In the biological domain, the interpretative operation corresponds to the expression, and subsequent testing for viability and reproduction success, of a newly emerging genotype in its phenotypic counterpart.

17. The potential for law-like hypotheses which make *negative* predictions is not affected by the epistemological constraint. Such law-like hypotheses predict that a particular event is not expected whatever future novelty will hold, see Hayek (1964) for an example. Natural laws can always be used for deriving negative predictions.

18. The enormous impact of culturally accumulated, socially shared knowledge on modern economic behavior can be grasped by studying the 'economy' of primates. The stage of cultural development of many primate groups living today is most likely comparable to that of very early hominids. It is plausible therefore that the production and consumption activities of our early ancestors resembled what we observe in modern primates. By comparison with present-day forms of human production and consumption the long path of cultural evolution which the human species has undergone becomes readily apparent.

19. Theories of motivation 'describe why a person in a given situation selects one response over another or makes a given response with greater energization or frequency' (Bargh et al. 2010, p. 286).

20. For a time series displaying all the mentioned variations of household expenditure shares over a span of one hundred years see US Bureau of Labor Statistics, Report 991, 2006.

21. See, for instance, Streeten and Burki (1978), Thomson (1987), and Scanlon's (1975) distinction according to the suggested urgency of different preferences, or even much older Pigouvian notions of differences in urgency expressed in terms of a decreasing marginal utility of money.

22. The deeper problem implied here is thus the much discussed relationship between group selection and individual selection. See Sober and Wilson (1998), Field (2001), Henrich (2004), Wilson and Wilson (2007).

23. An explanatory strategy in which the policymaker is endogenized is, however, pursued in public choice theory, albeit narrowly confined to applications of the rational-actor model, see, for example, Mueller (1993).

References

Aghion, P. and P. Howitt (1992), 'A Model of Growth through Creative Destruction', *Econometrica*, **60**, 323–51.

Alchian, A.A. (1950), 'Uncertainty, Evolution, and Economic Theory', *Journal of Political Economy*, **58**, 211–21.

Bargh, J.A., P.M. Gollwitzer and G. Oettingen (2010), 'Motivation', in S.T. Fiske, D.T. Gilbert and G. Lindzey (eds), *Handbook of Social Psychology*, New York: Wiley, 268–316.

Beck, N. (2015), 'The Garden of Orderly Polity: F.A. Hayek and T.H. Huxley's Views on Social Evolution', *Journal of Bioeconomics*, **17**, 83–96.

Boehm, C. (2012), *Moral Origins: The Evolution of Virtue, Altruism and Shame*, New York: Basic Books.

Brown, G.R. and P.J. Richerson (2014), 'Applying Evolutionary Theory to Human Behavior: Past Differences and Current Debates', *Journal of Bioeconomics*, **16**, 105–28.

Burnham, T., S.E.G. Lea, A. Bell, H. Gintis, P.W. Glimcher, R. Kurzban, L. Lades, K. McCabe, K. Panchanathan, M. Teschl and U. Witt (2015), 'Evolutionary Behavioral Economics', in D.S. Wilson and A. Kirman (eds), *Complexity and Evolution – A New Synthesis for Economics*, Cambridge, MA: MIT Press, in print.

Buss, D.M. (2003), *Evolutionary Psychology: The New Science of the Mind*, Boston: Allyn & Bacon.

Campbell, D.T. (1965), 'Variation and Selective Retention in Socio-cultural Evolution', in H.R. Barringer, G.I. Blankstein and R.W. Mack (eds), *Social Change in Developing Areas: A Re-interpretation of Evolutionary Theory*, Cambridge, MA: Schenkman, 19–49.

Coase, R.H. (1960), 'The Problem of Social Cost', *Journal of Law and Economics*, **3**, 1–44.

Cyert, R.M. and J.G. March (1963), *A Behavioral Theory of the Firm*, Englewood Cliffs, NJ: Prentice Hall.

Dawkins, R. (1983), 'Universal Darwinism', in D.S. Bendall (ed.), *Evolution from Molecules to Man*, Cambridge: Cambridge University Press, 403–25.

Dopfer, K., J. Foster and J. Potts (2004), 'Micro – Meso – Macro', *Journal of Evolutionary Economics*, **14**, 263–79.

Fagerberg, J. (2003), 'Schumpeter and the Revival of Evolutionary Economics: An Appraisal of the Literature', *Journal of Evolutionary Economics*, **13**, 125–59.

Fauconnier, G. and M. Turner (2002), *The Way We Think: Conceptual Blending and the Mind's Hidden Complexities*, New York: Basic Books.

Field, A. (2001), *Altruistically Inclined? The Behavioral Sciences, Evolutionary Theory, and the Origins of*

Reciprocity, Ann Arbor: University of Michigan Press.

Foster, J. (2011), 'Evolutionary Macroeconomics: A Research Agenda', *Journal of Evolutionary Economics*, **21**, 5–28.

Frank, R.H. (2010), *Luxury Fever: Weighing the Cost of Excess*, Princeton: Princeton University Press.

Frank, R.H. (2012), *The Darwin Economy: Liberty, Competition, and the Common Good*, Princeton: Princeton University Press.

Friedman, M. (1953), 'The Methodology of Positive Economics', in M. Friedman (ed.), *Essays in Positive Economics*, Chicago: University of Chicago Press, 3–43.

Georgescu-Roegen, N. (1971), *The Entropy Law and the Economic Process*, Cambridge, MA: Harvard University Press.

Gigerenzer, G. and D.G. Goldstein (1996), 'Reasoning the Fast and Frugal Way: Models of Bounded Rationality', *Psychological Review*, **103**, 650–69.

Glimcher, P. (2015), 'Proximate Mechanisms of Individual Decision-Making Behavior', in D.S. Wilson and A. Kirman (eds), *Complexity and Evolution – A New Synthesis for Economics*, Cambridge, MA: MIT Press, in print.

Gould, S.J. (1991), 'Exaptation: A Crucial Tool for an Evolutionary Psychology', *Journal of Social Issues*, **47**, 43–65.

Gowdy, J. (1994), *Coevolutionary Economics: The Economy, Society and the Environment*, Boston: Kluwer Academic Publishers.

Gray, J. (1998), *Hayek on Liberty*, London: Routledge.

Hayek, F.A. (1941), *The Pure Theory of Capital*, London: Routledge and Kegan Paul.

Hayek, F.A. (1964), 'The Theory of Complex Phenomena', in M.A. Bunge (ed.), *The Critical Approach to Science and Philosophy*, New York: Free Press, 22–42.

Hayek, F.A. (1979), *Law, Legislation, and Liberty, Vol. III: The Political Order of a Free People*, London: Routledge and Kegan Paul.

Hayek, F.A. (1981), 'The Flow of Goods and Services', Notes of a Lecture given at L.S.E., January 27, 1981.

Hayek, F.A. (1988), *The Fatal Conceit*, London: Routledge.

Henrich, J. (2004), 'Cultural Group Selection, Coevolutionary Processes and Large-scale Cooperation', *Journal of Economic Behavior and Organization*, **53**, 3–35.

Herrmann-Pillath, C. (2013), *Foundations of Economic Evolution – A Treatise on the Natural Philosophy of Economics*, Cheltenham, UK and Northampton, MA, USA: Edward Elgar Publishing.

Hodgson, G.M. (1995), 'The Evolution of Evolutionary Economics', *Scottish Journal of Political Economy*, **42**, 469–88.

Hodgson, G.M. (2004), *The Evolution of Institutional Economics*, London: Routledge.

Hodgson, G.M. and K. Huang (2012), 'Evolutionary Game Theory and Evolutionary Economics: Are They Different Species?', *Journal of Evolutionary Economics*, **22**, 345–66.

Hodgson, G.M. and T. Knudsen (2010), *Darwin's Conjecture – The Search for General Principles of Social and Economic Evolution*, Chicago: University of Chicago Press.

Hodgson, G.M., J. Järvinen and J.-A. Lamberg (2014), 'The Structure and Evolution of Evolutionary Research: A Bibliometric Analysis of the "Evolutionary" Literature in Management, Economics, and Sociology', Paper presented at the Annual Meetings of the European Association for Evolutionary Political Economy, Paris 2014.

Hull, D.L. (2001), *Science and Selection: Essays on Biological Evolution and the Philosophy of Science*, Cambridge: Cambridge University Press.

Jantsch, E. (1980), *The Self-Organizing Universe*, New York: Pergamon.

Kahneman, D. (2003), 'Maps of Bounded Rationality: Psychology for Behavioral Economics', *American Economic Review*, **93**, 1449–75.

Kobayashi, D. (2014), 'Effects of Anthropology and Archaeology Upon Early Innovation Studies', Paper presented at the International Schumpeter Society Conference, Jena 2014.

Koppl, R., S. Kauffman, T. Felin and G. Longo (2015), 'Economics for a Creative World', *Journal of Institutional Economics*, **11**, 1–31.

Leslie, J.C. (1996), *Principles of Behavioral Analysis*, Amsterdam: Harwood Academic Publishers.

Levit, G.S., U. Hossfeld and U. Witt (2011), 'Can Darwinism Be "Generalized" and of What Use Would This Be?', *Journal of Evolutionary Economics*, **21**, 545–62.

Loewenstein, G. (2000), 'Emotions in Economic Theory and Economic Behavior', *American Economic Review*, **90**, 426–32.

Loewenstein, G. (2004), 'Out of Control: Visceral Influences on Behavior', in C.F. Camerer, G. Loewenstein and M. Rabin (eds), *Advances in Behavioral Economics*, Princeton: Princeton University Press, 689–723.

March, J.G. and H.A. Simon (1958), *Organizations*, New York: Wiley.

Mas-Colell, A., M.D. Whinston and J.R. Green (1995), *Microeconomic Theory*, Oxford: Oxford University Press.

McCormick, B.J. (1992), *Hayek and the Keynesian Avalanche*, New York: Harvester Wheatsheaf.

Metcalfe, J.S. (1994), 'Evolutionary Economics and Technology Policy', *Economic Journal*, **104**, 931–44.

Metcalfe, J.S. (1998), *Evolutionary Economics and Creative Destruction*, London: Routledge.

Metcalfe, J.S. (2002), 'On the Optimality of the Competitive Process: Kimura's Theorem and Market Dynamics', *Journal of Bioeconomics*, **4**, 109–33.

Metcalfe, J.S. (2008), 'Accounting for Economic Evolution: Fitness and the Population Method', *Journal of Bioeconomics*, **10**, 23–50.

Mirowski, P. (1989), *More Heat Than Light – Economics as Social Physics, Physics as Nature's Economics*, Cambridge: Cambridge University Press.

Mueller, D.C. (1993), *The Public Choice Approach to Politics*, Aldershot, UK and Brookfield, VT, USA: Edward Elgar Publishing.

Nelson, R.R. (2006), 'Evolutionary Social Science and Universal Darwinism', *Journal of Evolutionary Economics*, **16**, 491–510.

Nelson, R.R. and S.G. Winter (1982), *An Evolutionary Theory of Economic Change*, Cambridge, MA: Harvard University Press.

Nelson, R.R. and S.G. Winter (2002), 'Evolutionary Theorizing in Economics', *Journal of Economic Perspectives*, **16**, 23–46.

North, D.C. (1997), *Institutions, Institutional Change and Economic Performance*, Cambridge: Cambridge University Press.

Penrose, E.T. (1952), 'Biological Analogies in the Theory of the Firm', *American Economic Review*, **42**, 804–19.

Popper, K.R. (1960), *The Poverty of Historicism*, London: Routledge and Kegan Paul.

Reinganum, J.F. (1985), 'Innovation and Industry Evolution', *Quarterly Journal of Economics*, **100**, 81–99.

Rice, C. and J. Smart (2011), 'Interdisciplinary Modeling: A Case Study of Evolutionary Economics', *Biology & Philosophy*, **26**, 655–75.

Richerson, P.J. and R. Boyd (2005), *Not by the Genes Alone: How Culture Transformed Human Evolution*, Chicago: University of Chicago Press.

Samuelson, L. (2002), 'Evolution and Game Theory', *Journal of Economic Perspectives*, **16**, 47–66.

Scanlon, T. (1975), 'Preference and Urgency', *Journal of Philosophy*, **72**, 655–69.

Schumpeter, J.A. (1934[1912]), *Theory of Economic Development*, Cambridge, MA: Harvard University Press (first published as *Theorie der Wirtschaftlichen Entwicklung*, 1912).

Schumpeter, J.A. (1942), *Capitalism, Socialism and Democracy*, New York: Harper.

Schumpeter, J.A. (1955), *History of Economics Analysis*, London: Allen & Unwin.

Schumpeter, J.A. (2002), 'The Economy as a Whole' (Seventh Chapter of *Theorie der Wirtschaftlichen Entwicklung*, 1912, English translation by U. Backhaus), *Industry and Innovation*, **9**, 93–145.

Scitovsky, T. (1962), 'On the Principle of Consumers' Sovereignty', *American Economic Review*, **52**, 262–8.

Scitovsky, T. (1981), 'The Desire for Excitement', *Kyklos*, **34**, 3–13.

Silva, S.T. and A.C. Teixeira (2009), 'On the Divergence of Evolutionary Research Paths in the Past 50 Years: A Comprehensive Bibliometric Account', *Journal of Evolutionary Economics*, **19**, 605–42.

Simon, H.A. (1955), 'A Behavioral Model of Rational Choice', *Quarterly Journal of Economics*, **69**, 99–118.

Smith, A. (1976[1776]), *An Inquiry into the Nature and Causes of the Wealth of Nations*, Oxford: Oxford University Press.

Sober, E. and D.S. Wilson (1998), *Unto Others – The Evolution and Psychology of Unselfish Behavior*, Cambridge MA: Harvard University Press.

Streeten, P. and S. Burki (1978), 'Basic Needs: Some Issues', *World Development*, **6**, 411–21.

Streissler, E. (1982), 'Schumpeter's Vienna and the Role of Credit in Innovation', in H. Frisch (ed.), *Schumpeterian Economics*, New York: Praeger, 60–83.

Thomson, G. (1987), *Needs*, London: Routledge and Kegan Paul.

Tinbergen, J. (1967), *Economic Policy: Principles and Design*, Amsterdam: North-Holland.

van den Bergh, J.C.J.M. (2007), 'Evolutionary Thinking in Environmental Economics', *Journal of Evolutionary Economics*, **17**, 521–49.

van den Bergh, J.C.J.M and G. Kallis (2013), 'A Survey of Evolutionary Policy: Normative and Positive Dimensions', *Journal of Bioeconomics*, **15**, 281–303.

Veblen, T. (1898), 'Why Is Economics Not an Evolutionary Science?', *Quarterly Journal of Economics*, **12**, 373–97.

Veblen, T.B. (1899), *The Theory of the Leisure Class – An Economic Study of Institutions*, New York: MacMillan.

Veblen, T.B. (1914), *The Instinct of Workmanship, and the State of the Industrial Arts*, New York: MacMillan.

Weibull, J.W. (1995), *Evolutionary Game Theory*, Cambridge, MA: MIT Press.

Wilson, D.S. (2015), 'Two Meanings of Complex Adaptive Systems', in D.S. Wilson and A. Kirman (eds), *Complexity and Evolution – A New Synthesis for Economics*, Cambridge, MA: MIT Press, in print.

Wilson, D.S. and E.O. Wilson (2007), 'Rethinking the Theoretical Foundation of Sociobiology', *The Quarterly Review of Biology*, **82**, 327–48.

Winter, S.G. (1964), 'Economic "Natural Selection" and the Theory of the Firm', *Yale Economic Essays*, **4**, 225–72.

Winter, S.G. (2014), 'The Future of Evolutionary Economics: From Early Intuitions to a New Paradigm?', *Journal of*

Institutional Economics, **10**, 613–44.

Witt, U. (1985), 'Coordination of Individual Economic Activities as an Evolving Process of Self-Organization', *Économie Appliquée*, **38**, 569–95.

Witt, U. (2001), 'Learning to Consume – A Theory of Wants and the Growth of Demand', *Journal of Evolutionary Economics*, **11**, 23–36.

Witt, U. (2010), 'Symbolic Consumption and the Social Construction of Product Characteristics', *Structural Change and Economic Dynamics*, **21**, 17–25.

Witt, U. (2011), 'Economic Behavior – Evolutionary Versus Behavioral Perspectives', *Biological Theory*, **6**, 388–98.

Witt, U. (2015), 'Causality and Regularity in a "Creative World"', *Journal of Institutional Economics*, **11**, 55–60.

PART I

THE ROAD MAP FOR EVOLUTIONARY ECONOMICS

[1]

evolutionary economics

Evolutionary economics focuses on the processes that transform the economy from within and investigates their implications for firms and industries, production, trade, employment and growth.

These processes emerge from the activities of agents with bounded rationality who learn from their own experience and that of others and who are capable of innovating. The diversity of individual capabilities, learning efforts, and innovative activities results in growing, distributed knowledge in the economy that supports the variety of coexisting technologies, institutions, and commercial enterprises. The variety drives competition and facilitates the discovery of better ways of doing things. The question in evolutionary economics is therefore not how, under varying conditions, economic resources are optimally allocated in equilibrium given the state of individual preferences, technology and institutional conditions. The questions are instead why and how knowledge, preferences, technology, and institutions change in the historical process, and what impact these changes have on the state of the economy at any point in time.

Posing the questions this way has consequences for the way theorizing is done in evolutionary economics. First, preferences, technology and institutions become objects of analysis rather than being treated as exogenously given. Second, following from the very notion that evolution is a process of self-transformation, the causes of economic change are in part considered to be endogenous, and not exclusively exogenous shocks. More specifically, these causes are identified with the motivation and capacity of economic agents to learn and to innovate. Third, the evolutionary process in the economy is assumed to follow regular patterns on which explanatory hypotheses can be based, rather than forming an erratic sequence of singular historical events.

These three meta-premises are widely shared in evolutionary economics. However, the details of the argument, methods, and even the specification of the attribute 'evolutionary' vary, corresponding to the different theoretical traditions in which evolutionary economics is rooted. The concept of evolution has a long history in economics and social philosophy. This antedates – and, to a certain extent, has influenced – Darwin's theory of the origin of species by means of natural selection. Where the concept of evolution originally stood for a process of betterment (of human society), the Darwinian revolution in the sciences purged these progressive, teleological connotations. Today, evolutionary thought usually defines itself in relation to the Darwinian theory of evolution, the contributions to evolutionary economics not excepted. Some authors consider Darwinian theory to be the master theory. Others borrow from it at a heuristic level for their analogy-driven theorizing in economics. Yet others explicitly dissociate themselves from Darwinian thought.

Schumpeter and the neo-Schumpeterian synthesis

Schumpeter avoided the term 'evolution'. He considered it a Darwinian concept and denied such concepts any economic relevance. However, in his theory of capitalist development, Schumpeter (1934) clearly subscribes to the three meta-premises above. The restructuring of the economy is explained as emerging endogenously from ever new waves of major innovations implemented by pioneering entrepreneurs with unique capabilities and motivation. Technology and the institutions of capitalism are endogenized. The transformation process of the economy is assumed to be governed by regular patterns, that is, cycles of investment and growth – booms and depressions – triggered by the innovations that occur 'in waves' and diffuse throughout the economy in competitive imitation processes.

In Schumpeter (1942, p. 83) innovations that 'incessantly revolutionize the economic structure from within' remain central, but the innovating agents change. Previously viewed as achievements of unique promoter-entrepreneurs, innovations now appear as the routine

output of trained specialists in large corporations. Correspondingly, the driving force of capitalist development is identified in the risky R&D investments of the large trusts – undertaken only if they expect proper returns to be earned. To protect these returns from being competed away immediately, the large, innovative corporations tend to engage in monopolistic practices. Such practices are incompatible with the ideal of perfect competition, but without them there would be significantly fewer R&D investments and innovations. Moreover, Schumpeter (1942, ch. 8) claims that monopolistic practices work for only a limited time before innovations are eventually imitated or invalidated by rival innovations. Despite temporary monopolistic practices, competition by innovation thus boosts economic growth and raises prosperity more than fiercer price competition could ever do. This notion of 'Schumpeterian competition' induced a long debate about the relationships between firm size, market structure and innovativeness in which, however, the broader concept of endogenous economic change was lost from sight.

Endogenous change returns to centre stage in Nelson and Winter's (1982) neo-Schumpeterian restatement of evolutionary economics that blends Schumpeter's ideas with Darwinian concepts on the one hand and elements of the behavioural theory of the firm on the other. Schumpeter (1942) had not been specific about the innovative operations of the large corporations. To fill the gap, Nelson and Winter assume that, because of bounded rationality, firms operate on the basis of organizational routines. Different firms develop different routines for producing, investing, price setting, using profits, searching for innovations, and so forth, resulting in a diversity of competitive behaviours in the industry. By analogy with the principle of natural selection, Nelson and Winter argue that this diversity tends to be eroded whenever competing routines lead to differences in the firms' market performance and profitability. The better the firms perform, the more likely they are to grow, and the less reason they have to change their routines. The opposite holds for poorly performing firms. Much as differential reproductive success raises the share of better adapted genes in the gene pool of a population, differential firm growth thus raises the relative frequency of the better adapted routines in the 'routine pool' of the entire industry.

Instead of being a matter of optimal, deliberate substitution between given alternatives, in this view, the firms' competitive adaptations to changing market conditions are forced on them by selection processes operating on their routines. However, in a Schumpeterian spirit, Nelson and Winter also account for innovative moves – a breaking away from old routines – in an industry's response to changing market conditions. New ways of doing things, for example in responding to rising input prices, are established by search processes which are themselves guided by higher-level routines. Modelled as random draws from a distribution of productivity increments, innovations raise the average performance of the industry and regenerate the diversity of firm behaviours for selection to operate on. Some of the firms are driven out of the market, while the surviving ones tend to grow. Under innovation competition, technology and industry structure thus co-evolve and feed a non-equilibrating economic growth process. Regarding the debate on Schumpeterian competition, Nelson and Winter's analysis suggests a reversal of cause and effect: a high degree of concentration within an industry (an indicator of monopolistic power) may evolve as a consequence of, rather than being a prerequisite for, a high rate of innovativeness in the industry.

Selection principles and processes
Analogies between natural selection and market competition are not new. Better-adapted variants of firm behaviour have often been argued to prevail in an industry just as better-adapted variants tend to prevail under natural selection pressure in the population of a species (an argument that has sometimes been misunderstood as vindicating profit-maximizing behaviour). The logic of the argument can be rendered more precise (Metcalfe, 1994). Consider an industry with firms $i = 1, \ldots, n$ producing a homogeneous output with unit cost $c_i = $ const. Assume that the firms use different organizational routines which result in a non-degenerate unit cost distribution. Let $s_i(t)$ denote the market share of firm i at time t measured by output. In a competitive market in which trade takes place at a uniform price $p(t)$,

$$p(t) = c(t) = \sum_i s_i(t) \cdot c_i, \qquad (1)$$

with $c(t)$ as the average level of unit cost in the industry. By eq. (1), the average profit in the industry is zero. For at least one firm i, however, individual profit $\pi_i = p(t) - c_i > 0$ unless the entire market is served by the firm with the lowest level of unit cost.

Let the firm's growth be expressed in terms of the rate of change of its market share $(ds_i(t)/dt)/s_i(t)$ that is assumed to be a monotonic function φ of the firm's profit. With (1) inserted into the individual profit equation, the rate of change of the firm's market share can therefore be written as

$$\frac{ds_i(t)/dt}{s_i(t)} = \varphi(c(t) - c_i) = \varphi(\pi_i(t) - \pi(t)). \qquad (2)$$

Hence, performance differences across firms and their routines translate into corresponding differential growth rates of the firms.

The 'replicator' eq. (2) corresponds to what is called 'Fisher's principle' in population genetics (Hofbauer and

Sigmund, 1988, ch. 3). Let the fitness of an organism carrying a certain genetic trait be a constant. If it exceeds the average fitness in a population, the relative share of that trait in the population increases and vice versa. Consequently, natural selection raises average fitness over time to the level of the highest individual fitness. The change of the mean population fitness is proportional to the variance of the individual fitness. Analogously, with $c(t)$ as the measure for 'population fitness' in eq. (2), $dc(t)/dt = f(\mathrm{Var}(c_i)) \leq 0$.

If individual fitness is not constant, Fisher's principle no longer applies. Suppose individual unit costs decrease with the firms' output, for example because of scale economies. The replicator equation can then have several fixed points representing multiple selection equilibria associated with a different average cost level (Metcalfe, 1994). Which of the multiple equilibria the process converges to – and, consequently, whether the *ex ante* most profitable cost practice is eventually selected – depends on the initial conditions. Selection does not necessarily drive fitness or, for that matter, profits to the largest maximum. (Replicator equations with multiple equilibria can also result if the individual fitness terms depend on the population shares of their carriers. Such a frequency dependency is characteristic of models in evolutionary game theory; see Hofbauer and Sigmund, 1988, ch. 16.)

To influence the underlying distribution of traits or behaviours, selection requires sufficiently inert conditions. In economic transformation processes this condition is often systematically violated. For example, firms facing a declining market share and/or profitability have strong incentives to modify their operations, that is, to replace inferior routines and/or to search for innovations. In general, with innovations playing a central role – as in Schumpeterian capitalist development – the volatility of the firms' environment increases and makes inertia rather unlikely. Industry dynamics are then more likely to be shaped by the generation and diffusion of innovations following their own time patterns rather than by selection processes. While in the case of selection processes theorizing focuses at the population level ('population thinking'), the explanation of the generation and diffusion of innovations can benefit from reconstructing motives and capabilities at the individual level.

Emergence and diffusion of innovations
Important as innovations are for economic transformation processes, the possibilities for analysing how they emerge are limited because the underlying cognitive processes are basically unknown. What can nonetheless be analysed is why and when agents are motivated to search for innovations, provided their motivation is not made contingent on the – as yet unknown – outcome of the search (as in models of optimal choices between known alternatives that are therefore not applicable here). Often search motivation is triggered by a state of

dissatisfaction or deprivation that the agents want to overcome by actions still to be found. Among the causes may be unsatisfied curiosity, a motivation to achieve something (Schumpeter, 1934), or an agent's aspiration level that is temporarily not satisfied (Nelson and Winter, 1982, ch. 9). Where individual motivations like these occur in an uncorrelated way, they induce a base rate of innovative activity in the economy. If, in contrast, search motivation arises in a correlated way, for example in an economic crisis or when an industry is exposed to major innovations, the rate of innovative activities can rise far above the base rate. This is the case, for example, when firms need to innovate or be fast imitators with sufficient absorptive capacity in order to survive and therefore routinely engage in R&D.

Once an innovation is created or discovered by an agent, its implications can be grasped. Suppose, after assessing its benefits and costs, an agent implements an innovation. The implementation can usually be observed by competitors and/or other potential users. Since, in the absence of independent, own experience, people often draw conclusions from observing what others do, some observers may thus infer that the innovation is profitable and may start imitating it. Other observers may draw this conclusion only after a number of competitors and/or potential users have also signalled that they expect to benefit from adopting the innovation. Observational learning of this kind implies a dependency of the individual imitation or adoption behaviour – and, hence, the diffusion of the innovation – on the relative frequency of adopters.

The logic of this dependency can be captured by a function $q(t) = g(F(t))$, depicting the probability $q(t)$ that an agent who decides in t will adopt the innovation against the relative frequency of adopters $F(t)$ at time t. For $q(t) > F(t)$ the expected relative share of adopters grows with each additional decision and vice versa for $q(t) < F(t)$. The diffusion dynamics

$$\frac{dF(t)}{dt} = q(t) - F(t) \qquad (3)$$

therefore hinge on the shape of the function g. For the quadratic function $q(t) = aF(t) - aF(t)^2$, $a > 1$, for instance, $F(t)$ converges to a fixed point F^a, $0 < F^a \leqslant 1$, that depends on the size of a. (By integration of eq. (3) the diffusion path can in this case be shown to follow the well-known S-shaped logistic trend.)

For the cubic function $q(t) = 3F(t)^2 - 2F(t)^3$, to take that example, the condition $q(t) = F(t)$ is satisfied if F equals $0, \frac{1}{2}$, or 1. Inserting the cubic function into eq. (3), $F = 0$ and $F = 1$ can be shown to represent stable fixed points of eq. (3) while $F^* = \frac{1}{2}$ represents an unstable fixed point. This implies that for $F(t) < F^*$ the probability of adopting the innovation is too small to induce a spontaneous diffusion process. If $F(t)$ were for some reason to exceed F^* – representing a 'critical mass' of

adopters – the innovation would however spread. The reason could be fluctuations of $F(t)$ that randomly cumulate, but are not represented in this simple deterministic model. (This explanation also plays a role in evolutionary game theory where the question is, for example, whether a new convention can emerge in a coordination game; see Young, 1993.) Another reason could be that somebody organizes a collective action by which the critical mass of agents is made to believe that more than the share F^* of agents will adopt the innovation.

With major technological innovations, competing variants or designs that serve the same user needs are often spawned simultaneously. The diffusion processes of the competing variants are interdependent if, for each of the variants, the users' utility varies with the number of adopters. Such 'economies to adoption' of alternative variants have been diagnosed, for example, for electric current transmission, video recorder systems, or the layout of typewriter keyboards. The underlying pattern is again a frequency-dependency effect that can be analysed as before, if only two rival variants are assumed and the decision of agents who adopt neither of these is neglected.

Let $q(t)$ denote the probability of adopting the first variant and $F(t)$ its share of adopters at time t. Suppose both variants become available simultaneously and offer the same inherent benefits. For the first variant the development is captured by the cubic function above, interpreted as the mean process of a stochastic adoption process. With an identical number of initial adopters, $F(0) = F^* = \frac{1}{2}$ and $q(t) = \frac{1}{2}$. Once $F(t) \neq \frac{1}{2}$ for $t > 0$, economies to adoption raise the individual adoption probability of one of the variants over that of the other. As a consequence, the realization of the stochastic diffusion process initially fluctuates around F^*. Over time, however, small historical events and cumulative random fluctuations drive the process in the direction of either $F = 0$ (first variant disappearing) or $F = 1$ (second variant disappearing). In competitive diffusion processes of this kind, the prevailing state of the technology is thus 'path-dependent', and the process can be 'locked in' to the one variant if it is assumed, in addition, that over time the number of adopters grows beyond all bounds (Arthur, 1994, ch. 3). This means that, for $t \rightarrow \infty$, the likelihood of passing F^* by cumulative random fluctuations goes to zero.

The evolution of industries and the institutions backing innovativeness

The substitution processes that the diffusion of new products and techniques induces shake up the established production structures. Factor owners and producers are forced to make adjustments – often painful ones that depreciate earlier investments and acquired competencies. While such 'pecuniary externalities' are inevitable

concomitants of innovations, the longer-run consequence of innovativeness is – as Schumpeter (1942)
had postulated – a rising standard of living of the masses.
As a result of innovativeness, labour productivity and
per capita income increase. New products and services
absorb the growing consumption expenditures where
established markets tend to be satiated. New employment
opportunities emerge in new industries. To understand
the working of the innovative transformation process and
its policy implications, it is often useful to reconstruct the
historical record of the evolution of entire industries
(Malerba et al., 1999). Many of them, like the auto
industry or the computer industry, grow out of a few
major innovations for which new markets can be established or existing ones can substantially be expanded.
Industries continue to grow over time under the pressure
of imitative competition, often following a path of technical improvements that evolves within a 'technological
paradigm' (cf. Dosi, 1988).

Such regular patterns of change at the industry level
can for many, though not all, industries be characterized
in a stylized way by a life-cycle metaphor (Klepper, 1997).
Soon after their markets have been established by early
innovators, the industries experience heavy entry and exit
activities by competitors who partly imitate and partly
add new varieties. While the market is expanding, a
drastic shake-out in the number of firms occurs so that
eventually a few large firms dominate the industry,
and diversity in products and processes is reduced. In
the beginning, product innovations are a main source
of competitive advantages. Over time, however, the
importance of process innovations increases. They raise
productivity, drive down unit costs, and tend to intensify
price competition. One cause of these patterns of industry evolution seems to be increasing returns to process
innovations. These favour first movers that have been
able to attain a sufficient size to spread development costs
over larger output bases. With fiercer price competition,
the firms with higher unit costs tend to be driven out of
the industry, as in the selection model discussed above.
Market concentration rises. With fewer innovations at
that stage in the industry, its growth slows down, if the
industry is not stagnating or declining.

Industry evolution is often connected with spatial
effects. Innovative production techniques and new products often grow out of initiatives, competencies, endowments, and institutional settings in particular locations
(Antonelli, 2001). If such complementary and interdependent local innovative activities gain momentum
and trigger a self-augmenting process of firm growth and
firm founding activities in close spatial proximity, an
'industrial cluster' can emerge. During early phases of the
industry life cycle, a substantial share of the corresponding national or international industrial innovative activity may even be concentrated in such locations, Silicon
Valley being the paradigmatic case. In such regions,
income and employment are boosted. For policymaking

the question therefore arises under what conditions
innovative industrial clusters emerge and how and when
their emergence can be fostered (Brenner, 2004).

The early growth of innovative industries creates new
employment opportunities. At later stages of the industry
life cycle, when price competition and substitution pressure from innovative industries force the industry to raise
labour productivity to reduce costs, employment is usually gradually lost. (For this reason, an industrial cluster
that dominates a region can, in later stages of the industry life cycle, become a drag on local employment and
prosperity.) At the macroeconomic level, the stages
reached in the life cycles of the industries interact in a
complex way with productivity and income growth rates,
and with the overall changes in employment (Metcalfe,
Foster and Ramlogan, 2006). Although these interactions
have not yet been fully explored, it seems clear that at
least two conditions must be met to maintain a high level
of aggregate employment. First, innovative industries
with new employment opportunities must emerge at the
right times to compensate for the labour-saving technical
progress. Second, the workforce must be able to adjust to
the qualification requirements of the innovative industries and technologies. Since there is no self-regulating
mechanism fulfilling the first condition, and because of
delays and frictions in satisfying the second condition,
the evolution of the industries is not necessarily a smooth
transformation process. Aggregate employment and
domestic income can vary substantially with the pace at
which innovative industries emerge and expand.

However, high levels of education and training are
likely to raise innovativeness and the qualifications of
the workforce. Ensuring this with an adequate institutional infrastructure – a productive national system of
innovations – is an important policy option in supporting and smoothing the transformation process. This is
even more true from a global perspective. A country's
growth potential and its competitive advantage in trade
hinge on when the country gains access to newly emerging technological opportunities and where in the
innovative industries' life cycle it enters the market.
History shows that differences between countries in
this respect correspond to differences in their national
innovation systems (Fagerberg, 2002).

Darwinian perspectives on economic evolution

The neo-Schumpeterian approach considers the concept
of selection as constitutive for evolutionary economics.
Economic selection processes, operating on the diversity
of individual behaviours, force adaptations on populations of agents who are prevented by their bounded
rationality from deliberately adapting optimally. The
import of the selection concept is not meant to extend
Darwinism to the economic domain. Such an extension
was, however, advocated by Veblen (1898) under the
influence of the Darwinian revolution of his time. He

coined the term 'evolutionary' economics for such an approach (Hodgson, 2004). A Darwinian perspective on the economic domain can indeed help to clarify how evolutionary economics fits with the Darwinian world view now prevailing in the sciences and in this way offer new insights (Witt, 2003).

In the economic domain, the bulk of change to be explained occurs within single generations. In contrast, the Darwinian theory of natural selection focuses on inter-generational change and is therefore relevant only for explaining the basis on which economic evolution rests. These are, first, the long-term constraints man-made economic evolution is subjected to and, second, the innate dispositions and adaptation mechanisms in humans (shaped earlier in human history by natural selection) that define the basic behavioural repertoire. Veblen (1898) focused on habits, including habits of thought, which he assumed to emerge from hereditary traits and past experiences, given the traditions, conventions and material circumstances of the time. (Habits play the crucial role in Veblen's explanation of the 'cumulative causation' of institutions which, in turn, he regarded as the key to understanding the different forms of economic life and their genesis.)

In a similar vein one may focus on human preferences that emerge from the interplay of inherited dispositions and innate conditioning learning mechanisms – both of these shared by all humans with the usual genetic variance. A prominent example of innate dispositions is the altruistic attitudes that play a prominent role in evolutionary game theory (Hofbauer and Sigmund, 1988, ch. 14). Other examples of innate dispositions can be found in certain forms of consumption. The genetically fixed learning mechanism accumulates the influence of a lifelong history of reinforcement and conditioning. It is responsible for the emerging variety of individual preferences and keeps them changing over time.

Following Hayek (1988, ch. 1), innate behaviour can be conjectured to play a key role in the evolution of human institutions. They emerge, he argues, through social learning of 'rules of conduct' that starts from primitive, genetically fixed, forms of social behaviour and add on new elements by trial and error. Over their history, different groups or whole societies thus build up a diversity of rules that regulate their interactions. The group members' innovativeness is channelled into economic activities provided institutional regulations do not discourage this or fail to protect the capital accumulation that is necessary to realize economic growth. Those groups that succeed in developing and passing on rules able to better meet these conditions can therefore be expected to grow and prosper in terms of population size and per capita income. Their differential success may enable such groups to conquer and/or absorb less well-equipped, competing groups and thus propagate better adapted institutions.

Economic evolution is, of course, also shaped in an essential way by human intelligence. By cognitive

learning, problem solving and inventiveness, knowledge about institutions, opportunities and technologies is created (Mokyr, 2002). In the longer run, the enabling effects of cumulative knowledge generation emerging over time matter more than the effects of economizing on scarce resources at each point in time. From a Darwinian perspective the most significant tendency in the use of cumulative knowledge is the manipulation of natural constraints to better accord them with human preferences. This has enlarged the niche for the human species and has improved living conditions for an ever-increasing number of its members. At the same time, however, knowledge accumulation has contributed to dramatically increasing the human share in the use of natural resources. According to Georgescu-Roegen's (1971) evolutionary approach to production theory, this way of solving problems implies a risky long-term impact on nature, the ultimate basis of the human economy. To account for these risks further innovative efforts that transform the economy from within seem indispensable.

ULRICH WITT

See also **analogy and metaphor; competition and selection; deterministic evolutionary dynamics; diffusion of technology; learning and evolution in games: an overview; path dependence; Schumpeter, Joseph Alois; Schumpeterian growth and growth policy design; structural change; Veblen, Thorstein Bunde.**

Bibliography

Antonelli, C. 2001. *The Microeconomics of Technological Systems.* Oxford: Oxford University Press.

Arthur, W. 1994. *Increasing Returns and Path Dependence in the Economy.* Ann Arbor: Michigan University Press.

Brenner, T. 2004. *Local Industrial Clusters – Existence, Emergence and Evolution.* London: Routledge.

Dosi, G. 1988. Sources, procedures, and microeconomic effects of innovation. *Journal of Economic Literature* 26, 1120–171.

Fagerberg, J. 2002. *Technology, Growth and Competitiveness.* Cheltenham: Edward Elgar.

Georgescu-Roegen, N. 1971. *The Entropy Law and the Economic Process.* Cambridge, MA: Harvard University Press.

Hayek, F. 1988. *The Fatal Conceit.* London: Routledge.

Hodgson, G. 2004. *The Evolution of Institutional Economics.* London: Routledge.

Hofbauer, J. and Sigmund, K. 1988. *The Theory of Evolution and Dynamical Systems.* Cambridge: Cambridge University Press.

Klepper, S. 1997. Industry life cycles. *Industrial and Corporate Change* 6, 145–81.

Malerba, F. Nelson, R., Orsenigo, L. and Winter, S. 1999. 'History-friendly' models of industry evolution: the computer industry. *Industrial and Corporate Change* 8, 3–40.

Metcalfe, J. 1994. Competition, Fisher's principle and increasing returns in the selection process. *Journal of Evolutionary Economics* 4, 327–46.

Metcalfe, S., Foster, J. and Ramlogan, R. 2006. Adaptive economic growth. *Cambridge Journal of Economics* 30, 7–32.

Mokyr, J. 2002. *The Gifts of Athena*. Princeton: Princeton University Press.

Nelson, R. and Winter, S. 1982. *An Evolutionary Theory of Economic Change*. Cambridge: Harvard University Press.

Schumpeter, J. 1934. *The Theory of Economic Development*. Cambridge: Harvard University Press.

Schumpeter, J. 1942. *Capitalism, Socialism and Democracy*. New York: Harper.

Veblen, T. 1898. Why is economics not an evolutionary science? *Quarterly Journal of Economics* 12, 373–97.

Witt, U. 2003. *The Evolving Economy*. Cheltenham: Edward Elgar.

Young, P. 1993. The evolution of conventions. *Econometrica* 61, 57–84.

[2]

A "Darwinian Revolution" in Economics?

by

U<small>LRICH</small> W<small>ITT</small>*

1. Neoclassical vs. Evolutionary Economics: The Inevitable Point of Departure?

In recent reappraisals of what has come to be labeled the "Darwinian revolution" at the turn of the century in biology there is a broad agreement that Darwin's formulation of the theory of the evolution of life on earth and the descent of species amounted to no less than the establishment of an entirely new scientific research program which rivaled the then dominant Newtonian world view (see M<small>AYR</small> [1991, ch. 5]). Studies of Darwin's diary and his correspondence with his contemporaries have shown that the ideas behind their ambitious endeavor were based on the upper class liberal social philosophy of Victorian England which was, in a sense, transferred to nature (Y<small>OUNG</small> [1988], D<small>ESMOND</small> and M<small>OORE</small> [1991], R<small>ICHARDS</small> [1992]). Looking back at what happened at the same time in economics, it appears ironical that the most influential group among the proponents of the "subjectivist revolution" then taking place in economic theory – Walras, Edgeworth, and Pareto – were just about to turn their backs on the social philosophy of Smith and Mill. Their aim, unlike that of the Darwinians, was the introduction into economics of a Newtonian approach, a rigorous formulation of the "mechanic of utility and self-interest" as Jevons had put it. Borrowing their basic concepts from the classical mechanics of gravitating systems, they focussed on a state of rest, the (total) market equilibrium, rather than on the actual market processes. Market equilibrium was considered not only as a state where all individual plans were mutually compatible, but also one in which the utility of all the agents involved reached a maximum subject to the mutually imposed constraints – the dual formulation of the concept of equilibrium in classical mechanics where the state of rest is associated with minimum free energy (see M<small>IROWSKI</small> [1988]).

The development of that Newtonian research program in economics reached its climax in S<small>AMUELSON</small>'s [1947] perfection of the analogy with classical mechanics. It coincided with a broad acceptance in the economics discipline of an idea that originated in a quite different strand of the subjectivist revolu-

* The author is grateful to J. Irving-Lessmann and C. Sartorius for helpful comments.

tion, namely Austrian economics. This was the conception of economics as the science dealing with "the use of scarce means for given ends." This idea not only brought about lasting confusion between the normative and explanatory aspects, it also encouraged the identification of the neoclassical synthesis of optimization calculus and equilibrium analysis with what was considered the proper algorithmic basis for formalizing economic theory. Although there has always been some opposition to these interpretations and some rival heterodox approaches, no paradigm has emerged which explicitly challenges the Newtonian underpinnings of economic theory like the Darwinian revolution did in the life sciences. More recently, some well-founded criticisms of the neoclassical synthesis of optimization calculus and equilibrium analysis have been launched under the label "evolutionary economics" which was successfully revived by Richard Nelson and Sidney Winter. However, as discussed elsewhere, the writers to whom that label can be attributed are far from pursuing a coherent research program.[1] In discussing the potential and future direction of an evolutionary approach to economics it may therefore be time to raise a provocative question: can evolutionary economic thought ever be expected to result in something like a Darwinian revolution in economics? If, as will be argued, chances are not too bad, then another question arises: what major changes would be implied by such a revolution? This question will be explored in what follows.

2. Evolution: Metaphor or Homomorphism?

At the turn of the century, VEBLEN [1898] – obviously influenced by the Darwinian revolution in biology – quite similarly asked whether economics could be made an evolutionary science in a Darwinian sense, a question for which he had no satisfactory answers. The revival of the label "evolutionary" economics in the seventies was not accidental. After a period of relative neglect, the potential of Darwinian thought for reshaping economics – Veblen's unanswered question – once more became an issue. However, the approach taken by major writers at the time, e. g. BOULDING [1981], NELSON and WINTER [1982], HIRSHLEIFER [1982], was not to rethink economics in a way that would result in a major shift comparable to the Darwinian revolution in the sciences. Rather, their strategy was a more limited one of looking for inspiration to explain certain economic phenomena through metaphors borrowed from evolutionary biology.

What figured most prominently in these attempts was the theory of natural selection. Competitive market processes with the entry and exit of firms, the

---

[1] See WITT [1992] and HODGSON [1995] for more recent developments. In particular, a strong current of contemporary evolutionary thought traces its roots back to work by Schumpeter who was explicitly opposed to any Darwinian analogies or metaphors in economics.

introduction and disappearance of products and manufacturing processes etc. were considered to operate as an instance of "economic natural selection" (WINTER [1964]). It is unclear, however, what the analogue to genes should be and how the analogue to genetic reproduction could be imagined to work in the economic domain, in particular, what would provide the continuity of the selection processes necessary to generate any systematic results. The problem is particularly pressing because of the human capacity to anticipate unfavorable systematic outcomes of "external" selection processes, if there are some, and to change the very basis of those processes by "internally" selecting different kinds of behavior through what is called cognitive problem solving.

The fact that in Darwin's contribution to evolutionary biology at least five different, but related, theories have been distinguished, of which the theory of natural selection is only one (MAYR [1991, ch. 4]), is indicative of the rather narrow aims informing the revival of evolutionary economics in the seventies – too narrow to get from a convincing criticism of neoclassical methods to laying the foundations for a truly persuasive alternative. The past few years have witnessed a real boost in the number of contributions to evolutionary economics with a huge increase in the breadth of the topics covered. Yet, a conclusive answer to Veblen's question is still pending and, it is submitted here, will not be found unless there is a clear concept of what evolution means in the economic domain. A metaphorical use of some notions selectively borrowed from evolutionary biology is not sufficient.[2] One possible way to arrive at such a concept is via abstraction. If abstract features can be identified wherever evolutionary processes are supposed to govern a domain – in nature, say, in languages, or in the economy – then it may be easier to determine what these abstract features imply specifically for the notion of evolution in the respective domain. Such a generalization strategy obviously presupposes some degree of homomorphy in the domains compared. Hence, what is suggested here is looking for commonalities at the level of homomorphic structures rather than at the metaphorical level.

3. General Features: Novelty, Historicity, and the Driving-Forces Problem

On an abstract level, evolution may be taken to mean the self-transformation of a system through the generation and dissemination of novelty. Novelty

---

[2] Note that for Darwin and his contemporaries the very notion of evolution in nature had philosophical and religious connotations which make it unsuitable to simply transfer it to the economic domain. The aim was to overcome the basically religiously motivated idea of a predetermined existence: if everything in the cosmos was already contained in the initial act of creation as postulated in Genesis, then development along the pre-established lines would be the issue. Against fierce religious opposition Darwin held that it is evolution that governs nature in a never ending process which keeps generating new species which did not previously exist. Corresponding to this, the theory of common descent postulated that each species developed from its predecessor as a result of the evolutionary process (see MAYR [1991, ch. 2]).

means different things in the biosphere, in the economy, and in languages. (In genetic reproduction, novelty is not necessarily to be equated with mutation. It may also result from recombining existing genetic information.) However, its key role for evolution is always the same.[3] A consequence of a system's capacity to create and disseminate novelty is the coexistence of a variety of forms within the system. Variety, and the differences in performance which it usually implies, is a crucial factor in explaining the dissemination processes which make up the lion's share of observable evolutionary processes. To talk about evolution in a specific field without knowing the variety, the phenomenological richness, which it has produced there would be pointless – hence the crucial role that the naturalists' empirical and historical descriptions, collections, and studies have played not only in Darwin's own work, but for the Darwinian revolution in general (BOWLER [1989, chs. 5–7]). However, beyond the mere taxonomic attempt to come to grips with morphological and geographical variety, the naturalists' efforts also turned out to be crucial for understanding and honoring the historical contingency, or historicity, of the evolutionary process.

Once a novel genetic variant has occurred, its further success or failure in terms of dissemination depends on the current state of its environment. Apart from the physical conditions, the other variants of life which are already present (and which stem from the preceding stages of evolution) and the traits these variants have are crucially important too. The influence of this well-known "occupancy effect" on the evolution of the species can be acknowledged in general terms, but its actual impact cannot be traced without careful studies of the historical and geographical contingencies. This explains the interest in evolutionary biology in phyletic structures and their paleontologic records. Quite similarly, knowledge about the ever changing institutional, technological, and commercial conditions is not only of interest for understanding what evolutionary economics is talking about. It is also necessary for identifying the influence of the historical contingencies – many of them similar to the occupancy effect – in economic processes of change.[4]

Historical contingency is an evident complication in tracing the causal structures in evolutionary processes, i. e. endogenous change. It is also relevant in exploring the circumstances under which novelty emerges. However, in such an

---

[3] Even the most casual experience shows economic processes and results around us which are less likely to be found the further back in time we go, and it shows that many of them are continuing to change more or less rapidly. All these changes have certainly not been imposed on the economy by exogeneous shocks – in spite of the fact this seems to be a fashionable idea in contemporary mainstream economics.

[4] Thus, investigations into the historical legal and customary (or cultural) framework of certain markets or entire economies may help, e. g., to understood how the occurrence of novelty may be *selectively* fostered or curbed, see e. g. HAGEN [1964], NORTH [1990] and SIEGENTHALER [1993]. The study of the history of technology may provide an understanding of the historical contingencies of industrial innovations and their diffusion in the markets as, e. g., in MOKYR [1990], CARON, ERKER and FISCHER [1995].

exploration, the question of generation must be kept separate from the question of causation. Economic novelties – or in the action oriented economic terminology: innovations – emerge from more or less actively pursued attempts to improve ideas about economic actions and purposes. Even though we may be unable to determine whether people succeed in coming up with new action possibilities and, if they do, to anticipate what these possibilites are, we are not necessarily unable to give reasons for why they have been trying. While the *outcome* of creative human problem-solving is, in this sense, theoretically "under-determined," our theories may allow us to conjecture about what *causes* people to use their creativity when they might otherwise have proceeded along established lines.[5] In fact, the motivational aspects which bring about the search for novelty may be sufficiently regular to be identified as the driving forces of economic evolution.

In Darwin's view the driving force of evolution in the biosphere appears to have been adaptation (BOWLER [1989, 154]). In the economic sphere the driving forces can be related to human endeavor, hence the relevance of motivational hypotheses. As explained earlier (e. g. in WITT [1993]), two motives may be conjectured to trigger the creation of novelty which are complementary but operate on distinct modes: curiosity and dissatisfaction or fear. As far as curiosity is concerned, people obviously find it entertaining to search for and experience novelty as such (not too much of it, not too little), and they are inventive enough to produce it. Therefore, with such a motivation, novelty is being sought at some basic rate, at all times and in all societies, though the economic significance of innovations thus induced may differ. As far as dissatisfaction with the status quo (or fear of imagined future developments) is concerned, search for novel, not yet known, ways of acting thus motivated is triggered increasingly in times of (sometime anticipated) crises. Thus, as expected, the driving forces behind economic evolution are themselves historically contingent to some extent, and this is why economic evolution is not steady, but is characterized instead by alternating phases of stasis and of rapid change.

4. Implications: Transition Laws, Non-Aprioristic Economics and Classical Questions

The initial question was: what changes could be required in economic theory, if something equivalent to the Darwinian revolution in the sciences were to happen? As mentioned above, under the double influence of the neoclassical writers and the narrow definition of economics, economic theory is presently

---

[5] In a recent paper HODGSON [1995] has argued in favor of the idea of an "uncaused cause" as something missing in the present author's approach to evolutionary economics. It seems that this argument fails to acknowledge the difference between the generation and the causation of novelty.

dominated by the idea of optimality. On the conceptual level, economists strive for, and are usually satisfied with, demonstrating, on the basis of an aprioristic approach, that observed behavior, institutions, technological and commercial phenomena can be rationalized in some way. Since the observed phenomena are to a large extent the outcome of interactions between individuals, the aprioristic rationalization strategy usually relies on a static equilibrium analysis to obtain consistent results. Correspondingly, at the algorithmic level, the optimization calculus dominates the scene and has been developed with admirable sophistication even into dynamic variants such as optimal control theory.

Under these conditions, a first conceptual step to be taken for the systematic foundation of an evolutionary approach is to overcome the narrow confines of economics as a science of optimization and the corresponding "tyranny of apriorism" (JONES [1994]). Economics can instead be interpreted as the theory of all kinds of human behavior (i. e. rational or not in terms of some scientific observer's reconstructing situational logic) in the context of what are usually considered economic activities like production, exchange, consumption, distribution, accumulation. In such a perspective, it is only natural for economic theorizing to ask why and how these activities have changed so differently in scope and speed at different places and times. As an immediate consequence of the suggested conceptual change a second, and corresponding, step has to be taken with respect to the algorithmic basis of evolutionary economics: the focus on optimization calculus has to be replaced by a focus on transition laws. Transition laws describe the regularities in the development of a system by determining how the system proceeds from one state to another. At the level of individual economic behavior, well-known hypotheses which imply transition laws cover adaptation behavior, learning, concept and opinion formation, preference change etc. Transition laws are obviously a prerequisite for any dynamic theory and can usually be given a formal expression in the form of recursive equations, difference and differential equations, or evolution algorithms. In evolutionary economics all of these tools are now being used for very different purposes.[6]

There are, of course, some limitations on the use of calculus in evolutionary theorizing which relate to the particular epistemological problems implied by novelty (see WITT [1993]). Since the meaning of novelty cannot positively be anticipated, the future development of evolutionary systems is, in principle, "open." Hence, the development cannot, in its entirety, be described by specifying some equation(s) of motion and some initial conditions. A hypothetical distinction can, however, be made between pre-revelation analysis and post-

---

[6] Examples are: simple Markoff models (e. g. WINTER [1971]), logistic diffusion models (e. g. FOSTER [1992]), replicator-dynamics (e. g. METCALFE [1994]), generalized Polya-urn schemes (ARTHUR [1994]), the master-equation approach (WEIDLICH and BRAUN [1993]), and evolution algorithms (e. g. MARENGO [1992]).

revelation analysis, i.e. before and after the meaning of novelty has been revealed. On such a basis many economic processes like, e.g., the diffusion of a new product, individual adaptation to new conditions, and differential selection in a market process can often reasonably be treated as post-revelation phenomena and described by equations of motion, subject to the condition that no further novelty is generated. Furthermore, economic evolution does seem to follow certain regularities which may be supposed to hold whatever the specific meaning of novelty revealed in the future. Nomological hypotheses referring to these regularities may well themselves have the form of transition laws claiming that, whichever novelty occurs, these laws will not be invalidated. If this condition holds, such laws may well be given a formal expression. [7]

A non-apriorist view of what is going on in the economy has certain aspects in common with the attitudes of many classical writers. Indeed, many of the questions which have been raised by pre-subjectivist economists appear as valuable objects of evolutionary theorizing: how do demographic growth and change interact with economic evolution? Are the division of labor and economic specialization prerequisites for economic development contingent on a certain institutional co-evolution? What is the lesson to be learned from the historical record concerning increasing specialization and the employment of labor in economic development? There are, of course, also many questions which have been raised more recently, not least in the growing number of contributions to evolutionary economics. What role is played by institutions and socially shared views and values; how do they themselves come into being and change? In which way is technological and commercial knowledge created, disseminated, and actually put to use? To what extent is innovativeness possible, and to what extent is it encouraged, so that behavioral variety can emerge and compete? What is the historical record for different forms of fostering innovativeness? In what institutional framework, and to what extent, does varying individual behavior result in differential success or failure and overall improvements in economic performance? How do all these factors feed back on one another both in general and in the historical detail? How can an ever growing production volume be sold without the consumers ending up satiated? What role is played in this context by the formation of and the change in tastes, and innovations and differentiation in the products and services?

Some of the questions to be raised point to connections between evolutionary economics and ecological economics (see GOWDY [1994]). Can the path of expanding production presently being pursued and the corresponding volume of inputs from nature be sustained? What actually are the factors of production when economic evolution in the very long run is considered as a continuing anthropogenic expansion of the natural dissipative system? As a matter of fact, for several questions related to long term development, Darwinian thought may

---

[7] Straight forward candidates are the laws of thermodynamic, see FABER and PROOPS [1990] for a contribution to evolutionary economics based on such a foundation.

even become a fruitful part of evolutionary economic theorizing, not through metaphorical use, but through direct application. Humans, and the inherited parts of their behavioral dispositions (preferences), are a result of evolution on this planet. It may therefore be conjectured that the common genetic elements in human preferences which dictate some average tendencies in the agents' endeavors could produce some "direction" in the path which economic evolution takes. It appears that almost any question relating to systematic features in the coming into being of economic phenomena and in changes in them is a valid problem for the evolutionary approach to economics. Any attempt to do justice to its potential research agenda is therefore beyond the present outline.

References

ARTHUR, W. B. [1994], *Increasing Returns and Path Dependence in the Economy*, Michigan University Press: Ann Arbor.

BOULDING, K. E. [1981], *Evolutionary Economics*, Sage Publications: Beverly Hills, CA.

BOWLER, P. J. [1989], *Evolution – the History of an Idea*, revised ed, University of California Press: Berkeley.

CARON, F., ERKER, P. and FISCHER, W. (eds.) [1995], *Innovations in the European Economy Between the Wars*, de Gruyter: Berlin-New York.

DESMOND, A. and MOORE, J. R. [1991], *Darwin*, Michael Joseph: London.

FABER, M. and PROOPS, J. L. R. [1990], *Evolution, Time, Production and the Environment*, Springer: Berlin-Heidelberg-New York.

FOSTER, J. [1992], "The Determination of Sterling M3, 1963–88: An Evolutionary Macroeconomic Approach," *Economic Journal*, 102, 481–496.

GOWDY, J. [1994], *Coevolution Economics: The Economy, Society and the Environment*, Kluwer: Boston.

HAGEN, E. E. [1964], *On the Theory of Social Change: How Economic Growth Begins*, Tavistock Publishers: London.

HIRSHLEIFER, J. [1982], "Evolutionary Models in Economics and Law," *Research in Law and Economics*, 4, 1–60.

HODGSON, G. M. [1995], "The Evolution of Evolutionary Economics," *Scottish Journal of Political Economy*, 42, 469–488.

JONES, E. [1994], "The Tyranny of Apriorism in Economic Thought," *History of Economics Review*, 22, 24–69.

MARENGO, L. [1992], "Coordination and Organizational Learning in the Firm," *Journal of Evolutionary Economics*, 2, 313–326.

MAYR, E. [1991], *One Long Argument*, Harvard University Press: Cambridge, MA.

METCALFE, S. [1994], "Competition, Fisher's Principle, and Increasing Returns in the Selection Process," *Journal of Evolutionary Economics*, 4, 327–346.

MIROWSKI, P. [1988], *Against Mechanism – Protecting Economics From Science*, Rowman & Littlefield: Totowa, NJ.

MOKYR, J. [1990], *The Lever of Riches – Technological Creativity and Economic Progress*, Oxford University Press: Oxford-New York.

NELSON, R. R. and WINTER, S. G. [1982], *An Evolutionary Theory of Economic Change*, Harvard University Press: Cambridge, MA.

NORTH, D. C. [1990], *Institutions, Institutional Change and Economic Performance*, Cambridge University Press: Cambridge.

RICHARDS, R. J. [1992], *The Meaning of Evolution: The Morphological Construction and Ideological Reconstruction of Darwin's Theory*, Chicago University Press: Chicago.

152/4 (1996)   *A "Darwinian Revolution" in Economics?*   715

SAMUELSON, P. A. [1947], *Foundations of Economic Analysis*, Harvard University Press: Cambridge, MA.

SIEGENTHALER, H. [1993], *Regelvertrauen, Prosperität und Krisen*, Mohr (Siebeck): Tübingen.

VEBLEN, T. B. [1898], "Why is Economics not an Evolutionary Science?" *Quarterly Journal of Economics*, 12, 373–397.

WEIDLICH, W. and BRAUN, M. [1993], "The Master Equation Approach to Non-Linear Economics," pp. 85–117 in: U. Witt (ed.), *Evolution in Markets and Institutions*, Physica: Heidelberg.

WINTER, S. G. [1964], "Economic 'Natural Selection' and the Theory of the Firm," *Yale Economic Essays*, 4, 225–272.

–– [1971], "Satisficing, Selection, and the Innovating Remnant," *Quarterly Journal of Economics*, 85, 237–261.

WITT, U. [1992], "Evolution as the Theme of a new Heterodoxy in Economics," pp. 3–20 in: U. Witt (ed.), *Explaining Process and Change – Approaches to Evolutionary Economics*, Michigan University Press: Ann Arbor.

–– [1993], "Emergence and Dissemination of Innovations: Some Principles of Evolutionary Economics," pp. 91–100 in: R. H. Day and P. Chen (eds.), *Nonlinear Dynamics and Evolutionary Economics*, Oxford University Press: Oxford-New York.

YOUNG, R. M. [1988], *Darwin's Metaphor: Nature's Place in Victorian Culture*, Cambridge University Press: Cambridge.

Professor Ulrich Witt
Abteilung für Evolutionsökonomik
Max-Planck-Institut zur
Erforschung von Wirtschaftssystemen
August-Bebel-Straße 9
07743 Jena
Germany

[3]

Journal of Economic Methodology 11:2, 125–146 June 2004

On the proper interpretation of 'evolution' in economics and its implications for production theory

Ulrich Witt

Abstract How relevant is the notion of evolution for economics? In view of the paradigmatic influence of Darwinian thought, several recently advocated interpretations are discussed first which rely on Darwinian concepts. As an alternative, a notion of evolution is suggested that is based on a few, abstract, common principles which all domain-specific evolutionary processes share, including those in the economy. A different, ontological question is whether and, if so, how the various domain-specific evolutionary processes are connected. As an answer, an evolutionary continuity hypothesis is postulated and its concrete economic implications are discussed exemplarily for the theory of production.

Keywords: evolutionary economics, novelty, selection metaphor, sociobiology, Universal Darwinism, production theory
JEL code: B41, B52, D20, O33

1 INTRODUCTION

The historical record of the economic transformations that have taken place over only the past few decades is dramatic. Few products and services have remained unaltered. Hundreds of thousands of them have been newly created. Rising real income has made all of them affordable for mass consumption. Production techniques and working lives have been deeply transformed. It may be doubted that the equilibrium-cum-optimization heuristic of modern economics – which focuses on states rather than processes – is helpful in conceptualizing this incessant historical transformation of the economy. An 'evolutionary' approach has therefore been proposed as an alternative. However, it is not clear what precisely is implied by the notion of evolution in an economic context and, hence, what progress can be made by adopting an evolutionary approach. 'Evolution' is usually associated today with the billion years old process in which the forms of life on earth emerged – the process that has become intelligible on the basis of Darwin's (1859) theory. Correspondingly, Darwinian principles and their more recent refinements have come to be *the* model of an evolutionary

Journal of Economic Methodology ISSN 1350-178X print/ISSN 1469-9427 online © 2004 Taylor & Francis Ltd
http://www.tandf.co.uk/journals
DOI: 10.1080/13501780410001694091

theory and pre-Darwinian evolutionary thought in social philosophy, law, and the humanities (cf. Hayek 1967) have been forgotten.

Indeed, the intellectual dominance of the Darwinian approach to evolution also has not failed to influence the modern attempts to conceive of an evolutionary approach to economics. However, these attempts differ significantly with respect to the extent to which they assume an ontological basis in common with the Darwinian theory and, thus, subscribe to the Darwinian world view now prevailing in the sciences. Some of the contributions to evolutionary economics, starting with Veblen (1898), endorse a common ontology. Other contributions, like that of Nelson and Winter (1982), borrow Darwinian concepts for analogous constructions or metaphorical use at a heuristic level and leave open whether there are ontological commonalities with Darwinism. (Some contributions explicitly deny this.) The differing views correspond with different interpretations of the very notion of evolution. In this paper therefore, the pros and cons of the different interpretations will be discussed. An attempt will be made to identify an interpretation which can lead to a fruitful theorizing about the record of the economic transformations. Since human production activities have occurred at all times and in all cultures, the particular aspect for which this will be demonstrated exemplarily are the historical changes in human production together with their implications for the economic theory of production.

The paper proceeds as follows. In view of the paradigmatic influence of Darwinian thought, Section 2 briefly reviews the different positions that have been taken more recently with respect to the role Darwinian concepts could, or should, play in economics. Section 3 extends the discussion to the notion of evolution. Given that the notion is used in various domains with quite different domain-specific connotations, an interpretation will be proposed which refers to a few, abstract, common principles which all domain-specific evolutionary processes share. A different, namely ontological, question is whether or not there are (inter-) dependencies between domain-specific evolutionary processes. To answer that question, the hypothesis of an ontological continuity between evolution in nature and in the economy will be introduced. Section 4 explains how the continuity hypothesis can be made fruitful for an analysis of evolutionary economic change with an exemplary reconstruction of the conditions from which human production started to evolve. The reconstruction requires an approach to production that is more 'naturalistic' than the one usually taken in economics where all efforts went into developing ever more abstract versions of production theory. Some of the implications of both the reconstruction of, and the concomitant 'naturalistic' approach to, changing human production activities for the theory of the factors of production and economic growth are then discussed in Section 5. Section 6 offers the conclusions.

2 DIFFERENT VIEWS OF THE ROLE OF DARWINIAN CONCEPTS

There are many ways of referring to Darwinian thought – with or without sharing its ontological assumptions – in the attempt to add substance to the notion of evolution in economics. Four heuristic strategies seem particularly worth mentioning here. A *first*, and most radical, strategy is the attempt to apply the neo-Darwinian theory of natural selection directly to human economic behavior.[1] The ontological basis of this interpretation is essentially the same as that of evolutionary biology in general and sociobiology in particular. The argument may be sketched as follows. Economic phenomena result from human behavior. Humans are themselves a product of natural selection. Accordingly, observable economic behavior should be explicable in terms of its contribution to genetic fitness.

The problem with such an explanation is, of course, that, strictly speaking, it applies only to genetically determined forms of behavior. Moreover, it requires assuming that selection pressure on humans is still tight enough to ensure that deviations from the best fit behavior (in terms of reproductive success) tend to be wiped out. While for the early, primitive, human economy this may be a reasonable working hypothesis, the conditions in the much more productive modern economy seem to be different. Indeed, in modern economies, the most significant part of the adaptations in economic behavior occur within one generation, i.e. at a pace much more rapid than that of inter-generational, genetic adaptation. The intra-generational adaptations result from learning and insight which can be associated with cultural, rather than natural, evolution and, as such, are inaccessible to neo-Darwinian theory.[2]

A *second* strategy for pursuing Darwinian ideas – the one currently most popular in evolutionary economics – not only rejects biological reductionism, but also denies the existence of a common ontological basis with evolutionary biology. Instead, an attempt is made to use Darwinian concepts in a purely heuristic fashion. This involves either aiming at constructing analogies between the principles of evolutionary economics and those of evolutionary biology, or at deriving metaphorical inspiration (cf. Hodgson 1999, Part II and Vromen 2001 for a discussion). However, because of obvious lack of anything in the economic domain comparable to the genetic reproduction mechanism, a true analogy cannot be expected to hold. Darwinian concepts, most notably the principle of natural selection, are therefore usually only borrowed as metaphors to conceptualize evolutionary change in the economic domain. Such a heuristic use of Darwinian concepts of course runs the risk of guiding theorizing away from the actual conditions prevailing in the economic domain. (A misleading heuristic resulted, e.g., in the case of the prominent attempt at constructing an analogy between classical mechanics and neoclassical economics, cf. Mirowski 1989.)

A major difference which a heuristic use of the selection principle tends to ignore lies in the fact that, whatever is supposed to be the unit of selection in the economic domains, it cannot be expected to show as much inertia as its biological analogue. This seems to be the problem, for example, in the use Nelson and Winter (1982), the leading proponents of evolutionary economics, make of the natural selection metaphor.[3] In order for natural selection to exert a systematic, shaping influence, some relative inertia are required to exist in the population subject to selection. In a turbulent environment characterized by many things changing simultaneously, natural selection is not capable of producing any systematic change. However, it is precisely such a turbulent environment that characterizes modern economies, not least because humans have sufficient intelligence and incentives to anticipate and avoid selection effects.[4] The selection metaphor may therefore divert attention from what seems to be crucially important for economic evolution – the role played by cognition, learning, and growing knowledge.[5] Adaptations which result from cognitive processes like hypothesis formation and learning from insight follow their own regularities which in both their dynamics and their outcome are unlikely to equal genetic selection processes.

A *third* strategy for pursuing Darwinian ideas, particularly the concept of natural selection, outside biology in general, and in evolutionary economics in particular, is that of 'Universal Darwinism' (Dawkins 1983). It has recently been clearly articulated by Hodgson (2002). Like the previous strategy focusing on metaphorical uses, this interpretation also suggests making use of Darwinian concepts but, unlike the previous strategy, in a substantial rather than in a heuristic form. As the label of Universal Darwinism indicates, the intention is to apply Darwinian concepts to all forms and levels of life. In contrast to the previous strategy, this presupposes that there is only one and the same ontological basis for all evolutionary phenomena. However, it is not this ontological assertion (which is also shared by the fourth position to be discussed in a minute) that appears as a problem. The problem rather is the general validity of the principles suggested by Darwin for explaining evolution in nature which is claimed for all forms of evolution.

As Hodgson (2002) points out, this third strategy of propagating Darwinian ideas as general purpose tools for coming to grips with evolutionary phenomena has a tradition in the post-Darwinian natural philosophy. A particularly popular version of it has been suggested by Campbell (1965). He argued that any theory of evolution is based on the abstract principles of variation, selection, and retention (or replication). Yet, as is easy to see, these principles are an abstract reduction of the neo-Darwinian theory in evolutionary biology.[6] Their invocation outside biology therefore amounts to nothing more than an attempt to construct an abstract analogy to the domain-specific model of evolutionary biology. As has just been outlined, such analogies – which are always already a result of abstraction – do not really work. Therefore, this strategy is likely to face interpretative problems like those just discussed in the context of the second strategy. Again, this is particularly obvious for the crucial test criterion for Darwin's theory of evolution: the absence of a systematic feedback between selection and variation. Such a feedback is characteristic, e.g., for economic evolution where people invent their way out when threatened by "selection forces". In the presence of a systematic feedback, the distinction between variation and selection, which is a fundamental premise of the neo-Darwinian theory, is no longer valid – a result that does not just live up to the expectations of Universal Darwinism.

A *fourth* strategy for making use of Darwinian thought for understanding economic evolution will be advocated in more detail in the remainder of this paper. As mentioned above, it also presumes one and the same ontological basis for all evolutionary phenomena, but tries to avoid over-expanding the domain of Darwinian concepts. The basis for doing so involves a somewhat more complex argument, labeled the 'continuity hypothesis', which connects evolutionary biology to, e.g., evolutionary economics (cf. Witt 1987: Ch. III; 1999, 2003). The fact that humans and their 'hardwired' endowment are a result of natural selection also figures prominently in this interpretation. (To recall, this is at the core of the first, above mentioned, strategy that tries to apply Darwinian theory directly to economic behavior). However, these genetic endowments are considered only as setting the stage for yet other forms of evolution which have emerged under the influence of the unfolding human culture. The latter forms follow their own regularities and interact both among themselves and with natural evolution in an increasingly richer and more complex way. Thus, an ontological continuity is assumed in which new forms of change have been generated within the freedom left by the constraints of Darwinian theory – and, hence, without invalidating that theory. To discuss and compare the different forms of evolution it is necessary, first, to develop some conceptual means by which the domain specific connotations of evolution can be transcended. This will be done in the next section to prepare the ground for the subsequent reflections on how evolution 'continues' within the economic domain.

3 DIFFERENT FORMS OF EVOLUTION AND THE CONTINUITY HYPOTHESIS

The notion of evolution was neither invented by Darwin, nor does evolution occur in nature alone. Culture, society, and the economy all evolve too. In fact, before Darwin, these were center stage in the thought of philosophers, lawyers, and social reformers who conceived the very notion of evolution as something emerging and systematically unfolding.[7] Defined in this broad sense, evolution can indeed be diagnosed in different domains which are today covered by different disciplines like, say, biology, linguistics, or economics. Does this mean that the evolution that occurs in the different domains takes on domain-specific forms? If so, do these different forms have some generic features in common, features that should be observable wherever evolution is said to take place – be it, say, in nature, in human languages, or in the human economy? It is presumably not controversial to answer both questions in the affirmative. Dissent is about what the generic features of evolution are.

As mentioned in the previous section, Universal Darwinism considers variation, selection, and retention/replication as generic features of evolution. However, these three principles and the relationships between them depend on a heuristic inspired by neo-Darwinian evolutionary biology and, as such, are still domain-specific. As argued elsewhere (Witt 1987: Ch. 1, 1993, 2003: Ch. 1), a way of arriving at generic features of evolution, and an alternative to constructing analogies, is the attempt to transcend the domain-specific conditions by generalization. Thus, by generalization it may be inferred that evolution is a dynamic governed by some regularities. Yet, even though this is a necessary condition, it is not sufficient for characterizing evolutionary processes. There are many dynamic processes displaying regularities which are usually not considered evolutionary – e.g. the stochastic process describing the motion of a particle suspended in a liquid known as Brownian motion. The necessary and sufficient condition is, it may therefore be claimed, that evolutionary dynamic processes have the capacity of expanding their state space through the generation of not previously existing states.

This means that the generation of novelty is considered generic here to all cases of evolution or, to put it differently, that evolution is the self-transformation over time of a system under consideration. The term 'transformation' means a process of change governed by regularities. The prefix in '*self*-transformation' points to the endogenous sources and causes of novelty.[8] Self-transformation can be split into two logically, and usually also ontologically, distinct processes: the emergence and the dissemination of novelty. These two processes, it will be submitted, are two characteristic, domain-transcending features of evolution. As expected, in the different disciplinary domains the two features appear in quite different forms. In biology, there is random mutation and genetic recombination on the one hand and selective replication in the gene pool of a population on the other. In linguistics, the invention of new idioms marks the emergence part and their popularization the dissemination part. In the economic domain, given the discipline's focus on human action, novelty is usually identified with new possibilities of action which, once taken, are called innovations. Any attempt to innovate is, of course, likely to be accompanied by learning which may trigger further novelty.[9]

At this point we can now return to the fourth strategy above mentioned for relating Darwinian thought to economic evolution. This strategy is based on the 'continuity hypothesis' and can perhaps best be epitomized as follows. In the autumn of the year 1835, on his five years trip around the world, Darwin arrived at the Galapagos Islands in the Pacific Ocean, some seven hundred miles west of what is now Ecuador on board of her Majesty's sailing ship Beagle. During his trip Darwin, like many other naturalists of his time, recorded nature's impressive richness of still unknown species. The isolated archipelagos of the Galapagos Islands were basically untouched by human settlement at those times and offered a rich and stunning variety of unique species. Among them was a variety of finches from the very different islands of the archipelagos. Darwin concluded that these populations of finches represented own species which, however, must have had one common ancestor that, most likely, had immigrated to the Galapagos Islands much earlier. This finding, which was later confirmed, had a crucial impact on how Darwin conceived a theory of speciation in his general evolutionary scheme (Mayr 1991: Ch. 1).

Scholars interested in recording the products of evolution who visited the Galapagos Islands today would obtain different findings. Instead of observing some new species they would find cottages, roads, landing fields, radar stations, and many other human artefacts not present in Darwin's time less than two hundred years ago. There is no indication of any genetic program to which these artefacts would have given expression, but some kind of program does seem to have been involved in their being made at the different points in time. In the light of this much different finding, scholars visiting the Galapagos Islands today would probably feel inclined to ask themselves what form of evolution could be held responsible for these kinds of changes and how it relates to evolution in nature. It is precisely this question that the continuity hypothesis addresses. As suggested by the generic characterization of evolution as processes of the emergence and dissemination of novelty, there are several different, domain-specific realizations of these processes. The differences between them not withstanding, it may be conjectured that their ontological basis is somehow related.

Indeed, it is this conjecture which allows the Darwinian world view to be expended to accommodate for the emergence of culture and its own forms of evolution. While natural evolution – 'the origin of the species by means of natural selection' as Darwin (1859) put it – is only one form in which evolution occurs in reality, it is the form that, in historical time, anteceded the other forms of evolution considered here. It has therefore shaped the ground, and still defines the constraints, for man-made, or cultural, evolution. In this sense there is, thus, also a historical ontological continuity, the fact not withstanding that the mechanisms and regularities of cultural evolution differ from those of natural evolution. The historical process of economic evolution can be conceived as emerging from, and being embedded in, the constraints shaped by evolution in nature. Darwinian theory is directly relevant to understanding the origin of economic evolution in human phylogeny and the fact that it has a lasting influence through innate elements of human behavior. Yet, in the further course of economic evolution, human behavior and, correspondingly, economic activities and their collective outcomes underwent a metamorphosis into the distinct, idiosyncratic forms observable in present-day economies. To explain the emergence of the latter, Darwinian theory is not sufficient. The many facets of cultural evolution require explanatory theories of their own.

The continuity just specified has two concrete implications for those explanatory theories. First, it suggests that innate dispositions and adaptation mechanisms in humans, which have been shaped by natural selection, determine the basic behavioral repertoire upon which other forms of evolution rest. In the early phases of human culture, natural and man-made evolution (including economic evolution) presumably interacted mutually or 'co-evolved'.[10] However, the synergisms between the natural and cultural results of natural selection eventually allowed forms of human behavior to emerge which gave a strong relative reproductive success compared to other species (Corning 2003). As a consequence, selection pressure was significantly reduced. Therefore, it can be argued that the basic genetic endowment of modern man is very similar to the one that was established by the time natural selection stopped being a shaping force. The more selection pressure faded during human phylogeny, the more behavioral variety that did not necessarily possess adaptive value in terms of genetic fitness could increase. This is now the room in which culture, institutions, technology, and economic activities evolve according to their own regularities. (These regularities still include, of course, the constraints on behavior resulting from the innate individual dispositions and adaptation mechanisms which are still in place.)

Second, in the development just characterized, the connection between natural and man-made evolution obviously resolves into an increasingly indirect one. Nonetheless, evolution in nature continues to represent a constraint for what can evolve in culture and the economy, albeit a dynamic one (Faber and Proops 1998). It has in recent times become looser as a result of human inventiveness. Indeed, the significant feature encountered when exploring the shifting constraints of an enlarging human niche and the corresponding decreasing selection pressure on mankind is human intelligence. As Veblen (1898) already had it, intention and learning from insight matter in as much as they permit cumulative problem solving and accumulation of knowledge (not so much, in contrast, in allowing economizing on scarce resources). Where natural evolution was once driven by newly emerging genetic variants and their selective diffusion processes, cultural and economic evolution is now driven by the dynamics of individual and collective human learning processes. The fundamentally different mechanisms by which evolution is brought about in the two cases result, not least, in a dramatically different pace of evolutionary change.

The question that remains now is: what do these conceptual reflections imply for economic theory proper? Do the identified generic features of evolution, the recognized domain-specific forms in which they materialize, and the suggested continuity hypothesis lead to reinterpretations in economic theory? If so, in what way? It may be useful to give at least an exemplary outline of how the consideration can indeed lead to a reframing of old economic problems and the identification of new ones. The ultimate aim is, of course, to derive explanatory hypotheses which can help in understanding the historical process of economic change. The case to be chosen for outlining these implications is human economic production and its growth over historical time.

4 RECONSTRUCTING THE POINT OF DEPARTURE IN HUMAN PRODUCTION

The current state of nature shaped by the evolutionary forces of natural selection has been said to represent a constraint on human productive activity. For most of human history it was experienced as the burden of 'nature's parsimony', as Ricardo once put it. And at all times, humans have tried to use their creativity and problem-solving capacity to work on that constraint in order to alleviate the burden. The long term evolution of human production reflects this constant endeavor.[11] How can this process be characterized in more detail? Are there any regularities which allow explanatory hypotheses to be formulated? The discussion on the continuity hypothesis suggests a basic conjecture: early in human phylogeny productive activities must have been mainly the result of genetically shaped, instinctive behavior until culturally shaped practices emerged which started to deviate from the innate programs. If this conjecture is true, an attempt can be made to reconstruct the point of departure of cultural and economic evolution in production practices by looking into the conditions under which early humans had to undertake their productive efforts.

An extraterrestrial observer visiting this planet some forty thousand years ago would presumably have had little reason to distinguish in principle between the productive activities of early man and those of other living beings like, e.g., higher mammals. If so, then it should be possible to reconstruct – in line with the continuity hypothesis – the conditions of early human production from what "production" means in non-human nature still today.[12] Prerequisite for such a study is obviously a more concrete, 'naturalistic' description of production than it is usual in economics (with the exception of engineering production approaches).[13] To start with, production can be characterized generically in physical terms as the generation or effecting of processes or objects (the 'output') by a controlled application of substances and/or forces (the 'input') according to the natural laws and the systemic relationships prevailing in a domain. Seen this way, production is ubiquitous in living nature, though the term 'production' is hardly ever used in that context.

Take, for example, the metabolism of living organisms. In this 'production process', the complex output is the maintained life function of the organisms, including the maintenance of the organized, living structure of which they are made up. The inputs are essentially the organized living structure itself, energy, minerals, water, and oxygen. The organized living structure, in turn, is generated and maintained by 'production processes' called anabolism (building up of cells, tissues, organs) and catabolism (breaking down tissue and splitting of larger protoplasmic molecules into smaller ones). All these natural production processes are governed by complex cascades of protein interactions which basically follow procedures which are genetically coded in nucleic acids.[14]

It is a built-in feature of these natural production processes that the genetic information is automatically reproduced over and again, subject to the shaping forces of natural selection. In a sense, thus, the 'technology' on which production in living nature operates hinges on the 'knowledge' that has evolved in the form of genetic information along with the bio-chemical reaction of its 'expressing' over millions of years in the gene pool of the living organisms. Further 'production technologies' have emerged in the animal kingdom, a comparatively late fruit of evolution in nature, namely those including, and based on, the anatomic and physical prerequisites for motility. Chemical energy has to be transformed into kinetic energy which, in turn, has to be transformed into physical work (force × distance), presupposing an anatomic apparatus capable of carrying out the mechanical transmissions. The "output" that becomes feasible in this way are more complex forms of behavior that enable the animal to escape from, and/or combat with, predators, to conquer and defend a habitat, to engage in territorial feeding and mating strategies, and many other forms of social behavior. Carnivores are enabled, moreover, to engage in hunting – often in socially organized ways.

A special form of genetically evolved 'production processes' in nature – particularly relevant to man as will turn out below – are the symbiotic ones. In these processes, 'output' produced by the exemplars of one species are not only "inputs" for the exemplars of another species, but the behavior of the species is also coordinated on the basis of either mutualism (a situation in which both parties involved benefit from each other), commensalism (in which cases the benefits are one-sided, but not detrimental to the non-profiting party) or parasitism (with one-sided benefits and damage caused to the exploited party).

The productive activities in the animal kingdom are largely an expression of instinct, i.e. genetically coded behavior dispositions. This means that they have been, and still are, shaped by natural selection, and that adaptation occurs in these activities only between – usually many – generations. There are also some more rapid forms of behavior adaptations within the some-times fairly broad limits left by what an animal is physically capable of doing. These adaptations are shown by the single organism, i.e. occur within one generation, as a result of reinforcement learning. Within very narrow limits, higher developed animals are also able to learn from observa-tion of what their own kind are doing ('imitation'), speeding up the dis-semination of better adapted behavior over what is feasible to mere reinforcement learning. However, in all these forms of adaptive behavior and, hence, the corresponding production, the underlying 'technology' basi-cally remains the one determined by the inherited behavioral repertoire. Only among the most advanced mammals do the intellectual capacity and the capacity of the anatomic apparatus to do fine-tuned physical work jointly allow those animals to invent or discover and use primitive tools which they create from suitable materials.[15] Tool creation is a qualitatively distinct, and very rare, form of production in nature and a first instance of 'round-about' production which is not based on genetic but on phenotypic knowledge.

5 SOME IMPLICATIONS FOR PRODUCTION THEORY

Following the continuity hypothesis it has been argued that the study of production in nature allows the conditions under which early man started an own, cultural, evolution in production practices to be reconstructed. Moreover, the reconstruction, should offer some insights on – and thus should put in perspective – how human production has evolved since. Such an approach obviously differs substantially from the traditional a-historic interpretations and therefore also invites some reflections on the ontological presumptions underlying the theory of production in economics. The two issues may be discussed jointly by making five points.

First, one insight that can be gained from the suggested reconstruction relates to the theory of the factors of production. The naturalistic perspective just outlined suggests the question of what the "factors of production" in nature would be, if those factors are defined as the basic means by which all sorts of output are generated. Portrayed at a very abstract level (and abstracting from human manipulations for the moment), production in nature is based on two generic inputs. One is the inputs coming from inanimate nature which can be classified in two categories: matter or materials and free energy. The other is a self-generated and, qua novelty, *self-transforming* input which may be labeled 'knowledge'. More specifically, this is production knowledge in a literal sense, namely the accumulated genetic information about the particular forms of synthesizing energy and materials for keeping up the organisms' life function. The information is contained as a genetic blueprint in the form of DNA and RNA strings in the cells of the carrying organisms. The unique procedural property here is that the genetic information contains instructions to *uno actu* interpret and express the blue prints in the form of building up and maintaining the organism during its ontogeny. Because of the finite lifetime of the single carrying organism, the genetic code is transferred, with or without some recombinatory changes to the next generation of organisms, allowing for some adaptation of the code in response to natural selection influences.

The naturalistic interpretation of materials, (free) energy, and genetically coded, self-expressing knowledge as factors of production has little in common with what are traditionally considered the factors of production, namely labor, capital, and land. The reason seem to be differing theoretical interests. From its inception onwards, political economy interpreted production a *social* activity, rather than a changing technical one. Accordingly, concern was not so much with how products and services were generated, but rather with how they were distributed among competing claims. The corresponding key notion was that of separate property. Labor, capital, and land reflect the property aspect (while, from a naturalistic point of view, their technical relationship to the basic means of materials, free energy, and knowledge is a very complex one). The earlier background in moral philosophy may have invited the question of what kind of (re-)distribution of the fruits of productive activities could be considered legitimate.[16] Soon it was also recognized that the distributional problem has implications for the incentives to take part in the expanding specialization, division of labor, and market exchange of the upcoming industrial revolution. Accordingly, the problem of production was increasingly framed in terms of a theory about the proper imputation of value to both the (property in the) inputs required for production and the (property in the) resulting output – paving the way for an understanding of economics as the 'science of value'.

Second, a related insight that can be gained from the reconstruction of the conditions of production in nature is the following. The 'natural' production factors, materials, free energy, genetic knowledge were all in place when modern humans entered the scene. Hence, something had to be added for the (cultural) evolutionary change in human production to occur. The additional component, it is claimed, was a new form of knowledge, qualitatively different from the genetically coded, self-expressing forms involved in nature's production. (To indicate the difference, the new form is usually called cultural knowledge.) What powered the creation of the new form of knowledge was the already mentioned, unique combination of intelligence and fine-tuned motility which allowed humans to instrumentalize simple material objects found in nature as tools for better achieving productive purposes – initially the very same as pursued before. It is precisely by this transformation that a new form of evolution was triggered on earth: cultural evolution. Insight into the tool character of certain material objects is the first occasion in the evolution of nature where at least a vague intentionality comes into play, one which is alien to the genetic adaptation process.

With respect to the factors of production, cultural evolution has, thus, added just one new element. Besides the inputs materials, free energy, and (from a human perspective: given) genetic knowledge there is now another generated and, qua novelty, *self-transforming* input. This is culturally accumulated, anthropogenic production knowledge, emerging in ever new pieces which potentially disseminate and accumulate. During the evolution of human production from the early times on, the quantities of materials, of renewable free energy, and of genetic knowledge existing on this planet have by and large been unchanging. What has been changing is the growing share of these quantities put to anthropogenic use and, in the case of energy, the tapping of fossil energy deposits. These changes would not have been possible without the growing amount and quality of human production knowledge that has been actively generated, applied, and disseminated between generations. Hence, the accumulation of this factor seems to have been decisive for the pace of economic evolution. This is not a new conjecture in economics. It also figures prominently in new growth theory.[17] But since new growth theory is basically still a value theory lacking a 'naturalistic' foundation, the question it cannot answer is *why* human production knowledge plays this role.

Third, the naturalistic approach taken here offers an answer to precisely that question. Production knowledge and its continuing, cumulative creation has enabled man to achieve two things: (i) the increasing manipulation of nature's production process in the direction of human ends; (ii) the extending implementation and fueling of artificial, i.e., not naturally occurring, production processes. The first achievement is mostly based on an expanding symbiotic exploitation of other species in agriculture and the domestication and breeding of animals. The second achievement is based on the large scale creation and use of tools. It is more difficult and has occurred much later. Tool creation is almost always a transformation of materials. Such transformations require a controlled application of free energy in the form of heat, pressure, chemical energy, or kinetic energy by appropriate technical devices. So too, does the use of the tools. Thus, free energy has to be made available and proper devices (themselves tools) for transmitting and applying energy must be found.

For long time both requirements had to be satisfied by natural means whose limited availability imposed tight constraints on human production: human muscle power as the source of free energy together with the mechanics of the human anatomy extended by simple mechanical tools adapted to it. The burden of work was later transferred to the trained and supervised muscle power of domesticated animals – still a natural production process.

With the invention of the wheel, a mechanical device for power transmission and application not inspired by the model of human anatomy had been found. The benefits of the new tools were significantly increased when devices were invented to tap, i.e., transmit and apply, wind and water power to drive those tools. The introduction of the steam engine meant a real boost both in tool use and production volume, particularly when devices were invented that allowed fossil sources of free energy to be tapped (cf. Rosenberg 1982). Once made available, the new source of energy was quickly found to be also applicable to many other purposes, in particular for heating in the chemical processing technology which developed in the nineteenth century into a powerful, independent paradigm of transforming materials, cf. Buenstorf (2004). Another prominent application, based not least on chemical processing technology, is the conversion into fertilizers used to expand by orders of magnitudes the returns on the symbiotic productions forms.

All these dramatic transformations and expansions of anthropogenic production are difficult to account for in terms of a theory of production if that theory is tailored primarily to answer the question of how well the various recipients of the produced output (labor, capital owners, landlords) fare. The problem is not changed much by adding to labor, capital, and land an additional production factor 'knowledge' whose ownership structure is – because of the implied public good problem – admittedly more complex. Much of the accumulated anthropogenic production knowledge can only be 'expressed' by incorporating it in tools in the broadest sense. Hence, a large share of this is represented in what, for reasons of political economy, is called the real capital stock. But, of course, much more knowledge is necessary to run the production process. That knowledge is not 'expressed' in the tools, but in what people do when they create and use tools. In fact, the acquisition, expression, and creation of knowledge is today probably one of the most important services of labor. If economic theory is determined to stick to its traditional notions of the factors of production, the question may thus be raised whether it is indeed possible to identify an additional factor 'knowledge' independently of capital and labor.

Fourth, it seems indeed much easier to discuss the role of knowledge and to understand its particularities on the basis of suggested naturalistic approach than on that of the abstract standard production theory. Again a comparison of some characteristic differences between the genetically coded knowledge in nature and human knowledge is illuminating here. Genetic 'knowledge' comes in a form which *uno actu* interprets, expresses, and replicates its meaning in terms of blue prints for manipulating materials and/or triggering and controlling processes, provided the necessary materials and free energy are available. Replication occurs with some variation between generations, and since genetic novelty originates from those variations, the emergence of novelty is a part of the programmed automatism. None of this holds in the case of cultural knowledge. The latter is coded and stored in a form lacking an automatic copying, interpreting, and self-expressing modus. The generation, storage, expression (utilization and application), and even the replication of cultural knowledge all need to be effected by human action and require at least a minimal level of intelligence.[18]

For this reason alone, the evolution of cultural knowledge is much different from that of automatically self-expressing genetic knowledge. On the other hand, its reproduction and transmission is not bound to the rather slow inter-generational pace of the genetic replication mechanism in nature, but is based instead on inter-individual communication and individual interpretation. Accordingly, the technology of communication can be expected to have a crucial influence on both the quality of cultural knowledge and the pace of cultural evolution. In early man, communication was constrained to oral face-to-face interaction, instruction, and observational learning. Since this was also the only way of transmitting knowledge between the generations, accumulation of production knowledge was severely constrained. Consequently, there was comparatively very little development in tool creation, tool making, and tool use. This did change with the invention of alphabetic writing some four thousand years ago. With written documents, both storage and transmission of knowledge become largely independent of the personal contingencies of oral instruction and the bottleneck which the memory of the single instructor represents. Yet as long as writing and reading were confined to a small elite which used it less for purposes of production and tool development than for religious and regulatory purposes, the potential of the new communication technology was not fully used. Only with the invention of the printing press in the fifteenth century, and the subsequently developing broader literacy in Europe, could writings in science and technology achive broad dissemination.[19]

The boost of human production knowledge over the past two centuries and, consequently, the growth of human production thus seem to have to do with the significant changes in the technology of generating, storing, expressing, and replication of cultural knowledge. With a break-through in codification and dissemination techniques, a rapidly rising rate of literacy, the spread of formal education, and the organization and institutionalization of (re-)search for new knowledge in science, a soaring growth of mostly (but not only) useful knowledge has become feasible. Because of the limited capacity of the individual mind, this growth requires increasing specialization and division of knowledge. There is no doubt that the (re-)production of the respective body of knowledge in the mind of every new user and every new generation of users is itself a substantial part of modern human production which has changed dramatically the character of both the work being done in the economy and the quality of labor (cf. Witt 1997).

This development has recently been topped by an automatization of information processing, independent from the human brain, on the basis of electronic signal processing technologies. However, the reproduction of individual knowledge in command of this new technology in each new generation of students still has to rely on the old, inherited information processing technology of the human brain. As long as intelligence cannot be shifted to machinery, this is likely to be a hard constraint.[20]

Fifth, a point that may finally be raised relates to the question of whether and why the accumulation of human production knowledge can (at least temporarily) result in 'increasing returns' in producing output. New growth theory has postulated this as a feature of a production factor knowledge without, however, giving any reasons for it. In the perspective of the present approach a reason can be given. Mere acceleration of the generation and dissemination of production knowledge is not sufficient to bring about an increasing returns effect. What induces the effect is an auto-catalytic feature that may temporarily govern the development of production (Witt 1997). New production knowledge which makes tools and the means of fueling them available usually means a reduction in the working time necessary for carrying out production of the same output. Assume that, in a reorganization of production, the spare time and effort is used for increasing specialization. Under an institutional regime which allows an extended division of labor, 'increasing returns' may then become feasible.[21]

All that seems necessary is that specialization also includes the acquisition of specialized know how and skills that are employed, in turn, for systematic searching for, and developing of, further innovations in tool and energy uses. As long as the net amount of human labor saved by further knowledge creation is positive, production knowledge can thus 'breed' further production knowledge. This seems to be precisely the autocatalytic cycle characteristic of modern economic growth – at least for present. Indeed, how long such an autocatalytic cycle can be maintained is highly uncertain. This depends not least on the properties of knowledge generated in the future which cannot be anticipated. Even more uncertain seems to be whether the auto-catalytic features of modern knowledge creation will continue to imply a growth of the human economy as it is known today.

One of the reasons for this uncertainty resides in the fact that the strong growth of anthropogenic production knowledge has been accompanied by an increasing disintegration of cultural and genetically coded knowledge. The correlate is an increasing lack of integration of man-made flows of energy and materials (the 'industrial metabolism', cf. Ayres 1996) within the natural recycling flows. While the latter have been harmonized in evolution through inter-species competition in eco-systems, the former have, as mentioned, temporarily been freed from the constraints of natural selection. Human problem solving behavior in expanding human production activities has paid little attention to the fact that, in the longer run, these constraints will still be binding. At a closer look, human problem solving indeed often turns out to result in the creation of new problems. Problem shifting may, of course, result in problems piling up in the future. Ever more of future human knowledge creation may therefore have to be devoted to attempts at solving the problems created in the past and the present by the expansion of man's artificial production processes.

6 CONCLUSIONS

This paper has tried to clarify the notion of evolution in more general terms and to discuss its relevance for economics. An evolutionary, Darwinian, world view is now widely held in the sciences. What role does this play for economics or, to put it the other way round, what is the place of human economic activity in such a world view? The answer given here has been epitomized by what was called the 'continuity hypothesis'. In contrast to two other positions that have also been discussed – on the one hand the metaphorical, heuristic use of Darwinian concepts and, on the other hand, 'Universal Darwinism' – the present interpretation of the continuity hypothesis suggests the following. Evolution in nature as explained by (neo) Darwinian theory is one form in which evolution occurs in reality. It is domain-specific in the sense that this form is now the object of the discipline of evolutionary biology. However, evolution in nature anteceded the other forms of man-made, or cultural, evolution considered here and explored by other disciplines, e.g., linguistics and economics, in their respective domains. Therefore there is a historical, ontological continuity in which evolution in nature shaped the ground and defines the constraints for the various other forms of cultural evolution. Nonetheless, it has been argued that the mechanisms and regularities of cultural evolution differ fundamentally from those of natural evolution. Darwinian theory is therefore not sufficient to explain them. The many facets of cultural evolution require explanatory theories of their own.

Some of the implications of that hypothesis have been pointed out for the context of human production activities and their evolution over time. To identify the point at which man-made evolution intervenes, the mode of production in a natural state has been reconstructed in a more 'naturalistic' approach than the one usually pursued in economic production theory. A new factor of production – human (cultural) knowledge – entered the scene at that point in history. New production knowledge which emerges and disseminates incessantly in the human economy has driven the changes that have occurred since. It has been instrumental in bringing about the soaring growth in human production output. Some regularities and contingencies of the evolution of production have been discussed in the paper together with some implications for the economic theory of production. What had to be left out here for reasons of space limitations is the historical record of how production and consumption have interacted. The no less dramatic changes in consumption are an essential part of the economic evolution. The suggested continuity hypothesis should provide a basis for analyzing them in a way similar in spirit to the analysis of the evolution of production given here. The interpretation of evolution advocated in this paper may therefore be expected to be a fruitful basis for also inquiring into the interactions between evolutionary change in production and consumption – an important target for future research.

Ulrich Witt
Max Planck Institute for Research into Economic Systems, Jena
ulrich.witt@mpiew-jena.mpg.de

NOTES

1   Cf., e.g., Hermann-Pillath (1991), Rubin (1982), Robson (2001), Corning (2003). A modified version of this strategy has informed anthropological research under the label of the co-evolution hypothesis. It is argued that cultural behavior in primitive societies can be explained by the joint fitness value of genetic and cultural traits, cf. Durham (1976), Boyd and Richerson (1994).

2   An intermediate position was taken by the late Hayek (1982: Ch. 1 and 8) in his theory of cultural evolution. Focusing on the change of more basic rules of conduct and economic attitudes – which indeed vary very slowly – he denies natural selection a direct impact, but argues that the process of change may here mimic the effect of group selection. The conditions to be met for this to happen are: the cultural communities which collectively share rules and attitudes are separable, e.g. geographically; their differing rules and attitudes cause differential economic success; success differentials induce significant survival inequalities or migration processes between the communities. If communities with less efficient rules decrease in size and those with more efficient rules increase, then the underlying social traits change in their relative frequency correspondingly (where it is assumed that migrants can indeed switch in their attitudes and rules of conduct).

3   They portray firm organizations and their activities – production planning, calculation, price setting, and even the allocation of research and development funds – as being based on organizational routines (ibid., Ch. 5). Despite the obvious absence in the economic domain of anything comparable to genetic reproduction, the firms' routines are interpreted as 'genotypes' and the specific decisions resulting from the applied routines as 'phenotypes'. They are assumed to affect the firms' performance so that different routines which lead to different decisions also lead to differences in the firms' growth. On the further assumption that organizational routines which successfully contribute to growth are not changed, the growth of the firm effects an increase in relative frequency of those 'genes-routines' in the entire population of firms, i.e. the industry. The opposite is supposed to hold for routines causing a deteriorating performance.

4   Thus, firms are usually eager to identify deficient organizational routines and to replace or improve them in a kind of intentionally produced mutation of their 'routine-genes' before they fall victim to selection forces. In markets, the

effects of 'external' selection are therefore likely to be largely replaced by what would have to be called effects of "internal" selection in the form of deliberate strategic anticipation based on insight and intention. "Internal" selection may be the outcome of higher organizational routines as Nelson and Winter (ibid.) argue. But the higher the level of the organizational hierarchy at which a routine (the 'genotype') is employed, the more the decisions actually made (the 'phenotypes') are influenced by managerial discretion and, hence, the situational logic applied by the decision maker(s). The properties of the higher organizational routine and the idiosyncrasies of individual decision making may become equally influential so that any observed differential success can no longer be uniquely attributed to the higher routine involved.

5   If the difference is acknowledged, economic evolution may be interpreted as Lamarckian rather than Darwinian in character, cf. Nelson and Winter (1982: 11). As Knudsen (2001) explains, Lamarckian evolution here means that a direct feedback from the phenotypic performance to genotypic traits is allowed as a systematic feature. However, the benefit of constructing an analogy to Lamarckian evolution in economics is not clear. In the sciences, the Lamarckian theory has never been worked out so that its implications and dynamics are unknown.

6   It omits, *inter alia*, the principles of descent and speciation which are important parts of Darwin's theory, cf. Mayr (1991: Ch. 4).

7   Cf. Hayek (1967). In the history of evolutionary biology there is broad agreement now that some of Darwin's inspiration for his theory of the origin of the species by means of natural selection came from his readings of Adam Smith and Malthus, cf., e.g., Desmond and Moore (1991). The main focus of the writings of Darwin's very influential contemporary, Herbert Spencer (a co-editor of *The Economist* for several years) was also on the evolution – in the sense of 'progress' and 'betterment' however – of the human society and economy, cf. Bowler (1986).

8   Self-transformation may be taken as a synonym for 'change from within' as Schumpeter (1934) put it without apparently realizing the generic character for all evolutionary processes. Attributing a prominent role in economic change to novelty is now indeed common to all strands of evolutionary economics, cf. Hodgson (1995) and Dopfer and Potts in this volume. The connotations associated with novelty and innovations vary greatly, of course. In the above definition, the term "system" is just a dummy for the different disciplinary objects that evolve: nature in the case of biology, language in the case of linguistics, society in the case of sociology, or the economy in the case of economics.

9   The distinction between emergence and dissemination of novelty not only accounts for ontological differences. It is significant also for epistemological reasons because, by novelty's very nature, its meaning, and hence its future consequences, cannot fully be anticipated. For a discussion of the implications cf. Witt (1987: Ch. 1, 1993).

10 This co-evolution hypothesis figures prominently in the anthropological literature. For a statement of that hypothesis from the point of view of sociobiology cf. Lumsden and Wilson (1981).

11 The motivation to seek a better way of living is closely related to human wants and preferences which represent another, significant, co-evolving phenomenon that has been dealt with elsewhere, cf. Witt (2001).

12 The idea of setting economic production in perspective by comparison with the conditions in nature is not new. However, the comparison usually focuses on the implications of the laws of thermodynamics for theorizing about economic production, cf. Georgescu-Roegen (1971), Gowdy (1994), Faber *et al.* (1998).

13   For an exemplary rethinking of production theory in 'naturalistic' terms cf. Buenstorf (2004).

14   It may be noted in passing that under the influence of natural selection, i.e. driven by competition between the species in a given habitat or ecological system for reproductive success and an expansion of the own niche, production in living nature frequently effects substantial 'investments' in biomass which do not directly improve or expand the organisms' metabolism. Instead, these investments prevent the chances of the organisms of a given species from suffering in reproductive competition with other species, a phenomenon known as the 'red queen effect', see Stenseth and Maynard-Smith (1984).

15   Tools are defined as equipments which, as an outcome of an intelligent act, are created by, but not physically integrated into, an organism. The intelligent act at the origin of tools is what makes the difference to "investments" made by animals which, as discussed before, are guided by instinct.

16   This guiding interest is still very much visible in Quesnay (1736) and the physiocratic school. The school had a concrete understanding of the fact that the symbiotic forms of production in agriculture allow man (with the input of some additional human labor) to grow and reap the crops which themselves are 'produced' not by labor but by nature. Yet, the school's theoretical concern was to establish a theory of value which would explain whose property contributes how much to the overall expansion of wealth in the economy and what distribution of income could therefore be theoretically justified.

17   Cf., e.g., Grossman and Helpman (1991). New growth theory also postulates a more than linearly increasing functional relationship between human production knowledge – however measured – and output. On this see the fifth point below.

18   At least for its expression in tools, materials and the dissipation of free energy are needed as well. As in all cases of human action, the intention and understanding of the particular individuals involved also play a role for when and how cultural knowledge changes. These individualities, in turn, depend systematically on institutional features of the respective economies, cf. Witt (1987: Ch. 4).

19   With the printing press, the audience that could be instructed or informed could be multiplied. Since reading is a parallel process, information could much more rapidly be diffused than by spoken word.

20   Should ways be found sometime in the future to create a truly intelligent machinery, cultural evolution will have reached a stage in which humans are no longer in control of its outcome. The future fate of human production, indeed of the human species in general, may then hinge on whether the finite human problem solving capacity will be able to force the new intelligent beings into symbiotic forms of production of knowledge under human guidance or vice versa (cf. Wadmann 2001).

21   Drawing on Adam Smith, Marshall (1920, book IV) strongly emphasized this insight. Note that 'increasing returns' in this sense differ from increasing returns to scale. The latter concept is based on the notion of a production function defined over a set of factors of unchanging quality. In contrast, the very essence of the notion of specialization is that the quality of at least one factor involved in production changes. Increasing returns in the present sense has therefore sometimes been attributed to technical progress.

REFERENCES

Ayres, R.U. (1996) *Industrial Ecology*, Cheltenham: Edward Elgar.
Bowler, P.J. (1986) *Theories of Human Evolution: A Century of Debate 1844–1944*, Oxford: Blackwell.

'*Evolution' in economics and its implications for production theory* 145

Boyd, R. and Richerson, J.P. (1994) 'The evolution of norms: an anthropological view', *Journal of Institutional and Theoretical Economics* 150: 72–87.
Buenstorf, G. (2004) *Energy Use in Production: A long-term Analysis*, Cheltenham: Edward Elgar.
Campbell, D.T. (1965) 'Variation and selective retention in socio-cultural evolution', in H.R. Barringer, G.I. Blankenstein and R.W. Mack (eds). *Social Change in Developing Areas: A Reinterpretation of Evolutionary Theory*, Cambridge, MA: Schenkman, pp. 19–49.
Corning, P.A. (2003) *Nature's Magic: Synergy in Evolution and the Fate of the Humankind*, Cambridge: Cambridge University Press.
Darwin, C. (1859) *On the Origin of the Species by Means of Natural Selection*, London: J. Murray.
Dawkins, R. (1983) 'Universal Darwinism', in D.S. Bendall (ed.). *Evolution from Molecules to Man*, Cambridge: Cambridge University Press, pp. 403–25.
Desmond, A. and Moore, J.R. (1991) *Darwin*, London: Michall Joseph.
Durham, W.H. (1976) 'The adaptive significance of cultural behavior', *Human Ecology* 4: 89–121.
Faber, M. and Proops, J.L.R. (1998) *Evolution, Time, Production and the Environment*, Berlin: Springer.
Faber, M. and Proops, J.L.R. and Baumgaertner, S. (1998) 'All production is joint production – a thermodynamic analysis', in S. Faucheux, J. Gowdy, I. Nicolai. (eds). *Sustainability and Firms*, Cheltenham: Edward Elgar, pp. 131–58.
Georgescu-Roegen, N. (1971) *The Entropy Law and the Economic Process*, Cambridge, MA.: Harvard Univ. Press.
Gowdy, J.M. (1994) *Coevolutionary Economics: The Economy, Society and the Environment*. Boston: Kluwer.
Grossman, G.M. and Helpman, E. (1991) *Innovation and Growth in the Global Economy*. Cambridge, MA: MIT Press.
Hayek F.A. (1967) *Dr. Bernhard Mandeville*, Proceedings of the British Academy, Oxford: Oxford University Press.
Hayek, F.A. (1982) *The Fatal Conceit*, London: Routledge.
Hermann-Pillath, C. (1991) 'A Darwinian framework for the economic analysis of institutional change in history', *Journal of Social and Biological Structures* 14: 127–48.
Hodgson, G.M. (1995) 'The evolution of evolutionary economics', *Scottish Journal of Political Economy* 42: 469–88.
Hodgson, G.M. (1999) *Evolution and Institutions*, Cheltenham: Edward Elgar.
Hodgson, G.M. (2002) 'Darwinism in economics: from analogy to ontology', *Journal of Evolutionary Economics* 12: 259–81.
Knudsen, T. (2001) 'Nesting Lamarckism within Darwinian explanations: necessity in economics and possibility in biology?', in J. Laurent and J. Nightingale (eds). *Darwinism and Evolutionary Economic*, Cheltenham: Edward Elgar, pp. 121–59.
Lumsden, C.J. and Wilson, E.O. (1981) *Genes, Mind and Culture: The Coevolutionary Process*, Cambridge: Harvard University Press.
Marshall, A. (1920) *Principles of Economics*, London: MacMillan.
Mayr, E. (1991) *One Long Argument*, Cambridge, MA.: Havard University Press.
Mirowski, P. (1989) *More Heat than Light. Economics as Social Physics – Physics as Nature's Economics*, Cambridge: Cambridge University Press.
Nelson, R.R. and Winter, S.G. (1982) *An Evolutionary Theory of Economic Change*, Cambridge, MA.: Harvard University Press.
Quesnay, F. (1736) *Essai physique sur l'économie animale*, Paris: Guillaume Cavelier.
Robson, A.J. (2001) 'The biological basis of economic behavior', *Journal of Economic Literature* 39: 11–33.

146   *Articles*

Rosenberg, N. (1982) *Inside the Black Box: Technology and Economics*, Cambridge: Cambridge University Press.

Rubin, P.H. (1982) 'Evolved ethics and efficient ethics', *Journal of Economic Behavior and Organization* 3: 161–74.

Schumpeter, J.A. (1934) *The Theory of Economic Development*, Cambridge, MA: Harvard University Press.

Stenseth, N.C. and Maynard-Smith, J. (1984) 'Coevolution in ecosystems: red queen evolution or stasis?', *Evolution* 38: 870–80.

Veblen, T.B. (1898) 'Why is economics not an evolutionary science?', *Quarterly Journal of Economics* 12: 373–97.

Vromen, J.J. (2001) 'The human agent in evolutionary economics', in J. Laurent and J. Nightingale (eds). *Darwinism and Evolutionary Economics,* Cheltenham: Edward Elgar Publ, pp. 184–208.

Wadman, W.M. (2001) 'Technological change, human capital and extinction', *Journal of Bioeconomics* 3: 65–8.

Witt, U. (1987) *Individualistische Grundlagen der evolutorischen Ökonomik*, Tübingen: Mohr-Siebeck.

Witt, U. (1993) 'Emergence and dissemination of innovations: some principles of evolutionary economics', in R. Day and P. Chen, (eds). *Nonlinear Dynamics and Evolutionary Economics*, Oxford: Oxford University Press, pp. 91–100.

Witt, U. (1997) 'Self-organization and economics – what is new?', *Structural Change and Economic Dynamics* 8: 489–507.

Witt, U. (1999) 'Bioeconomics as Economics from a Darwinian perspective', *Journal of Bioeconomics* 1: 19–34.

Witt, U. (2001) 'Learning to consume – a theory of wants and the growth of demand', *Journal of Evolutionary Economics* 11: 23–36.

Witt, U. (2003) *The Evolving Economy*, Cheltenham: Edward Elgar.

J Evol Econ
DOI 10.1007/s00191-008-0107-7

REGULAR ARTICLE

What is specific about evolutionary economics?

Ulrich Witt

Abstract Ever since an "evolutionary" perspective on the economy has been suggested, there have been differing, and partly incommensurable, views on what specifically this means. By working out where the differences lie and what motivates them, this paper identifies four major approaches to evolutionary economics. The differences between them can be traced back to opposite positions regarding the basic assumptions about reality and the proper conceptualization of evolution. The same differences can also be found in evolutionary game theory. Achievements of the major approaches to evolutionary economics and their prospects for future research are assessed by means of a peer survey.

Keywords Evolution · Evolutionary economics · Evolutionary game theory · Neo-Schumpeterian economics · Universal Darwinism · Institutional economics

JEL Classification B15 · B25 · B41 · B52 · C73 · O10 · O30

1 Introduction

The question of what is specific about an evolutionary approach to economics has been discussed ever since the label "evolutionary" was introduced into an economic context in the late 19th century. A commonly accepted answer is still pending. Nevertheless, interest in applying evolutionary thought to economics has increased in recent years. In their bibliometric analysis of the

U. Witt (✉)
Max Planck Institute of Economics, Jena, Germany
e-mail: ulrich.witt@econ.mpg.de

 Springer

EconLit database, Silva and Teixeira (2006) find that the number of articles published in economic journals using the term "evolutionary" as a keyword grew roughly exponentially between 1986 and 2005. In 2005, such articles were about 1% of all journal publications covered by EconLit in that year. However, Silva and Teixeira also find that the increasing use of the term does not correspond with anything like growing coherence in what it is supposed to refer to. There is still no agreement about the specific features associated with the label "evolutionary" in economic analysis, not to speak of a commonly accepted paradigmatic "hard core" like, e.g., the equilibrium-cum-optimization framework in canonical economic theory.

Under these conditions it seems desirable to reflect on the differences in interpretations, topics, and methods in evolutionary economics and on their reasons—not least in order to explore the chances for reconciling the different positions. This is particularly warranted in view of some recent developments in the field. On the one hand, there is an ongoing interest in the role played by evolutionary biology and Darwinism in evolutionary economics (see, e.g., Nelson 1995; Foster 1997; Witt 1999; Laurent and Nightingale 2001; Knudsen 2002; Andersen 2004)—an interest driven by the search for a unified evolutionary approach. On the other hand, there are signs of disintegration. Evolutionary game theory, for instance, takes little notice of the research that is more broadly associated with evolutionary economics and vice versa (see, e.g., Samuelson 2002 on the one side and Nelson and Winter 2002 on the other). An attempt will therefore be made in this paper to identify the main sources of disagreement on what is meant by the label "evolutionary" in the economic context. In this attempt, the prospects for, or the limits of, a unified evolutionary approach should become apparent. Such a clarification should also benefit the assessment of the new developments in the field.

Scientific approaches can differ in many respects. The most consequential differences usually occur at three levels of scientific reasoning. These are the ontological level (what basic assumptions are made about the structure of reality), the heuristic level (how the problems are framed to induce hypotheses), and the methodological level (what methods are used to express and verify theories). A key to a better understanding of evolutionary economics, it will be argued, is to distinguish between these three levels and the corresponding, often only implicit, assumptions. What different authors consider special about the evolutionary approach, for instance, is likely to depend on how they conceptualize "evolution" in the economic context. This is a decision at the *heuristic* level, i.e. about what concepts to use to frame problems and their interpretations. A different issue is how the authors define the agenda of evolutionary economics. Economic phenomena can be seen as forming an own sphere of reality, e.g., a sphere of subjective likings and beliefs. The agenda then differs from the one that results when economic activities are seen, e.g., in a Darwinian world view, that is, as an interaction with nature's constraints and contingent on the human genetic endowment. This is a decision at the *ontological* level where the assumptions about the structure of reality shape the perception of objects and disciplinary boundaries (see Dopfer 2005).

 Springer

In many neo-Schumpeterian contributions to evolutionary economics, metaphors based on analogies to the Darwinian theory of natural selection are strongly endorsed at the heuristic level (i.e. as a means of conceptualizing evolution in the economic domain). At the same time, the challenge of a naturalistic, Darwinian world view on the economy is usually ignored, if not rejected, at the ontological level. Conversely, authors like Veblen (1898), Georgescu-Roegen (1971), Hayek (1988), and North (2005) who have adopted a naturalistic approach to evolutionary economics—but differ widely in most other respects—do not work with analogies to Darwinian concepts at the heuristic level. In contrast, the new approach of Universal Darwinism advocates just such a combination of a heuristic based on an abstract analogy to Darwinian concepts and a naturalistic ontological position (Hodgson 2002; Hodgson and Knudsen 2006). Evolutionary game theory basically ignores the conceptual debates and controversies in evolutionary economics. Yet, as will be explained, within evolutionary game theory the opinions are divided exactly along the same lines.

Finally, there is a third, the *methodological*, level where controversial assumptions can be made. Here, a truly enduring controversy relates to the question of whether and how to account for the role of history in economic theorizing. As will turn out, however, this question is much less controversial in evolutionary economics, probably because, in all of its different interpretations, the historical contingency of evolutionary processes is clearly acknowledged. Different positions at the methodological level therefore usually mean that they suggest different methods for coming to grips with the historical dimension. However, in most cases the choice of the method is determined by the particularities of the problems investigated. Often the methods are complementary rather than alternatives. The decisions at the methodological level are therefore more a matter of pragmatics than principles and not the reason for the differences in the views about what is specific about evolutionary economics.

In this paper it will therefore be argued that differing interpretations of evolutionary economics have their origin in the, often not explicitly stated, divergent ontological and heuristic positions. To elaborate on this argument in more detail, Section 2 digs more deeply into the controversies at each of the different levels of scientific reasoning—the ontological, the heuristic, and the methodological levels. Section 3 shows that, once the contrasting views about the first two levels are recognized, these can be used to identify four different approaches to evolutionary economics. These approaches also differ significantly in the main research topics they focus on. Section 4 turns to evolutionary game theory and argues that, although there is hardly any exchange with evolutionary economics, evolutionary game theory is faced with exactly the same kind of ontological and heuristic controversies. In Section 5 achievements and prospects for future research in evolutionary economics are assessed in relation to the different approaches. To provide a more representative picture, the assessment is based on the results of a peer survey. Section 6 offers the conclusions.

 Springer

2 Why ontology and heuristics matter and methodology matters less so

As mentioned in the introduction, the question of what is specific about evolutionary economics has several facets that correspond to different levels of scientific reasoning: the ontological, the heuristic, and the methodological levels. By tracing the various interpretations of evolutionary economics back to different assumptions made at these three levels, the causes of the controversy become more transparent, and the difficulties in reconciling the diverging views can be assessed better.

To start at the ontological level, i.e. at the basic assumption about the structure of reality, one possible position is ontological monism. This means to assume that both change in the economy and change in nature belong to connected spheres of reality and are therefore potentially interdependent processes. Such an ontological continuity assumption is favored by the adherents of an ideal of the unity of the sciences (see Wilson 1998) and it involves adopting a naturalistic perspective on the human sphere. As explained elsewhere (Witt 2004), the ontological continuity hypothesis does not imply that evolution in the economy and evolution in nature are similar or even identical. The mechanisms by which the species have evolved in nature under natural selection pressure, and are still evolving, have shaped the ground for, and still influence the constraints of, man-made, cultural forms of evolution, including the evolution of the human economy. But the mechanisms of man-made evolution that have emerged *on* that ground differ substantially from those of natural selection and descent. Human creativity, insight, social learning, and imitative capacity have established mechanisms of a high-pace, intra-generational adaptation (Vromen 2004).[1]

The implication of the ontological continuity assumption—that the economy and economic change are connected with a naturalistic substratum—is an idea that is often neglected, ignored, or even explicitly rejected in favor of a dualistic ontology. The latter treats economic and biological evolutionary processes as belonging to different, disconnected, spheres of reality.[2] As a consequence, possible influences on economic evolution that result from its historical embeddedness in evolution in nature—such as, e.g., the influences of the human genetic endowment on economic behavior—are ignored. Since

---

[1] From the point of view of the continuity hypothesis, the relevance of the Darwinian theory of evolution for explaining economic change is therefore that of a meta-theory. Not unlike in evolutionary psychology (see Tooby and Cosmides 1992), it allows the genetic endowment, fixed at times when early humans were under fierce selection pressure, to be reconstructed along with the influence it still has on economic behavior today. Furthermore, on this basis, the conditions under which economic evolution took off in the early human phylogeny can be reconstructed. A comparison with the conditions of modern economies is not only conducive to taking a naturalistic perspective on the latter, but it also helps to better grasp the historical path of the development, see Witt (2003, Chap. 1) for a more detailed discussion.

[2] A dualistic ontology is often justified with reference to the Cartesian divide between the *Geisteswissenschaften* (humanities)—to which economics is considered to belong—and the sciences, see the discussion in Herrmann-Pillath (2001) and Dopfer and Potts (2004).

 Springer

these basic assumptions about reality cannot be subjected to a test, they are sometimes classified as metaphysical. They are part of a researcher's informal world view and will therefore be dubbed her or his 'ontological stance'.

The second level of controversy relates to the heuristic devices that guide the framing of problems and thus the way in which one arrives at conjectures and hypotheses in evolutionary economics. At this level, some authors argue that the use of particular analytical tools and models borrowed from evolutionary biology is the specific feature that distinguishes "evolutionary" from canonical economics. Here, they find themselves in the company of other social sciences where analogy constructions to biological selection models and population dynamics similarly provide the heuristic basis for conceptualizing evolution in the own domain. This may not be surprising in view of the fact that the Darwinian theory of natural selection is widely considered to be the prototype of an evolutionary theory today.

Supported by attempts at extending the Darwinian theory universally beyond the domain of evolutionary biology (Dawkins 1983), three principles of evolution have now become increasingly popular as a heuristic for evolutionary theorizing: blind variation, selection, and retention (Campbell 1965). These have been derived by abstract reduction of some key elements of the Darwinian theory of natural selection, and have been applied to conceptualizing the evolution of technology, science, language, human society, and the economy (Ziman 2000; Hull 2001; Hashimoto 2006; Hallpike 1985, 1986; Nelson 1995, respectively). The borrowing of these domain-specific abstractions by other disciplines means, of course, that they still rely on an analogy construction, albeit an abstract one. Analogy constructions and metaphors are frequently used heuristic devices in scientific work and can be very fruitful. The problem is that there is always also a risk of being lead astray by biases in, and incompleteness of, analogies. The analogy between classical mechanics and utility and demand theory in canonical economics is a well known example (see Mirowski 1989, Chap. 5). The analogy constructions in evolutionary economics are no less problematic (see Vromen 2006; Witt and Cordes 2007).

There are other heuristic strategies for conceptualizing evolution inspired not by analogies, but by a generic concept of evolution. Consider something that evolves, be it the gene pool of a species, a language spoken in a human community, the technology and institutions of an economy, or the set of ideas produced by the human mind. Although such entities can change over time in response to exogenous, unexplained forces ("shocks"), their genuinely evolutionary feature is that they are capable of transforming themselves endogenously over time. The ultimate cause of their endogenous change is the capacity to create novelty. The way in which this happens varies greatly across different domains. In the biological domain, for instance, the crucial processes are genetic recombination and mutation. These are very different from, say, the cultural processes by which new grammatical rules or new idioms emerge in the evolution of a language. Both these cases differ, in turn, from the invention of new production techniques or the emergence of new institutions in an economy.

 Springer

In all these cases, the generic feature that transcends the disciplinary do-mains is the endogenous emergence of novelty. Yet this is not all. While novelty can be the trigger of qualitative change in the evolving entity, the actual process of transformation also depends on whether and how the novelty created disseminates and, by doing so, transforms the entity. The dissemination of novelty—the twin concept that characterizes evolution generically—is usually contingent on many factors and comes in many forms. Among them are multi-level competitive diffusion processes, like natural selection in the biological sphere, or successive adoption processes resulting from a non-selective imi-tation behavior as is often the case in the dissemination of human thought, practices, and artifacts. "Evolution" can thus be characterized generically—in a way that is not domain-specific—as a process of self-transformation whose basic elements are the endogenous generation of novelty and its contingent dissemination (Witt 2003, Chap.1). The generic concepts of novelty emergence and dissemination provide an overarching heuristic for interpreting problems and inducing hypotheses in the evolutionary sciences.

Since one's ontological stance is independent of the heuristic strategy one can choose to conceptualize evolution in economics, using any one of the two-by-two combinations—monism vs. dualism and generalized Darwinian heuristic vs. generic evolutionary heuristic—is, in principle, possible. Indeed, each of the four combinations is the basis for a different interpretation of what is specific about evolutionary economics. These interpretations will be discussed in more detail in the next section. Before doing this, however, the discussion of the three levels of controversy needs to be completed with a short digression into the problems at the methodological level. Here the controversy revolves around the question of how to account for the fact that the evolution of the economy at any particular point in time results in conditions and events that are historically unique.

The controversy begins with Veblen who, in formulating his version of evolutionary economics, took the methodological position of the German Historical School (see Hodgson 2001, Chap. 1). The controversy thus has its prelude in the *Methodenstreit* of the late 19th century. Here is not the place to discuss that prelude. Suffice to say that Veblen's partisanship is difficult to understand, if one were to follow the popular caricature of the Historical School's position as an entirely descriptive, a-theoretic historicism that denies the possibility of general hypotheses and deductive reasoning in economics. There was indeed much emphasis put on working in the historical archives to register and reproduce, in a very descriptive fashion, data about the economic conditions prevailing under different institutional regimes in earlier times. However, this was not meant to imply that theoretical reasoning was not possible.

The Historical School can be seen as part of the post Enlightenment em-piricism that was in vogue in the nineteenth century. In the sciences, this kind of empiricism—determined to uncover what historical reality is, what fossil remnants look like, and to record the findings—was characteristic of the Naturalist movement associated with names like Humboldt, Lyell, Herschel,

 Springer

Wallace, and others (Yeo 1993). After traveling all around the world, researchers filled books, journals, and session of scientific academies with reports on their observations and discoveries.[3] To understand nature meant primarily grasping its enormous variety. Something analogous to the Naturalists' attitude seems to have appealed to Veblen, who wanted to extend the naturalistic perspective to economic evolution. Hence, his sympathy for a methodology that set out primarily to reconstruct the historical habits, institutions, technologies, etc. and the order in which they occurred over time.

Of course, if historical description were the only method to account for the fact that, at any particular point in time, the state of nature or the economy is historically unique, evolutionary biology would reduce to natural history, and evolutionary economics to economic history. Yet this did not happen. Theoretical speculations about the general causal relationships and mechanisms that manifest themselves in the historical record turned out to be possible and fruitful. Darwin's theory of natural selection, the laws of heredity, and their more recent biophysical underpinnings are all general hypotheses about how the historical record has come about. Similarly, the particular economic conditions and events characteristic of a certain epoch may be historically unique. But this is not necessarily the case for the way in which they are generated and the patterns of transition between the states. It may be conjectured that the mechanisms of change are of more general nature, so that they produce recurrent features of change in economic history that can be explained by general hypotheses.

The methodological challenge that the historical contingency of economic phenomena poses leaves a variety of options to respond. These options are realized in different contributions to evolutionary economics, independent of their specific ontological and heuristic positions. Indeed, there seems to be a tendency across all ontological and heuristic positions to accept that different explanatory challenges require different methodological responses. One way to respond is to construct historical narratives for observed changes in technology and its knowledge base that identify, record, and make sense of, the historical sequence of events. As the work of Mokyr (1998, 2000) shows, qualitative theoretical inquiries into economic history like these can be based on a heuristic of selection analogies and metaphors. On the same basis, another methodological option is, for example, the development of sophisticated quantitative survival models to explain the historical record of the entry and exit dynamics over an industry's life cycle (Klepper 1997).

A method of historical reconstruction that is compatible also with other heuristic strategies is the "history-friendly, appreciative" modeling approach (Malerba et al. 1999). It makes use of numerical models whose simulations

---

[3]In broader perspective, the historical contingency of empirical phenomena is by no means exclusively a problem in economics. It is center stage in the great transition in the sciences from the a-historic, Newtonian world view to an evolutionary one during the Darwinian revolution (Moore 1979). It is worth noting that the ground for the transition was prepared by the Naturalists' empiricism (Mayr 1991, Chap. 1).

 Springer

can be made to fit an observed sequence of historical events or empirical time series. To match the general theoretical claims with the historical contingency condition, the models can be used to simulate counter-factual sequences of events (see Cowan and Foray 2002). Independent of the choice of the heuristic strategy, a frequently adopted methodological approach is to focus on the explanation of recurrent features of the evolutionary process rather than its historically unique outcomes. This means theorizing, e.g., about some underlying mechanisms of change or some typical transition patterns (assumed to be involved in generating historically unique outcomes without themselves being equally historically unique). A wide variety of modeling approaches is based on this methodology: diffusion models describing technological change as a result of innovativeness (Metcalfe 1988), selection models emulating competitive industrial change (Metcalfe 1994), models of path-dependence, lock-in, and critical masses in technological or institutional change (Arthur 1994; David 1993; Witt 1989). Last but not least, there is, of course, the option to develop explanatory hypotheses on the historical process of evolution itself, like, e.g., Hayek's (1988) theory of societal evolution.

There is thus a large variety of very different methodological choices in evolutionary economics (Cantner and Hanusch 2002). They can be, and in fact are, employed in a pragmatic way to cope with the historical contingencies of evolutionary processes. It may therefore be claimed that, at least in evolutionary economics, the *Methodenstreit* has no longer any relevance as a source of significant controversy. It is not at the methodological level, but at the ontological and heuristic levels, that enduring controversies split the opinions in evolutionary economics and trigger some of the new developments in the field.

3 A guide to evolutionary economics

In the previous section it was argued that the differences relating to ontological stance and heuristic strategies are decisive for understanding the different approaches to evolutionary economics. They can be conveniently represented in a 2 × 2 matrix by depicting the two ontological positions against the two heuristic strategies in Fig. 1. This representation provides a guide to both the evolutionary heterodoxy and some new developments in this field. In view of the great number and variety of contributions to evolutionary economics, no attempt can, of course, be made here to discuss them in detail in the form of a survey. The more limited purpose rather is to identify what the different, overarching approaches are, and why they differ.

In the *lower right cell* in the matrix of Fig. 1, a dualistic, non-naturalistic ontological perspective on economics is combined with a heuristic strategy based on a generic concept of evolution. This is the position of Schumpeter (1912) in his *Theory of Economic Development*. It is the basis for his unique interpretation of economic development that is usually considered a seminal contribution to evolutionary economics. Schumpeter did not use of the terms "evolution" and "evolutionary" precisely because he wanted to avoid the

What is specific about evolutionary economics?

		ontological stance	
		monistic	dualistic
heuristic strategy	generalized Darwinian concepts (variation, selection, retention)	**Universal Darwinism**	**neo-Schumpeterians** *(Nelson and Winter)* <u>topics:</u> innovation, technology, R&D, firm routines, industrial dynamics, competition, growth, institutional basis of innovations
	generic concept of evolution (novelty emergence & dissemination)	**naturalistic approaches** *(Veblen, Georgescu-Roegen, Hayek, North)* <u>topics:</u> long-run development, institutional evolution, production, consumption, growth & sustainability	**Schumpeter** (1912)

Fig. 1 Interpretations of evolutionary economics

association with the monistic Darwinian interpretation that, in his mind, the term evolution suggested.[4] When he elaborated his theory, he was guided by the notion that the economic transformation process is "intrinsically generated from within itself" (ibid. p. 75). As the source of change, he identified entrepreneurial innovations. If successful, they disseminate through imitation throughout the economy and thus transform its structure. This is exactly the generic evolutionary heuristic that focuses on the endogenous emergence of novelty and its dissemination.

However, Schumpeter did not fully exploit his ingenious insight. He used the distinction between invention and innovation to belittle the role of novelty creation (invention) and instead emphasized, in a voluntaristic fashion, the heroic character of entrepreneurship that he deemed necessary in order to be able to carry out innovations. Attention was thus shifted away from how the new knowledge on which innovations are based is being created and how the corresponding search and experimentation activities—the sources of novelty—are motivated. Furthermore, Schumpeter's theory was inspired not least by the ongoing debate on the crisis-driven capitalist development and his own experience of the uneven growth and wealth generating industrialization process at the turn of the 19th century. This may explain why his theory of

---

[4]See Schumpeter (1912, Chap.7). The chapter was omitted from later editions and the English translation of 1934. It has appeared only recently in English translation (Schumpeter 2002). In this chapter, Schumpeter is quite explicit in criticizing the pure theory of economics of his time because of its flawed Newtonian equilibrium heuristic. But he did not distance himself from the dualistic ontological position of that theory.

economic development is presented in terms of a theory about the unsteadiness of capitalist development, i.e. a business cycle theory. Entrepreneurs who trigger a wave of innovations and imitation occur "in swarms" and therefore induce the economy to move through phases of "prosperity and depression" in cyclical pattern.

At that time, explaining the business cycle was cutting edge research in economics. In presenting his theory of economic development as a contribution to the unfolding business cycle research, Schumpeter was able to earn himself a reputation as leading theorist in economics. But this way of selling his theory detracted attention from its non-Newtonian, evolutionary foundations. When Schumpeter (1942) later modified important parts of his theory, the evolutionary impetus was weakened even further. He claimed that, in the further development of capitalism, the role of the promoter-entrepreneur would be replaced by large, bureaucratic corporations and trusts (ibid., Chap. 7 and 12) and, thus, omitted the original psychological, motivational foundations of his entrepreneurial theory (that were difficult to reconcile with the equilibrium-cum-optimization paradigm). What he emphasized instead were the concomitants of the routine-like innovativeness of the large trusts: unprecedented economic growth and productivity increases on the one side and monopolistic practices necessary to protect the investments into innovations on the other. By arguing that it is not possible to have the one without the other, he challenged the established ideal of perfect competition. This interpretation of the competitive process—later dubbed the "Schumpeterian hypothesis"—stirred a long debate with a huge number of empirical and theoretical contributions (see Baldwin and Scott 1987). However, the broader, evolutionary connotations were increasingly lost from sight.

The unique heuristic strategy developed in Schumpeter (1912) did not find followers. None of Schumpeter's prominent Harvard students carried it further with, perhaps, the exception of Georgescu-Roegen (see below). A resurgence of interest in Schumpeter's pioneering evolutionary contribution had to wait until the work of Nelson and Winter (1982) and their neo-Schumpeterian synthesis. Yet this synthesis is based on a different heuristic strategy. In the debate on "economic natural selection" in the 1950s, analogies and metaphors relating to the theory of natural selection had made their appearance as a possible heuristic strategy in economics.[5] Nelson and Winter introduce this heuristic that makes metaphorical use of Darwinian concepts as a central element of their conceptualization of the transformation process in firms and industries. They thus replace the generic evolutionary heuristic that Schumpeter had used in avoiding Darwinian concepts. Indeed, within the

---

[5]Alchian (1950), Penrose (1952), Friedman (1953). The core of the debate was whether, in a competitive market, a firm can survive if it is not profit maximizing—an attempt to employ the selection metaphor to rectify profit maximizing behavior. However, on closer inspection, it turns out that the profit level sufficient to ensure survival at a particular time, and in a particular market, varies with so many factors that no unique profit maximum can be determined, see Winter (1964), Metcalfe (2002).

neo-Schumpeterian camp, this switch to, and the reliance on, the Darwinian selection metaphor are often considered to be the constitutive element of evolutionary economics (e.g. in Dosi and Nelson 1994; Nelson 1995; Zollo and Winter 2002). Schumpeter's non-monistic ontological stance in defining the disciplinary bounds of economics is factually maintained (see Nelson 2001). The neo-Schumpeterian approach therefore represents the combination of the *upper right cell* in Fig. 1.

In Nelson and Winter (1982), the heuristic based on Darwinian metaphors is the inspiration for an idea that has become a core concept of the neo-Schumpeterian approach: the organizational routine as a unit of selection in economic contexts. Schumpeter (1942) did not back a crucial assumption of his innovation competition hypothesis—that the corporate organizations of the large trusts have taken over the innovation process in the economy—with any specific hypotheses as to how these organizations do this. The concept of the organizational routine fills the gap. This is derived from the behavioral theory of the firm (March and Simon 1958; Cyert and March 1963)—another constitutive element of Nelson and Winter's neo-Schumpeterian synthesis. Based on the assumption of bounded rationality, Nelson and Winter (1982, Chap. 5) argue that, in their internal interactions, firm organizations are therefore bound to use rules of thumb and develop organizational routines. Production, calculation, price setting, the allocation of R&D funds, etc. are all represented as rule-bound behavior and organizational routines.

Informed by a heuristic based on the selection metaphor, Nelson and Winter interpret organizational routines as sufficiently inert to function as the unit of selection. Accordingly, the firms' routines are taken as the analogue to the genotypes in biology. The specific decisions resulting from the routines applied are taken as the analogue to biological phenotypes. The latter are supposed to affect the firms' overall performance. Different routines and different decisions lead to differences in the firms' growth. On the assumption that routines which successfully contribute to growth are not changed, the firms' differential growth can be understood as increasing the relative frequency of successful "genes-routines". In contrast, routines that result in a deteriorating performance are unlikely to multiply, so that their relative frequency in an industry decreases.

There is no doubt that the re-formulation of Schumpeter's conjectures on innovativeness, industrial change, and growth in terms of selection processes operating on the organizational underpinnings of firms and industries yields important insights. Nelson and Winter demonstrate that the firms' competitive adaptations to changing market conditions do not necessarily have to be understood as a deliberate, optimizing choice between given alternatives. Rather the adaptations may be forced on the industry by selection processes operating on the diversity of routines used in that industry. At the same time, Nelson and Winter are also able to account for the effects of innovative activities, the breaking away from old routines, in an industry's response to changing market conditions. New ways of doing things result from search processes which are themselves guided by higher level routines. Modeled as random draws

 Springer

from a distribution of productivity increments, innovations raise the average performance of the industry and regenerate the diversity of firm behaviors. Selection then drives out some of the firms, while the surviving ones tend to grow. Under innovation competition, technology and industry structure thus co-evolve and feed a non-equilibrating economic growth process.

Although the concept of the organizational routine, exposed to selection, has now become something of an icon of the neo-Schumpeterian approach to evolutionary economics, the perhaps even more momentous effect that Nelson and Winter's synthesis triggered was a different one. It prepared the ground for taking advantage of the rich body of insights on knowledge creation (neglected by Schumpeter) that in the meantime had become available in innovation research (see Dosi 1988). Indeed, the blending of innovation studies with the classical Schumpeterian themes of technological change, industrial dynamics, and economic growth has generated thriving empirical research that, in many cases, makes little, if any, use of the notion of routines and Darwinian metaphors (see Fagerberg 2003 for a survey).

On the methodological side, Nelson and Winter (1982) strongly rely on a simulation-based analysis of the implications of the selection processes operating on populations of firm routines—a methodology that has found many followers in the neo-Schumpeterian camp (e.g., Andersen 1994; Malerba and Orsenigo 1995; Kwasnicki 1996). As an analytically solvable alternative an approach based on the replicator dynamics has been suggested by Metcalfe (1994). It raises the heuristic of the selection metaphor to the level of a more stringent analogy construction. Unlike the modeling tradition in economics that focuses on the situational logic of (representative) individual behavior and its motives, the replicator dynamics—an abstract model of natural selection—focuses on the changing composition of populations and thus requires "population thinking"—a point much emphasized by Metcalfe.[6] In this version, the analogy-based heuristic then allows even the economic analogue of main theorems of population genetics to be derived.[7]

---

[6]The flip side of the coin is that the assumption of selection operating on routines and population thinking makes it difficult to account for individual learning, problem solving, and strategic reorientation—as important as they may be for the firms' adaptations to changing market conditions. Focus is at the industry level. Improved average performance in the industry is explained exclusively in terms of changing relative frequencies of the organizational routines that are themselves unchanging.

[7]These are Fisher's principle and Kimura's theorem, see Metcalfe (2002). The former states that natural selection raises average fitness in a population to the level of the highest individual fitness, the pace of change of the mean population fitness being proportional to the variance of the individual fitness. In the economic analogue, fitness is expressed by profit differentials between competing firms. In population genetics, mutation and cross-over again increase variety continuously. The analogue in economics, Metcalfe (1998) argues, is Schumpeter's notion of the creative (innovative) destruction. By improving products, technology, organizational routines, etc.

In the neo-Schumpeterian approach, a non-monistic ontological stance is combined with a heuristic using Darwinian metaphors to conceptualize economic evolution. However, such a heuristic strategy is also compatible with a monistic ontological stance that suggests extending the naturalistic view of the sciences to economic behavior and the economy. This is the combination in the *upper left cell* in Fig. 1. It corresponds to the approach advocated by the proponents of "Universal Darwinism" (Hodgson 2002; Hodgson and Knudsen 2006). The characteristic of this approach is that it relies on an abstract analogy to, rather than a metaphorical use of, Darwinian principles: Campbell's (Campbell 1965) variation, selection, retention principles. As already mentioned in the previous section, these have been derived by an abstract reduction of real processes in evolutionary biology and are claimed to govern evolutionary processes in all spheres of reality.

Regarding evolutionary processes in the economy, the latter claim has been met with skepticism (see Nelson 2006). Some critics object to the inevitable risks of being misled in economic theorizing by the domain specific abstractions of Universal Darwinism (Buenstorf 2006; Cordes 2006). The reasons for using a particular heuristic strategy have to do with expectations regarding the fecundity of the strategy. The question will therefore be whether the advocates of Universal Darwinism can dispel the concerns of their critics by demonstrating the fruitfulness of their heuristic in the economic domain. Up to now, not enough concrete research has been done in economics on the basis of Universal Darwinism (see, however, Hodgson and Knudsen 2004). An assessment of the pros and cons is therefore not yet possible.

Finally, the *lower left cell* in Fig. 1 represents the combination of a monistic ontological stance and a heuristic strategy focusing on the emergence and dissemination of novelty as generic concepts of evolution.[8] The combination is characteristic of a naturalistic interpretation of evolutionary economics that has been advocated by several writers. Since they come from quite different strands of thought, they are, however, often not recognized as following a common approach, nor is their approach usually perceived as a coherent alternative to the position of the neo-Schumpeterians. There are good reasons to associate Veblen with this position (see Cordes 2007). The arguments by which Veblen (1898) introduced the very notion of evolutionary economics to the discipline clearly indicate that what he had in mind was a naturalistic ontology, based on a Darwinian world view. His heuristic strategy is less clear. He did not provide any generic characterization of evolution. But he repeatedly emphasized human inventiveness and imitation as important

[8]Unlike Universal Darwinism, this position does not claim that the explanation of evolution in nature and evolution in the economy can identically be reduced to the abstract Darwinian principles of variation, selection, and retention. Instead, the latter are seen as special, and therefore often not relevant, materializations of what drives evolution generically: the emergence and dissemination of novelty. Consequently, for this position, the role which the Darwinian theory plays is defined by the ontological continuity hypothesis, see footnote 1 above.

 Springer

drivers of the development of institutions and technology, just as the heuristic strategy in the lower left cell in Fig. 1 would suggest.

An eminent contribution to evolutionary economics, that is very explicit about taking this position, is the work of Georgescu-Roegen (1971). In line with his ontological and heuristic position, major recurring themes in his writings are the role of novelty in driving evolution and the role of entropy in constraining evolution. Both issues are given a broad methodological and conceptual discussion and are finally applied to reformulating economic production theory. In reflecting on the conditions and the evolution of production, he strongly conveys the gist of what has been called here the continuity hypothesis. This is perhaps even more true of his inquiry into the technology and institutions of peasant economies in contrast to modern industrial economies (see Georgescu and Roegen 1976, Chapters 6 and 8). His concern with the fact that natural resources represent finite stocks that are degraded by human production activities induced him to criticize the abstract logic and subjective value accounting of canonical production theories that tend to play down these concerns.

A similar criticism also motivates works in the tradition of Georgescu-Roegen's naturalistic interpretation of evolutionary economics that link up with the emerging ecological economics movement like Gowdy (1994) and Faber and Proops (1998). Gowdy and Faber and Proops emphasize the role of the emergence of novelty, and they focus in a naturalistic perspective on production processes, their time structure, and their impact on natural resources and the environment. Blending positive evolutionary theorizing with normative environmental concerns, Gowdy and Faber and Proops also expand on the policy implications focusing on core issues of ecological economics, thus explicitly connecting the agenda of evolutionary and ecological economics.

Another eminent contribution that explicitly takes the naturalistic position, albeit with an entirely different motivation and background, is the late works of Hayek (1971, 1979, 1988, Chap. 1) on societal evolution. Hayek distinguishes between three different layers where human society evolves. A first layer is that of biological evolution during human phylogeny where primitive forms of social behavior, values, and attitudes became genetically fixed as a result of selection processes. These imply an order of social interactions for which sociobiology provides the explanatory model. (Once genetically fixed, these attitudes and values continue to be part of the genetic endowment of modern humans, even though biological selection pressure has now been largely relaxed.) At the second layer of evolution, that of human reason, evolution is driven by intention, understanding and human creativity resulting in new knowledge and its diffusion. The crucial point of Hayek's theory is, however, that between these two layers of evolution, i.e. "between instinct and reason" (Hayek 1971), there is a third layer of evolution. This is a layer at which rules of conduct are learnt and passed on in cultural rather than genetic transmission. The process is often not even consciously recognized. Accordingly, the emergence of, and the changes in, the rules of conduct that

 Springer

shape human interactions and create the orderly forms of civilization are not deliberately planned or controlled.

While these conjectures correspond to the ontological continuity hypothesis discussed in Section 2, Hayek goes a step further by adding a group selection hypothesis. Which rules are transmitted and maintained, he claims, depends on whether, and to what extent, they contribute to a groups' success in terms of economic prosperity and population growth. The latter can be brought about either as a result of successful procreation or through the attraction and integration of outsiders. A growing population fosters specialization and division of labor, and this will be the more so the case, the more reliably a group's rules of conduct coordinate individual activities and prevent social dilemmas. By the same logic, groups that do not adopt appropriate rules are likely to decline. Hayek thus interprets cultural evolution as a differential growth process operating on human sub-populations that are defined by their common rules of conduct. The criterion of the process is the—not necessarily genetic—reproductive success which the group's rules enable. From his hypotheses Hayek draws far-reaching conclusions regarding the political economy of the "extended order of the markets" that he considers the main human cultural achievement (see Hayek 1988).

It is worth noting that Hayek's group selection hypothesis does not necessarily involve natural selection operating at the level of the genes. It thus differs from the "dual inheritance hypothesis" in anthropology (see Henrich 2004; Richerson and Boyd 2005). The latter holds that gene-based natural selection processes and cultural learning jointly developed an impact on reproductive success in early phases of human phylogeny in which selection pressure was high. In the dual inheritance model, the cultural learning component explains why group selection is possible where natural selection alone would be bound to kin selection.

Unlike both Hayek's (tacit) cultural learning theory and the dual-inheritance hypothesis, the theory of economic change recently put forward by North (2005) emphasizes the role of human cognition. Culture, institutions, and technology matter for economic evolution, not least through their influence on transaction costs as a measure of social efficiency. But the true driving forces in North's view are human intentionality, beliefs, insight (i.e. cognitive learning), and knowledge. These make economic change for the most part a deliberate process. Accordingly, North directs attention to what is learned and how it is shared among the members of a society. The emphasis he puts on human learning and knowledge creation—i.e. the emergence of novelty—and the sharing of experience-based knowledge within and between generations— i.e. dissemination of novelty—points to a heuristic similar to the one based on the generic concept of evolution. Moreover, unlike his early contributions to new institutional economics (see Vromen 1995), North (2005) clearly takes a naturalistic ontological stance. Much like Hayek, he is eager to define the relationship between his explanatory sketch of economic evolution and the Darwinian world view, and the way he does so correlates with the ontological continuity hypotheses. Hence, North (2005) can be assessed as an important recent contribution to the naturalist interpretation of evolutionary economics.

As the discussion has shown, the four combinations of ontological stances and heuristic strategies in Fig. 1 correspond to four different interpretations of what is specific about evolutionary economics. Of these interpretations, the neo-Schumpeterian and the naturalistic interpretation have been those most actively elaborated in recent times, the former clearly more so than the latter. These two schools of thought differ significantly in the main research topics they focus on. In a nutshell, the neo-Schumpeterian themes are innovation, technology, R&D, organizational routines, industrial dynamics, competition, growth, and the institutional basis of innovation and technology. The themes of the naturalistic approach are long-term development, cultural and institutional evolution, production, consumption, and economic growth and sustainability.

The difference in perspective is not accidental. The naturalistic interpretation offers substantial new insights, particularly in a comparative, long-run analysis of the economic evolutionary process, while it makes less of a difference, e.g., for economic theorizing on short run industrial dynamics and competitiveness. However, this does not mean that the naturalistic approach cannot fruitfully be extended to the neo-Schumpeterian agenda. For example, production and consumption are important, but somewhat neglected, research topics that are relevant also for the neo-Schumpeterian agenda. Integrating the naturalistic approach with these topics can therefore be expected to add significantly to the understanding of the structural transformation of industries, economies, and international trade patterns.

4 Ontology and heuristics in evolutionary game theory

Many references in Hayek's work on his theory of societal evolution show that he draws to a considerable extent on the early sociobiology debate for which the introduction of game-theoretic arguments played a constitutive role (Caplan 1978). On the basis of a qualitative analysis, Hayek's theory of how societal evolution works therefore anticipates results that were later established in a more rigorous form in the unfolding field of evolutionary game theory in economics. In fact, his hypotheses on cultural learning at the layer "between instinct and reason", and the key role that rules of conduct play for coordination and prevention of social dilemmas, can be reproduced in elaborate game-theoretic terms (see, e.g., Witt 2008). In a sense, Hayek's contribution can thus be seen as an early outline of what a naturalistic approach to evolutionary game theory could mean. With regard to ontological stances and heuristic strategies, there is indeed a similar divide between the different interpretations of evolutionary game theory in economics as diagnosed in the previous section for evolutionary economics. Furthermore, as in the case of evolutionary economics, the authors often do not seem aware of the assumptions they implicitly make.

 Springer

Compared to rational game theory, the distinctive features of evolutionary game theory are special assumptions about how strategies are determined and, as a consequence, special solution concepts.[9] These assumptions follow from, and are designed to meet, the explanatory requirements of evolutionary biology, particularly sociobiology (Trivers 1971; Wilson 1975; Maynard Smith 1982). With the rise of game theory as a major field of research in economics, the interest of some authors was also attracted to evolutionary game theory. This interest may sometimes be due more to the formal properties of evolutionary game theory than to an intention to seek applications to economic problems (see, e.g., Weibull 1995). Because of the special assumption built into evolutionary game theory, such applications are indeed not easy to find (Friedman 1998). These assumptions make sense in sociobiology when arguing how certain forms of genetically determined social behavior, e.g. altruistic forms, can emerge under natural selection. It is not evident, however, what kind of economic behavior is supposed to meet the assumptions of evolutionary game theory.

Applications of evolutionary game theory in the economic domain follow basically two interpretations. A first interpretation takes over models of interactive selection mechanism and the corresponding algorithms from evolutionary biology in order to model human interactive learning processes in an economic context (usually non-cognitive learning behavior like reinforcement or stimulus-response learning, see Brenner 1999, Chap. 6). This is not meant to claim that the biological mechanisms apply directly to economic behavior—an idea that would not make sense because human learning is a non-genetic adaptation process. The interpretation is rather based on the heuristic strategy of assuming an analogy between genetic adaptation mechanisms and the non-genetic adaptation through non-cognitive learning. The formal background for the analogy is replicator dynamics that covers a very broad class of adjustment process (see Hofbauer and Sigmund 1988; Joosten 2006). In ontological terms, i.e. with respect to the basic assumptions about the structure of reality, the analogy construction typically neglects the question of whether, and how, economic processes modeled in that way connect with the naturalistic foundation of human behavior. This combination is thus the same as the one in the upper right cell in Fig. 1.

For the second interpretation of evolutionary game theory, by contrast, the biological context for which evolutionary game theory was originally developed is directly relevant to the political economy applications this interpretation deals with. It is claimed that certain very basic features of human economic behavior, like altruism, moral behavior, fairness, and other rules of conduct, have a genetic background and can therefore be best explained as a

---

[9]A player does not choose among strategies, but rather represents one fixed strategy out of a set of strategies present in a population of potentially interacting players. Players (or strategies) are matched randomly for single interactions. Their pay-offs are defined in terms of fitness values. Differences between the players' pay-offs result in a corresponding marginal change of the relative frequencies of the respective strategies in the population. See, e.g., Friedman (1998).

 Springer

result of natural selection (see, e.g., Güth and Yaari 1992; Binmore 1998; Gintis 2007). Similar to the continuity hypothesis, the existence of such features of human behavior is traced back to their conjectured emergence at the times of early human phylogeny when natural selection pressure on the human species was still high enough to shape behavior according to what can be speculated to have raised genetic fitness. Unlike in the former interpretation, such a view obviously presumes a monistic, naturalistic ontology. The heuristic strategy is not explicitly dealt with, but it has some similarity with Hayek's theory of societal evolution. In Binmore (1998) the game-theoretic argumentation is used to establish the particular content, e.g. in terms of the notion of fairness and justice, of the rules of conduct that emerged initially in human phylogeny. Because of its genetic background, the content is still effective and is argued to imply two basic coordination mechanisms for human societies, leadership and fairness (see also Binmore 2001).

In view of the two interpretations, it is striking how similar the understanding of the specific meaning of the attribute "evolutionary" is in evolutionary game theory and evolutionary economics. They share similar ontological stances and heuristic strategies and even develop a similar schism in these respects. But researchers in these two fields take little notice of each other. There is hardly any cross reference between the two fields, even when scholars from both camps join in symposia or conferences.[10] In a rare attempt to explain the mutual lack of exchange, Nelson (2001) argues that evolutionary game theory differs in two ways from evolutionary economics. First, it is more equilibrium oriented—even when the adjustment dynamics are explored this mainly serves the understanding of the resulting equilibrium configurations. Second, evolutionary game theory is less empirically oriented, paying little tribute to analyzing the historical record of the evolutionary process. For these reasons, Nelson argues, the two research communities have less in common than might be expect. In a similar vein, Dosi and Winter (2002) argue that evolutionary game theory is mostly theory-driven while evolutionary economics is more experience-driven, leaving little common ground for exchange.

In the light of the present discussion, a distinction can, however, be made between the naturalistic and the non-naturalistic approaches to evolutionary game theory on the one side and to evolutionary economics on the other. The non-naturalistic approaches do not have much more in common than the construction of analogies to natural selection—in the one case with, in the other without, strategic interaction—by means of concepts imported from evolutionary biology. In such a situation, there seems to be little opportunity to gain from trade. The naturalistic approaches, in contrast, share the explanation of human economic behavior by recourse to genetic and behavioral dispositions. This creates much more commonality in substance (as, e.g., the line of thought reaching from Hayek's theory of societal evolution to Binmore's

---

[10]See, e.g., the papers in Nicita and Pagano (2001) or the *Journal of Economic Perspectives* symposium on evolutionary economics (Samuelson 2002; Nelson and Winter 2002).

theory of social contract may show). Factual lack of exchange may here simply be due to the small number of researchers who follow, at one time, a naturalistic approach in their own field.

5 Recent trends in the evolutionary agenda—a peer survey

It has been argued above that Schumpeter's original interpretation has no more followers today and that Universal Darwinism is only just starting substantial work in economics. Of the four different interpretations of evolutionary economics in Table 1 only two—the neo-Schumpeterian and the naturalistic—are therefore currently leading to significant research output. These two differ significantly in the topics they deal with. If there were only the diverging research interests, the two schools could be seen as complementary. However, there is also a difference between the two in the basic assumption they make about reality and the way in which they approach, and theorize about, evolutionary processes in the economy. This is not easily reconcilable. In this section, an attempt will be made to assess the achievements and prospects for future research in evolutionary economics in relation to these two main interpretations.

In order to put this assessment on a broader basis, this section draws on the results of a survey conducted in 2004. A questionnaire in which they were asked about their opinion was sent out by e-mail to 149 academic scholars all over the world. The scholars were selected according to the criterion of whether they had at least one publication where they had dealt with, and had explicitly used the term, evolutionary economics.[11] The questionnaire contained several questions.

The first question aimed at getting an assessment from the respondents about what has been accomplished by past research into evolutionary economics. The precise formulation was: *"Summarizing evolutionary economics' achievements, what would you consider the most significant insights that have so far been gained? (Please give 4 or 5 keywords or names of contributors.)"* In order to derive a survey statistic from the answers, the keywords quoted in the questionnaires returned were categorized into classes of synonyms and near-synonyms that were given a representative label, and the number of designations that fell into the various keyword classes were counted. The keyword class then had to be identified, if possible, with one of the interpretations of evolutionary economics in Fig. 1, an identification that was done according to the author's best knowledge. In view of the fate of Schumpeter's position, and

---

[11] Although this is an objective selection criterion, it cannot be claimed that the selection of scholars is free from subjective biases and that it forms a representative sample of all authors who satisfy the criterion. Furthermore, the lack of anonymity in the e-mail based response mode may have had an impact on who was willing to respond and in what way. The survey results may therefore be subject to selection biases.

Table 1 Keyword labels quoted as "most significant insights so far"

Keywords	Named by % of all respondents	Ranked by		Significant for agenda of
		Professors	Younger scholars	
Innovation and technological change	26	1st	3rd	Neo-Schumpeterians
Evolution of institutions and norms	26	1st	3rd	Both approaches
Learning behavior	21	3rd	2nd	Both approaches
Knowledge creation and use	19	5th	1st	Both approaches
Variation and selection mechanism	17	2nd	5th	Neo-Schumpeterians
Diversity and population thinking	17	3rd	6th	Neo-Schumpeterians
Industry evolution and life cycles	17	4th	1st	Neo-Schumpeterians
Path dependence	17	3rd	4th	Both approaches
Non-equilibrium market dynamics	15	4th	4th	Unclear
Novelty and invention	13	7th	2nd	Both approaches
Bounded rationality	11	5th	5th	Both approaches
Co-evolution institutions/technology	11	6th	4th	Neo-Schumpeterians
General features of evolution	9	6th	5th	Both approaches
Routines	9	6th	5th	Neo-Schumpeterians
Spontaneous order	9	7th	4th	Naturalists
Evolutionary game theory	9	7th	4th	Unclear

because of the early stage in which Universal Darwinism currently is, the neo-Schumpeterian interpretation and that of the naturalist approaches are most likely the research programs to be associated here.

Of the 149 questionnaires sent out, 53 (36%) were returned.[12] Since some of the keywords given in the questionnaires could not be associated with any, or only very few, other keywords, a relatively large number of 48 different keyword classes resulted. For space reasons, only the 16 keyword classes with at least five designations—i.e. keywords quoted by at least roughly one tenth of all respondents—are reported in Table 1 together with the percentage of the 53 respondents that quoted the (near-) synonyms. The table also ranks the number of designations of the keyword classes differentiated by the professional status of the respondents. Furthermore, in the last column of Table 1, the keyword classes are associated with one of the interpretations of evolutionary economics.

For characterizing the achievements of evolutionary economics, the two keyword classes quoted most often in the sample were: "innovations and endogenous technological change" and "evolution of institutions and norms". With only one fourth of all respondents mentioning these keyword classes—and even smaller shares mentioning other classes—there is only modest agreement as to what the most significant insights in evolutionary economics are. Furthermore, the differences between professors and younger scholars in what they assess as an achievement or an insight in evolutionary economics are striking. The Spearman rank correlation coefficient for the two rank orders in Table 1 is very small ($r_s = 0.051$), indicating that there is almost no correlation between them. Given that the class label "innovations and endogenous technological change" seems highly significant for the dominant neo-Schumpeterian agenda, a share of only 26% may be surprising. Yet, in view of the fact that 6 of the 16 class labels can also be identified with the neo-Schumpeterian research agenda, this agenda is not under-represented. On the contrary, if the identification in Table 1 of the keyword classes with the alternative research programs is accepted, the neo-Schumpeterian school is obviously perceived by the respondents as the most important and successful. As indicated, seven of the remaining keyword classes can be claimed for both research programs, two seem unclear, and only one—"spontaneous order"—can, with some right, be considered associated with the naturalistic program.[13]

---

[12] By geographical status came 43 from Europeans and 10 non-Europeans. By professional status, 37 respondents were professors and 16 were at an earlier stage of their career (post-docs, lecturers, researchers, etc.—because of their average age denoted "younger scholars" below).

[13] The keyword class "evolution of institutions and norms" demonstrates the difficulties involved in the identification task. It can be identified with Veblen's institutionalist agenda, with Hayek's and North's agenda, and with that of evolutionary game theory (evolutionary game theory itself was only among the less frequently (9%) mentioned achievements)—mostly naturalistic interpretations. However, the keyword class could also be claimed to be significant for the institutional underpinnings of national innovation systems, a neo-Schumpeterian theme.

 Springer

A second issue addressed by the questionnaire concerned the opinions about promising topics for future research in evolutionary economics. The precise formulation of the question was: *"What would you consider the most promising new developments in evolutionary economics since 1990? (Please give 4 or 5 keywords or names of contributors.)"* Again, the procedure was to form classes of keywords from synonyms and near synonyms and to check how far they are associated with any of the two schools. For this question, 44 different keyword classes resulted of which 13 obtained at least five designations. These are presented in Table 2, together again with the percentage of the respondents, the ranks of the number of designations differentiated by the professional status of the respondents, and the associations with the research agendas of the different schools in evolutionary economics.

To characterize the most promising new developments, the keyword class "integrating the institutional side" was quoted most often in the sample. This is a conceptual issue that presently figures prominently in the neo-Schumpeterian camp (see, e.g., Nelson and Sampat 2001) that has up to now been strongly technology-oriented. Second in designation frequency are "agent-based modeling tools and computational methods" and "cognitive aspects" (of the evolutionary approach to economics)—the former a methodological/technical point that is not specific to any of the two schools, the latter again a conceptual issue relevant to both schools. The keyword label "industry evolution and life cycles" that is next in relative frequency already appeared in Table 1 as major insight and is therefore in italics. The same holds for "knowledge creation and use" and "evolutionary game theory". Unlike the other ten keyword classes that signal a certain shift in interest or emphasis when turning from the past to the future, the keywords in italics seem to be considered as topics with continuing high potential.

As far as the identification with the two schools is concerned, the neo-Schumpeterian themes are represented somewhat less than before, but the naturalists' topics have not gained more support. What does seem to be gaining ground is the interest in formal modeling and the corresponding tools ("agent-based and computational methods", "network models", "complex economic dynamics"). The differences between professors and younger scholars in what they consider promising new developments in evolutionary economics are once again remarkable, albeit less spectacular than in Table 1. (For the two rank orders in Table 2, $r_s = 0.345$, at a significance level 0.248).

The results of the peer survey show that, of the two main interpretations of evolutionary economics, the neo-Schumpeterian approach is perceived more prominently and its achievements are more widely appreciated than is the case for the naturalistic interpretation. This is not surprising in view of the fact that these days, the majority of research activities in evolutionary economics focus on innovations, technology, R&D, organizational routines, industrial dynamics, competition, growth, and the institutional basis of innovations and technology. These topics reflect the strong impact that Nelson and Winter (1982) and their neo-Schumpeterian synthesis had, and still have, on the field and on the self-perception of many scholars contributing to evolution-

 Springer

What is specific about evolutionary economics?

Table 2 Keyword labels quoted as "most promising new developments"

Keywords	Named by % of all respondents	Ranked by Professors	Ranked by Younger scholars	Significant for agenda of
Integrating the institutional side	23	1st	3rd	Neo-Schumpeterians
Agent-based and computational methods	21	2nd	2nd	Unspecific
Cognitive aspects	21	3rd	1st	Both approaches
Industry evolution and life cycles	19	4th	1st	Neo-Schumpeterians
Preference evolution	17	3rd	2nd	Naturalists
Knowledge creation and use	13	4th	3rd	Both approaches
Evolutionary game theory	13	5th	2nd	Unspecific
Evolutionary theory of the firm	11	4th	4th	Neo-Schumpeterians
Network models	9	6th	3rd	Unspecific
Complex economic dynamics	9	5th	4th	Unspecific
Universal Darwinism	9	5th	4th	Universal Darwinism
Evolutionary theory of policy making	9	6th	3rd	Unspecific
Evolutionary psychology	9	4th	5th	Naturalists

 Springer

ary economics today. If judged by the survey results, the contributions to the naturalistic interpretation—from Veblen (the inventor of "evolutionary" economics) to Georgescu-Roegen, Hayek, North, and others—do not seem to have much resonance in evolutionary economics today.

Regarding the promising prospects for future research, the situation is less one-sided. In part this is due, however, to the stronger influence of formal methods. These attract the interest particularly of the younger participants in the survey, and they have no particular association with any of the alternative interpretations. There are no signs of convergence as far as the two main interpretations of evolutionary economics are concerned. The potential of the naturalistic interpretation is still not really recognized by the evolutionary economists. Its characteristic topics—long-term development, cultural and institutional evolution, production, consumption, and economic growth and sustainability—deserve more attention. They can help to avoid the impression one can get today that evolutionary economics is basically a competitor to canonical industrial economics. By embracing a wider range of topics, among them traditional themes since the classics, the naturalistic agenda broadens the scope of evolutionary economics. What is more, with its foundations in a Darwinian world view, it can also challenge canonical economics and its mix of Newtonian thought and radical subjectivism.

6 Conclusions

There is little agreement among the researchers in the field when it comes to deciding what is specific about evolutionary economics. As has been shown in this paper, some interpretations of evolutionary economics consider the Darwinian theory of evolution relevant for understanding economic behavior and the transformation of economic institutions and technology. Other interpretations do not embrace, or even explicitly reject, that idea. At the core, this is a controversy about the basic (ontological) assumption about the structure of reality. It relates to the question of whether evolutionary change in nature and in the economy represent connected spheres of reality, making them likely to mutually influence each other.

In a different sense, the role of Darwinian theory is also relevant for a second controversy. This revolves around the question of whether evolutionary theorizing in economics can profit from borrowing analytical tools from evolutionary biology, e.g. models of selection processes and population dynamics. As has been explained, some authors consider the application of such models to economic processes on the basis of analogies or metaphors to be the specific feature of the evolutionary approach to economics. Other authors have different ideas. To construct analogies between, and to use metaphors originating from, different disciplinary domains is a heuristic device, i.e. a way of framing problems and of arriving at hypotheses. Unlike the previous controversy, the one about whether or not to borrow analytical tools from evolutionary biology thus refers to the heuristic level. The way it is decided is independent of the ontological position taken, but is decisive for the form of theorizing in evolutionary economics.

Finally, there is a controversy relating to the methodological level, particularly to the problem that economic evolution is a historical process producing historically unique conditions and events: how should this fact be accounted for in evolutionary economics? The controversy has been claimed to be independent of the other two. As was discussed in the paper, some authors have tried to account for the question by relying on qualitative reasoning. Others have responded by developing a "history friendly" modeling strategy. However, it can also be argued that, while at any given time the results of evolution may be historically unique, the processes by which they are generated are not necessarily historically unique. (In fact, if this were not so, it would be pointless to claim that the way in which evolution works can be explained by more general hypotheses.) It can therefore be concluded that with the variety of choices, and the usually pragmatic decision making as to which of them to select, the methodological level is not the reason for the views on what is specific about evolutionary economics being different.

The major differences indeed result from diverging ontological stances and heuristic strategies. This turned out to be true also for evolutionary game theory which is faced with exactly the same kind of ontological and heuristic controversies. Juxtaposing the two positions that have been identified at each of the two levels results in a convenient two-by-two matrix. In the paper this matrix has served as a guide to the various interpretations of evolutionary economics that can be found in the literature. Not all interpretations corresponding to the four cells in the matrix have received equal attention. In recent years, the combination of Darwinian concepts at the heuristic level and neglect or rejection of a naturalistic monism at the ontological level is most frequent. This combination is characteristic of the neo-Schumpeterian approach. As was shown, this has not always been so. Schumpeter's own approach differed from that of the neo-Schumpeterian. There has also been a naturalistic interpretation of evolutionary economics advocated by such diverse scholars as Veblen, Georgescu-Roegen, Hayek, and North. The most recent development—Universal Darwinism—has been recommended as an approach to evolutionary economics that favors yet another combination of ontological stance and heuristic strategy.

The scientific value of the alternatives should be measured in terms of the insights they deliver on the transformation processes in the economy. To assess the fruitfulness of the alternative interpretations, a peer survey was conducted to identify achievements in past research and promises for future research in evolutionary economics. In the overall ranking of past achievements expressed in the opinion poll, the neo-Schumpeterian position was found to stand out. In the assessment of promising future research the picture is somewhat different. However, there is little evidence for convergence, or for a real resurgence of interest in the naturalistic approach to evolutionary economics. Such a resurgence would seem desirable in order to broaden the agenda of evolutionary economics beyond the neo-Schumpeterian themes that basically rival the

 Springer

canonical theories of industrial economics and technological change. Not only would topics like long-term development, cultural and institutional evolution, production, consumption, and economic growth and sustainability have a come-back on the evolutionary agenda. Founded on a Darwinian (naturalistic) world view, evolutionary economics would also challenge in principle terms the mix of Newtonian thought and radical subjectivism characteristic of canonical economics.

Acknowledgements   I should like to thank Guido Buenstorf, John Gowdy, Hardy Hanappi, Christian Schubert and two referees of this journal for helpful comments on an earlier version of this paper.

References

Alchian AA (1950) Uncertainty, evolution, and economic theory. J Polit Econ 58:211–221
Andersen ES (1994) Evolutionary economics—post-Schumpeterian contributions. Pinter, London
Andersen ES (2004) Population thinking, Price's equation and the analysis of economic evolution. Evol Inst Econ Rev 1:127–148
Arthur WB (1994) Increasing returns and path dependence in the economy. University of Michigan Press, Ann Arbor
Baldwin WL, Scott JT (1987) Market structure and technological change. Harwood Academic Publishers, Chur
Binmore K (1998) Just playing-game theory and the social contract II. MIT Press, Cambridge, MA
Binmore K (2001) Natural justice and political stability. Journal of Institutional and Theoretical Economics 157:133–151
Brenner T (1999) Modelling learning in economics. Edward Elgar, Cheltenham
Buenstorf G (2006) How useful is generalized Darwinism as a framework to study competition and industrial evolution? J Evol Econ 16:511–527
Campbell DT (1965) Variation and selective retention in socio-cultural evolution. In: Barringer HR, Blankstein GI, Mack RW (eds) Social change in developing areas: a re-interpretation of evolutionary theory. Schenkman, Cambridge, MA, pp 19–49
Cantner U, Hanusch H (2002) Evolutionary economics, its basic concepts and methods. In: Lim H, Park UK, Harcourt GC (eds) Editing economics. Routledge, London, pp 182–207
Caplan AL (ed) (1978) The sociobiology debate. Harper, New York
Cordes C (2006) Darwinism in economics: from analogy to continuity. J Evol Econ 16:529–541
Cordes C (2007) Turning economics into an evolutionary science: Veblen, the selection metaphor, and analogical thinking. J Econ Issues 41:135–154
Cowan R, Foray D (2002) Evolutionary economics and the counterfactual threat: on the nature and role of counterfactual history as an empirical tool in economics. J Evol Econ 12:539–562
Cyert RM, March JG (1963) A behavioral theory of the firm. Prentice Hall, Englewood Cliffs, NJ
Dawkins R (1983) Universal Darwinism. In: Bendall DS (ed) Evolution from molecules to man. Cambridge University Press, Cambridge, pp 403–425
David PA (1993) Path-dependence and predictability in dynamical systems with local network externalities: a paradigm for historical economics. In: Foray DG, Freeman C (eds) Technology and the wealth of nations. Pinter, London, pp 208–231
Dopfer K (2005) Evolutionary economics: a theoretical framework. In: Dopfer K (ed) The evolutionary foundations of economics. Cambridge University Press, Cambridge, pp 3–55

Dopfer K, Potts J (2004) Evolutionary realism: a new ontology for economics. J Econ Methodol 11:195–212

Dosi G (1988) Sources, procedures, and microeconomic effects of innovation. J Econ Lit 26:1120–1171

Dosi G, Nelson RR (1994) An introduction to evolutionary theories in economics. J Evol Econ 4:153–172

Dosi G, Winter SG (2002) Interpreting economic change: evolution, structures and games. In: Augier M, March JG (eds) The economics of choice, change and organization. Edward Elgar, Cheltenham, pp 337–353

Faber M, Proops JLR (1998) Evolution, time, production and the environment. Springer, Berlin

Fagerberg J (2003) Schumpeter and the revival of evolutionary economics. J Evol Econ 13:125–159

Foster J (1997) The analytical foundations of evolutionary economics: from biological analogy to economic self-organization. Struct Chang Econ Dyn 8:427–451

Friedman D (1998) On economic applications of evolutionary game theory. J Evol Econ 8:15–43

Friedman M (1953) The methodology of positive economics. In: Friedman M (ed) Essays in positive economics. University of Chicago Press, Chicago, pp 3–43

Georgescu-Roegen N (1971) The entropy law and the economic process. Harvard Univ. Press, Cambridge, MA

Georgescu-Roegen N (1976) Energy and economic myths—institutional and analytical economic essays. Pergamon, New York

Gintis H (2007) A framework for the unification of the behavioral sciences. Behav Brain Sci 30:1–61

Gowdy J (1994) Coevolutionary economics: the economy, society and the environment. Kluwer, Boston

Güth W, Yaari M (1992) Explaining reciprocal behavior in simple strategic games: an evolutionary approach. In: Witt U (ed) Explaining process and change—approaches to evolutionary economics. University of Michigan Press, Ann Arbor, pp 23–34

Hallpike CR (1985) Social and biological evolution I. Darwinism and social evolution. J Soc Biol Syst 8:129–146

Hallpike CR (1986) Social and biological evolution II. Some basic principles of social evolution. J Soc Biol Syst 9:5–31

Hashimoto T (2006) Evolutionary linguistics and evolutionary economics. Evol Inst Econ Rev 3:27–46

Hayek FA (1971) Nature vs. nurture once again. Encounter 36:81–83

Hayek FA (1979) Law, legislation and liberty. The political order of a free people, vol 3. Routledge, London

Hayek FA (1988) The fatal conceit. Routledge, London

Henrich J (2004) Cultural group selection, coevolutionary processes and large-scale cooperation. J Econ Behav Organ 53:3–35

Herrmann-Pillath C (2001) On the ontological foundations of evolutionary economics. In: Dopfer K (ed) Evolutionary economics—program and scope. Kluwer, Boston, pp 89–139

Hodgson GM (2001) How economics forgot history: the problem of historical specificity in social science. Routledge, London

Hodgson GM (2002) Darwinism in economics: from analogy to ontology. J Evol Econ 12:259–281

Hodgson GM, Knudsen T (2004) The firm as an interactor: firms as vehicles for habits and routines. J Evol Econ 14:281–307

Hodgson GM, Knudsen T (2006) Why We need a generalized Darwinism, and why generalized Darwinism is not enough. J Econ Behav Organ 61:1–19

Hofbauer J, Sigmund K (1988) The theory of evolution and dynamical systems. Cambridge Univ. Press, Cambridge.

Hull DL (2001) Science and selection: essays on biological evolution and the philosophy of science. Cambridge University Press, Cambridge

Joosten R (2006) Walras and Darwin: an odd couple? J Evol Econ 16:561–573

Klepper S (1997) Industry life cycles. Ind Corp Change 6:145–181

Knudsen T (2002) Economic selection theory. J Evol Econ 12:443–470

Kwasnicki W (1996) Knowledge, innovation and economy—an evolutionary exploration. Edward Elgar, Aldershot

Laurent J, Nightingale J (eds) (2001) Darwinism and evolutionary economics. Edward Elgar, Cheltenham

Malerba F, Orsenigo L (1995) Schumpeterian patterns of innovation. Camb J Econ 19:47–65

Malerba F, Nelson RR, Orsenigo L, Winter SG (1999) 'History-friendly' models of industry evolution: the computer industry. Ind Corp Change 8:3–41

March JG, Simon HA (1958) Organizations. Wiley, New York

Maynard Smith J (1982) Evolution and the theory of games. Cambridge Univ. Press, Cambridge

Mayr E (1991) One long argument. Harvard Univ. Press, Cambridge, Mass

Metcalfe JS (1988) The diffusion of innovations: an interpretative survey. In: Dosi G, Freeman C, Nelson RR, Silverberg G, Soete L (eds) Technical change and economic theory. Pinter Publishers, London, pp 560–589

Metcalfe JS (1994) Competition, Fisher's principle and increasing returns in the selection process. J Evol Econ 4:327–346

Metcalfe JS (1998) Evolutionary economics and creative destruction. Routledge, London

Metcalfe S (2002) On the optimality of the competitive process: Kimura's theorem and market dynamics. J Bioecon 4:109–133

Mirowski P (1989) More heat than light—economics as social physics, physics as nature's economics. Cambridge University Press, Cambridge

Mokyr J (1998) Induced technical innovations and medical history: an evolutionary approach. J Evol Econ 8:119–137

Mokyr J (2000) Evolutionary phenomena in technological change. In: Ziman J (ed) Technological innovation as an evolutionary process. Cambridge Univ. Press, Cambridge, pp 52–65

Moore JR (1979) The post-Darwinian controversies. Cambridge Univ. Press, Cambridge

Nelson RR (1995) Recent evolutionary theorizing about economic change. J Econ Lit 33:48–90

Nelson RR (2001) Evolutionary theories of economic change. In: Nicita A, Pagano U (eds) The evolution of economic diversity. Routledge, London, pp 199–215

Nelson RR (2006) Evolutionary social science and universal Darwinism. J Evol Econ 16:491–510

Nelson RR, Sampat B (2001) Making sense of institutions as a factor shaping economic performance. J Econ Behav Organ 44:31–54

Nelson RR, Winter SG (1982) An evolutionary theory of economic change. Harvard Univ. Press, Cambridge, MA

Nelson RR, Winter SG (2002) Evolutionary theorizing in economics. J Econ Perspect 16:23–46

Nicita A, Pagano U (eds) (2001) The evolution of economic diversity. Routledge, London

North DC (2005) Understanding the process of economic change. Princeton Univ. Press, Princeton

Penrose ET (1952) Biological analogies in the theory of the firm. Am Econ Rev 42:804–819

Richerson P, Boyd R (2005) Not by genes alone: how culture transformed human evolution. The University of Chicago Press, Chicago

Samuelson L (2002) Evolution and game theory. J Econ Perspect 16:47–66

Schumpeter JA (1912) Theorie der wirtschaftlichen Entwicklung, 1st edn. Duncker & Humblot, Leipzig (English translation 1934: Theory of Economic Development. Harvard Univ. Press, Cambridge, MA)

Schumpeter JA (1942) Capitalism, socialism and democracy. Harper, New York

Schumpeter JA (2002) The economy as a whole. (7th Chapter of Schumpeter 1912, translation by Backhaus U) Industry and Innovation 9:93–145

Silva ST, Teixeira AC (2006) On the divergence of research paths in evolutionary economics: a comprehensive bibliometric account. Papers on Economics and Evolution #0624: Max Planck Institute of Economics, Jena

Tooby J, Cosmides L (1992) The psychological foundations of culture. In: Barkow JH, Cosmides L, Tooby J (eds) The adapted mind: evolutionary psychology and the generation of culture. Oxford University Press, Oxford, pp 19–136

Trivers RL (1971) The evolution of reciprocal altruism. Q Rev Biol 46:35–57

Veblen T (1898) Why is economics not an evolutionary science? Q J Econ 12:373–397

Vromen J (1995) Economic evolution: an enquiry into the foundations of new institutional economics. Routledge, London

Vromen J (2004) Conjectural revisionary economic ontology: outline of an ambitious research agenda for evolutionary economics. J Econ Methodol 11:213–247

Vromen J (2006) Routines, genes, and program-based behavior. J Evol Econ 16:543–560

What is specific about evolutionary economics?

Weibull JW (1995) Evolutionary game theory. MIT Press, Cambridge, Mass

Wilson EO (1975) Sociobiology—the new synthesis. Belknap Press, Cambridge, MA

Wilson EO (1998) Consilience—the unity of knowledge. Knopf, New York

Winter SG (1964) Economic 'natural selection' and the theory of the firm. Yale Econ Essays 4: 225–272

Witt U (1989) The evolution of economic institutions as a propagation process. Public Choice 62:155–172

Witt U (1999) Bioeconomics as economics from a Darwinian perspective. J Bioecon 1:19–34

Witt U (2003) The evolving economy. Edward Elgar, Cheltenham

Witt U (2004) On the proper interpretation of 'evolution' in economics and its implications for production theory. J Econ Methodol 11:125–146

Witt U (2008) Observational learning, group selection, and societal evolution. J Inst Econ 4:1–24

Witt U, Cordes C (2007) Selection, learning, and Schumpeterian dynamics—a conceptual debate. In: Hanusch H, Pyka A (eds) The Elgar companion to neo-Schumpeterian economics. Edward Elgar, Cheltenham, pp 316–328

Yeo R (1993) Defining science: William Whewell, natural knowledge and public debate in early Victorian Britain. Cambridge Univ. Press, Cambridge

Ziman J (ed) (2000) Technological innovation as an evolutionary process. Cambridge Univ. Press, Cambridge

Zollo M, Winter SG (2002) Deliberate learning and the evolution of dynamic capabilities. Organ Sci 13:339–351

PART II

THE ROLE OF NOVELTY FOR EVOLUTION AND EVOLUTIONARY METHODOLOGY

PART II

THE ROLE OF NOVELTY FOR EVOLUTION AND EVOLUTIONARY METHODOLOGY

Industry and Innovation, Volume 9, Numbers 1/2, 7-22, April/August 2002 Carfax Publishing
Taylor & Francis Group

HOW EVOLUTIONARY IS SCHUMPETER'S THEORY OF ECONOMIC DEVELOPMENT?

ULRICH WITT

D espite the enormous prominence of the work of Joseph A. Schumpeter in terms of citations there is nothing like a Schumpeterian school in economics—even though, particularly during his tenure at Harvard University from 1932 until his death in 1950, Schumpeter had extremely talented students in his classes. Many of them—Bergson, Georgescu-Roegen, Goodwin, Hirshleifer, Musgrave, Samuelson, Stolper, and Tobin, to mention just a few—became eminent economists in their own right, and usually recalled Schumpeter's classes with sympathy, if not admiration. In their research, however, they went their own, diverse ways without carrying Schumpeter's thought on the development of modern capitalism much further. The reason, it will be claimed here, is that Schumpeter left no conclusive theoretical system to his students, as did Mill or Marshall before him, and Samuelson after him. What he left rather was an oeuvre dealing with an enormously broad range of topics in a rather eclectic fashion, albeit framed by, and interpreted within, a distinct economic world-view.

It is especially in his two great, and undisputedly most original, works—*The Theory of Economic Development* (1912/1934) and *Capitalism, Socialism and Democracy* (1942)—that Schumpeter most clearly reveals his world-view. It seems to be shaped partly by Schumpeter's own historical experience of the unsteady and unbalanced economic growth process in the period of "promoterism" and rapid industrial expansion in Europe in the late 19th and early 20th centuries, and partly by the impact and the repercussion of the popular Marxist teachings of a crisis-prone capitalist development. While passing through booms and crises, prosperity and depression, capitalist economic development had created previously unknown levels of economic achievement in production, consumption, exchange, and even in the institutional set-up of the economy. Any attempt to theorize that historical record (and, indeed, the continuing development since) can hardly fail to take account of the role of innovations and innovativeness, of entrepreneurship, and of incessant economic change at all levels of the economy. Yet, when the young Schumpeter was writing, all these concepts and the corresponding theoretical conjectures were, at best, discussed loosely at the margins of economic theory. In fact, these concepts stood outside the Newtonian paradigm of an ever-equilibrating economy, a paradigm that, under the influence of writers like Jevons, Walras, Edgeworth, Pareto, Clark, and Marshall had gained increasing adherence by the early years of the 20th century.

Schumpeter was fully aware of all this. In his habilitation thesis (Schumpeter 1908) he had given a survey-like discussion of precisely those recent developments in "pure" economic theory in the non-Germanic world; this was published as his first book, *Das Wesen und der Hauptinhalt der theoretischen Nationalökonomie* [*The Essence and Principal Contents of Economic Theory*]. In the later omitted Chapter 7 of his second

1366-2716 print/1469-8390 online/02/01/20007-16 © 2002 Taylor & Francis Ltd
DOI: 10.1080/13662710220123590

book, *Theorie der wirtschaftlichen Entwicklung* [*The Theory of Economic Develop-ment*] (Schumpeter 1912)—the focus of the present issue—he clearly recognized the heuristic analogy to gravitating systems underlying that "pure" theory. He argued that, even though this is rarely explicitly stated, "pure" economic theory, which he equated to "static" (or comparative static) theory, excludes any possibility of development occurring from within the economic system. Schumpeter (1912) therefore felt the need to supplement that theory, and he summed up in Chapter 7 what he called the "developmental" method. The book of 1912 is actually an elaboration of an earlier exposé (Schumpeter 1910) that presented the hypotheses about capitalist develop-ment framed within a business cycle theory. Perhaps this theoretical frame may have occurred straightforward to Schumpeter, given the connotations of his economic world-view. Perhaps, he also expected his interpretation to be more easily acceptable in such a form to the adherents of the neo-classical approach.

Yet, the great fame of the book of 1912 notwithstanding, its main concern—to estab-lish a developmental approach—was irreconcilable with, and therefore never inte-grated within, neo-classical doctrine. Even within business cycle theory, the influence he undoubtedly had (cf. Haberler 1937), has faded. Schumpeter's endeavour to improve his grasp of the business cycle phenomenon by ever more descriptive and "technical" extensions, culminating in the two monumental volumes of Schumpeter (1939), could not prevent the Keynesian and later neo-classical interpretations from dominating the scene. While of minor importance in Schumpeter (1939), developmental considera-tions were forcefully reintroduced in new form and quality in Schumpeter (1942). The encompassing reflections on the future of capitalist development in that book are clearly a response to his impressions of American capitalism after his move to Harvard. But the perspective from which the book is written is still that of the Old-World debate in which the repercussions of Marxian projections figure prominently.

In an economic world-view in which the incessant change of the capitalist economy plays the central part, it seems natural to ask what possible historical regularities may exist within, and what driving forces are behind, those changes. It was Schumpeter's ingenious insight that a theoretical approach conceived to deal with features of gravitating, rather than self-transforming, systems is not well suited to provide answers to these questions. He concluded that it would be his mission to provide a theoretical approach that could account for the features of a self-transforming system, based on its internal dynamics rather than seeking change through external causes or stimuli. But, as can clearly be noted in Chapter 7 of *The Theory of Economic Development* (TED), he was determined to do so entirely on the basis of received economic concepts that involve few, if any, developmental ideas. In particular, Schumpeter avoided the term "evolution" and a more general inquiry into the character of evolutionary change. He consistently denied biological thought any relevance both on the formal and the substantive level.[1] As will be argued in this paper, it may have

---

1   This is in remarkable contrast to the Darwinian undertones in more recent writings reviving Schumpeterian ideas in evolutionary economics (as in Nelson and Winter 1982). It must be left to biographical inquiries whether and when Schumpeter became familiar in any detail with the Darwinian theory of evolution. At the only place in Chapter 7 of Schumpeter (1912) in which he touched on possible formal or material relationships between his theory and biology, he did not refer to the Darwinian notion of phylogenetic evolution, but to the process of ontogenetic development of the organism—and rejected it.

been precisely because of his reluctance to consider the evolutionary character of change in more abstract terms that Schumpeter failed to reach a level of generality necessary for elaborating a conclusive theoretical system to explain economic change.

Even though in Schumpeter (1912) the general features of an evolutionary theory show up, Hodgson (1993: Chap. 10) is right in his verdict that Schumpeter's wrestling with an economic reasoning that had originated from comparative statics could not produce a coherent alternative to the neo-classical paradigm. Instead, we find a rich set of original and fruitful conjectures and observations which are hampered, from the beginning, by theoretical *ad hoc* constructions induced by the business cycle framework and, later, by the weaknesses of a philosophy of history in a Marxian spirit. To substantiate these claims the present paper proceeds as follows. In order to establish a conceptual frame of reference for assessing Schumpeter's theory of economic development, the first section outlines some abstract characteristics of evolutionary theories. With this as background, the next section discusses the argument in Schumpeter (1912)—which, as mentioned, is cast in terms of a business cycle theory. The paper then turns to Schumpeter (1942) and tries to identify the problems emerging in his historical thought, impressive and inspiring as it undoubtedly is, from the point of view of evolutionary theory. The paper closes with some concluding comments.

WHAT IS AN EVOLUTIONARY THEORY?

The concept of evolution is an offspring of late 18th and early 19th century debates within philosophy and the social sciences (cf. Schumpeter 1954: Part III, Chap. 3; Bowler 1989: Chaps 3 and 4). Modern notions of evolution, by contrast, are usually informed by the more recent and much more successful Darwinian theory of natural selection with all its powerful extensions developed in biology. This also holds true in economics where a characterization of an evolutionary approach is often attempted by referring to Darwinian theory in evolutionary biology—usually by way of analogy (e.g. Boulding 1981; Nelson and Winter 1982; Hodgson 1993). The explanatory power of the (neo-) Darwinian theory in relation to evolutionary phenomena within the biosphere can hardly be denied, but its relevance for the human sphere, where human intelligence and intentionality are of significant importance, is unclear and disputed. In place of debating the suitability of transferring biological analogies to economics, with all the dangers this implies, the discussion of the meaning and form of an evolutionary approach to economics would therefore be better founded on a generalized notion of evolution.

Accordingly, let us start by introducing a general definition of evolution as the self-transformation over time of a system under investigation. Such a system may be a population of living organisms, a collection of interacting individuals as in an economy or some of its parts, or even the set of ideas produced by the human mind (Popper 1972). Self-transformation, it will be argued here, follows regularities, yet these regularities are too weak to allow for reliable prediction of the future results of evolution. Evolution is an "open" process in which the capacity of a system to produce novelty is reflected, but, as the notion of novelty indicates, it is only the way in which this happens that can be expected to be anticipated as a regularity, not the outcome itself.

In general, evolutionary theories, in whatever discipline they may be moulded, have certain properties which enable them to describe and explain processes of self-transformation (cf. Witt 1993). An evolutionary theory is:

  (i) dynamic—such that the dynamics of the processes, or some of their parts, can be represented;
  (ii) historical—in that it deals with historical processes which are irrevocable and path-dependent;
  (iii) self-transformation explaining—in that it includes hypotheses relating to the source and driving force of the self-transformation of the system.

Concerning property (i) there is little to say, if it is agreed upon that the aim of the theory is to trace the path of evolution. (Dynamic theories are commonly understood to refer to a time-scale such that the events to be described or explained can be explicitly dated.) An immediate consequence is of course that, with regard to economics, the methods of static and comparative static analysis lose the prominence that they have traditionally been accorded. Property (ii) implies additional demands on the kind of dynamics being discussed. The precise meaning to be attached to terms like irrevocability and path-dependency, is open to interpretation. The following is assumed here. Even though in the historical process recurrent patterns may occur, the process does not repeat itself identically and, hence, it is "irrevocable" (Georgescu-Roegen 1971: 196–197). Accordingly, deterministic difference or differential equations may, for example, be used in evolutionary theories as an idealized expression of a recurrent pattern without necessarily violating the irrevocability condition. However, it may be the case that such difference or differential equations do not necessarily satisfy the path-dependency criterion. The latter excludes, for example, all cases of unique equilibria from the domain of evolutionary theories.[2] In the Newtonian world-view, the dynamic patterns of convergence to unique equilibria have traditionally preoccupied the sciences. Dynamic systems that display strangely converging, irregular or even divergent motions have received little attention. However, if incessant change, i.e. the unending series of transitions, is the crucial feature, then the dynamics of a system cannot completely be captured in terms of convergence properties leading to an equilibrium, that is, a state of rest.

Even if evolutionary processes pass through equilibrium states, the crucial question is how the divergence from equilibrium comes about. In the Newtonian physics of closed systems—and in neo-classical economics—the causes of divergence are considered to be exogenous. Forces outside the system and, hence, outside the explanatory domain of the respective theory, trigger disturbances or "shocks" that

---

2 This is so because, if a globally asymptotically stable equilibrium exists for an autonomous dynamical system, then each solution of the system is bound to converge to the equilibrium independent of the initial condition and, hence, independent of the path which is taken. Path-dependency of a process is compatible, however, with the existence of multiple equilibria for those processes which are either locally asymptotically stable or unstable. This is to say that, if the basic dynamic pattern of convergence to an equilibrium appears at all in the domain of an evolutionary theory, the theory can be expected to be faced with the task of explaining why multiple equilibria exist or emerge and whether the process may be biased towards one or the other solution by the path it is taking.

push the system out of its state of rest.[3] But since evolution cannot be conceptualized as a sequence of external disruptions and internal equilibrations alone, there must exist endogenous causes of change. Indeed, it is at this point that property (iii) comes in. While properties (i) and (ii) can be satisfied by theories not usually associated with the notion of evolution as, for instance, neo-classical theories of non-tâtonnement market processes (cf. Fisher 1983), property (iii) is the generic feature that must be exhibited by all evolutionary theories.

To the extent that change is endogenously caused (as the notion of self-transformation suggests), evolutionary theories need to explain the source(s) and regularities of that kind of change. Not surprisingly, sources and regularities vary greatly between the different domains in which evolution occurs. In biological evolution, genetic recombination and mutation follow regularities very different from those involved in the creation of, say, new grammatical habits and the coining of new idioms in the evolution of language. Both these cases differ, in turn, from the invention and adoption of new production techniques or of new consumer goods in the evolving economy. Yet, in all these cases there seems to be a common, abstract causation of evolutionary change: the emergence of novelty within, and its dissemination throughout, the system under consideration. If this is true, endogenous change originates, in the last resort, from *the capacity of the system under investigation to produce novelty*. The novelty is specific to each field of study. Unless it is investigated in its concrete meaning in the respective disciplinary context, novelty becomes a rather amorphous concept which is difficult to deal with. In the following discussion of Schumpeter's theory of economic development in the light of the criteria for evolutionary theories given above, we will therefore focus on the economic context in which novelty emerges and is disseminated.

THE "THEORY OF ECONOMIC DEVELOPMENT"—A CRITICAL ASSESSMENT

As already mentioned, the approach in Schumpeter (1912), published with several revisions—and without the original seventh chapter—in the English edition of 1934, emerged in the context of, and with reference to, contemporaneous equilibrium theories.[4] As compared with these Schumpeter suggested two crucial changes. First, he wanted to abandon the static method of analysis in favour of a dynamic approach. Accordingly, he re-interpreted the (static) notion of equilibrium in terms of a dynamic approach as a stationary state of an economy. Taken literally, such a state is rarely attained in reality because of disruptions emanating from outside the sphere of economics. Schumpeter therefore used the notion of a "circular flow" to characterize

---

3   Evolving systems are, of course, not closed systems. None the less, it may even here be useless to try to explain all causes of changes that affect them. Some of them simply reside outside the domain proper of the respective evolutionary theory. In the case of economics, for example, such causes may be changing weather conditions, natural disasters, wars, or political upheavals.

4   To the disapproval of some members of the Austrian school (see Mises 1978: 36; Boehm 1990) Schumpeter had originally started out in his habilitation thesis submitted to the University of Vienna (Schumpeter 1908) with a review of the contemporaneous equilibrium theories of Cournot, Walras, Edgeworth, Pareto, Marshall, and Fisher—in an obvious attempt to distinguish himself from the received teachings in Vienna. Only shortly after, and apparently inspired by ideas of J.B. Clark and W.G. Lanworth Taylor (cf. Schneider 1951), he outlined an alternative interpretation in Schumpeter (1910) which anticipated the core of his book of 1912.

the state of affairs in which ordinary businesses and routines prevail in the behaviour of economic agents, and where nothing significantly new happens even if some data change due to exogenous disturbances. Consistent with this understanding, the second innovation Schumpeter introduced was the idea that there are also changes in the economy that are caused endogenously.[5] Since actual economic development— according to Schumpeter (1934: 58) consisting of a sequence of historical states where each particular one can only be understood in the light of the preceding ones—is obviously not caught in a circular flow at all times, economic theory is confronted with the question of what makes the development depart from states of circular flow. Schumpeter (ibid.) argued that an answer could not be achieved in terms of an equilibrium theory, as such a theory describes a development that "contains nothing, which suggests the possibility of development *intrinsically gener-ated from within itself"*.[6]

With the emphasis on the dynamics, the historical interpretation of the development process, and the endogenous causes of economic change, all the characteristics of an evolutionary theory summarized in criteria (i)-(iii) of the previous section are seen to be already mentioned in Schumpeter's interpretation of economic development. How are they dealt with in substance in his theory? A key concept is the notion of "new combinations", that is the innovative reallocation of economic resources and changes in organizational forms.[7] These innovations cause considerable adjustment problems. They emerge, it is claimed, in coexistence with established activities before beginning to supplant them, often by competing with the preceding forms of economic behaviour in goods and/or factor markets.[8] To Schumpeter, the carrying out of new combinations is a unique achievement which only "entrepreneurs" are able to accomplish where, contrary to the usual definition, being an "entrepreneur" is not denoting an occupation or a profession (and even less capital ownership), but rather denotes a capacity or function. The characteristic attitudes of such entrepreneurs are claimed to be initiative, authority, imaginative foresight, leadership, best personified by the figure of a "promoter", a "captain of industry" (as long as he or

---

5   Despite his frequent admiring acknowledgments of Walras' achievements in improving "pure" economic theory (cf. Swedberg 1991: Chap. 2), Schumpeter was clearly critical of the limitations of "pure" economic theory—and, hence, Walras'—which he wanted to overcome with this second innovation. The assessment of Schumpeter's attitude towards Walras given in Hodgson (1993: Chap. 10) is therefore misleading.

6   Schumpeter (1912: 75, my italics and translation, U.W.); the quotation is from the Appendix to Chapter 1, which has been omitted from the English edition of 1934. In Schumpeter (1934: 63) a similar reasoning can be found: "Should it turn out that there are no such changes arising in the economic sphere itself, and that the phenomenon that we call economic development is in practice simply founded upon the fact that the data change and that the economy continuously adapts itself to them, then we should say that there is *no* economic development. By this we should mean that economic development is not a phenomenon to be explained economically, but that the economy, in itself without development, is dragged along by the changes in the surrounding world, that the causes and hence the explanation of the development must be sought outside the group of facts which are described by economic theory."

7   Schumpeter (ibid.: 66) enumerates product innovation and major differentiations in the product quality, process innovation in production or selling techniques, opening up of new outlets at home and abroad, opening up of new input markets and sources at home and abroad, changes in market and/or firm organization, as in cartelization, promotion of mergers, and formation of trusts.

8   As has often been noted (cf., e.g. Streissler 1981), the role of banks assisting innovators in acquiring the necessary resources for new combinations seems to be perceived quite naively by Schumpeter. Banks are prepared, at every ruling interest rate, to satisfy every innovator's demand for credit through money creation (Schumpeter 1934: 137).

she is innovative) as opposed to the "plain businessman" or manager who only does business as usual (ibid.: 74-94).

Considerable emphasis is given to the explanation of the entrepreneur's motivation. Typically, it is claimed, an entrepreneur shows little interest in "hedonistic satisfaction" that might result from his or her efforts (ibid.: 92). She works restlessly out of what, in more modern terminology, would be called achievement motivation (McClelland 1961) and a craving for recognition. Dreams and wishes to found a private kingdom are mentioned; the sensation of power, leadership and authority, whose fascination is particularly strong for such people who have no other chance of achieving social distinction; the will to conquer, the impulse to fight, and the satisfaction derived from getting great things going. Only later, in the context of a discussion of the surplus (ibid.: 128-156) is the profit motive mentioned. A successful carrying out of new combinations promises "promoters' profits". As the innovation is imitated and eventually becomes routine, these profits will, however, be competed away. (None the less, promoters' profits are, according to Schumpeter, by far the most important source for making large fortunes.)

In short, referring to criterion (iii) of the previous section, we can summarize the main hypothesis on the source and driving force of self-transformation in Schumpeter's theory of economic development as follows:

Hypothesis 1: Change that is endogenously generated within the economy is brought about by the innovative activities of entrepreneurs, the only agents who are capable of carrying out new combinations of resources and transforming organizational forms.

It is important to note that information regarding innovation possibilities is considered to be readily available by Schumpeter (1934: 88). He holds that inventiveness and creativity have no great role to play in entrepreneurial capacity. It is not the entrepreneur who figures out new possibilities. These are already present, often in the form of common knowledge, abundantly accumulated by all sorts of people. It is the "doing the thing"; the will to demonstrate that mere possibilities can be turned into reality, that constitutes the specific contribution of Schumpeter's entrepreneur. Given these exceptional qualities it stands to reason that entrepreneurs are rare—in any case much less numerous than those, who as factory owners, managers, or administrators, personify the "plain businessmen". This means, however, that the crucial prerequisite for entrepreneurial activity—novelty—is actually treated as exogenously given. Its emergence is left unexplained by Schumpeter's theory, a delicate point to which we will return below.

If new ideas and new knowledge are always amply available, then one might expect that entrepreneurs would be able to draw on such a supply in a steady manner, so that there would be a continuous flow of innovations in the economy. Yet Schumpeter argues that the innovations disrupting the circular flow of the economy periodically come in waves (ibid.: 214). The explanation he gives for the periodical patterns is based on two rather peculiar hypotheses. First, it is submitted that conditions in the circular flow are such that carrying out the new combinations meets serious obstacles and many forms of resistance. Only the most gifted entrepreneurs, the "pioneers" and the "leaders" are able to overcome these. Once this has been achieved, however, the way is paved for less and less gifted entrepreneurs. Underlying this view is the assumption that among those businessmen or businesswomen who are able to innovate at all, entrepreneurial capacity is a normally distributed phenomenon. On the one extreme of the distribution of entrepreneurial talent are the pioneering innovators, on the other the least daring imitators. Second, it is claimed that the consequences of carrying out new combinations are not equally intelligible in different states of the economy (Schumpeter 1910: Sect. 6). It is only in the circular flow that the future of the economy appears calculable. Apparently, Schumpeter (1934: 243) considers this a necessary condition for the pioneering entrepreneurs to dare to undertake new ventures.

Taken together, the two arguments imply that entrepreneurs appear "swarm-like" in an order of decreasing innovative capacity. A new swarm enters the scene only after the state of "circular flow" has each time been restored. To put it in the form of another simple hypothesis which reflects the dissemination of novelty in the course of evolution:

Hypothesis 2: A necessary condition for the first, most skilled entrepreneurs in a swarm to introduce a major innovation is a state of circular flow where the economic situation is calculable. The frequency with which ever more imitative entrepreneurs follow, in the course of time, is a monotonous transformation of the density function of a normal distribution of entrepreneurial capability.

The special conditions summarized by Hypothesis 2 turn Schumpeter's theory of economic development into one of an unsteady growth process passing through "prosperity and depression" (Schumpeter 1910: Sect. IV), that is, into a business cycle theory (as discussed in detail in Schumpeter 1934: 212-255). The example which the pioneering innovators set and the multiplier effects which they trigger off in various industries enable less capable imitative entrepreneurs to implement new combinations on their part. Eventually, the wave of innovations fades out in imitative adjustments where no further entrepreneurial talent is required. At this point what was originally innovation, becomes a matter of routine. Overcapacity has been built up, and prices tend to decline. The promoters' profits are competed away. The boom comes to an end. Deflation caused by credit repayment induces a demand contraction. Depression results and lasts until all those producers who are not able to cover their costs have been driven out of business and a new, stationary phase of circular flow has been reached—albeit a phase where the economy is operating at a higher level. Thus, the "achievements of the boom" are presumed to be preserved in the form of an increased flow of goods and services, reorganized production, reduced production costs, and promoters' profits being transformed into real income growth (ibid.: 241-251). The necessary condition for the next innovation-driven business cycle to start is thereby restored.

In assessing Schumpeter's theory of development there can be no doubt that it deserves the merit of having identified, in an original and independent way (particularly independent of Darwinian analogies), crucial ingredients of an evolutionary theory in economics. This is indeed an ingenious creative achievement. Yet, the particular hypotheses of his developmental theory fail to actually realize the potential of an evolutionary approach; their relevance may therefore be debated. Consider the problems related to Hypothesis 1 first. Schumpeter draws attention to the crucial role of innovations or the "carrying out of new combinations". Innovations have ever since been appreciated as a core concept in Schumpeterian economics. In Hypothesis 1 the concept is, however, tied to the figure of the "entrepreneur"; in fact, this is the figure on whom the whole burden of explaining economic evolution has been imposed by Schumpeter. In support of the explanation little more is offered than a psychological characterization of the exceptional entrepreneurial personality resembling a kind of an elite theory.[9]

In terms of understanding the driving forces behind economic evolution, the truly serious constriction implied by Schumpeter's interpretation of the entrepreneurial role lies in his treatment of novelty. In his methodological considerations Schumpeter emphasizes the endogenous causation of economic change. In his theory of economic development, by contrast, the exclusive focus on innovations—submitting that entrepreneurs do not have to search for, discover, or invent the new combinations—is, in effect an attempt to avoid an explanation of the emergence of novelty. (It corresponds to the somewhat artificial distinction between inventive and innovative activities that Schumpeter makes.) An explanation of how new knowledge is created, and what the feedback relationships between search, discovery, experimentation, and adoption of new possibilities look like, and the respective motivations—all this would be necessary in order to really be able to treat economic change as being endogenously caused.

With the focus on entrepreneurial skills in *promoting* innovations, rather than conceiving them, attention is diverted from general human creativity and inventiveness and the motivations underlying it as crucial elements of evolutionary change. Relatedly, with the exclusive emphasis on innovations carried through by heroic entrepreneurs, the role of all unspectacular innovation-driven forms of economic change is played down in Schumpeter's approach. His discounting of the idea that gradually ongoing change—and the inventiveness underlying it—could transform the economy, is brought home by his powerful metaphor of stagecoaches being added in any quantity you like, but never adding up to a railroad. "Dime a dozen" innovations which may well be argued to be important carriers of gradual economic change are discarded. But, in a developing market, to give an example, many small-scale innovative activities may sum up to a major breakthrough not carried out, not designed, and possibly not even expected by single (entrepreneurial) individuals. It is not unlikely that "plain businessmen" and even consumers contribute to this kind of innovation in a significant way. Schumpeter (1934: 65), by contrast, explicitly attributes a passive and non-innovative attitude to these agents, treating changes of tastes and behaviour of consumers as "data changes". This ignores such features as innovative buying and consumption activities, attempts to gain new sources of information, or to improve one's own situation by setting up a bargaining position. The same can be said for the

9   Interestingly, Schumpeter not only sees entrepreneurs as the single driving force in the continuous reorganization and further development of the capitalist economy. He also holds that, due to their acquisition of financial wealth, they are the recruiting base for the "the upper strata of society" (Schumpeter 1934: 155-156). According to Streissler (1981) this glorification of the entrepreneur is not consistent with the actual social conditions in Imperial Austria of Schumpeter's time. But there seems to have been an academic tradition behind this idealization—with the very same view of the entrepreneur, and even the same terminology, in the work of Schumpeter's teacher Friedrich von Wieser (cf. Streissler 1983).

supply side of the factor markets. Thus, because of his rather one-sided interpretation of the source and driving force of self-transformation (as summarized by Hypothesis 1), Schumpeter fails to acknowledge other important facets of economic evolution.

Several questions can also be raised with regard to the dissemination of the fruits of innovation throughout the economy, as portrayed by Hypothesis 2 and the rather arbitrary "ratchet effect" which it postulates. For example, if, for pioneer innovations, an extraordinary personality, motivation, and creativity are necessary attributes, is it convincing then that these same personalities simply accept their promoters' profits being competed away via imitation in the later stages? A more plausible assumption would have been that these extraordinary entrepreneurs are eager to, and have the means to, counter the dwindling of their leading position by converting more of the supposedly abundant inventions into innovations. This would mean, of course, that there is a feedback from the performance of the pioneering entrepreneurs in the course of the diffusion process to their motivation to trigger further innovative activities. A declining innovative lead would tend to induce individual innovative activities. Clearly such an "individualized" feedback is at odds with the "ratchet effect" hypothesis, as it is with the notion of business cycle patterns.[10] It was only half a century later that, as a result of a reconsideration of the evolutionary concepts in Schumpeter's work, the implications of an individualized feedback were seriously considered by Winter (1971).[11]

American Experiences and the Turn to Historicism

Thirty years after the German edition of *The Theory of Economic Development* had appeared, Schumpeter published a book which documents the direction into which his evolutionary thought developed further, namely his *Capitalism, Socialism and Democracy* (1942). In this new publication, the business cycle framework is dropped. The reader is offered instead a long run view of the historical transformation of firms, markets, and capitalism as a whole. In a sense this seems only logical. If the theory discussed in the previous section is stripped of the specific elaborations on cyclical patterns of development, what remains but a scenario of perpetuated economic growth and increase of material welfare due to the incessant innovative efforts of carrying out new combinations? However, Schumpeter (1942) chooses to embed these considerations in the framework of an ambitious edifice of historical speculation, and references at various places point to Marx's philosophy of history as the source of inspiration. The grand view of the historical fate of capitalism which Schumpeter gives, builds upon one major modification of Hypothesis 1. The entrepreneur is replaced by the impersonal organization—the large corporation, the trust—as the driving force of economic evolution.

Schumpeter develops this modification by advancing two arguments. First, he holds

---

10 Schumpeter seems to have been well aware of this. He concedes (ibid.: 224): "If the new enterprises in our sense were to appear independently of one another, there would be no boom and no depression as special, distinguishable, striking, regularly recurring phenomena."

11 Furthermore, one may ask: if the entrepreneurs initiating a new wave, whom Schumpeter considered the most gifted, must be able to calculate the consequences of their carrying out of new combinations, how then does the growing number of follow-up innovators, considered to be less gifted, reach decisions on their ventures? Do the latter not actually face increasingly turbulent conditions? Apparently, Schumpeter assumes that the possibility of imitating renders all calculation needs unnecessary.

that large enterprises have gained a comparative advantage in the process of "industrial mutation ... that incessantly revolutionizes the economic structure *from within*" (ibid.: 83), that is, in the carrying out of new combinations. As a rule the big industrial units have greater capital resources and obtain credit more easily to finance new methods of production, organization and distribution. Second, the entrepreneurs are divested of the exclusive position as the ones capable of carrying out new combinations—because innovation is being reduced to routine. "Economic progress tends to become depersonalized and automatized. Bureau and committee work tends to replace individual action" (ibid.: 133). Schumpeter goes on not only to surmise a decline in the figure of the promoter, the industrial leader, but an ultimate decline of the bourgeoisie in general, of which the entrepreneur is portrayed as pillar. By their central planning procedures the large trusts are able to efficiently command an increasing share of the resources in the economy. According to Schumpeter this transforms the basis for running the economy, and a transition from capitalism to socialism is eventually apt to come about in a natural way.

With this prognosis Schumpeter (1942) obviously leaves the basis of an empirical evolutionary theory in the direction of a philosophy of history.[12] He extrapolates a stylized historical trend which he seems to have inferred from his observations of the rise of large corporations and trusts in the USA. But an extrapolation like this violates a binding constraint for any theory of evolution. Because of the special epistemological status of novelty created in evolution, the implications of future evolution cannot be positively anticipated. Evolutionary theories can only claim that certain developments or consequences will not occur—an empirically testable conjecture. Indeed, the same objection has been raised by Popper (1960) against historical materialism that also claimed to be able to predict societal evolution.[13]

Leaving Schumpeter's speculations on the fate of capitalism aside there are other ideas in his book of 1942 which point to significant revisions of his earlier views, and these have had a substantial impact on the discipline of economics: the consideration of innovativeness, and the dynamics of competition or, as he puts it, the "perennial gale of creative destruction" (ibid.: 81–106). The obvious result of incessant innovations, which revolutionize the production process, the organization of the economy, and the supply of goods, is a historically unique rise over time in living standard of the masses. Schumpeter holds that incessant innovations are the outcome of a competitive process of its own. In this process many features may bring to mind monopolistic practices, but it would be mistaken to assess the observed forms of competition, the corresponding market performance and market structure, against the measuring rod of static price theory and its notion of perfect competition with given goods, qualities, and production processes. Much as Schumpeter's rejection of the static theory of perfect competition as inappropriate for dealing with the emergence and dissemination of innovations deserves support, the way in which he presents his argument is itself problematic from the point of view of an evolutionary approach. Despite his criticism of static price theory he basically adopts its mode of reasoning. Considerations on profitability and risk take precedence. Information is

---

12 Cf. the discussion in Stolper (1994: Chap. 8) on Schumpeter's own assessment of this dilemma.

13 Cf., e.g. Marx (1976: Chaps 21–26). There is broad agreement that Marx seems to have been an inspiration for Schumpeter in writing his book of 1942, cf. Swedberg (1991: Chap. 7) and Stolper (1994: Chap. 8).

tacitly presupposed which is typically assumed to be available in static price theory although this information is, in principle, not feasible in the case of innovations which, after all, incorporate yet unknown novelty.

In order to illustrate Schumpeter's argumentation consider the case of a corporation which is just about to introduce an innovation (i.e. a new combination). Apparently, Schumpeter thinks of a decision that will typically involve large capital outlays. As distinct from the entrepreneurial motivation as he viewed it in 1912, the motivation of large corporations is profit seeking: the venture will only be undertaken and the expenses needed to break from routine be made, if the prospective gains appear sufficiently high. In order for this to happen, there must be a way of safeguarding the returns on an innovation from spilling over to competitor firms. Two sorts of competitors must be checked: those who copy, with lower or no expenses, the innovation once it becomes known (i.e. the imitators) and those who introduce a further, superior innovation (i.e. the next generation of innovators). Protection against the former can be provided by patent settlements, by temporary trade or production secrets, and by long-term contracts or other means which bind subcontractors and customers. Protection against the latter sort of competitors is more difficult to obtain. Schumpeter emphasizes, as a general measure, a pricing policy aiming at two targets: a more rapid amortization of innovative investments and an acceleration of investment in order to build up overcapacities which may then serve to attack or defend against potential competition.

Unquestionably, any such measure (and there are many, see Schumpeter 1942: 92–98) amounts to monopolistic practices. But, to attain such a monopolistic position means in the first place to out-compete all rivals working with the old standards. To achieve a monopolistic position is therefore only possible—and this is Schumpeter's crucial point—if the advantage which the innovation entails is shared to some extent with the customers: in order to induce them to substitute the new offer for the old the former must be available at a lower price and/or a higher quality. As the monopolistic practices do not provide permanent protection (unless erected by government intervention, ibid.: 99), in particular against competitors who break down the erected barriers by introducing superior innovations, competition through innovation means that the welfare of the customers and thus, in the last resort, of the masses of consumers, will be continuously improved. Indeed, a situation can easily be imagined in which the monopoly price is lower and the monopoly output larger in an innovative industry than prices and output would be under conditions of perfect competition, which discourage innovative activities.

Let us again summarize these arguments put forward in Schumpeter (1942) in two hypotheses:

Hypothesis 3: The prospect of attaining a market position in which monopolistic practices can be used against (potential) competitors positively affects a firm's willingness to innovate; where such prospects prevail the number of innovations per unit of time increases.

Hypothesis 4: Innovations increase welfare in the long run; to the extent that monopolistic practices are an attribute of competition through innovation they have therefore, given the preceding thesis, a welfare increasing rather than decreasing effect in the long run.

The conjecture summarized in Hypothesis 3 is known in the literature as the "Schumpeterian hypothesis"; it poses several problems and has sparked off extensive empirical and theoretical work (cf., e.g. Kamien and Schwartz 1982; Cohen and Levin 1989). A detailed discussion doing justice to the huge literature is beyond what is feasible here. However, it may be argued that much of the motivation behind the long debate on the Schumpeterian hypothesis derives, at least in part, from the companion Hypothesis 4 on which we will therefore concentrate. If its premise is accepted, the standard view in competition policy on monopoly pricing, aggressive capacity policy, and other attempts to impede market entry would indeed have to be dramatically revised—at least to the extent to which they are informed by the ideal of perfect competition. However, there are two problems with Hypothesis 4 preventing such a conclusion to be easily drawn, even when taking Hypothesis 3 for granted.

The first problem is related to the claim that innovative activities increase welfare in the long run. In retrospect it can hardly be denied that innovations, more precisely improvements in technical knowledge and skills, have in the very long run been the major source of an impressive growth of economic production and wealth. The indubitable growth-enhancing effects of innovations do not, of course, necessarily lead to welfare increases in the sense of Pareto-improvements—since the pecuniary external effects induced by innovations may induce net losses for some agents which are not compensated for (cf. Witt 1996 for a more detailed discussion). Schumpeter possibly had in mind that, in the past hundred years, the legion of innovations induced enough economic growth providing indirect compensation by a secular rise of average income to those who suffered from pecuniary externalities so that, at least in the industrialized countries, there have remained few net losers in the longer run. However, even if this assessment were shared in retrospect, an unconditional extrapolation of this historical experience into the future would be fallacious. Schumpeter (1942) seems to have been tempted here once more to extrapolate a trend that he saw prevailing in the past.

The second problem which Hypothesis 4 poses is, from the perspective of an evolutionary theory, more serious. What is being considered by Schumpeter is not the emergence of a welfare increase of indeterminate size. Rather, his argument presupposes that a specific quantitative relation can be determined: welfare gains from innovations have to be compared with welfare losses resulting from the innovator's use of the monopoly power (s)he achieves. Hypothesis 4 claims, in more precise terms, that the somehow determined value of a stream of welfare gains accruing from innovations in the long run, is strictly greater than the value of a corresponding stream of welfare losses. Since, however, the gains or losses depend on the properties of the particular innovation to come, and since, by the very meaning of novelty, these properties cannot positively be anticipated, a prediction of the size of future gains or losses is not possible.

The problem can be illustrated in a slightly different way. Imagine that the waiting time between the occurrence of two successive innovations becomes almost infinitely long, in other words, the process of creative destruction runs almost infinitely slowly. In this case monopolistic practices would cause an enduring welfare loss to society that could well be avoided, without great sacrifices, by policy action aimed at intensifying competition. This is to say that even in a naive view Hypothesis 4 cannot claim to make sense, if the process of innovation in the economy is too slow. (How slow it may be in order not to fall under this verdict depends on the non-anticipatable welfare gains it creates.) Schumpeter submits that in the past the process has been sufficiently fast, and it may well continue to be in the future—though this cannot be more than a personal expectation. If we object, in this way, against calculating with quantitative properties of innovations—which are, in principle, not anticipatable—this is tantamount to opposing the very concepts of profitability and risk calculations which underpin neo-classical innovation theory. In contrast, in his attempt to over-come the notion of perfect competition Schumpeter has perhaps inadvertently, paved the way for a kind of reasoning which is not adequate for dealing with the phenom-enon of novelty.

Thus, in comparing the 1912 and 1942 versions of Schumpeter's discussion of the process of economic development, from an evolutionary point of view, the latter seems to have created serious additional problems without solving those of the former. Schumpeter (1942) remained reluctant to address the problem of how novelty emerges in the economy and therefore made no progress in broadening the grasp of his evolutionary approach. He abandoned the figure of the entrepreneur as the driving force of evolutionary change together with its psychological underpinnings which are irreconcilable with a neo-classical approach. Later this has turned out to be conducive to the efforts of neo-classical writers of the past decades to recast the Schumpeterian hypothesis in terms of optimal "innovation" race strategies and equilibrium investments into "innovative" activities. No doubt, nothing in Schum-peter's huge oeuvre has been given more attention in neo-classical economics than the conjecture (in a rather isolated form) summarized in Hypothesis 3. At the same time, however, the last traces of evolutionary thought originally created out of the young Schumpeter's concern with the inadequacies of "pure" economics for explaining economic change were eventually eliminated.

CONCLUSIONS

In this paper it has been argued that Schumpeter's work on the theory of economic development proceeded through two quite different stages resulting in his books of 1912 and 1942. Although Schumpeter had obviously a clear understanding of the general character of an evolutionary theory—an understanding which he derived in an original way without borrowing from Darwinian analogies as is fashionable today in evolutionary economics—he did not succeed in formulating a satisfactory, general theory of economic evolution. Rather his approach to economic development is actually a special theory of the unsteady capitalist growth process passing though booms and crises. Throughout his entire oeuvre Schumpeter was therefore occupied with improving his grasp of the business cycle phenomenon. This special heuristic framing implies not only some rather peculiar hypotheses which are difficult to accept within an evolutionary framework, but also some shortcomings in his understanding of (what he refused to call) the economic evolutionary process.

Central to Schumpeter's theory of economic development is the role of a promoter-entrepreneur. The image of the entrepreneur who propels development has become a popular metaphor for the evolutionary approach, yet as has been argued, it draws a rather one-sided portrait of the source and driving force of the self-transformation process in the economy. Schumpeter later abandoned his entrepreneur-centred theory. In a speculative grand view of the historical trend of capitalism obviously inspired by Marx's historical materialism, Schumpeter argued that the innovative entrepreneur had become obsolete. The entrepreneur's role had been absorbed, as a matter of routine, into the bureaucracies of the large trusts. In order to protect their large-scale innovation ventures these trusts use precautionary measures which result in monopolistic practices. These practices (if successful) allow returns to be earned on innovative activities, yet, at the same time the profits attract further innovation efforts, thereby inducing what Schumpeter calls a "perennial gale of creative destruction" of monopolistic market positions and profits.

Although these conjectures have spawned a vast theoretical and empirical literature their contribution to a more general theory of the evolutionary process in the economy has been a limited one. None of the problems facing Schumpeter's earlier interpretation of economic development could thus be solved. While innovation research, triggered not least by the debate on the "Schumpeterian hypothesis" concerning the relationships between innovativeness and market structure, has made great progress, the proper place of innovations and the motivation to pursue them within an evolutionary theory of the economic process still needs clarification. Neo-classical models of optimal innovation decisions and innovation races, which have emerged in large number in recent years, cannot serve as substitutes. The reason is that they assume—not unlike Schumpeter's theory of economic development—an exogenously given flow of innovation possibilities with largely known properties. They thus presuppose what, in an evolutionary perspective, needs to be explained in the first place.

REFERENCES

Boehm, S. 1990: The Austrian tradition: Schumpeter and Mises, in K. Hennings and Warren J. Samuels (eds.), *Neoclassical Economic Theory 1870 to 1930*. Boston, MA: Kluwer, pp. 201–241.

Boulding, K.E. 1981: *Evolutionary Economics*. Beverly Hills, CA: Sage.

Bowler, P.J. 1989: *Evolution—the History of an Idea*. Berkeley, CA: University of California Press.

Cohen, M.W. and Levin, R.C. 1989: Empirical studies of innovation and market structure, in R. Schmalensee and R.D. Willig (eds.), *Handbook of Industrial Organization*, Vol. II. Amsterdam: North-Holland.

Fisher, F.M. 1983: *Disequilibrium Foundations of Equilibrium Economics*. Cambridge: Cambridge University Press.

Georgescu-Roegen, N. 1971: *The Entropy Law and the Economic Process*. Cambridge, MA: Harvard University Press.

Haberler, G. 1937: *Prosperity and Depression*. Geneva: League of Nations.

Hodgson, G. 1993: *Economics and Evolution—Bringing Life Back into Economics*. Ann Arbor, MI: Michigan University Press.

Kamien, M.I. and Schwartz, N.L. 1982: *Market Structure and Innovation*. Cambridge: Cambridge University Press.

Marx, K. 1976: *Capital*, Vol. I. Harmondsworth: Penguin.

McClelland, D.C. 1961: *The Achieving Society*. Princeton, NJ: Van Nostrand.

Mises, L. von 1978: *Notes and Recollections*. South-Holland: Libertarian Press.

Nelson, R.R. and Winter, S.G. 1982: *An Evolutionary Theory of Economic Change*. Cambridge, MA: Harvard University Press.

Popper, K.R. 1960: *The Poverty of Historicism*, 2nd edn. London: Routledge & Kegan Paul.

Popper, K.R. 1972: *Objective Knowledge—an Evolutionary View*. Oxford: Oxford University Press.

Schneider, E. 1951: Schumpeter's early German work, 1906-1917, *Review of Economics and Statistics*, 33: 104-108.

Schumpeter, J.A. 1908: *Das Wesen und der Hauptinhalt der theoretischen Nationalökonomie* [*The Essence and Principal Contents of Economic Theory*]. Leipzig: Duncker & Humblot.

Schumpeter, J.A. 1910: Über das Wesen der Wirtschaftskrisen [On the essence of economic crises], *Zeitschrift für Volkswirtschaft, Sozialpolitik und Verwaltung*, 19: 271-325.

Schumpeter, J.A. 1912/1934: *Theorie der wirtschaftlichen Entwicklung*. Leipzig: Duncker & Humblot. English translation published in 1934 as *The Theory of Economic Development*. Cambridge, MA: Harvard University Press.

Schumpeter, J.A. 1939: *Business Cycles*, 2 vols. New York: McGraw-Hill.

Schumpeter, J.A. 1942: *Capitalism, Socialism and Democracy*. New York: Harper.

Schumpeter, J.A. 1954: *History of Economic Analysis*. New York: Oxford University Press.

Stolper, W.F. 1994: *Joseph Alois Schumpeter—The Public Life of a Private Man*. Princeton, NJ: Princeton University Press.

Streissler, E. 1981: Schumpeter's Vienna and the role of credit in innovation, in H. Frisch (ed.), *Schumpeterian Economics*. New York: Praeger, pp. 60-83.

Streissler, E. 1983: Schumpeter and Hayek: on some similarities in their thought, in F. Machlup, G. Fels and H. Müller-Groeling (eds.), *Reflections on a Troubled World Economy*, pp. 356-364. London: Macmillan.

Swedberg, R. 1991: *Schumpeter: A Biography*. Princeton, NJ: Princeton University Press.

Winter, S.G. 1971: Satisficing, selection, and the innovating remnant, *Quarterly Journal of Economics*, 86: 237-261.

Witt, U. 1993: Emergence and dissemination of innovations: some principles in evolutionary economics, in R.H. Day and P. Chen (eds.), *Non-linear Dynamics and Evolutionary Economics*. Oxford: Oxford University Press, pp. 91-100.

Witt, U. 1996: Innovations, externalities and the problem of economic progress, *Public Choice*, 89: 113-130.

[6]

Generic Features of Evolution and Its Continuity: A Transdisciplinary Perspective

Ulrich WITT

ABSTRACT: Because of the intellectual attraction of the neo-Darwinian theory of evolution, its concepts are often borrowed to conceptualized evolutionary change also in non-biological domains. However, a heuristic strategy like that is problematic. An attempt is therefore made to identify generic features of evolution which transcend domain-specific characteristics. Epistemological, conceptual, and methodological implications are discussed, and the ontological question is raised how non-biological evolutionary theories can be accommodated within the Darwinian world view of modern sciences.

Keywords: Darwinism, emergence, evolution, evolutionary ontology, novelty.

I. Introduction

The integration of Darwin's theory, and later the neo-Darwinian synthesis, into the modern scientific world view was probably the most challenging intellectual endeavor of the last century. It reflects the overwhelming success of the "Darwinian revolution" (Ruse 1979) in the sciences. However, some questions remain. One that will be discussed here relates to the role which a Darwinian world view offers for understanding evolution as a general phenomenon. Evolution is not specific to the realm of nature. Phenomena of evolution also occur in other domains. The social sciences are a case in point. What is the relevance of Darwinism, e.g., for understanding societal evolution? Early attempts at applying Darwinian thought to the human society resulted in Social Darwinism (Hawkins 1997). This proved to be a misinterpretation with disastrous consequences. For long time this experience made many social scientists reluctant to even consider the possibility of a connection between Darwinian thought and the social sciences.

These discouraging experiences not withstanding, the issue deserves attention, given the enormous impact of Darwinism on modern scientific thought. It can be dealt with in a more abstract way (which, as far as the social sciences are concerned, is less prone to the fallacies of Social Darwinism) by asking whether Darwinian concepts are sufficiently general to explain evolutionary processes wherever they are thought to occur. There is a strong tendency nowadays to explicitly or implicitly answer this question in the affirmative. Many writers openly or tacitly borrow from evolutionary biology. It has become something of "the" model for evolutionary theorizing in many disciplines, and the neo-Darwinian approach to evolution in nature has in the meantime mutated to "Universal Darwinism" (Dawkins 1983).

However, as will be argued in this paper, for understanding phenomena of evolution outside the domain of biology, such an approach is neither necessary nor does it seem well suited. The idea that Universal Darwinism has identified the generic features of evolution can be contested. To make that point, the case of the social sciences, and more specifically, of economics will be discussed exemplarily. Since neo-Darwinian theory could be considered relevant at several levels in the economic domain, a rather complex argument will be necessary, one which results in the hypothesis of an ontological continuity of evolution. Section II prepares the ground by briefly reviewing some attempts to come to grips with the role which evolution plays in economics. In this light, Section III discusses the concepts for explaining evolution suggested by Universal Darwinism and develops an alternative approach to identifying the generic features of evolution. Section IV elaborates on the epistemological implications of those generic features and some of their methodological consequences. Section V then returns to the question of what relevance can be attributed to Darwinian thought in the trans-disciplinary approach taken here. Section VI offers some conclusions.

II. Responses in Economics to the Challenge of Darwinism

The influence of contemporary Darwinian thought on the first efforts to conceive an evolutionary approach to economics more than a century ago is quite obvious. Thorstein Veblen, then a widely read author, published an article with the provocative title "Why is Economics not an Evolutionary Science?" (Veblen 1898). His article was more of a criticism of the static economic theory of his time than an outline of an alternative evolutionary program. Nevertheless, in later work, Veblen (1899, 1914) tried to reconstruct and interpret the anthropological record of how institutions and technologies had developed from a primitive state of human society. As he had already posited in his programmatic article, to him the historical change in man-made evolution was cumulative and followed the path of the evolution of the habits of thought. Unfortunately, despite his impressive elaboration of the historical process inspired by the scientific ideals of the German historical school (cf. Hodgson 2001), Veblen failed to provide a systematic theoretical account of economic evolution and its relationship to Darwinian theory[1].

While Veblen's approach to evolutionary economics was clearly inspired by a Darwinian world view, the other early attempt to address the issue was explicitly anti-Darwinian. It was undertaken by Joseph Schumpeter in his influential theory of economic development (Schumpeter 1912/34). He denied Darwinism any relevance for understanding economic evolution, in fact, he even avoided using the term "evolution" in this context. The inspiration for his approach seems to have come from another major intellectual controversy of the time, namely the debate on Marx's theory of a crisis-prone capitalist development of the economy (which may be subsumed to the class of pre-Darwinian evolutionary thought). The growth process in the period of "promoterism" in Europe in the late 19th and early 20th century had created previously unknown forms of economic reality in production, consumption, exchange, and even in the institutional set up of the economy. In Schumpeter's view, theorizing about capitalist development would be pointless, if it failed to take account of innovations and the role of entrepreneurship. Since he rejected biological analogies, Schumpeter had to

---

[1] Cf. Rutherford (1998). The theoretical deficit left the school which Veblen founded (American Institutionalism) somewhat disoriented and was never compensated in that school -- perhaps one of the reasons for why this first attempt to establish "evolutionary economics" was later lost from sight (Hodgson 1999, Chap. 5).

find a way to make sense of economic evolution without recourse to Darwinian concepts. He tried to achieve this by focusing on entrepreneurial innovations and their diffusion.

However, Schumpeter fell short of realizing the potential of his ingenious insight which could have led him to recognize the emergence and dissemination of novelty as generic features of evolution. With a somewhat artificial distinction between invention and innovation, and the assumption that inventions are always already given, he stopped half way in his investigation of endogenously generated economic change. By refusing to consider inventions -- or, more generally, novelty -- more closely, an explanation of how knowledge is created, and why, is made exogenous to Schumpeter's theory. By the same token, the question of whether a feed-back between search, discovery, experimentation, and adoption of new possibilities (and the respective motivations) exists is excluded. Moreover, perhaps as a tribute to the debate on Marxism, Schumpeter chose to cast what he called his "developmental method" in terms of a theory of unsteady capitalist development, i.e. of business cycle theory. When he discussed how entrepreneurs carry out innovations and, by doing so induce development "from within the economy", the upshot of his discussion was that these innovative activities occur in regular cyclical patterns of economic growth.

For reasons discussed elsewhere (Witt 2002), Schumpeter was unable to establish what could have been a Schumpeterian evolutionary school. It was only in a more recent manifesto by Nelson and Winter (1982) -- which triggered a new wave of evolutionary economics (Nelson 1995) -- that his ideas about capitalist development have been revived. Remarkably enough, in this revival, his ideas are blended with Darwinian conceptions -- despite Schumpeter's own rejection of any analogies to Darwinian thought. This is an obvious tribute to the above mentioned increasing impact which (neo-) Darwinian evolutionary biology has had as "the" model of an evolutionary science. This impact is also visible in the recent surge of interest of economists in evolutionary game theory which originated from evolutionary biology[2].

It may therefore be asked at this point how pertinent Darwinian thought is for coming to grips with evolution in the economic domain. The answer to this question is complicated by the fact that there are many possible ways of referring to Darwinian thought. One point in which the diverse ways differ is their ontological foundation. In fact, there seem to be only two alternative ontological positions. Either evolutionary economics is assumed to share its ontological basis with neo-Darwinian evolutionary biology or the idea of a common ontological basis is (often implicitly) rejected. Prominent examples of the latter position are the various attempts to construction analogies to, and the metaphorical uses of, Darwinian concepts to be discussed now in mo-

---

[2] Cf. Maynard Smith (1982). Symptomatic of the current situation in economics, the development in evolutionary game theory is entirely disconnected from the revival of Schumpeterian evolutionary economics. No attempt is made to identify a common ontological basis as is clearly brought out in a recent symposium on evolutionary economics (Bergstrom 2002, Nelson and Winter 2002, Robson 2002, Samuelson 2002). In fact, few attempts are made at all in evolutionary game theory to explicate the relevance of this theory for economics. For notable exceptions cf. Binmore (1998) and Young (1998).

re detail. Examples of differing versions of the former position will be considered in later sections.

A popular strategy for pursuing Darwinian ideas for heuristic purposes is the construction of analogies. Without pretending to imply any commonality at the ontological level, analogies are drawn between principles of evolution in the biological domain on the one hand and the economic domain on the other. However, because of obvious differences between the two domains, analogies rarely really hold. Other than by way of a (probably unnoticed) mistaken analogy, the actual use made of Darwinian concepts in evolutionary economics is therefore often only a metaphorical one. This means borrowing Darwinian concepts to conceive and express conjectures about evolution in the economic domain. Particularly popular is the recourse to the selection metaphor (see below). The value of these heuristic strategies is difficult to assess in general. The potentially fruitful heuristic of a metaphor has to be weighed against the potential perils of being attracted to, and trapped in, mistaken analogies which may then for long time be difficult to correct. The way in which Darwinian concepts have been made part of neo-Schumpeterian evolutionary economics illustrates the pros and cons.

In the 1950s a first debate about "economic natural selection" started in the context of rivaling hypotheses about the pricing setting behavior of firms (Alchian 1950, Penrose 1952). These hypotheses either postulated profit maximizing behavior or some form of non-maximization. Observational problems prevented a conclusive discrimination between the rivaling hypotheses being made on an empirical basis. The question was therefore raised as to whether a logical argument for discriminating between the alternative hypotheses could be derived from an analogy to natural selection. The basic rationale that was proposed assumed that, under conditions of competitive markets, all forms of non-maximizing firm behavior would fall victim to selection forces. However, the profit level that actually suffices to survive in a particular market at a particular time hinges on the behavior of the competitors -- a dependency called "occupancy effect" in the biological analogue. No analogue to a genetic continuity being present in the highly volatile pricing behavior of firms, the occupancy effect in this context hinges on a large number of situational factors so that, as a survival criterion, profitability says very little (cf. Winter 1964, Metcalfe 2003). In this context, "economic natural selection" is therefore a rather superficial metaphor of uncertain heuristic value.

Nonetheless, it has also been used in the "loose analogy" (as they call it) in Nelson and Winter's (1982) revival of Schumpeterian evolutionary economics. Informed by the notion of bounded rationality, they argue (ibid., Chap. 5) that in their internal interactions organizations are based on behavioral routines, rules of thumb, and regular interaction patterns. Production planning, calculation, price setting, and even the allocation of research and development funds, are all seen as following routine and rule-bound behavior. Borrowing the Darwinian notions, the firms' routines are then interpreted as "genotypes" and the specific decisions resulting from the applied routines as "phenotypes". The latter are supposed to affect the firms' overall performance.

Different routines and different decisions are assumed to imply differences in the firms' growth. On the assumption that routines which successfully contribute to growth are not changed, the actual expansion is interpreted as an increase in relative frequency of those "genes-routines", while routines which cause a deteriorating performance are unlikely to expand. Their relative frequency is therefore supposed to decline. Analogously to the principles of natural selection, the changing composition of behavioral routines within an industry is thus considered to be a significant instance of economic evolution. Yet, there is little to support the assumption that there are sufficient inertia in this development for the selection mechanism to effect systematic changes. The reason is that it is most likely that firms facing deteriorations will be induced to identify the deficient routines and to replace or improve them in a kind of intentionally produced mutation of their "genes" [3].

Indeed, a more general limitation of the analogy between natural selection and "economic natural selection" turns up here. In the genetic context, selective forces operate on a given population and change the relative frequencies of the genes in the pool. The individual members of the population have little, if any, room for escaping from these pressures or for adjusting to them. In this sense, selection forces may be labeled "external". In a similar way, the anonymous competitive forces of the markets can be seen as external to the individual. The market participants unintentionally impose constraints on each other in their multilateral interactions, and these constraints may even force some of them out of business. Thus the population of agents on the supply and/or demand sides of a market may systematically change over time. But, unlike in the genetic case, the agents are not helpless when exposed to these changes. In fact, the systematic changes observable in markets may be attributed to a large extent to the individuals' attempts to anticipate the effects of the market forces and to take account of them. If successful, the effects of "external" selection are replaced by what would have to be labeled "internal" selection.

The deliberate, discretionary character of behavior adaptation in the economy has no equivalent in the domain of genetically coded behavior considered in evolutionary biology. The notion of natural selection therefore runs the risk of inducing a misleading heuristic which fails to (sufficiently) acknowledge a genuine feature of economic evolution -- the role played by learning and cognition. [4] Cognitive processes like hy-

---

[3] Nelson and Winter (ibid.) argue that such improvement or replacement activities are themselves subject to higher routines, and that the differential growth argument therefore applies once again. It may indeed be that firms activate higher problem solving routines on a regular basis when a crisis occurs or is expected to occur. Yet, the outcome of these problem solving routines is often more likely to depend on whose problem solving capacity is involved in those routines than on the routines themselves. In this case, the differential success of the problem solving process triggered cannot be derived from differences in those routines. Differential success is basically unpredictable (much like mutation in the genetic sphere). When different people are involved in the same routines at different times, development may be different. The inertia in what has been suggested as the analogue of the selection mechanism is lost.

[4] The individuals' capacity to anticipate consequences of their behavior and to take account of them deliberately by searching for better solutions may be interpreted as a case of Lamarckian rather than Darwinian evolution (Nelson and Winter 1982, p.11). Allowing for a direct feedback from the phenotypic performance to genotypic traits is said

pothesis formation and learning from insight are likely to produce adaptations which follow their own regularities. Emerging from a limited human information processing capacity -- which means that people are constrained in what they sense, learn, and perceive -- the regularities reflect mental processes which in both their dynamics and their outcome are not necessarily the same as the process of genetic selection.

III. Generic Features of Evolution

The social sciences have an independent, pre-Darwinian tradition of evolutionary thought (cf. Hayek 1967a; for its influence on Darwin, cf. Richards 1992). Social philosophers and lawyers of the eighteenth and nineteenth century reflected on what would nowadays be called "cultural evolution". Some of this thought had strong normative connotations, equating societal evolution with progress in some sense. [5] However, this entire tradition is largely forgotten today. The intellectual impact of Darwin's thought has been so strong that the notion of evolution is now almost exclusively associated with the meaning given to it in evolutionary biology. As discussed in the previous section, attempts at conceptualizing evolution in the domain of the social sciences make use of doubtful analogies and metaphors borrowed from evolutionary biology rather than reflecting on proper domain-specific concepts of their own. This intellectual habit coincides (and is occasionally mixed up with) an attitude cultivated in the post-Darwinian natural philosophy of claiming general empirical relevance for the Darwinian conception of evolution under the heading of "Universal Darwinism" (Dawkins 1983).

As the label indicates, Universal Darwinism suggests applying Darwinian notions as general tools for explaining evolutionary phenomena wherever such phenomena are thought to be present. In practice this may not appear much different from the borrowing of concepts discussed in the previous section. Yet, the ontological presumption is a different one. It is claimed that the general applicability of certain Darwinian concepts rests on the fact that they represent the generic features of evolution. What are the concepts considered generally valid by Universal Darwinism? A frequently cited list has been given by Campbell (1965). He suggested the interactive concepts of variation, selection, and retention or replication of competing variants from a population of variants. Similarly, Dawkins (1986) speaks of "replicators" like genes or "memes" as units of selection whose variation and selective multiplication are behind all forms of evolution on this planet.

There is no doubt that these concepts -- gained by abstraction from the neo-Darwinian synthesis in evolutionary biology -- characterize very general features of

---

to imply a "Lamarckian" -- rather than Darwinian -- theory of evolution (Knudsen 2001). Note, however, that hardly any Lamarckian population dynamics have ever been worked out and studied in the sciences and that, unlike those of an analogy to the advanced Darwinian dynamics, the implications (and the benefits) of an analogy to Lamarckian interpretations are therefore unclear.

[5] A special variant are theories of evolution in which society goes through a sequence of progressive stages as, e.g., in Marxian historical materialism. The problems of these theories are well known from the criticism articulated in Popper (1960).

evolution *in nature*. [6] But, as abstract reductions of the Darwinian principles, they are still domain-specific. *Per se* there is little reason to believe that principles derived by an isolated abstraction from evolution in one domain do indeed carry over to evolution in other domains. The proposition that the population based principles of variation, selection, and replication are generic to all forms of evolution -- evolution in nature as much as cultural evolution, say -- is not self-evident. Conclusive empirical support for the alleged general relevance of the abstract Darwinian principles has not yet been provided. It may therefore be argued that their application to the non-biological domain (such as the economic domain) is actually only yet another attempt to construct analogies -- just more abstract ones. Indeed, several of the concrete objections to the attempted analogies raised in the previous section may be repeated similarly here.

To give an example, consider the relationship between selection and variation. In evolutionary biology the absence of a systematic feedback between selection and variation is a test criterion for Darwin's theory. In the economic domain this is different. The comparatively recent achievements of intelligence and codified knowledge often allow people to invent their way out when threatened by selection forces. Such a feedback would have to be given the status of a systematic feature of adaptation, if adaption were to be cast in terms of an interplay between selection and variation. The consequences of this difference with respect to the character and the pace of the adaptive process are dramatic. The meaning of both selection and variation would actually have to change significantly when going from one domain to the other. Similar objections could be raised against the Darwinian assumption of "blindness" or randomness of the variation process which does not do justice to human intuition and creativity. Hence, even at a very abstract level, it is hard to see how analogies suggested by Universal Darwinism can hold.

This is not to say, however, that the idea of identifying generic features of evolution -- which is a good part of the motivation underlying Universal Darwinism -- is mistaken. This idea is based on the ontological assumption of some commonalities shared by all forms of evolution. What has just been criticized is neither the basic idea nor its underlying ontological presumption, but the particular way of trying to realize the idea: the abstract reduction of Darwinian principles does not lead to generic features of evolution. To identify the latter, an attempt needs to be made to transcend all domain-specific characteristics by abstracting from specific forms of evolution in several domains. The question thus is, by what features can evolution be characterized if its particularities in, say, nature, in human culture in general, or in the human economy in particular, are recognized.

The social philosopher John Morley (1874) argued long ago that "evolution is not a force but a process, not a cause but a law". Of course there are forces driving the process of evolution and causes playing a role in it. But Morley is right in claiming that these are not constituent features of evolution. Constituents rather are the dynamically unfolding character and the lawfulness, i.e. regularity, of the changes brought about by

---

[6] They abstract, among other things, from the principles of descent and speciation which figure prominently in Darwin's original understanding, cf. Mayr (1991, Chap.4).

evolution wherever it occurs. However, Morley's two properties are not sufficient. There are many processes which display regularities that are not evolutionary, e.g. the stochastic process describing the motion of a particle suspended in a liquid, known as Brownian motion. Thus, evolution is more than just dynamics. As has been explained in detail elsewhere (Witt 1987, Chap. 1), the crucial qualification that makes dynamics an *evolutionary* dynamics is the emergence and dissemination of novelty in the evolutionary process. To put it differently, evolution is always a process that has the capacity of expanding its state space through the generation of not previously existing states. Hence, the generation of novelty is generic to all cases of evolution.

On this basis, evolution can be defined in an abstract way as the self-transformation over time of a system under consideration. In this definition, the term "transformation" means a process of change governed by regularities. [7] The prefix in "*self*-transformation" points to the endogenous sources and causes of novelty. For epistemological reasons it is useful to split self-transformation into two logically, and usually also ontologically, distinct processes: the emergence and the dissemination of novelty. With the emergence and dissemination of novelty, it is submitted here, the generic, domain-unspecific features of evolution have been identified. The two features materialize in quite different forms in the different disciplines. In biology, we have random mutation and genetic recombination on the one hand and selective replication in the gene pool of a population on the other. In linguistics, to take that example, the invention of new idioms marks the emergence part and their popularization the dissemination part. In the economic domain, given that discipline's focus on human action, novelty is usually seen as emerging from a newly discovered possibility for action which, once taken, is called an innovation. However, any attempt to innovate is likely to trigger learning and be accompanied by it. When the news of the innovation spreads the innovation can disseminate by imitative learning.

IV. Some Methodological Implications

The generic features of emergence and dissemination of novelty help to understand the epistemological problems which all evolutionary theories face -- independent of their disciplinary domains. By novelty's very nature, its meaning, and hence its future consequences, cannot be completely anticipated. In a deliberate search for a particular novelty, e.g. a solution to a specific problem, it may appear possible to define ex ante necessary conditions which any solution must satisfy. But those necessary conditions rest on the current understanding of the problem. In many cases, the novelty or invention actually discovered re-frames the understanding of the problem. Ex post, the corresponding problem-shift then renders the ex ante postulated necessary conditions

---

[7] Note that the choice of the term "system" is not meant to necessarily imply a system-theoretic interpretation of evolution as suggested by Luhmann and others (cf. Hutter 1994). Rather, it is just a dummy for the different disciplinary objects that evolve: nature in the case of biology, language in the case of linguistics, society in the case of sociology, or the economy in the case of economics. From a physical point of view, as living systems, all evolving entities depend on free energy being accessible to them to maintain their life functions. Availability of free energy is therefore also a necessary, but not sufficient, condition for their further evolution.

obsolete or irrelevant. Moreover, even if this is not the case, ex ante formulated necessary conditions cannot cover all properties of the novel solution -- otherwise it would no longer be novelty. Some features, perhaps important ones, cannot positively be anticipated. (The many, often only much later discovered, negative side effects of technological innovations are a case in point.) This trivial fact is responsible for the constrained predictive power of all evolutionary theories. Because of novelty's very nature, the outcome of evolution cannot be positively anticipated. Yet, since it is possible to derive hypotheses that *exclude* the occurrence of certain kinds of novelty some testable propositions do always seem feasible [8]-- though they usually imply rather weak predictions.

If the epistemological constraint is taken seriously, what are the implications? As discussed elsewhere (Witt 1987, Chap. 1; 1993), evolutionary theory faces two different kinds of explanatory problem with strongly differing epistemological connotations. The first is to provide explanations for phenomena and conditions without knowing the meaning of the next emerging novelty ("pre-revelation analysis"). The second kind of problem is to explain what happens once novelty has revealed its meaning ("post-revelation analysis"). Roughly speaking, this distinction corresponds to the two tasks of any theory of evolution. The first task is to explain how, and under what conditions, novelty is being generated within the domain of a theory. The second task is to explain what happens as a consequence of novelty having emerged within the domain. The "epistemological boundary" between the problem of emergence and the problem of dissemination not only establishes the constraints on the predictive power of evolutionary theories, but it also implies differing methodological options for the different explanatory tasks.

The bulk of explanatory efforts usually focuses on the second task. [9] These explanations are indeed much less complicated. This is particularly so under two widely used idealizing assumptions. One assumption is that all relevant properties of a newly generated novelty are already known to the scientific observer. The other assumption is that no further novelty will intervene in the post-revelation analysis. Under these two assumptions, novelty is factually removed from the period of analysis, and its occurrence and revelation is shifted to the antecedent conditions. Under these conditions, the effects triggered by an exogenously given novelty can often be described mathematically by means of ordinary difference or differential equations and their derivatives and solutions. Since there are hardly any mathematical concepts for the emergence of novelty and virtually no algorithmic basis for solving the meaning attri-

---

[8] Take, to use the example given by Hayek (1967b), the neo-Darwinian theory of evolution. Because of the complexity of the genetic recombinatory process there is no way for it to positively anticipate all properties of future generations. But the theory definitely excludes certain novelties from occurring. Even if a forepaw of parent dogs were to be amputated over several generations, the theory predicts that no puppy will ever be born that has no forepaw. However arbitrary this hypothesis may appear on first sight, it offers the possibility for a test that discriminates between Darwin's theory and the rivaling Lamarckian hypothesis of the heredity of acquired traits.

[9] This is even true in evolutionary biology, where the lion's share of theorizing deals with what may be classified as "selection" and "retention" processes according to the scheme of Campbell (1965). The production of genetic novelty by mutation and recombination ("variation") is a comparatively special topic.

bution problem (cf. the discussion in Egidi 1992), this condition defines the presently binding boundary for mathematical modeling in evolutionary economics.

For analyzing the effects and characteristic phenomena of dissemination processes, formal modeling is useful. In fact, many implications can otherwise hardly be derived[10]. As discussed in Witt (1992), these phenomena include frequency-dependency effects and occupancy effects. Furthermore, there are effects of critical mass thresholds and lock-in effects. These effects often occur as "emerging properties", which is to say that they only turn up if, in the evolutionary process, certain ranges of parameter values are exceeded. These dynamic phenomena help in understanding the peculiar coexistence of two apparently conflicting ideas in evolutionary theories. On the one hand there is a belief in general procedural regularities. On the other hand, there can be no doubt about the historical specificity of the evolutionary process. Can regularity and historicity go together? A tentative answer could be: even if history is made up of a sequence of unique episodes, in these episodes, and in the transition between them, something can repeat itself, i.e. regularities can occur. Regularities may reside in learning and imitation phenomena, in diffusion and selection phenomena, and even in the very generation of novelty. Among the recurrent features one can expect, for example, frequency-dependency and occupancy effects, critical mass and lock-in effects. This is to say on the one hand that nomological knowledge by means of which at least some aspects of historical particularities can be explained is feasible. On the other hand, the evolutionary process in its entirety is "irrevocable" (Georgescu-Roegen 1971, pp.196-197). It cannot repeat itself identically even though, as a consequence of its regularity, it may display some recurrent patterns.

V. Ontological Claims: the Continuity Hypothesis

In the previous section some generic features which are supposed to characterize evolution -- the emergence and dissemination of novelty -- have been discussed. This means that all domain-specific evolutionary processes are expected to share these features and some abstract principles that may follow. At the ontological level, this implies that all evolutionary processes have something in common without necessarily being connected to one another. Indeed, whether or not there are also (inter-) dependencies between the various domain-specific processes of evolution, or whether some of them even refer to the same phenomena in reality, is a different ontological question. It is the subject of this section. In order to discuss it, two further views of how Darwinian evolutionary biology and, for that matter, evolutionary economics, relate at the ontological level will be surveyed.

---

[10] Examples in evolutionary economics are individual learning, imitation, and the resulting collective dynamics. As Brenner (1999) shows, they can be represented by diffusion processes on the basis of some version of the master equation. In some cases, the replicator dynamics equation (now popular in evolutionary game theory, cf. Hofbauer and Sigmund 1988, Chap. 4) which gives an abstract account also of selection processes can be used.

The first, and most radical, view assumes that the neo-Darwinian theory of natural selection can be extended to also explain economic behavior of modern man.[11] Thus, the ontological basis of evolutionary economics, evolutionary biology in general, and sociobiology in particular is assumed to be essentially the same. By implication, the emergence and dissemination of novelty would have to be understood as referring to the genetic level only. The justification for this assumption may be sketched as follows. Economic phenomena result from human behavior. Humans are themselves a product of natural selection. Accordingly, the Darwinian theory of evolution may be considered directly relevant to the explanation of human economic behavior. Observable economic behavior should therefore be explicable in terms of its contribution to genetic fitness.

The problem with such an explanation is, of course, that it would be valid only if selection pressure on humans is still tight enough for deviations from the best fit behavior (in terms of reproductive success) to be wiped out. While this may be a reasonable working hypothesis for early, primitive economies, the conditions in the much more productive modern economies seem to be different. Indeed, in the latter, the most significant part of the adaptations in economic behavior usually occur within one generation, i.e. at a pace much more rapid than that of inter-generational, genetic adaptation. These adaptations reflect the emergence and dissemination of novelty at the cultural level: ideas, practices, habits, artefacts etc. They result from the evolutionary dynamics of learning and insight which are inaccessible to the neo-Darwinian theory of natural selection.

The second view, advocated by the present author (cf. Witt 1987, Chap. 3; 1991; 1996; 1999), is epitomized by what may be called the "continuity hypothesis". In this view, the fact that humans and their "hardwired" endowment are a result of natural selection also figures prominently. However, these genetic endowments are considered as only setting the stage for yet other forms of evolution which have emerged under the influence of the unfolding human culture. They follow their own regularities and interact both among themselves and with natural evolution in an increasingly richer and more complex way. This means that an ontological continuity over time is assumed in which new forms of change have been generated within the freedom left by the constraints of Darwinian theory -- and, hence, without invalidating that theory.

Under natural selection, innate dispositions and adaptation mechanisms and programs in humans have been shaped which define the basic behavioral repertoire upon which other forms of evolution rest. In the early phases of human culture it is likely that the two forms of evolution have interacted. However, the synergisms between the natural and cultural results of natural selection eventually allowed forms of human behavior to emerge which had a strong relative reproductive success compared to other species (Corning 1983). As a consequence, selection pressure was significantly reduced

[11] Cf., e.g., Hermann-Pillath (1991), Rubin (1982), Robson (2001); for a critical view cf. Witt (1985) and Hallpike (1996). A modified version of this strategy has informed anthropological research under the label of the co-evolution hypothesis. It is argued that cultural behavior in primitive societies can be explained by the joint fitness value of genetic and cultural traits, cf. Durham (1976), Boyd and Richerson (1994).

and man's genetic endowment has remained much the same since then. The more selection pressure faded, the less systematically selected was behavior which contributed to genetic fitness. Behavioral variety could increase and include variants which had little or no adaptive value. This gave room for human culture, institutions, and advances in economy and technology to evolve according to their own regularities. These regularities are compatible with, and build on, the fact that the innate individual dispositions and adaptation mechanisms are still in place.

Thus, the continuity hypothesis postulates a historical transition. "The origin of the species by means of natural selection", as Darwin (1859) put it, is that form of evolution occuring in reality which antedates, in historical time, other forms of evolution considered here. It is exclusively characterized by the emergence and dissemination of novelty at the genetic level. But this has shaped the ground, and still defines the constraints, for man-made, or cultural, evolution. A plurality of partly interactive evolutionary processes could thus develop in which novelty of very different quality emerges and disseminates at diverse levels. Darwinian theory is directly relevant for understanding both the origin of economic evolution in human phylogeny and continuing influence of innate elements on human economic behavior. Yet, in the further course of economic evolution, human behavior and, correspondingly, economic activities and their collective outcomes underwent a metamorphosis into the distinct, idiosyncratic forms observable in present-day economies. To explain the emergence of the latter, Darwinian theory is not sufficient. What is needed in addition are theories which explain the several facets of cultural evolution.

The continuity hypothesis just specified has important implications for a broadly conceived research program in evolutionary economics. To give an example: the hypothesis suggests ways substance can be added to the theory of human preferences which, by and large, has been treated until now as a "black box" in economics. To escape from the unnecessarily agnostic preference subjectivism in modern economic theory and to reconstruct and explain some objective features of revealed human preferences, recourse can be taken to the remnants of the different, simultaneously operating forms of evolution: the genetic dispositions, the behaviorally reinforced attitudes, and the cognitively acquired knowledge and beliefs. The resulting theory (cf. Witt 2001) explains how human preferences emerge from some innate dispositions and non-cognitive learning mechanisms, and how their revelation is affected by socially shared cognitive frames and subjective experience.

To give another example: the proposed continuity hypothesis allows us to better come to grips with the evolutionary change in the constraints on human productive and consumptive activities. At present, economic theory reflects on these constraints only in an extremely abstract form, namely, to the extent to which they affect the transformation of unspecified inputs into unspecified outputs in anthropogenic production. The continuity hypothesis offers a more concrete approach (cf. Witt 2003). Since evolution in nature has defined the constraints for what can evolve elsewhere, the changing production forms in human phylogeny can easily be reconstructed against that background. The crucial effect of cultural evolution that comes to the fore here is not so much the economizing on scarce resources (which is usually emphasi-

zed in economics), but rather the cumulative problem solving and knowledge generation on the one side, and a successive creation of new problems on the other. On balance, the human economy's growing capacity to generate, apply, and improve cultural
knowledge has up to now increasingly allowed the natural constraints on human economic activity to be slackened.

A significant feature worth mentioning is the massively enhanced access to free
energy, particularly fossil energy resources. The increasing release of large parts of the
human society from being limited to the age-old uses of human time for physical work
has enabled humankind to generate and apply ever more knowledge -- a kind of auto-
catalytic cycle (cf. Buenstorf 2000). It has allowed the niche for the human species to
be enlarged, at least temporarily. Moreover, the command over natural resources has
increased dramatically for almost all its members currently alive. (In economic growth
theory these consequences are usually reflected by growing per capita income world-
wide and unprecedented increases in labor productivity.) On the other hand, the evolutionary process that has produced these amenities has also triggered developments
with an uncertain, and possibly highly problematic, longer term impact on nature, the
ultimate foundation of the human economy. Unfortunately, the epistemological
boundary discussed in the previous section prevents us from making predictions of
the meaning of future new knowledge. How the balance between problem solving and
problem generating will develop in the future is therefore unknown. It is a matter, alternatively, of optimistic hopes or pessimistic fears.

VI. Conclusions

An attempt has been made here to clarify the generic features of evolution and some
of the implications that follow from these features. The attempt was motivated by the
fact that evolution is believed to occur in many disciplines. As a tribute to the intellectual attraction of the neo-Darwinian theory of evolution, the evolutionary processes in
other domains are often also conceptualized in terms of Darwinian concepts. Some
modern Darwinists even propagate the concepts of variation, selection, and replication as universally applicable. However, as has been argued, when it comes to making
sense of evolution in non-biological domains, recourse to Darwinian concepts is neither a necessary heuristic strategy nor is it always a helpful one. There are good reasons
to search for generic features of evolution in a way that transcends all domain-specific
characteristics. These reasons have been discussed and a way of identifying generic
features has been pointed out. Two concrete generic features have been suggested and
some of their implications, which are relevant for analyzing evolution in all domain-
specific manifestations, have been outlined.

Finally, an attempt has been made to confront the findings with an issue that
seems of some importance for the post-Darwinian natural philosophy. How does the
idea that various forms of evolution have emerged in different domains fit the Darwinian world view? And, accordingly, how can the various domain-specific evolutionary
theories such as, for instance, evolutionary economics, be accommodated by the
world view of the moderns sciences which is strongly influenced by the neo-
Darwinian theory of evolution? The answer that has been suggested is a specific onto-

logical claim which has been dubbed the "continuity hypothesis". The hypothesis does attribute relevance to the neo-Darwinian theory of evolution for explaining evolutionary phenomena in non-biological disciplinary domains such as the economic domain. Hence it subscribes to a Darwinian world view. However, unlike in some contributions inspired by sociobiology, the relevance does not lie in its direct applicability to explaining the evolution of economic behavior. Nor is the relevance that of a master theory which provides abstract tools, as Universal Darwinism has it. Instead, the relevance of neo-Darwinian theory rather is the following. It is the theory that explains how the basis has been generated and constraints are still shaped for those forms of evolution which have emerged later under the influence of the unfolding human culture. The human economy and its tremendous historical change is a congenial example.

BIBLIOGRAPHY

Alchian, A.A. (1950). "Uncertainty, Evolution, and Economic Theory", *Journal of Political Economy* 58, 211-221.

Bergstrom, T.C. (2002). "Evolution of Social Behavior: Individual and Group Selection", *Journal of Economic Perspectives* 16, 67-88.

Binmore, K. (1994). *Playing Fair - Game Theory and the Social Contract I.* Cambridge, MA: MIT Press.

—— (1998). *Just Playing - Game Theory and the Social Contract II.* Cambridge, MA: MIT Press.

Boyd, R, and Richerson, P.J. (1994). "The Evolution of Norms: An Anthropological View", *Journal of Institutional and Theoretical Economics* 150, 72-87.

Brenner, T. (1999). *Modelling Learning in Economics.* Cheltenham: Edward Elgar.

Buenstorf, G. (2000). "Self-organization and Sustainability: Energetics of Evolution and Implications for Ecological Economics", *Ecological Economics* 33, 119-134.

Campbell, D.T. (1965). "Variation and Selective Retention in Socio-cultural Evolution", in Barringer, H.R., Blankstein, G.I., Mack, R.W. (eds.). *Social Change in Developing Areas: A Re-interpretation of Evolutionary Theory.* Cambridge, MA: Schenkman, 19-49.

Corning, P.A. (1983). *The Synergism Hypothesis: A Theory of Progressive Evolution.* New York: McGraw-Hill.

Darwin, C. (1859). *On the Origin of the Species by Means of Natural Selection or the Preservation of Favored Races in the Struggle of Life.* London: John Murray.

Dawkins, R. (1983). "Universal Darwinism", in Bendall, D.S. (ed.). *Evolution from Molecules to Man.* Cambridge: Cambridge University Press, 403-425.

—— (1986). *The Blind Watchmaker.* Harlow: Longman.

Durham, W.H. (1976). "The Adaptive Significance of Cultural Behavior", *Human Ecology* 4, 89-121.

Egidi, M. (1992). "Organizational Learning, Problem Solving and the Division of Labor", in Egidi, M., Marris, R. (eds.). *Economics, Bounded Rationality and the Cognitive Revolution.* Aldershot: Edward Elgar, 148-173.

Georgescu-Roegen, N. (1971). *The Entropy Law and the Economic Process.* Cambridge, MA: Harvard University Press.

Hallpike, C.R. (1996). "Social Evolution", *Journal of Institutional and Theoretical Economics* 152, 682-689.

Hawkins, M. (1997). *Social Darwinism in European and American Thought, 1860-1945.* Cambridge: Cambridge University Press.

Hayek, F.A. (1967a). "Dr. Bernhard Mandeville", *Proceedings of the British Academy* 12, London: Oxford University Press.

—— (1967b). "The Theory of Complex Phenomena", in Hayek, F.A. *Studies in Philosophy, Politics and Economics.* Routledge & Kegan Paul, 22-42.

Hermann-Pillath, C. (1991). "A Darwinian Framework for the Economic Analysis of Institutional Change in History", *Journal of Social and Biological Structures* 14, 127-148.

Hodgson, G.M. (1999). *Evolution and Institutions.* Cheltenham: Edward Elgar.

—— (2001). *How Economics Forgot History: The Problem of Historical Specificity in Social Science.* London: Routledge

Hofbauer, J., Sigmund, K. (1988). *The Theory of Evolution and Dynamical Systems.* Cambridge: Cambridge University Press.

Hutter, M. (1994). "The Unit that Evolves: Linking Self-Reproduction and Self-Interest", in Magnussen, L. (ed.). *Evolutionary and Neo-Schumpeterian Approaches to Economics.* Dordrecht: Kluwer, 49-64.

Knudsen, T. (2001). "Nesting Lamarckism within Darwinian Explanations: Necessity in Economics and Possibility in Biology?", in Laurent, J., Nightingale, J. (eds.). *Darwinism and Evolutionary Economics.* Cheltenham: Edward Elgar, 121-159.

Maynard Smith, J. (1982). *Evolution and the Theory of Games.* Cambridge: Cambridge University Press.

Mayr, E. (1991). *One Long Argument.* Cambridge, MA: Harvard University Press.

Metcalfe, J.S. (2002). "On the Optimality of the Competitive Process: Kimura's Theorem and Market Dynamics", *Journal of Bioeconomics*, forthcoming.

Morley, J. (1874). *On Compromise.* London: Chapman and Hall.

Nelson, R.R. (1995). "Recent Evolutionary Theorizing About Economic Change", *Journal of Economic Literature* 33, 48-90.

Nelson, R.R, Winter, S.G. (1982). *An Evolutionary Theory of Economic Change.* Cambridge, MA: Harvard University Press.

—— (2002). "Evolutionary Theorizing in Economics", *Journal of Economic Perspectives* 2, 23-46.

Penrose, E.T. (1952). "Biological Analogies in the Theory of the Firm", *American Economic Review* 42, 804-819.

Popper, K. (1960). *The Poverty of Historicism.* London: Routledge & Kegan Paul, 2nd edit.

Richards, R.J. (1992). *The Meaning of Evolution: the Morphological Construction and the Ideological Reconstruction of Darwin's Theory.* Chicago: Chicago University Press.

Robson, A.J. (2001). "The Biological Basis of Economic Behavior", *Journal of Economic Literature* 39, 11-33.

—— (2002). "Evolution and Human Nature", *Journal of Economic Perspectives* 2, 89-106.

Rubin, P.H. (1982). "Evolved Ethics and Efficient Ethics", *Journal of Economic Behavior and Organization* 3, 161-174.

Ruse, M. (1979). *The Darwinian Revolution.* Chicago: University of Chicago Press.

Rutherford, M. (1998). "Veblen's Evolutionary Programme: A Promise Unfulfilled", *Cambridge Journal of Economics* 22, 463-477.

Samuelson, L. (2002). "Evolution and Game Theory", *Journal of Economic Perspectives* 2, 47-66.

Schumpeter, J.A. (1912/34). *Theorie der wirtschaftlichen Entwicklung.* Leipzig: Duncker & Humblot, 1912; first English edition *Theory of Economic Development.* Cambridge, MA: Harvard University Press, 1934.

Veblen, T. (1898). "Why Is Economics Not an Evolutionary Science?" *Quarterly Journal of Economics* 12, 373-397.

—— (1899). *The Theory of the Leisure Class - An Economic Study of Institutions.* New York: MacMillan.

—— (1914). *The Instinct of Workmanship, and the State of the Industrial Arts.* New York: MacMillan.

Winter, S.G. (1964). "Economic 'Natural Selection' and the Theory of the Firm", *Yale Economic Essays* 4, 225-272.

Witt, U. (1985). "Economic Behavior and Biological Evolution: Some Remarks on the Sociobiology Debate", *Journal of Theoretical and Institutional Economics* (formerly *Zeitschrift fuer die gesamte Staatswissenschaft*), 141, 365-389.

—— (1987). *Individualistische Grundlagen der evolutorischen Oekonomik.* Tuebingen: Mohr-Siebeck.

—— (1991). "Economics, Sociobiology, and Behavioral Psychology on Preferences", *Journal of Economic Psychology* 12, 557-573.

—— (1992). "Evolutionary Concepts in Economics", *Eastern Economic Journal* 18, 405-419.

—— (1993). "Emergence and dissemination of Innovations: Some Principles of Evolutionary Economics", in: Day, R.H., Chen, P. (eds.). *Nonlinear Dynamics and Evolutionary Economics.* Oxford: Oxford University Press, 91-100.

—— (1996). "A Darwinian Revolution in Economics?", *Journal of Institutional and Theoretical Economics* 152, 707-715.

—— (1999). "Evolutionary Economics and Evolutionary Biology" in: Koslowski, P. (ed.). *Sociobiology and Bioeconomics.* Berlin: Springer, 279-298.

—— (2001). "Learning to Consume - A Theory of Wants and the Growth of Demand", *Journal of Evolutionary Economics* 11, 23-36.

—— (2002). "How Evolutionary is Schumpeter's Theory of Economic Development?", *Industry and Innovation* 9, 7-22.

—— (2003). "Production in Nature and Production in the Economy - Second Thoughts about Some Basic Economic Concepts".

Young, P. (1998). *Individual Strategy and Social Structure: An Evolutionary Theory of Social Institutions.* Princeton: Princeton University Press.

Ulrich WITT is the director of the Evolutionary Economics Unit of the Max Planck Institute for Research into Economic Systems and professor of economics at the Friedrich Schiller University, both in Jena, Germany. He did his Ph.D. in economics at the University of Goettingen in 1979 and finished his habilitation at the University of Mannheim in 1985. From 1988-1995 he held a chair in economic theory at the University of Freiburg in Germany before he assumed his current position.

Address: Evolutionary Economics Group, Max-Planck-Institute for Research Into Economic Systems. Kahlaische Str. 10, D-07745 Jena, Germany. E-mail: witt@mpiew-jena.mpg.de

Journal of Economic Behavior & Organization 70 (2009) 311–320

Contents lists available at ScienceDirect

Journal of Economic Behavior & Organization

journal homepage: www.elsevier.com/locate/econbase

Propositions about novelty[☆]

Ulrich Witt

Max Planck Institute of Economics, Kahlaische Str. 10, 07745 Jena, Germany

ARTICLE INFO

Article history:
Received 15 June 2007
Received in revised form 19 January 2009
Accepted 19 January 2009
Available online 30 January 2009

JEL classification:
D 80
D 83
O 30
O 31

Keywords:
Novelty
Creativity
Evolution
Uncertainty
Knowledge growth

ABSTRACT

The emergence of novelty is a ubiquitous feature in science, technology, and economic life. It is the crucial input to the growth of human knowledge. At the same time, novelty is one of the most amorphous concepts in scientific thought. Theorizing about novelty and its emergence faces notorious problems. This paper explores why this is so and what can be done to deal in a more systematic fashion with novelty. The notion of degrees of novelty is introduced, and its relationship with the concept of uncertainty is discussed. The results of the inquiry are summarized by a number of hypotheses.

© 2009 Elsevier B.V. All rights reserved.

1. Introduction

The emergence of novelty is a pervasive feature of modern life and an important driver of economic development. New ideas, practices, and artefacts transform culture, commerce, and technology. When considering options to innovate, every businessman is contemplating, and often trying out, new speculations, beliefs, and know-how. More broadly seen, in nature too, the emergence of genetic and epigenetic novelty is a driving agent of evolution. Both in nature and the sphere of human action, novelty adds to already existing variety and fuels the competitive transformation processes with manifest consequences. In the economy, the continuing creation of novelty feeds the growth of useful (problem-solving) knowledge that, in turn, has been the mainstay of the soaring economic growth of the past few centuries.

Despite the importance of emerging novelty as an agent of change, a comprehensive, structured theory of novelty does not exist, and it does not even seem clear whether such a theory is feasible at all. The complexity of the act from which novelty emerges and its epistemic peculiarity (the fact that the informational content of novelty cannot be anticipated) make novelty a difficult research topic. Some insights that are relevant for the mental production of novelty can be found in the vast literature on human creativity (see, e.g., Sternberg, 1999), cognitive science (e.g., in the work on problem-solving, see Newell and Simon, 1972), and the formation of cognitive concepts (Finke et al., 1992; Hofstadter, 1995; Fauconnier and Turner, 2002). There have even been some first attempts at dealing with novelty analytically (e.g., in Zabell, 1992). In contrast,

---

☆ The author is grateful to the participants of seminars in Jena, Great Barrington, St. Gall, and Pollenzo for helpful comments on earlier drafts.
E-mail address: Ulrich.Witt@econ.mpg.de.

0167-2681/$ – see front matter © 2009 Elsevier B.V. All rights reserved.
doi:10.1016/j.jebo.2009.01.008

312   *U. Witt / Journal of Economic Behavior & Organization 70 (2009) 311–320*

with the exception of historical studies of the emergence of man-made novelty in technology and production (e.g., Usher, 1954; Vincenti, 1990; Mokyr, 1990), in economics the emergence of novelty is usually treated as an exogenous shock. If novelty is considered at all, the focus is on its diffusion in an industry or the economy.

In this paper, the emergence of novelty will therefore be put at center stage. What the processes that lead to novelty emergence look like and what kind of hypotheses are possible *ex ante* about their outcome (i.e. about the emerging informational content) will be explored. The paper proceeds as follows. Section 2 clarifies some conceptual ambiguities that often hamper the discussion about novelty. Section 3 introduces a procedural approach to novelty that distinguishes between a generative operation and an interpretative operation that are involved in the emergence of novelty. These two operations are shown to be logically independent of each other and to have profoundly differing implications. In the light of the procedural approach suggested, Section 4 discusses the epistemic peculiarities in the creation of novelty, the logical structure of the interpretative operation, and the conclusions to be drawn regarding the role that novelty plays for the evolution of human knowledge. Section 5 elaborates on the observation that, in retrospect, it makes a difference whether novelty means only a minor variation in known details or an entirely new thought that eludes existing frameworks. The notion of degrees of novelty is introduced and is compared with the concepts of degrees of likelihood or belief. Section 6 offers the conclusions.

2. Some prolegomena

When an attempt is made in this paper to explore the possibilities for and some features of a theory of novelty and its emergence, one problem that must be faced is the ambiguity of the term "novelty". Usually, what is meant can be captured as follows:

Definition. Novelty is something that was unknown before a particular point in time and that, hence, was discovered or created at that point in time.

Some qualifications are, however, necessary. Novelty is defined here relative to existing propositional or procedural knowledge on facts, rules, or theories. This relationship implies several contingencies. What is not known in one domain j up to a time t_j can already have become known in a different domain i at a time $t_i < t_j$. It is thus new only to the specific domain j. Therefore, it is necessary to distinguish between something novel to a specific domain and something that is universally novel. Universal novelty emerges somewhere at a time τ, so that there is no domain i for which $t_i < \tau$.

The distinctive epistemological feature of novelty is expressed by the difference it makes when the *ex ante* view of what is novel (i.e. the view at a time $t < \tau$) is compared to the view one can take *ex post* (i.e. at time $t \geq \tau$). Unlike in the *ex ante* case, *ex post* a (fictitious) observer is able, and typically is assumed, to know the relevant properties and meaning of what has emerged or is being created. However, what has become known in this way is no longer "novelty" in the epistemic sense. It is an ordinary piece of information labeled "novel" only in a retrospective sense. Depending on which perspective is taken, theorizing about novelty thus amounts to either pre-revelation or post-revelation analysis, two epistemologically fundamentally different approaches (Witt, 1993). One of the consequences of the epistemic limitations that are binding up to time τ is the predictive weakness of scientific disciplines in whose domains novelty is regularly generated in the course of events, economics being a case in point.

As far as anthropogenic novelty is concerned, its origin can be exogenously triggered new sensory perceptions (and their mental representation) or the endogenous formation of new thought. Discovering, for example, the flavor of a not-yet-tasted fruit certainly satisfies the above definition of novelty. However, this may, but does not have to, involve a creative act of the mind, something that, in contrast, is always the case when new thought is formed. This distinction is relevant for clarifying the relationship between discovery and invention. Discovery can, but does not necessarily, involve a creative act. Invention, in contrast, always presupposes the creation of some new thought that materializes in the form of new artefact and/or practice. On the one side there are thus some discoveries that do not involve a creative act while, on the other side, there are both discoveries and inventions that do.

New ideas, beliefs, and know-how induce the agents to develop new behaviors, strategies, practices, and artefacts (innovations). The differences between domain-specific and universal novelty turns up here again in the guise of subjective vs. objective novelty (Machlup, 1980, Chapter 8; Witt, 1993; in Boden, 1999 as historic vs. psychological novelty). Subjective novelty is something that is new for a particular agent k who gets to know it at time t_k. Being new relative to k's knowledge domain does not exclude the possibility that its meaning is already known to some other agent(s), for example, a scientific observer h, if $\tau \leq t_h < t_k$. Already knowing what is going to be revealed to other individuals later provides a basis for conjecturing about their likely reactions when they become aware of the particular novelty. This is indeed the epistemic position regularly adopted in research on the diffusion of innovations (see Rogers, 1995), the arena of post-revelation analysis. In the case of objective, that is, universal, novelty (the arena of pre-revelation analysis), this epistemic position is not possible.

3. The procedural approach: operations by which novelty is being created

What can be said more precisely about how new ideas, beliefs, and knowledge emerge, given that, as Shackle (1973, p. 26) noted, such statements cannot be logically deduced from already existing ideas, beliefs, and knowledge? What is the logical relationship between already existing thought and new thought established by the creative act? In his inquiry into the emergence of cognitive novelty, Koestler (1964, p. 120) claims that "the creative act...does not create something out

U. Witt / Journal of Economic Behavior & Organization 70 (2009) 311–320 313

of nothing; it uncovers, selects, re-shuffles, combines, synthesizes already existing facts, ideas, faculties, skills". By a more or less accidental displacement of attention to something not previously noted, new elements are introduced into a given context with which they have not been previously associated.

The idea that novelty can emerge from cross-over or, more generally, (re-) combination of existing elements (including combination with omissions), is not a new one, but it needs some qualifications. An arbitrary (re-) combination of something with something else is rarely what leads to new ideas or imaginings.[1] A cognitive concept carries meaning only in relation to some context. To combine concepts in an accidental way therefore usually means mixing up contexts that are foreign to one another. New meaning can only be induced if there is a chance of aligning the different contexts (Gentner and Markman, 1997). However, even if the contextual constraint of some similarity between the things to be (re-) combined is met, the subsequent reshuffling does not by itself lend a new meaning to the resulting combinations. For this to be accomplished, a meaningful association between them must be induced, be it a "conceptual integration" based on the common elements or features or a categorical reduction by which commonalities are induced via a memorized more general category (Finke et al., 1992, Chapters 2 and 5, Fauconnier and Turner, 2002, Chapter 3).

At a closer look it thus appears that a qualified reshuffling of existing elements is one thing. Finding sense in the resulting combinations, if there is any, for example, aligning the multiple contexts that have been mingled, is something else. From a procedural point of view on what happens when novelty emerges, one may thus conclude

Hypothesis 1. The creation of new cognitive concepts (ideas, imaginings) involves two operations. One is a generative operation that produces new (re-) combinations of elements. The other is an interpretative operation by which the new (re-) combination is integrated into a newly emerging or a more general already existing concept.

Even though they coincide in time, the two operations are logically distinct. How they work and interact can be illustrated by a simple example of a conceptual integration.

Economic activities can sometimes be described by simple factual statements such as, "agent X sells commodity Y". In a semantic representation, the cognitive concepts involved are depicted by subject S, predicate P, and object O in the corresponding basic sentence. (Using a semantic representation has some advantages. First, the criteria constraining the generative operation can easily be identified. Second, at the semantic level, it is possible to grasp intuitively the similarity of cognitive concepts and the meaning that emerges in the act of conceptual integration.) Consider the following simple statements

(i-a) "kiosks (S_1) sell (P_a) *convenience goods* (O_{1a})"
and
(i-b) "kiosks (S_1) have (P_b) extended business hours (O_b)".

Statements like these, sharing the same subject (kiosks), are simple propositional networks by which contextual knowledge or beliefs about the subject are encoded (Anderson, 2000, Chapter 5). Imagine a test person who is asked to write down what she associates with "kiosk" (i.e. retrieves from her memory as the relevant context). The results typically are statements such as (i-a) and (i-b). Let us denote the structure of the corresponding propositional network by

(1)

Now suppose that the test person is given the cognitive concept "gas station" (S_2), and that she associates the following statements:

(ii-a) "gas stations (S_2) sell (P_a) gas (O_{2a})"
and
(ii-b) "gas stations (S_2) have (P_b) extended business hours (O_b)".

---

[1] Jonathan Swift (1934, p. 172, reprint of 1st edition of 1726) parodied the absurdity of such a notion nicely in Section III of Gulliver's Travels, "A Voyage to Laputa", with a mechanical reshuffling of words. The protagonist Gulliver visits the academy of science, meeting the "projector of speculative learning" who shows him. ". . . a Frame, about the Sides whereof all his Pupils stood in Ranks. It was Twenty Foot square. The Superficies was composed of several Bits of Wood, about the Bigness of a Dye, but some larger than others. They were all linked together by slender Wires. These Bits of Wood were covered on every Square with Papers pasted on them; and on these Papers were written all the Words of their Language. . .without any Order. The Professor then desired me to observe, for he was going to set his Engine at work. The Pupils at his Command took each of them hold of an Iron Handle, whereof there were Forty fixed round the Edges of the Frame; and giving them a sudden Turn, the whole Disposition of Words was entirely changed. He then commanded Six and Thirty of the Lads to read the several Lines softly as they appeared upon the frame; and where they found three or four Words together that might make Part of the Sentence, they dictated to the four remaining Boys. . ."

314   *U. Witt / Journal of Economic Behavior & Organization 70 (2009) 311–320*

The corresponding propositional network can be denoted by

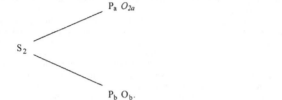

$$\text{(2)}$$

The propositional networks (1) and (2) have P_a, P_b, and O_b in common. To avoid nonsensical statements that would result from an arbitrary reshuffling of subjects, predicates, and objects (as in Swift's parody), the commonalities can be used as a basis for cross-overs or recombinations. The generative operation is then subjected to the constraint of retaining the syntactic order. This means that, in the recombination, precisely the non-common elements (set in italics) are crossed over as shown by the scheme in (3).

$$\text{(3)}$$

For the two statements thus generated, the question is whether, in the new combination, the original contexts can be aligned so that a new meaning is induced. This question is answered by the interpretative operation. In the present case, the original contexts are so similar that they suggest a *combinatory extension* of the original factual statements (i-a) and (ii-a) into

(i-c): "kiosks sell convenience goods *and* gas"
(ii-c): "gas stations sell gas *and* convenience goods".[2]

The combinatory extensions (i-c) and (ii-c) evoke the interpretation of a possible extension of the business strategies of kiosks and gas stations, respectively. Despite the extremely simple structure of the propositional networks used in the generative operation, when interpreted as a combinatory extension, its outcome yields meaningful new concepts. In the 1960s this extension was indeed an innovation strategy in the services industry. In the U.S., convenience store chains such as "7-eleven" started adding gas to their assortment of products and services. About a decade later, gas stations in Europe started to sell convenience goods in addition to gas to take advantage of their extended business hours.

4. Some implications of the procedural approach to novelty

The example in the previous section served to highlight the different functions of the generative and the interpretative operation. Due to the simple structure of the factual statements in the example, both the generative operation and the combinatory extensions identified by the interpretative operation are rather special. They can easily be extended to explain the use of metaphors and analogies by which the acts of recombining and conceptual integration in creating novelty are often systematized (see, e.g., the work on concept formation by Nersessian, 2002). In other cases, the associative basis for attributing new meaning may, of course, require a more complex semantic representation and/or logic, such as, when meaning is induced by categorical reduction and generic abstraction. Furthermore, before a conceptual integration succeeds, several iterations may often be necessary in which the conceptual inputs to the generative operation are modified or replaced over and over again (Finke et al., 1992, Chapter 2). In addition, if objects other than semantically represented ones are involved, the two

---

[2] An equivalent result can be derived if the statements (i-a) and (ii-a) are interpreted as definitions of the form "kiosks are businesses that sell convenience goods" and "gas stations are businesses that sell gas". A mere recombinant exchange of O_{1a} and O_{2a} would result in a violation of these definitions. Only by expanding the definitions of kiosks and gas stations in the form of the combinatory extension do the new, conceptually integrated definitions "kiosks are businesses that sell convenience goods and gas" and "gas stations are businesses that sell gas and convenience goods" emerge.

U. Witt / Journal of Economic Behavior & Organization 70 (2009) 311–320

operations may have to be suitably adjusted. However, these reservations notwithstanding, both the generative operation and the interpretative operation are generic to the creation of mental novelty. Their exemplary discussion can therefore be used to derive some more general insights about novelty and its emergence that will be discussed now.

A first inference that can be made relates to the generative operation. With reference to Campbell (1960), the adherents of an evolutionary epistemology often claim that novelty emerges from "blind" variation (see, e.g., Hodgson and Knudsen, 2006). Blindness here means that the contextual constraints on the (re-) combination process discussed above are not binding. Any arbitrarily chosen sets such as, for example, the English vocabulary and the data set of daily Dow-Jones stock exchange indices from 1950 to 2000 could be commingled irrespective of whether or not there is some commonality on the basis of which the disparate elements could be conceptually integrated. Furthermore, in choosing which elements of the sets are to be (re-) combined, blind variation would also mean ignoring the internal structure of the sets such as, for example, the syntactic structure of the propositional networks in scheme (3) above.

However, even in genetics, the model for evolutionary epistemology, variation is not blind (not even in the case of muta- tions which are, after all, *local* copying errors in DNA strings). In sexual reproduction, for instance, the lion's share of variation results from the recombination of parental genes. This is subject to strict matching rules for the nucleotide chains in the breakage and reunion of homologous chromosomes, a biochemical form of rigid contextuality. Even in the analogously mod- eled genetic algorithms, the crossing over is confined to elements or sections of binary coded strings, and it exchanges only equivalently formatted sections. The following may therefore be inferred:

Hypothesis 2. The generative operation is based on a contextual pre-selection of sets and elements of sets to be recombined that follows some similarity or conformity criterion.

Because of the similarity and conformity criteria underlying the choice of what is (re-) combined, the generative operation is a more or less strongly guided process and, hence, is far from a "blind" variation.

A further conclusion concerns the interpretative operation and a significant feature in which it differs from the generative operation. Unlike the generative operation with its plain logic, the associative act by which the human mind accomplishes a conceptual integration in the interpretative operation is not fully understood.[3] In discussing examples of the associative act such as the one above, the unresolved problem of how exactly the conceptual integration comes about is by-passed by letting our intuition doing the trick. In view of this it is important that, by Hypothesis 1, the generative operation and the interpretative operation are logically distinct and, hence, can be carried out separately from one another. From this follows

Hypothesis 3. While the generative operation can be automatized mechanically or electronically outside the human mind, for example, by numerical algorithms and programs, the carrying out of the interpretative operation is bound to the medium of the human mind and can therefore not be automatized.

A remark is necessary here. The generative and the interpretative operations are given a constitutive role in the creation of mental novelty. This does not necessarily mean that these two operations are also sufficient for the creative act. Yet another operation can often be observed to accompany the interpretative operation, namely an evaluative one. However, where the interpretative operation answers the question of what it is that emerges, the evaluative operation is concerned with what the utility, advantage, benefit of this is. Even if coinciding with the interpretative operation, the act of evaluating the novel outcome is therefore logically distinct and, from the procedural point of view, not necessary for novelty to be created. On the other hand, where novelty creation is an iterated process, a concomitant evaluative operation can feed back on the generative operation. This happens if the criteria on which, according to Hypothesis 2, the pre-selection of sets and elements involved in the generative operation is made contingent on how the preceding outcomes of the interpretative operation are evaluated. Though not itself involved in the creation of novelty, an evaluative operation can in this way influence what novelty emerges.

The fact that an evaluative operation is logically distinct from the interpretative operation makes it possible to carry this out outside the human mind and to automatize it. Recently, steps in that direction have indeed been taken by modeling the feedback of the evaluative operation on the generative operation by way of an analogy to natural selection in genetic or, more generally, evolution algorithms (see Holland, 1992; Bäck, 1996). In nature, the generative operation is the recombination of specifically selected genetic material. The equivalent to the interpretative operation is the epigenetic expression of the varied gene code in the development of the phenotype. The evaluation is indirectly produced at an extra-somatic level by the competition for reproductive success between the different phenotypes that develop from the population's gene pool. The systematic feedback between the adaptive value of the traits of the phenotypes (evaluation) and the selective admission of their genes to the recombination (generative operation) in the next generation is called natural selection.

Analogously, in genetic algorithms, elements or segments of binary strings are recombined in a computer-based generative operation. If not skipped altogether, the interpretative operation is degenerated into pre-specified mapping instructions

---

[3] To say nothing of the underlying neural processes (cf. Koch and Crick, 2000; Edelman and Tononi, 2000, Chapter 10). Johnson-Laird (2005) considers the associative act as something that is outside the scope of current psychological theories and their computer implementations. It has been conjectured, however, that the associative act is a search process in an extremely high dimensional memory space (cf. Kohonen, 1987). By searching the space, connections are traced to cognitive concepts that have been laid out by earlier experience. These concepts can be imagined to be sampled with a probability that depends on how closely they appear to be connected to the new concept under consideration, yet thus far it has not been possible to derive the measure of coherence that is required to determine the 'closeness' of concepts.

written into the computer program. The resulting "new" variant is launched into a simulated environment where it is subjected to an evaluative operation that measures the performance relative to that of competing variants produced in the same way. If better performing variants are used more frequently or exclusively for recombination in a next round of the simulated generative operation, this can shape the kind of novelty that emerges in the simulation over time.

By recognizing the role of such complex numerically iterated dynamic systems in generating novelty, yet another conclusion can be drawn. Assume that the algorithm of the generative operation is known and that it does not produce a chaotic time series. In addition, let the interpretative and/or evaluative operations be pre-specified. If it is nonetheless not possible to deduce the implications logically from the premises, this is usually because of the complexity of the recursive relation between the generative, interpretative, and evaluative operations. Novelty in the sense of not previously known implications can then be discovered (rather than created) by the human experimenter through numerical simulations. Hence, the process of revealing novelty by simulating complex recursive programs and the creative act of the human mind have something in common. The commonality is a key to understanding the peculiar epistemic features of novelty.

Hypothesis 4.   Novelty is revealed through inductive operations whose outcome, by definition, cannot be derived from the premises. Carrying out the inductive operations requires time, and thus prevents the meaning of novelty being instantaneously accessible.

The inductive nature of the simulations discussed is obvious. Notwithstanding the fact that the creation of novelty in the human mind is not fully understood, the inductive nature of the associative act underlying conceptual integration, categorical reduction, or generic abstraction seems equally obvious. Moreover, it has been argued that the interpretative operation is inaccessible to deductive reasoning on grounds of principle (see Markose, 2004, 2005 referring to Gödel's incompleteness theorem). The generative operation requires inductive methods whenever it is chaotic (which can even be the case for simple recombination dynamics; see Prigogine, 1993) or too complex to be solved analytically. Note that the time constraint stated in Hypothesis 4 still holds even if someday it would be possible to automatize the interpretative operation in a non-trivial way outside the human mind.

A final inference that can be drawn from the approach taken here concerns the role that novelty plays for the evolution of human thought and knowledge. In the example in the previous section, the meaning of the elements (the cognitive concepts in the propositional networks) from which the combinatory extension emerged were all known beforehand. Moreover, it seems likely that the primitive concepts ("gas station", "kiosk") themselves emerged through conceptual integration from other, still more primitive cognitive concepts. It can therefore be conjectured that the emergence of novelty is not only a process that is iterated over and over again, but that it is also a cumulative, potentially autocatalytic process. This suggests

Hypothesis 5.   By re-using newly created concepts in further iterations of the generative operation, an infinitely growing number of concepts can emerge from a finite number of initial elements, provided that the share of combinations to which a new meaning can be attributed is non-vanishing.

In the light of Hypothesis 5, the evolution of human thought appears to be the creation of increasingly more complex chains of concepts composed of an ever-larger set of known elements. (What carries novelty are, in each case, the recombined elements that did not previously exit.) This fact is hidden only by the complexity-reducing habit of denoting longer chains, or parts of them, with own shorthand terms. For example, instead of using the combinatory extension (ii-c) "gas stations selling gas *and* convenience goods", a shorthand has already emerged, calling the new hybrid a "supercenter". In this example, Hypothesis 5 would thus presuppose that "supercenter" can be entered into the formation of new propositional networks, perhaps as subject or object, without any of the now three concepts "kiosks", "gas stations", and "supercenter" being a substitute for any other.

If Hypothesis 5 is correct, it follows by backward induction that at the beginning of the chain of cumulative novelty creation, there must have been some ultimate prior concepts that were themselves not cognitively created. To put it differently, the cumulative process must have started from some innate concepts, a conclusion that accords with the "embodied knowledge" hypothesis (cf. Hayek, 1952 for an early discussion).

The conjecture of an autocatalytic expansion of the number of concepts in human thought (i.e. of an expansion that, driven by a growth-of-base effect, fuels itself) is in agreement with the observable accumulation of the human knowledge. At the symbolic level of the alphabet, the novelty-by-extension phenomenon finds its equivalent in the ever-longer strings of letters by which the expanding body of thought (the "library of human thought" that has been growing since the invention of writing) is documented. However, given that it is not known what exactly happens in the interpretative operation, it is hard to assess what chances there are for the condition to hold that the share of combinations to which a new meaning can be attributed is indeed non-vanishing. Furthermore, it cannot be excluded that, because of both memory and communication constraints, it is increasingly more difficult to make the ever-growing body of concepts available for further (re-) combinations.[4]

---

[4] For a discussion of the economic implications of an auto-catalytic growth of economically useful knowledge see Weitzman (1998). For scientific knowledge it has been claimed that there is evidence for a fading auto-catalytic growth of knowledge primarily because there is a declining share of significant new results from search and experimentation; see de Solla Price (1963) and Rescher (1989).

U. Witt / Journal of Economic Behavior & Organization 70 (2009) 311–320 317

5. Degrees of novelty and uncertainty

Novelty has been defined here as something that was unknown before a particular point in time and that, hence, was discovered or created at that point in time. However, whether a particular novelty is only a more or less minor detail of something that is otherwise well known or whether it is altogether new seems to make a big difference. The invention of a new ignition device like the sparking plug, for instance, created a new and more reliable way of running a combustion engine, but in retrospect, this seems to be a less significant novelty than the invention of the combustion engine itself. Observations such as these give rise to the conjecture that there are degrees of novelty that can differ from case to case. In fact, such an *ex post* distinction between degrees of novelty is often made in innovation research, for example, by contrasting basic innovations with follow-up innovations.[5] The question is whether different degrees of novelty can also be distinguished *ex ante*. Such differences correlate with the uncertainty surrounding an up-coming novelty. The higher the degree of novelty, the more novelty-induced uncertainty seems to loom. To determine the extent of novelty-induced uncertainty, it would therefore be desirable to have a measure for the *ex ante* degree of novelty.

In a procedural approach to novelty it is straightforward to try to derive differences in the degree of novelty from constraints that can be imposed on the generative and/or interpretative operation on a priori grounds. An example of such constraints was given above with the contextual constraints relevant for the combinatory extensions (i-c) and (ii-c). Indeed, if the generative operation and its outcomes are known, those combinations that *cannot* be generated by that operation can be excluded from the subsequent interpretative operation, thus reducing substantially the input set on which it is based.

A simple example is an urn with 49 balls numbered from 1 to 49 and a mechanical device by which 6 balls are drawn from that urn at random in an unbiased way without replacement and without observing the order of the drawings. (This is the basis of a popular weekly bet offered by the state lottery in some European countries.) In this example, no outcome other than a combination of 6 different integers between 1 and 49 can ever be generated. To give another example, imagine a unit box that is subjected to the "baker transformation" (Prigogine, 1993). This means that the box is squashed to half its height and double its length, cut in the middle, and re-composed by putting the cut-off right half on top of the left. The outcome of the transformation is the spatial relocation of the coordinates of all points in the unit box by a deterministic rule, yet the future coordinates of any two initially chosen points disappear quickly from sight, the further ahead an iteration of the transformation is. All that can (trivially) be excluded in this example is that no point will ever fall outside the unit box.

Regarding the interpretative operation, the fact that it is not fully understood makes it difficult, if not impossible, to impose *ex ante* constraints on it or its outcome. What can often be observed, but should not be confused with the desirable constraints, is that criteria are invoked *ex ante* by which the outcome of the interpretative operation is to be assessed *ex post*. For example, for a given technical or economic problem, some desirable features of its unknown solution may be specified in advance. The novelty resulting from the subsequent creative search process may then be assessed *ex post* as to whether it represents a solution to the problem with the desired features.

The deviation of actually emerging novelty from the expectations formed before may *ex post* be taken as a measure of subjective surprise. It is clear, though, that such an *ex post* assessment of surprise cannot have any bearing on an *ex ante* degree of novelty, nor can an *ex ante* assessment of "potential surprise" have any bearing. The cardinal measure of potential surprise was suggested by Shackle (1949) as an alternative for deriving subjective probabilities. It rates events that are *ex ante* imagined (and hence anticipated) by a decision maker according to how surprising their later occurrence would subjectively be felt by the decision maker. In contrast, novelty is something that, by definition, is not anticipated.[6]

It seems, thus, that the interpretative operation is either non-trivial, so that no constraint can *ex ante* be imposed on the operation and its outcomes,[7] or it is a trivial operation in the sense that the meaning of all possible outcomes is already known beforehand. This is, in particular, the case when the generative operation implies a binding interpretation for all its outcomes as in the examples of the (stochastic) lottery and the (deterministic) baker transformation. No associative act is needed anymore for making sense of the results. In view of this condition, the conclusion that can be derived from the feasible *ex ante* constraints is rather weak.

Hypothesis 6. The *ex ante* degree of novelty is minimal (but not necessarily zero) if the generative operation is known and the interpretative operation is trivial in the sense that the meaning of all its possible outcomes is known beforehand. The

---

[5] See the examples in Silverberg and Verspagen (2003). The distinction can be traced back to Schumpeter (1934, pp. 64–66) who stresses in his theory of entrepreneurial innovations the role of novelty that discontinues previous lines of technological and organizational development. The deeper issue here are the gradualist vs. saltationalist theories of evolution (see Rosser, 1992 for a discussion) that implicitly presuppose a distinction of different degrees of novelty.

[6] A striking example is the "Arcanum" story (Gleeson, 1999). In 1703 the German alchemist Johann Friedrich Boettger was imprisoned by August the Strong of Saxonia, because it was believed that he would be able to synthesize gold. A laboratory was set up for him at the fortress in Meissen. He probed and sifted there using several processes and materials, but instead of finding a recipe for making gold, 6 years later he invented a way to make white porcelain. A non-anticipated outcome like this (it is actually a case of a domain-specific novelty as, unknown to the western world, the way to make white porcelain had been known in China since ancient times) cannot be made part of an *ex ante* rating of potential surprise.

[7] Note that even an apparently trivial constraint like that of logical truth is not binding here. The construction of an erroneous mathematical proof may be as much novelty as the construction of a logically true one. The same holds for the validity of an empirical conjecture created by inductive inference; it is new independent of whether or not it can be confirmed. This is indeed the very basis for running science as a process of conjectures and refutations.

318   *U. Witt / Journal of Economic Behavior & Organization 70 (2009) 311–320*

degree of novelty is maximal where the generative operation is not known and no constraint can be imposed on the outcome of the interpretative operation.

Turning to the relationship between the degree of novelty and uncertainty, two questions can be posed. First, while the limiting case of a maximal degree of novelty is obviously associated with a state of complete (novelty-induced) uncertainty about what is going to be created, what is the nature of novelty-induced uncertainty in the other limiting case? Second, and following-up an answer to this question, what can be said about the degree of novelty, or novelty-induced uncertainty, in the range between the two extremes?

In the case of a minimal degree of novelty, to start with that question, there is still something not known *ex ante*. Consider the lottery example. Assuming that the true bias status of the drawing device is known, all possible outcomes of a future run can be anticipated. However, because it is generated by a random mechanism, what is not yet known is the particular subset of integers drawn at a certain date or iteration in the future. However, precisely because all possible outcomes and the nature of the sampling mechanism are known, there is a basis for deriving probabilities. Lacking evidence to the contrary, all possible outcomes can be treated as equally probable so that degrees of likelihood of, or belief in, all possible outcomes can be constructed as a cardinal measure of uncertainty in the probabilistic sense.

More generally speaking, the feature that is still unknown in a state where the degree of novelty is minimal is exactly the object on which probability theory focuses when arguing that something is not yet known with certainty. An instance indicative of this constellation is Zabell (1992) attempt at "predicting the unpredictable". Zabell explores the emergence of novelty under the assumption that the emergence is a serial phenomenon. His example is the emergence of a new species. A finite number of organisms already exist. They are classified into different species. New organisms are continually added. They can either represent an already known species or a new one (the so-called "sampling of species problem"). Zabell is able to derive the probability for the event that a newly added organism represents a new species. In terms of the present approach, what Zabell predicts has a minimal degree of novelty. As in the case of the lottery, all possible outcomes of the generative operation can be anticipated. The interpretative operation is trivial, adding no new meaning to any of the two possible outcomes. What is not known with certainty is whether or not the next living organism added will indeed increase the number of existing species by 1.

Regarding the second question above, it can be more specifically asked now whether the reduction of novelty-induced uncertainty to uncertainty in the probabilistic sense is also possible for a degree of novelty in the range between minimal and the maximal ones. By Hypothesis 6, the degree of novelty is greater than minimal, but less than maximal, if one of the following conditions holds. Either the outcome of the interpretative operation is non-trivial, but possible outcomes of the generative operation are known *ex ante*, or the outcome of the interpretative operation is trivial, but the outcome of the generative operation cannot be anticipated.

Consider the first condition. Since the meaning of what comes out of the interpretative operation is not known beforehand, the information available *ex ante* is no longer sufficient to specify the state space required for constructing a probability measure. Zabell's "sampling of species problem" can be used to illustrate the difference. The outcome of the interpretative operation would not be trivial (and, hence, the *ex ante* degree of novelty would be greater than minimal) if, instead of predicting the mere occurrence of a new species, the problem were to predict the *properties* of the new species. However, in contrast to Zabell's probability model in which the state space can recursively be determined by adding a further organism of either an already existing species or a new one, the state space would now have to be made dependent on the number of different properties of the new species, something not yet known.[8]

Now consider the case where the interpretative operation is trivial, but the outcome of the generative operation cannot be anticipated. Again, there is no basis for specifying the state space required for a probability model. An instructive example is the process resulting from Prigogine's iterated baker transformation. Whatever the transformation generates, its interpretation is indeed known beforehand: it will always be the coordinates of two points in the unit box. In fact, even the generative operation is clearly defined by the deterministic relocation rule. Nonetheless, in many cases, the position which two initially chosen points subsequently take can no longer be anticipated for iterations further ahead into the future.[9] The outcome needs to be induced by carrying out the generative operation over and over again.

For the relationships between the concept of novelty-induced uncertainty on the one hand and the probabilistic concept of uncertainty on the other, it follows from these considerations:

---

[8] When such information is lacking, probability theory traditionally resorts to the notion of equi-probability or equi-possibility to compensate for the information deficit (see Hacking, 1975, Chapter 14). However, these notions cannot be extended to an as yet unknown number of cases or variants, except in the trivial sense that everything is possible, see Shackle (1973, Chapter 1) and his "residual hypothesis" verdict.

[9] It is sufficient here to demonstrate this for the horizontal distance d, $0 < d \leq 1$, between the two points (cp. Prigogine, 1993). d is multiplied by a "factor 2 modulo 1" transforming d into $d' = \begin{cases} 2d, & \text{if } 0 < 2d \leq 1, \\ 2d - 1, & \text{if } 2d > 1. \end{cases}$ Any value that d can take can be represented as the sum of some elements of the geometric series 2^{-n}, $n = 0, 1, 2, \ldots$ Mark the position of each of the elements in the geometric series that sum up to d with 1 and all other positions up to the smallest element of the sum with 0. This results in a binary string of varying length. Each iteration of the baker transformation can then be expressed in terms of a Bernoulli shift (i.e. a shift by which the zeros and ones of the binary string are moved by one position) to the left. Now let $d = \sqrt{2} - 1$. In this case, the number of elements in the geometric series required to represent this value, and hence the corresponding binary string, are infinite. It is not possible, therefore, to derive the evolution of d by extrapolation of the Bernoulli shift. This is a simple case of a chaotic time series in which novelty can emerge (cp. also Smale's 1967 "horseshoe" model).

U. Witt / Journal of Economic Behavior & Organization 70 (2009) 311–320   319

Hypothesis 7. Novelty-induced uncertainty reduces to uncertainty in the probabilistic sense measured by the degree of likelihood or belief if, and only if, the degree of novelty is minimal. In the limiting case of a degree of novelty equal to zero, known outcomes occur with probability 1(certainty).

On a priori grounds our knowledge does not suffice to weigh how lacking information about the generative operation impacts the degree of novelty compared to the impact of a lack of information about the interpretative operation. A comparative assessment of the number, relevance, and/or conditionality of possible constraints on the two operations is not feasible. For this reasons there is no possibility of deriving a consistent ranking for the *ex ante* degree of novelty between the minimal and the maximal degrees, not to speak of a cardinal measure. Consequently, what our knowledge allows is only the weakest possible ordering (cp. Keynes, 1921, Chapter II).

Hypothesis 8. The *ex ante* degree of novelty (and, hence, novelty-induced uncertainty) can, on a priori grounds, be determined as being maximal, less than maximal but greater than minimal, or minimal (with limiting case of a zero degree of novelty).

Because of its peculiar epistemological status, novelty-induced uncertainty is a much less structured concept than uncertainty in the probabilistic sense.[10]

6. Conclusions

Why is it so difficult to work with the notion of novelty? How does novelty emerge? Are there different degrees of novelty, and if so, how do they relate to the concepts of uncertainty? In this paper an attempt has been made to answer these questions. Novelty was defined as something that was unknown before a particular point in time and that, hence, was discovered or created at that point in time. It was argued that novelty emerges from two logically distinct operations, a generative one and an interpretative one. To take advantage of our capacity to grasp the meaning of novelty intuitively, a semantic representation of novelty was chosen to explain this in more detail. The generative operation was shown to (re-) combine conceptual inputs given here in the form of propositional networks. With respect to the interpretative operation, it had to be acknowledged that the way in which meaning (if any) is attributed in a conceptual integration to the newly generated combinations is not yet understood and that it therefore cannot be carried out outside the human mind. Nonetheless, the insights into the generative and the interpretative operations that are feasible allow some conclusion to be drawn.

One of the conclusions is that the peculiar epistemic status of novelty is caused by the inductive nature of the operations from which it emerges. These operations need to be carried out in real time before any novelty can be revealed. Another conclusion is that, by the very operation by which they are generated, all newly created cognitive concepts are made up of elements that have previously been known. Since newly created concepts can be used, in turn, as inputs for iterating the generative operation, ever more extended compositions of known elements evolve. Starting from conceptual input sets with a finite number of elements, an infinite number of new concepts can be created. The expansion of human thought is thus a cumulative process that feeds itself.

Since it seems to make a big difference whether a particular novelty is only a minor variation of something already known or whether it is altogether new, the paper also discussed the possibility of distinguishing between different degrees of novelty *ex ante*. Differences in this degree correlate with the uncertainty surrounding an up-coming novelty. In the procedural approach to novelty that was chosen in this paper, differences in the degree of novelty are likely to result from constraints that can be imposed on the generative and/or interpretative operations on a priori grounds. Such constraints were shown to relate to how much is known about the properties of the two operations and their possible outcomes.

Accordingly, the degree of novelty and, hence, the uncertainty surrounding an up-coming novelty were argued to be maximal where the generative operation is not known and no constraint can be imposed on the outcomes of the interpretative operation. It could be demonstrated that, at the other end of the range, the *ex ante* degree of novelty is minimal, but not necessarily zero, if the outcomes of the generative operation and the meaning of all possible outcomes of the interpretative operation are known beforehand. There may then still be features of up-coming novelty that are not known with certainty, but for these it is possible to derive degrees of likelihood. Hence, novelty-induced uncertainty in this special case reduces to uncertainty in the probabilistic sense. For degrees of novelty between the two extremes, novelty-induced uncertainty cannot be reduced to uncertainty in the probabilistic sense, nor can, for epistemological reasons, an ordinal or even cardinal measure of the degree of novelty be established.

References

Anderson, J.R., 2000. Cognitive Psychology and Its Implications, 5th edition. Worth Publishers, New York.
Bäck, T., 1996. Evolutionary Algorithms in Theory and Practice. Oxford University Press, Oxford.
Boden, M.A., 1999. Computer models of creativity. In: Sternberg, R.J. (Ed.), Handbook of Creativity. Cambridge University Press, Cambridge, pp. 351–372.
Campbell, D.T., 1960. Blind variation and selective retention in creative thought as in other knowledge processes. Psychological Review 67, 380–400.
de Solla Price, D.J., 1963. Little Science, Big Science. Columbia University Press, New York.

---

[10] If a distinction between risk and uncertainty as in Knight (1921, Chapter VII) is made, novelty-induced uncertainty is a case of Knightian uncertainty.

Edelman, G.M., Tononi, G., 2000. A Universe of Consciousness: How Matter Becomes Imagination. Basic Books, New York.
Fauconnier, G., Turner, M., 2002. The Way We Think – Conceptual Blending and the Mind's Hidden Complexities. Basic Books, New York.
Finke, R.A., Ward, T.B., Smith, S.M., 1992. Creative Cognition – Theory, Research, and Applications. MIT Press, Cambridge, MA.
Gentner, D., Markman, A.B., 1997. Structure mapping in analogy and similarity. American Psychologist 52, 45–56.
Gleeson, J., 1999. Arcanum. Warner Books, New York.
Hacking, I., 1975. The Emergence of Probability. Cambridge University Press, Cambridge.
Hayek, F.A., 1952. The Sensory Order – An Inquiry into the Foundations of Theoretical Psychology. Routledge and Kegan Paul, London.
Hodgson, G.M., Knudsen, T., 2006. Why we need a generalized Darwinism, and why generalized Darwinism is not enough. Journal of Economic Behavior and Organization 61, 1–19.
Hofstadter, D.R., Fluid Analogies Research Group, 1995. Fluid Concepts and Creative Analogies. Basic Books, New York.
Holland, J.H., 1992. Adaptation in Natural and Artificial Systems, 2nd edition. MIT Press, Cambridge, MA.
Johnson-Laird, P.N., 2005. Flying bicycles: How the Wright Brothers invented the airplane. Mind & Society 4, 27–48.
Keynes, J.M., 1921. A Treatise on Probability. MacMillan, London.
Knight, F.H., 1921. Risk, Uncertainty and Profit. Chicago University Press, Chicago.
Koch, C., Crick, F., 2000. Some thoughts on consciousness and neuroscience. In: Gazzaniga, M.S. (Ed.), The New Cognitive Neurosciences, 2nd edition. MIT Press, Cambridge, MA, pp. 1285–1294.
Koestler, A., 1964. The Act of Creation. Hutchinson & Co., London.
Kohonen, T., 1987. Self-organization and Associative Memory, 2nd edition. Springer, Berlin.
Machlup, F., 1980. Knowledge and Knowledge Production. Princeton University Press, Princeton.
Markose, S.M., 2004. Novelty in complex adaptive systems (CAS) dynamics: a computational theory of actor innovation. Physica A: Statistical Mechanics and Its Applications 344, 41–49.
Markose, S.M., 2005. Computability and evolutionary complexity: markets as complex adaptive systems. Economic Journal 115, F159–F192.
Mokyr, J., 1990. Twenty-Five Centuries of Technological Change – An Historical Survey. Harwood, Chur (Switzerland).
Nersessian, N.J., 2002. Abstraction via generic modeling in concept formation in science. Mind & Society 3, 129–154.
Newell, A., Simon, H.A., 1972. Human Problem Solving. Englewood Cliffs, Prentice Hall.
Prigogine, I., 1993. Bounded rationality: from dynamical systems to socio-economic models. In: Day, R.H., Chen, P. (Eds.), Nonlinear Dynamics and Evolutionary Economics. Oxford University Press, Oxford, pp. 3–13.
Rescher, N., 1989. Cognitive Economy: The Economic Dimension of the Theory of Knowledge. University of Pittsburgh Press, Pittsburgh.
Rogers, E., 1995. Diffusion of Innovations. Free Press, New York.
Rosser Jr., J.B., 1992. The dialogue between the economic and the ecologic theories of evolution. Journal of Economic Behavior and Organization 17, 195–215.
Schumpeter, J.A., 1934. Theory of Economic Development. Harvard University Press, Cambridge, MA.
Shackle, G.L.S., 1949. Expectation in Economics. Cambridge University Press, Cambridge.
Shackle, G.L.S., 1973. Epistemics and Economics – A Critique of Economic Doctrines. Cambridge University Press, Cambridge.
Silverberg, G., Verspagen, B., 2003. Breaking the waves: a Poisson regression approach to Schumpeterian clustering of basic innovations. Cambridge Journal of Economics 27, 671–693.
Smale, S., 1967. Differentiable dynamical systems. Bulletin of the American Mathematical Society 73, 747–817.
Sternberg, R.J. (Ed.), 1999. Handbook of Creativity. Cambridge University Press, Cambridge.
Swift, J., 1934. In: Hayward, J. (Ed.), Gulliver's Travels and Selected Writings in Prose and Verse. Random House, New York.
Usher, A.P., 1954. A History of Mechanical Inventions. Harvard University Press, Cambridge, MA.
Vincenti, W.G., 1990. What Engineers Know and How They Know It. Johns Hopkins University Press, Baltimore.
Weitzman, M.L., 1998. Recombinant growth. The Quarterly Journal of Economics 113, 331–360.
Witt, U., 1993. Emergence and dissemination of innovations: some principles of evolutionary economics. In: Day, R.H., Chen, P. (Eds.), Nonlinear Dynamics and Evolutionary Economics. Oxford University Press, Oxford, pp. 91–100.
Zabell, S.L., 1992. Predicting the unpredictable. Synthése 90, 205–232.

[8]

Novelty and the bounds of unknowledge in economics

Ulrich Witt*

Max Planck Institute of Economics, Germany

Economic development and growth are driven by the emergence of new technologies, new products and services, new institutions, new policies, and so on. Important though it is, the emergence of novelty is not well understood. Epistemological and methodological problems make it a difficult research topic. They imply a 'bound of unknowledge' (Shackle) for economic theorizing wherever novelty occurs in economic life. To make progress, this paper takes stock of the problems. The methodological consequences for causal explanations and the modelling of economics dynamics are discussed, and some possibilities for positively theorizing about novelty are outlined.

Keywords: novelty; epistemic bounds; abduction; causation; dynamical systems; economic change; evolution

I Introduction

Innovations are a constitutive element of economic life today. They revolutionize production and trade, employment and consumption, and fuel competition, structural change, and economic growth. These developments, in turn, trigger innovative political responses that induce regulatory and institutional change. At the core of all these innovations is novelty, one of the most amorphous scientific objects. To deal with innovations in the economy thus means grappling with novelty, this ubiquitous agent of change. How does it come about? How can economic theorizing account for the fact that, by its very nature, novelty is something unpredictable? What constitutes the epistemic bounds? Given the enormous economic impact of innovations, taking a closer look at the nature of novelty seems warranted.

Novelty, in the sense of something not previously existing, occurs in many forms and guises. To the extent to which novelty is man-made, its ultimate source is the creative activity of the human mind. Research into human creativity (e.g. Sternberg 1999), cognitive science and linguistics (e.g. Finke, Ward, and Smith 1992; Hofstadter and the Fluid Analogies Research Group 1995; Fauconnier and Turner 2002), and the history of science and technology (e.g. Usher 1954; Vincenti 1990; Mokyr 2002 to mention just a few) have provided many insights into how people arrive at novelty. Yet, none of these different strands of thought have directly focused on, or resulted in, a systematic account of novelty itself and its properties. One of the reasons for this neglect may be the problems associated with the very nature of novelty.

With respect to the point in time at which novelty emerges and reveals its meaning, theorizing about novelty can be done alternatively from *ex ante* or *ex post* points of view. The epistemological difference is that, in the first case, novelty is synonymous with

ISSN 1350-178X print/ISSN 1469-9427 online
© 2009 Taylor & Francis
DOI: 10.1080/13501780903339269
http://www.informaworld.com

something 'unknowable' while, in the latter case, it is synonymous with something 'not previously known'. Distinctions similar to these have often been suggested (Machlup 1980, chap. 8; Witt 1993; Boden 1999). Yet, their epistemological implications, which complicate the scientific analysis of novelty in a characteristic way, have rarely been addressed. As far as novelty created in the human mind is concerned, there is an additional problem. The explanation of how it emerges hinges critically on what happens in our minds when we think, experience, or do something new. Despite considerable progress in the past, these mental processes are still far from being known. The act by which new meaning is created is neither well understood (not to speak of the underlying neuronal processes in the brain, see Koch and Crick 2000; Edelman and Tononi 2000), nor can its outcome be predicted. For this reason, the 'bounds of unknowledge' (Shackle 1983) seem to be a hard constraint – not only for economic theorizing.

In this paper, the underlying problems will be discussed in more detail with the intention to explore where precisely the bounds to positively dealing with novelty are. Section II suggests a procedural approach to the emergence of novelty. Using the example of new cognitive concepts, the approach identifies two different operations involved in the creation of novelty. The distinction helps to understand what happens in the human mind when novelty emerges. Section III turns to the sources of the conceptual and epistemological problems induced by novelty and derives the conditions for post-revelation analysis in economic theorizing (the usual case) as opposed to a pre-revelation analysis of novelty. On this basis, section IV discusses some practices of modelling economic dynamics. In view of the role of novelty it is argued that the domain in which analytically solvable models can be applied is confined to the context of post-revelation analysis. In the light of the findings, section V addresses the question of whether the emergence of novelty is indeed an exogenous shock (as it is usually treated in economics), and relates the question to the more general problem of causation. Section VI offers the conclusions and a brief outlook on what the novelty-induced bounds of unknowledge might imply for the direction of future economic analysis.

II   Novelty emerging from (re-) combination and intuitive inductive inference

To the extent to which novelty originates from human thought, its imagining or discovery is the result of an inductive mental act of the brain (Knight 1996). If it informs and motivates new action, this is an input to the transformation of economic reality that comes from within the economy, and that is, in this sense, endogenous. But is it also endogenous in the sense that its explanation is covered by economic theory? Obviously, this depends on what can be said more specifically about that creative, mental act. It has often been argued to be some form of recombinatory, inductive logic. In his treatise on the act of creation, Arthur Koestler (1964, Part II) refers to a large number of proponents of such a combinatory principle and provides several compelling examples. He argues that a displacement of attention to something not previously noted brings new elements into focus in a given context, elements that have not previously been associated with that context. Although they come from a different frame of reference, the new elements must in some way be similar to the already familiar elements, so that some associative basis is given. Identifying a previously hidden analogy – an act which Koestler calls 'bisociation' – gives rise to the discovery of novelty.

It is indeed important to note that simply recombining some elements is not sufficient for arriving at novel insights. An element that is drawn, perhaps accidentally, from a different context, and therefore represents something foreign to the given context does not induce a new meaning unless the difference can be aligned with the given context (Gentner and Markman 1997). Only if the conceptual inputs to be blended have some kind of similarity – some common element – can their non-common elements be integrated in an associative act into a new, meaningful concept (Fauconnier and Turner 2002, chap. 3). Whether or not there is some kind of similarity is, of course, a matter of conceptual judgement that needs to be exerted independent of the actual recombination. Often the similarity criterion is implicitly ensured by admitting only sufficiently similar input sets or input spaces to the recombination. As long as the similarity requirement is satisfied, the recombination – or, more generally, the generative operation – can, in principle, be done by any arbitrary device. The integration of what is newly recombined into a newly emerging, meaningful concept requires an own, interpretative operation. In the human mind, generating recombinations and interpreting them may coincide. From an analytical point of view, however, the generative and the interpretative operations are logically distinct.

The difference between the two operations can best be demonstrated by a semantic representation. (At the semantic level we can take advantage of our capacity to recognize similarity and difference spontaneously and to grasp the induced new meaning intuitively.) Consider cognitive concepts which are so simple that they can be represented by sentences with just a subject, a predicate, and an object, for instance, the two factual statements: 'grain grows in tufts' and 'grain can be cut by scythes'. The two statements have the subject 'grain' in common. In cognitive psychology, such statements, sharing a concept indicated by the same subject, are taken as representations of what is called 'propositional networks' (Anderson 2000, chap. 5). The structure of the propositional network can be denoted more formally by:

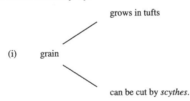

$$\text{(i)} \quad \text{grain} \begin{array}{c} \diagup \ \ \text{grows in tufts} \\ \\ \diagdown \ \ \text{can be cut by } \textit{scythes.} \end{array}$$

Propositional networks like (i) are used to encode conceptual knowledge that people associate with a cognitive concept like 'grain'. If people are given such a concept, they start associating several things connected with the concept in their memory. If people are given another concept, say 'hair', and are asked to come up with what they associate with this concept, it may happen that the result is the factual statements 'hair grows in tufts' and 'hair can be cut by clippers'. The corresponding propositional network would be:

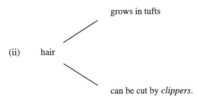

$$\text{(ii)} \quad \text{hair} \begin{array}{c} \diagup \ \ \text{grows in tufts} \\ \\ \diagdown \ \ \text{can be cut by } \textit{clippers.} \end{array}$$

The propositional networks (i) and (ii) have a certain similarity. More specifically, the syntactic structure is identical, and they share the elements not in italics. The recombinant, generative operation then means using the common elements as the basis to recombine the non-common ones (put in italics). Thus, exchanging the subjects 'grain' and 'hair' for each other in (i) and in (ii) results in two new combinations: '*grain* can be cut *by clippers*', and '*hair* can be cut *by scythes*'. Our intuition tells us that the latter statement does not appear to make sense. Not so, however, the former. Here the common element may allow a conceptual integration. As a matter of fact, this association is said to have inspired McCormack's invention of the mechanical reaper (Martindale 1999).

For logical completeness, it should be mentioned that the original statement '*grain* can be cut *by scythes*' is not invalidated. The newly created statement can therefore be combined into what will be called here a combinatory extension of the form

(iii)   '*grain* can be cut *by scythes and clippers*'.

It may be stated in passing that the fact that meaningful recombinations often result in combinatory extensions is important for understanding the relationships between novelty and the extension of knowledge.

Independent of their meaning, any two different propositional networks like (i) and (ii) that satisfy a formal similarity requirement can be recombined in a similar way. Hence, the generative operation itself requires no semantic knowledge. It is an arbitrary procedure and can easily be imagined to be carried out mechanically or by an alpha-numerical algorithm laid down in a computer program. However, carrying out the generative procedure – whether mechanically or electronically – is only one and, in fact, the easier part of the problem. What is lacking is a way of discriminating between combinatory extensions that do make sense and those that do not. This is the interpretative operation by which conceptual similarity is identified and semantic meaning or sense is attributed. Is there anything more specific that can be said about the interpretative operation which, in the above example, has been left for our intuitive comprehension to be carried out?

Referring to Peirce (1934), it is sometimes argued that the logic by which novelty is found is that of an abductive inference (Magnani 2002; Aliseda 2006, chap. 2). An abduction is a logical operation by which conjectures about possible reasons for an observed fact (in need of being explained) are derived. Finding a possible, not yet known reason or explanation for an observed fact certainly involves creating novelty, albeit a kind of novelty slightly different from discovering possible new facts (as in the previous example). However, to logically reconstruct in terms of an abductive inference the relationship between an observed fact and its conjectured reason is not the same as inquiring into what happens in the creative act on which the interpretative operation is based.[1] With its focus on the conditions of the conceptual integration of (i) and (ii) invited by the suggestive cross-over, the procedural approach taken here offers a somewhat closer grip on the creative act.[2] Yet even this approach is not sufficient to discriminate between statement 'grain can be cut by scythes and clippers' and statement 'hair can be cut by scythes and clippers'. The understanding of why the one seems to make sense, while the other does not, hinges on the still pending explanation of how the human brain accomplishes the spontaneous interpretative operation.

In cognitive science, it has been suggested to interpret the creative act as a search process in an extremely high-dimensional memory space looking for possible connections on the basis of some probabilistic measure of 'closeness' of cognitive concepts (Kohonen 1987). However, this abstract description is not specific enough to explain the intuitive associative act in the human mind nor does its algorithmic representation allow the act to be carried out artificially. To do so in the form of a computer algorithm, say, would require being able to handle the complexity of a myriad of selectively activated neural nets – something which is currently out of reach (see Edelman and Tononi 2000, chap. 10). For this reason, unlike in the case of the generative operation, the interpretative operation cannot (at present) be transferred to non-human intelligence, not to speak of any device by which its outcome could be predicted. Instead, what is needed for the interpretative operation to be carried out is to draw the intuitive inductive inference *in vivo* by the human mind *pace* its not yet understood associative power.

III The epistemic problem

Speculative imaginings that have emerged from recombinations as discussed in the previous section often precede inventions and discoveries. More or less vague, or even erroneous, new ideas may inspire and motivate people to search for ways of turning their visions into reality – McCormack's invention of the mechanical reaper being a case in point. However, the search processes induced often transcend the sphere of the individual and become an object of collective efforts. Unlike the very conceiving of novelty, its further use and practical application may employ a whole population of agents who have somehow learned about a new idea. In logical terms, when the information about novelty propagates, this is, of course, no longer the emergence, but rather the dissemination of novelty. For each single agent encountering the artefact or idea for the first time, it may then feel like a discovery or experience of novelty. This fact connects to the already mentioned asymmetry in viewing novelty *ex ante* vs. viewing it *ex post*. The asymmetry – also holding for novelty not originating from, but experienced by, the human mind implies that there are actually two epistemologically different usages of the term 'novelty'.

An agent who is exposed for the first time to something that other people already know, encounters the novelty only relative to her current state of knowledge. This kind of novelty can be classified as *subjective* or psychological. If, in contrast, an agent encounters novelty that no one else has ever experienced before, then this is novelty in an *objective* or historical sense. From an epistemological point of view, the constraints to theorizing about subjective novelty on the one hand, and objective novelty on the other, differ significantly. In the case of subjective novelty, other people, including, perhaps, a scientific observer, already hold some knowledge about the properties and implications of that particular novelty. On that basis, it may be possible to formulate hypotheses about, e.g. the reaction patterns of the agents exposed to that novelty. Indeed, this is common practice in diffusion research (cf. Rogers 1995). In the case of objective novelty, in contrast, there is nobody – not even a scientific observer – who has any experience which theorizing about that novelty could be based on.

What implications does this epistemological constraint – the 'bounds of unknowledge' as Shackle (1983) put it – have? One consequence is that, in all scientific domains in which novelty can emerge, all predictions and projections are contingent on the possible intervention of as yet unknown, newly generated novelty. Obviously, this contingency hampers the predictive power in scientific disciplines in whose domains novelty is a generically occurring feature. These are, in particular, the evolutionary sciences that face endogenously generated novelty. For example, the potential emergence of genetic novelty makes it impossible to predict the future course of evolution in evolutionary biology. Likewise, the potential creation of mental novelty constrains the ambition to predict cultural, scientific, or economic developments. However, regarding the scientific practice, the contingency on non-predictable novelty may not always be equally relevant. In dealing with the explanation of phenomena and conditions relating to the creation of novelty, the fact that the meaning of novelty cannot be anticipated is a crucial constraint. But when it comes to explaining what effects and consequences a just created novelty has, assuming that the informational content or meaning of that novelty has already fully been revealed, may often seem justified. The difference again relates to the *ex ante* vs. *ex post* asymmetry or, more specifically, the difference between *pre*-revelation analysis and *post*-revelation analysis (Witt 1993).

The methodological implications of this difference are significant. In post-revelation analysis it is usually assumed that the scientific observer knows all the relevant properties of the novelty under consideration. If, in addition, it is assumed that no further novelty will intervene in the post-revelation analysis, the epistemological constraint is factually eliminated. (The occurrence and revelation of the particular novelty considered is shifted to the antecedent conditions.) Most diffusion theories that deal with the adoption of subjective novelty make these assumptions – often tacitly. These are, of course, simplifying assumptions that may be counter-factual. Important implications of some particular novelty are very often discovered only after significant delay. Harmful side effects of scientific and technological innovations that become evident only years, or even decades, after their large-scale introduction are cases in point. Similarly, the no-further-novelty-intervening assumption is often illusionary, particularly in the domain of evolutionary theories where the generation of novelty is endemic and is often triggered by novelty that has occurred before (Witt 2003). Thus, the predictive strength of post-revelation analysis is a contingent one. Pre-revelation analysis does not hinge on such provisos, but its power obviously suffers from the lack of predictability.

IV   Limitations of dynamic economic models in dealing with novelty

The methodological consequences of novelty discussed so far seem obvious. Nonetheless, when dynamic models are used in disciplines like economics where the emergence of novelty is a ubiquitous feature these consequences are often not accounted for or not even recognized. The notion of dynamics is originally an outgrowth of the deterministic Newtonian physics of celestial bodies where novelty has no role to play. The main interest there is the mathematical description of equilibrium orbits of gravitating systems and the analysis of the stability conditions, i.e. patterns of convergence to these unique states of rest. The appeal of this kind of dynamics is that it allows the use of differential equations whose implications can be derived analytically, and, hence, be anticipated, once the specification and the initial conditions are known.

Despite the fact that it is a characteristic for the economy and its history that novelty/innovations emerge over and again, general equilibrium theory in economics extends this 'closed' version of dynamics to the economic domain. It is claimed (Fisher 1983) that this kind of economic theorizing is concerned only with the price system's stability or capacity to return to the state of general equilibrium after an 'exogenous shock', i.e. an unexplained effect that disrupts the equilibrium state in the markets from outside. The emergence of novelty is accounted for (if at all) by treating it as one sort of such exogenous shocks. The sole purpose of these models is thus to demonstrate whether, and under what assumptions, a convergence to the equilibrium is *logically* possible, and whether the convergence is monotonous or cyclical; or whether it is even approaching a limit cycle.

Taking such a restricted view on theorizing in economics has often been criticized, particularly by authors who focus on economic change and consider innovations central to its understanding (e.g. Nelson and Winter 1982, chap. 2). When it comes to modelling economic change, the critics of course also make use of dynamic models (deterministic and stochastic differential or difference equations). The goal is to analyse not the stability conditions of unique equilibria but rather the out-of-equilibrium features of the processes of change. On closer inspection it turns out, however, that the nature of the dynamics in the two cases is not all that much different even when assuming stochastic processes.

Consider, for example, the analysis of the diffusion or adoption processes of innovations (see Metcalfe 1988). The basic idea here can be put as follows. The utility that can be derived from adopting an innovation, and hence the agents' probability to adopt, systematically change with the number of adopters. The quality or versatility of an innovation may, for example, decline with a rising relative frequency of adopters. Or the individual competitive advantage accruing from an innovation may fade away as more competitors in the market adopt the innovation too. In more abstract terms, this is the logic of a frequency-dependency effect. The underlying mean process can be captured by the simple quasi-deterministic function $q(t) = f(F(t))$ that maps the relative frequency of adopters $F(t)$ at time t (via the implicit utility assessment) into the expected probability $q(t)$ that an agent who decides in t will adopt the innovation. If $q(t) > F(t)$, the expected relative share of adopters increases and it decreases of $q(t) < F(t)$.

Obviously, the shape of function f determines what happens on average during the diffusion process. For example, in the case of a quadratic specification $q(t) = aF(t) - aF(t)^2$, with $a > 0$, $F(t)$ grows to an upper bound F_a, $0 < F_a \leq 1$, that depends on the size of a. The expected change in F over time can be approximated by $[F(t + \Delta t) - F(t)] / \Delta t = q(t)/m$. Let the number m of potential adopters be very large. Inserting the quadratic specification above and taking the limit then results in:

$$dF(t)/dt = \alpha F(t) - \alpha F(t)^2 \qquad (1)$$

with $\alpha = a/m$. By integration of Equation (1) the diffusion path can be shown to follow an S-shaped logistic trend as it has been associated with the diffusion of innovations since the seminal study by Griliches (1957).

Another example of a frequently found model of out-of-equilibrium dynamics is given by selection processes. Selection can be assumed to operate, e.g. on cost differentials between competing firms that result if some of the competitors innovate (see Metcalfe 1994). Consider a competitive market with a uniform price $p(t)$. Let $s_i(t)$ denote the market share of firm $i = 1, \ldots, n$ at time t measured in terms of output. The average level of unit cost in the industry is given by $c(t) = \Sigma_i s_i(t) \times c_i$, where c_i is the constant unit cost of firm i. Because in a competitive market $p(t) = c(t)$, the average profit (per unit) in the industry, $\pi(t) = 0$. For at least one firm i, however, the individual profit $\pi_i = p(t) - c_i > 0$ unless the entire market is served by the firm with the lowest level of unit cost. Now let the change of the size of firm i over time be expressed by the increment of its market share $ds_i(t)/dt$. Assume furthermore that the latter is a monotonic function φ of the firm's profit per unit – the very core of the selection analogy – weighed by its market share. After trivial transformations one then obtains:

$$ds_i(t)/dt = \varphi(c(t) - c_i)s_i(t) = \varphi(\pi_i(t) - \pi(t))s_i(t) \qquad (2)$$

Equation (2) is a 'replicator equation' (Hofbauer and Sigmund 1988, chap. 16). Analogously to the natural selection argument, it states that the performance differences between firms (fitness differences between reproducing organisms) translate into corresponding differential growth rates across the firms (differential growth rates of the corresponding gene frequencies in the population).

From a purely formal point of view, the diffusion model (1) and the selection model (2) have basically the same structure as the Walrasian auctioneer model in general equilibrium economics (Joosten 2006). The latter represents the out-of-equilibrium price adjustment dynamics by:

$$dp_j(t)/dt = g(x_{dj}(\mathbf{p}(t)) - x_{sj}) \tag{3}$$

where p_j denotes the price of commodity $j = 1, \ldots$ k, $\mathbf{p}(t)$ the price vector for all k commodities, x_{dj} the demand for, and x_{sj} the (fixed) supply of, commodity j. (The excess demand function g is assumed to be a sign preserving function with $g(0) = 0$.)

In Equation (1) to (3), the time increment of the dependent variable (the adopter frequency, the firms' market share, the price of a commodity) is made dependent on a measure for the distance from a state of rest which is characterized by the right-hand side of the equations taking the value 0. This means that all three models are based on the same 'closed' version of dynamics that is good for analysing the convergence to equilibria.[3] Hence, even when they do not explicitly call the generation of novelty/innovations an exogenous shock, diffusion and selection models actually relegate the emergence and revelation of novelty to the antecedent conditions. Moreover, they assume that no further novelty emerges during the convergence process. These are all the assumptions of post-revelation analysis, and it is this that the diffusion and selection models do – all mentioned contingencies included.

The same holds, in principle, for more sophisticated stochastic, dynamic models with multiple equilibria or attractors that are used to model the diffusion of competing innovations. The question here is which of the multiple equilibria will eventually be reached. The new feature is that, because of the multiplicity of the attractors, the answer depends no longer on the specification of the equations and the initial conditions alone, but also on the random influences the trajectory actually realized is subject to. This condition has been called the 'path-dependence' of such processes (Arthur 1994). Suppose that, unlike in the former diffusion model, there are two variants or standards of an innovation that serve the same user needs and therefore compete in their diffusion. Assume further that, for each of the variants, the users' utility rises with the number of adopters. Such 'increasing returns to adoption' have been found for e.g. electric current transmission, video recorder systems or the layout of typewriter keyboards (David 1985). In more abstract terms, the mean process is again based on the frequency dependency effect $q(t) = f(F(t))$, except that it now has inverse effects on the rival innovations: $q(t)$ now denotes the probability of adopting the first variant, $F(t)$ its share of adopters, and $1-q(t)$ and $(1-F(t))$ the respective values for the second variant.[4]

The simplest way of expressing a frequency dependency effect with these features is a cubic specification of the function f, i.e. $q(t) = 3F(t)^2 - 2F(t)^3$. With the same approximation for the change of $F(t)$ over time as before, this results in:

$$dF(t)/dt = \beta F(t)^2 - \gamma F(t)^3 \tag{4}$$

where $F(t)$ in Equation (4) is now the mean value and $\beta, \gamma > 0$, $\gamma/\beta = 2/3$. Suppose both variants become available simultaneously and offer the same inherent benefits. Hence, $q(0) = \frac{1}{2}$ and $F(0) = \frac{1}{2}$. Once $F(t) \neq \frac{1}{2}$, increasing returns to adoption raise the individual adoption probability more than proportionately for one of the variants. The realization of the stochastic diffusion process $F(t)$ initially fluctuates around $\frac{1}{2}$, but small historical events and cumulative random fluctuations drive the process in the direction of either $F = 0$ or $F = 1$ where the first or the second variant are gradually disappearing respectively. In fact, for t ∞ 4 the process will be 'locked in' to either one or the other attractor with probability

1 (Arthur, Ermoliev, and Kaniovski 1984). This amounts to a more complex convergence process, but still one that represents a 'closed' dynamics. Not surprisingly, the typical assumptions of post-revelation analysis can be found: the emergence of novelty – in this case the two competing innovations – is relegated to the antecedent conditions; no further novelty is assumed to emerge during the convergence process.

V   Causality issues – is the emergence of novelty an exogenous shock?

The discussion of the nature and role of novelty in this paper has been based on three hypotheses: first, that economic novelty is to a significant extent the result of human creative acts; second, that, to this extent, novelty emerges endogenously in the economy; third, that the emergence of novelty is a caused event. All three hypotheses can be contested (see Hodgson 1995 and 1999, chap. 6). One may raise objections to the idea of tracing the origins of novelty back to the activity of the human mind. Furthermore, one may object to the notion that the emergence of novelty has a cause (or many causes). Finally, even when conceding that man-made novelty is significant in the economic sphere and is a caused event, one may consider its emergence exogenous in the sense that the cause(s) fall outside the explanatory domain of economic theory. It seems appropriate, therefore, to discuss the hypotheses and their counter-arguments in more detail now.

Concerning the first hypothesis, it may be doubted that events like the Japanese–US war 1941–1945 in the Pacific or the breakdown of an institution like the Bretton Woods system of monetary alignment – which obviously qualify as historic novelty – are the result of a human creative act. The particular feature of such novel historic events is that they involve collective action and, as usually in cases of collective action, are not master-minded by one, however creative, single agent. To the contrary, at the level of the involved agents they are often not intended or even considered unwelcome outcomes. Nonetheless, it does not necessarily follow that such historic events are entirely unrelated to creative mental acts of individual agents (as Hodgson 1999, chap. 6 suggests). Unlike historic events not caused by human action, e.g. a natural disaster, collective action is, after all, originating from individual behaviour. Moreover, the trigger for the historic events can well be an innovative change of behaviour by some individuals. Thus, even if, say, the sudden collapse of an institution, e.g. a bank, can be attributed to the formation of a critical mass of agents who openly distrust the persistence of the institution as a proximate cause, the ultimate cause is the formation of this critical mass through innovative moves of some of the agent(s) involved that can rest on creative acts.

Regarding the causation hypothesis, it does not seem plausible that novelty is entirely uncaused.[5] A safe way to prove this assertion is to state the cause(s). Prior to that it needs to be recognized, however, that the causality question actually arises at two different levels of explanation. At the first level, the question is what causes the activities (searching, seeking inspiration, tinkering) from which novelty emerges. At the second level, the question is what causes the particular informational content of the novelty that those activities result in. Since the causes are likely to be different at the two level of explanation, it is sensible to decide what aspects of the emergence of novelty one wishes to attribute causes to. A concrete example may help to highlight the difference.

In the 1880s, Herman Hollerith invented a punch card based mechanism for electro-mechanically tabulating and sorting information.[6] The novelty that he created was a combination of three elements which, taken in isolation, were not all new: punch cards, coding numbers by a specifically placed hole on the card, and a mechanical reading device using spring-mounted needles that make an electrical connection while passing through the holes. Referring to the second level of explanation, it can be asked what caused this particular new combination to make sense in Hollerith's perception. This is the question of what the cause or causes for the creation of the special novel meaning was or were. It has repeatedly been mentioned that the associative act underlying the interpretative operation in the human brain is not well understood. Hence, even though there is no indication that the complex interpretative outcome (the particular meaning of the new combination of elements) was uncaused, it is admittedly difficult to state, even in principle, what the causes of the emergence of the specific new meaning were.

A different question, relating to the first level of explanation, is what caused Hollerith to seek to make such an invention in the first place. It refers to Hollerith's motivation to engage in explorative activities, a question not subject to the bounds of unknowledge. In Hollerith's case, it has been speculated (Austrian 1982) that, due to his family background, a high aspiration level both in terms of achievement and material status and a strong technological curiosity came together in motivating his extended search and experiment activities – two typical causal factors (see below).

To distinguish the two causality questions is helpful also for clarifying the endogeneity vs. exogeneity issue or, to put it another way, for deciding whether or not the emergence of novelty in the economy has to be interpreted as an exogenous shock.[7] Man-made novelty – originating from the creative activity of the human mind – is as much part of the agents' behaviour as are the agents' choices. Both bring about the incessant transformations of the economy. That the emergence of novelty is relevant for economics can therefore hardly be doubted. A different question is, of course, whether the causes of novelty fall into the explanatory domain of economics, or whether they belong to the domain of other disciplines, e.g. psychology, or are inaccessible by whatever discipline. Only in the first case the emergence of novelty would have to be considered endogenous, implying a need for economic theorizing to explain it. Else novelty would legitimately be treated as unexplained shock affecting the economy from outside.

What position is to be taken in this respect hinges on which of the two levels of explaining the causes of novelty emergence one is interested in. While the reasons for the particular new meaning lie in the dark and, thus, cannot reasonably be claimed to be made endogenous, the motivational causes inducing people to search and try out novelty can. (Even more so do the causes of the possible diffusion of novelty and its effects, e.g. on collective action, qualify as endogenous to the economic process.) To come up with novelty is the result of behaviour motivated in a particular way that can be explained in terms of a behavioural theory rather than representing it as an exogenous shock. This behaviour is economically relevant even though it does not lend itself to an explanation in terms of utility maximization under constraints. The optimization hypothesis (as any hypothesis in which individual motivation is explained by the expected consequences of a chosen behaviour) is not applicable here, because the bounds of unknowledge prevent the agents from knowing in advance whether, and if so what kind of, novelty will result from their effort. Instead of claiming (illusionary) foresight, the behavioural theory required here can refer to the individuals' past or present situation as a source of motivation for search into the unknown.

At least two behavioural theories fitting that criterion can be suggested for the explanation of the motivational causes of novelty creation. One is associated with the long-established concept of 'satisficing' (Siegel 1957; March and Simon 1958, chap. 2). According to this theory, it is dissatisfaction with the status quo, relative to an agent's aspiration level, that provides the motivation for, and determines the amount of time and effort going into, search and experimentation. The current aspiration level is subject to adjustments that reflect earlier successes and failures in the attempt to reach previously valid aspiration levels. Consider an event – perhaps a competitor's innovative activity – that negatively affects the alternatives feasible for the agent. Assume that the best choice available to the agent after the event is inferior to the best one before. Such a situation usually violates the current aspiration level. Accordingly, the satisficing hypothesis would predict that motivation to search for new, not yet known, choices is generated, even though it is not known whether the search will be successful. The motivation to search declines, the longer the search is continued without a successful novelty being found, because the aspiration level declines. The latter may eventually converge to the best option currently feasible and the motivation to search thus fades away. If, on the other hand, the search turns out to be successful, in the sense that an option better than the best one currently feasible is discovered, then the aspiration level will increase to this new level.

The other theory that offers an explanation for the motivation to search for yet unknown outcomes suggests that experiencing novelty, as such, is a rewarding experience (see Scitovsky 1976). This motivational force can be related to what is commonly called curiosity. This means assuming a preference for novel mental or sensory stimuli that again hinges on the present situation of the agents. More specifically, it varies with the degree of relative deprivation: the more boring a life otherwise is, the more the novel stimuli are appreciated and, hence, longed for and searched for. Where the environment does not offer such stimuli (or not enough of them) the agents may be motivated, with the usual inter-individual variance, to create them by inventing something and/or trying something new.

The two motivation theories are complementary. However, the causes of searching and coming up with novelty are different. In some cases they may coincide (as in the Hollerith example). In other cases, the conditions under which they become relevant differ. The satisficing model suggests that a search for novelty is typically triggered in situations of challenge or crisis (including anticipated crises). The preference-for-experiencing-novelty hypothesis predicts a short-term fluctuation of this preference between deprivation and satiation, so that novelty is sought with a, perhaps rather low but constant, basic rate. Taken together, individual novelty creation can be expected to take place at a basic rate independently of the specific time and place, but to increase significantly beyond this rate in situations of challenge and crisis. At a social or organizational level, selective reinforcement in one or the other direction channels innovativeness and may foster, or impede, the individuals' creation of novelty.

VI Conclusions

The emergence of novelty is a major driving agent in economic development, but it is difficult to account for in economic analysis. In this paper an attempt has been made to identify where the problems are, what consequences they have at the methodological level, and what room there is for positively dealing with the creation of novelty in economics. The procedural approach that was pursued here suggests distinguishing between two operations involved in novelty creation, a generative one and an interpretative one. In the generative operation, it was argued, conceptual inputs (the epistemic base of novelty) are recombined. More specifically, these input sets were expressed by propositional networks that have to satisfy certain similarity criteria. It was shown that, if the recombined elements can be integrated, meaningful combinatory extensions of the original propositional networks emerge. The integration itself is done by the interpretative operation that is, at present, not well understood. However, the insights that are possible already suffice to better understand the generic features of novelty and the epistemological and methodological consequences that follow.

The fact that the creative inductive inference intuitively made in the human mind during the interpretative operation is currently not accessible to scientific explanations results in an epistemological constraint on theorizing about the emergence of novelty. The practical implication is that, in scientific disciplines in whose domains the emergence of this kind of novelty is a generic feature, there are limits to both causal explanations and predictions concerning the further course of events. In the case of universal laws of nature (which are supposed to be invariable and independent of whatever novelty occurs), laws of motion may exist whose implications can be anticipated by dynamic systems *qua* their *a priori* determined solutions. Something similar cannot be expected where, as in the economic domain, the agents' creation of novelty is a constitutive part of the course of events. In more or less conscious response to this epistemological constraint, economic analysis focusing on the course of events in the economy (rather than on equilibrium states and their properties) is usually confined to a post-revelation analysis in which the epistemic 'bound of unknowledge' is removed by idealizing assumptions: the informational content or meaning of emerging novelty is assumed to be revealed instantaneously and completely, and it is assumed that no further novelty will emerge during the post-revelation period of analysis. As has been shown, these are the typical assumptions made when dynamical models are used in economics.

One may wonder what form of economic analysis would be less impacted by the epistemological bound following from the emergence of novelty. Although it goes beyond the frame of the present inquiry, it is interesting to note in regard to this question that among the first attempts to discuss the role of epistemic constraints for economic theorizing were those that made a connection not only to probability theory (Keynes 1921; Shackle 1949), but also one to expectations in investment and finance (Keynes 1936; Shackle 1938). And it is also not accidental that the first major theory about the impact of innovations on the economy – Schumpeter's (1934) *Theory of Economic Development* – emphasizes the critical role of finance in enabling innovation-induced booms and busts. In fact, nowhere else in the economy does the emergence of novelty seem to be able to trigger correlated expectations and reactions – with unintended collective outcome – with so much effect as in financial markets.

Taking up these earlier considerations, it may be a worthwhile task for future research to find out whether investment and finance indeed have a congenial role to play for the economic analysis of novelty. Usually, the flow of emerging novelty is considered to find its economic expression in the industrial innovation dynamics. As was mentioned, they are often modelled as diffusion dynamics which, assuming the absence of any further novelty intervening, converge to equilibrium states. The most immediate economic response to novelty is, however, that of the decision makers faced with the problem of whether and how to proceed with novelty created. These decisions are heavily conditioned by the decision makers' financial situation. Conversely, the potency of financial markets heavily depends on the prospects of a continuing, but not necessarily steady, inflow of economically significant novelty.

The epistemological limitations notwithstanding, it may therefore be conjectured that the mediation of economic novelty, whatever its yet unknown meaning will be, will strongly be affected by the institutional make up of the net of expectations and financial activities. The correlated responses to which the financial markets seem to be susceptible can amplify, or even overdo, the impact of emerging novelty on the real economic sphere with the necessary corrections sooner or later being due. In its technological and commercial diffusion processes the imponderables of emerging novelty may sooner or later become assessable. But the uncertainty resulting from the repercussions that novelty has by then triggered in the financial markets may go on and may contribute to keeping the economy far from a state of general equilibrium.

Notes

1. A simple example can make this clear. Let the observed fact be (F) 'the demand for cars in the US decreased in 2008' and the conjectured causal hypothesis be (H) 'when prices are increased, demand decreases'. If (H) and the condition (C) 'prices for cars in the US increased in 2008' were the valid premises, the classical syllogistic deduction would lead to (F) as the conclusion. (Conversely, in an induction one would infer from (C) and (F) as premises to (H) as the conclusion.) The abductive inference, in contrast, starts from the observation (F) to be explained. If the observer were to imagine (H) as additional premise, (F) and (H) together would imply (C) as hypothetical reason contingent on (H), see Magnani (2002) for a discussion. Obviously, how the observer arrives at the (potentially creative) choice of (H) is not addressed by this reconstruction.
2. Something similar holds in comparison to reconstructions of the logic by which novelty is derived in terms of categorical reductions or generic abstractions, see Finke et al. (1992, chap. 2) and Nersessian (2002).
3. In the case of the simple replicator equation (2) this follows immediately from the assumption that, in a perfectly competitive economy, the average profit $\pi(t) = \text{const.} = 0$. In general, the average population fitness (measured here in profit terms) does not have to be a constant, but can adjust as a consequence of the selection process. Nonetheless, as long as selection pressure prevails, it pushes the average population fitness to the value of the best adapted individual fitness value and, hence, the dynamics converge to a fixed point. A replicator equation can, of course, be extended by adding a mutation equation that describes the random event of a new variant entering the population (see Hofbauer and Sigmund 1988, pp. 249–250). It should be noted, however, that such a variant is 'new' only in the ex post sense – all its properties are already contained in the mathematical specification of the compound selection-mutation-equation so that even the compound dynamics usually have a fixed point.
4. Thus, the tail probability (tail frequency) do not, as in the diffusion model before, denote the probability of not adopting (the relative frequency of non-adopters). Agents who refrain from adopting any of the rivaling variants are not considered. For a discussion see Witt (1997).
5. Hodgson himself has more recently revised his earlier view, expressed in Hodgson (1995 and 1999, chap. 6), that novelty is a case of an 'uncaused cause', see Hodgson (2004, chap. 3).
6. For details see Kistermann (1991). Hollerith's invention was exploited commercially by his Tabulating Machine Company, later sold to the Computer Tabulating Recoding Company renamed IBM in 1924.
7. Hodgson (1999, chap. 6) opposes the focus on endogeneity vs. exogeneity of novelty as missing the decisive point. He suggests replacing it by a distinction that he considers the relevant one – that between open and closed systems. The capacity to generate novelty endogenously is indeed sufficient for a system to be an open one, more specifically an evolving system. Yet the opposite is not true, and the suggested substitution is therefore incomplete. Knowing that a system is open is not sufficient to determine whether or not novelty can emerge endogenously, because there may be other reasons why a system is open or closed, e.g. whether or not it has systematic exchange with its environment.

References

Aliseda, A. (2006), *Abductive Reasoning – Logical Investigations into Discovery and Explanation*, Dordrecht: Springer.

Anderson, J.R. (2000), *Cognitive Psychology and Its Implications* (5th ed.), New York: Worth.

Arthur, W.B. (1994), *Increasing Returns and Path Dependence in the Economy*, Ann Arbor: Michigan University Press.

Arthur, W.B., Ermoliev, Y.M., and Kaniovski, Y.M. (1984), 'Strong Laws for a Class of Path-Dependent Stochastic Processes With Applications', in *Proceedings of the International Conference on Stochastic Optimization*, Berlin: Springer, pp. 287–300.

Austrian, G.D. (1982), *Herman Hollerith: The Forgotten Giant of Information Processing*, New York: Columbia University Press.

Boden, M.A. (1999), 'Computer Models of Creativity', in *Handbook of Creativity*, ed. R.J. Sternberg, Cambridge: Cambridge University Press, pp. 351–372.

David, P.A. (1985), 'Clio and the Economics of QWERTY', *American Economic Review, Papers and Proceedings*, 75, 332–337.

Edelman, G.M., and Tononi, G. (2000), *A Universe of Consciousness: How Matter Becomes Imagination*, New York: Basic Books.

Fauconnier, G., and Turner, M. (2002), *The Way We Think – Conceptual Blending and the Mind's Hidden Complexities*, New York: Basic Books.

Finke, R.A., Ward, T.B., and Smith, S.M. (1992), *Creative Cognition – Theory, Research, and Applications*, Cambridge, MA: MIT Press.

Fisher, F.M. (1983), *Disequilibrium Foundations of Equilibrium Economics*, Cambridge: Cambridge University Press.

Gentner, D., and Markman, A.B. (1997), 'Structure Mapping in Analogy and Similarity', *American Psychologist*, 52(1), 45–56.

Griliches, Z. (1957), 'Hybrid Corn: An Exploration in the Economics of Technological Change', *Econometrica*, 25, 501–522.

Hodgson, G.M. (1995), 'The Evolution of Evolutionary Economics', *Scottish Journal of Political Economy*, 42, 469–488.

—— (1999), *Evolution and Institutions*, Cheltenham: Edward Elgar.

—— (2004), *The Evolution of Institutional Economics*, London: Routledge.

Hofbauer, J., and Sigmund, K. (1988), *The Theory of Evolution and Dynamical Systems*, Cambridge: Cambridge University Press.

Hofstadter, D.R., and the Fluid Analogies Research Group (1995), *Fluid Concepts and Creative Analogies*, New York: Basic Books.

Joosten, R. (2006), 'Walras and Darwin: An Odd Couple?', *Journal of Evolutionary Economics*, 16, 561–573.

Keynes, J.M. (1921), *A Treatise on Probability*, London: Macmillan.

—— (1936), *The General Theory of Employment, Interest, and Money*, New York: Harcourt, Brace, Jovanovich.

Kistermann, F.W. (1991), 'The Invention and Development of the Hollerith Punched Card', *IEEE Annals of the History of Computing*, 13, 245–259.

Knight, R.T. (1996), 'Contribution of Human Hippocampal Region to Novelty Detection', *Nature*, 383, 256–259.

Koch, C., and Crick, F. (2000), 'Some Thoughts on Consciousness and Neuroscience', in *The New Cognitive Neurosciences* (2nd ed.), ed. M.S. Gazzaniga, Cambridge, MA: MIT Press, pp. 1285–1294.

Koestler, A. (1964), *The Act of Creation*, London: Hutchinson & Co.

Kohonen, T. (1987), *Self-Organization and Associative Memory* (2nd ed.), Berlin: Springer.

Machlup, F. (1980), *Knowledge and Knowledge Production*, Princeton: Princeton University Press.

Magnani, L. (2002), 'Conjectures and Manipulations: External Representations of Scientific Reasoning', *Mind and Society*, 3, 9–31.

March, J.G., and Simon, H.A. (1958), *Organizations*, New York: Wiley.

Martindale, C. (1999), 'Biological Bases of Creativity', in *Handbook of Creativity*, ed. R.J. Sternberg, Cambridge: Cambridge University Press, pp. 137–152.

Metcalfe, J.S. (1988), 'The Diffusion of Innovations: An Interpretative Survey', in *Technical Change and Economic Theory*, eds. G. Dosi, C. Freeman, R.R. Nelson, G. Silverberg, and L. Soete, London: Pinter Publishers, pp. 560–589.

—— (1994), 'Competition, Fisher's Principle and Increasing Returns in the Selection Process', *Journal of Evolutionary Economics*, 4, 327–346.

Mokyr, J. (2002), *The Gifts of Athena: Historical Origins of the Knowledge Economy*, Princeton: Princeton University Press.

Nelson, R.R., and Winter, S.G. (1982), *An Evolutionary Theory of Economic Change*, Cambridge, MA: Harvard University Press.

Nersessian, N.J. (2002), 'Abstraction via Generic Modeling in Concept Formation in Science', *Mind and Society*, 3, 129–154.

Peirce, C.S. (1934), *Pragmatism and Pragmaticism, Collected Papers of Charles Sanders Peirce* (vol. 5), eds. C. Hartshorne and P. Weiss, Cambridge, MA: Harvard University Press.

Rogers, E. (1995), *Diffusion of Innovations*, New York: Free Press.

Schumpeter, J.A. (1934), *The Theory of Economic Development*, Cambridge, MA: Harvard University Press.

Scitovsky, T. (1976), *The Joyless Economy*, Oxford: Oxford University Press.

Shackle, G.L.S. (1938), *Expectations, Investment, and Income*, Oxford: Oxford University Press.

——— (1949), *Expectations in Economics*, Cambridge: Cambridge University Press.

——— (1983), 'The Bounds of Unknowledge', in *Beyond Positive Economics*, ed. J. Wiseman, London: Macmillan, pp. 28–37.

Siegel, S. (1957), 'Level of Aspiration and Decision Making', *Psychological Review*, 64, 253–262.

Sternberg R.J. (ed.) (1999), *Handbook of Creativity*, Cambridge: Cambridge University Press.

Usher, A.P. (1954), *History of Mechanical Inventions*, Cambridge, MA: Harvard University Press.

Vincenti, W.G. (1990), *What Engineers Know and How They Know It*, Baltimore: Johns Hopkins University Press.

Witt, U. (1993), 'Emergence and Dissemination of Innovations: Some Principles of Evolutionary Economics', in *Non-linear Dynamics and Evolutionary Economics*, eds. R.H. Day and P. Chen, Oxford: Oxford University Press, pp. 91–100.

——— (1997), '"Lock-in" vs. "Critical Masses" – Industrial Change Under Network Externalities', *International Journal of Industrial Organization*, 15, 753–773.

——— (2003), 'Generic Features of Evolution and Its Continuity: A Transdisciplinary Perspective', *Theoria*, 18, 273–288.

PART III

EVOLUTIONARY THINKING AT WORK

9

20 Evolutionary economics and psychology

ULRICH WITT

20.1 Introduction

Evolutionary economics focuses on the transformation of the economy over time and the consequences this has for the current conditions of production and consumption. The sources of the transformation process are human learning, problem solving, and the accumulation of knowledge and capital. The diversity of individual efforts and capabilities with respect to both learning and innovation results at any time in the generation and diffusion of a variety of innovative technologies, institutions, and commercial activities that compete with each other. The competition between them, and the economic and social adaptations triggered by that competition, fuel the process of transformation from within the economy (see Nelson 1995, Foster and Metcalfe 2001, Fagerberg 2003, Witt 2008 for recent surveys).

The concept of evolution thus has a meaning in evolutionary economics that differs from the one in evolutionary psychology. In the latter, "evolution" – in the sense of the Darwinian theory (see Mayr 1991, chap. 4) – is part of the explanans. It provides the meta-hypothesis on the basis of which capabilities and constraints of the human brain – and the corresponding features of the cognition and choice – are reconstructed as, it is assumed, natural selection has created them at times when early humans were under fierce selection pressure (see Lea, chapter 21 in this volume). In evolutionary economics, in contrast, "evolution" is a synonym for the economic transformation process and, hence, part of the explanandum. However, because of the causal reduction of endogenous economic change to human learning, creativity, and innovative action, there is a basis and a need for engaging in a dialogue with psychological theories on these dynamic aspects of human behavior.

In order to explain the economic transformation process and the results it is generating, it is necessary, thus, to go beyond static decision-making theories. These are theories of choice that take alternatives as given. In some cases, as in evolutionary psychology, they focus on how framing effects bias the perception of the alternatives and how choices follow simple decision heuristics (see Gigerenzer and Goldstein 1996). In evolutionary economics, in contrast, the role of choice alternatives that newly emerge is crucial (see Witt 2003). Accordingly, the focus is on what motivations drive learning and innovativeness from which the newly perceived options arise. How are new insights and actions created, and what behavioral adaptations do they trigger? Obviously, these questions transcend a mode of reasoning often to be found in contemporary economic theorizing which is preoccupied with the characteristics and implications of equilibrium states of the economy. In that mode of reasoning, the complexities of human behavior and its adaptative potential are not considered. The present reflections on the adaptations in economic behavior and their driving forces may therefore be seen as an attempt to broaden the foundation of the theory of economic behavior more generally.

The argumentation in this chapter proceeds as follows. Adaptations in human behavior can be distinguished by the different time scales in which they occur. In rough approximation, three levels can be identified. One level is that of the genes that code certain forms of behavior. Another level is that of innate, non-cognitive learning mechanisms that govern instrumental conditioning and conditioned reinforcement. Last, but not least, there is the level of cognitive reflection, insight, and observational learning. As argued in section 20.2, adaptations at the genetic level – for which the Darwinian theory of evolution would be relevant – need many generations to appear. Given that, in the economic domain, the bulk of change occurs within single generations, the pace of that kind of behavioral adaptation seems too slow to matter for economic evolution. Moreover, systematic behavior adaptations of the kind explained by sociobiology only occur under sufficient natural selection pressure – an assumption that is controversial as far as modern humans are concerned. The facts notwithstanding, it will be argued that, for similar reasons as in evolutionary psychology, the Darwinian theory of evolution in general, and sociobiology in particular, can be considered a relevant meta-hypothesis for evolutionary economics too.

In elaborating this argument, section 20.3 explores the influence of the innate, non-cognitive learning mechanisms on behavior adaptations as they occur in the course of the economic transformation process. To account for these influences within the utilitarian model of economic behavior, a connection to the concepts of utility functions and their logical equivalent, individual preference orderings, needs to be made. These concepts, central to microeconomic theorizing, play no similar role in psychology. In economics the questions of what generates utility and how are left open, as, for that matter, are questions of what becomes the object of preference orders and why. However, as will be explained, it is precisely in answering these questions that the influences of innate dispositions and non-cognitive learning mechanisms are relevant. Section 20.4 turns to the cognitive influences on economic behavior and the systematic changes they are responsible for in interaction with the non-cognitive learning processes. In a short digression, the section also discusses what motivations drive innovativeness from which new choice alternatives emerge. Section 20.5 elaborates in an exemplary fashion on the implications of the theory presented in the previous sections for explaining the economic transformation process. The example chosen is the apparently incessant growth and structural change of consumption. Section 20.6 briefly concludes.

20.2   Setting the frame: the role of the human genetic endowment

When economic evolution is identified with the ongoing transformation processes of the economy, what relevance does the Darwinian theory of evolution then have for evolutionary economics? Opinions on this point are split. If a Darwinian world-view is accepted as a unifying frame for scientific inquiry (see Wilson 1998), a straightforward answer would be to interpret the Darwinian theory as a meta-hypothesis from which the initial conditions and some of the underlying constraints of the historical process of economic change in the long run can be derived. Influenced by the Darwinian revolution of his time, this position had already been suggested by Veblen (1898) – who also introduced the label "evolutionary" economics. But his position was not pursued further in the school he founded (see Hodgson 2004). The discussion on the relevance of the Darwinian world-view for evolutionary economics and on what it implies has therefore only recently reappeared on the agenda of evolutionary economics.[1]

Another way of making use of Darwinian thought in evolutionary economics is a purely heuristic one. Negating the idea of a common ontology of the sciences, this approach borrows key notions and models from evolutionary biology to conveniently conceptualize the economic evolutionary process on the basis of analogy constructions. Analogy constructions to natural selection and recourse to models of population dynamics are characteristic, in particular, of the neo-Schumpeterian branch of evolutionary economics initiated by the work of Nelson and Winter (1982).[2] Yet, population thinking and analogy constructions can be more of a hindrance than a help when it comes to explaining the causal role that behavior adaptations play in economic change. Nelson and Winter (1982, chap. 5) assume that, because of their bounded rationality, economic agents operate on the basis of behavioral routines. When different agents follow different routines this usually means that a variety of more or less successful behaviors emerge. Analogously to the principle of natural selection, selection forces implied by market competition are argued to erode that variety and, thus, to produce adaptations in average behavior. Hence, what is considered to improve average performance is not individual behavior adaption, for

---

[1] See Witt (1996), Vromen (2001), Hodgson (2002), Witt (2003, chap. 1); see also the special issue of the *Journal of Evolutionary Economics*, vol. 16, no. 5, 2006 on "Evolutionary Concepts in Economics and Biology."

[2] See Metcalfe (1998), Nelson and Winter (2002), Fagerberg (2003). In his seminal work on the self-transformation of the economy, Schumpeter (1934) had avoided the term "evolution." He considered it a Darwinian concept and, as such, irrelevant for the social sciences. He also opposed the use of biological analogies.

example through learning and problem solving, and the corresponding motivations, but the changing relative frequencies in a population of behavioral routines that are themselves unchanging.

In order to be able to account for the impact of individual behavior adaptations on the economic transformation process – the focal point of the present chapter – the neo-Schumpeterian approach will therefore not be adopted here. The Darwinian theory will not be used as a source for constructing analogies but as a meta-theory that, though not directly relevant for the economic transformation process, can shed light on the behavioral foundations of this process. Not unlike in evolutionary psychology, it can be used to reconstruct the genetic influences on behavior, deriving from times when early humans were under fierce selection pressure. The consequences of these influences can be put in perspective with culturally acquired forms of economic behavior.

As far as animals are concerned, there is little doubt that important parts of their behavioral repertoire are innate, i.e. develop as an expression of their genes. Cases in point are elementary behavior dispositions and adaptation patterns like instrumental conditioning and conditioned reinforcement (Dugatkin 2003, chap. 4). With their direct or indirect effect on reproductive success, innate dispositions and adaptation patterns are likely to have been shaped by natural selection in a way that enhances individual fitness of the organisms carrying the corresponding behavior genes. In sociobiology, this hypothesis is extended to the animals' behavior in social interactions (Wilson 1975). Prominent examples are rearing offspring, the joint stalking of prey, food sharing, support of mating and breeding activities of other animals, and – most puzzling – "altruistic" forms of behavior, for example in self-sacrifices that increase the survival chances of others. These and other social forms of behavior are explicable in terms of the theory of natural selection by substituting the concept of "inclusive fitness" (Hamilton 1964) for the concept of individual genetic fitness.[3]

Some basic behavioral dispositions and adaptation patterns seem to be innate also in humans. The question of whether the sociobiological approach can be extended to explaining human social behavior is, however, highly controversial (see Caplan 1978). Particularly in the context of early (and of still living, primitive) human societies, the problems of coordination of joint activities, mutual support, reciprocity, and "altruism" seem to present themselves somewhat similarly to those in higher animal societies. Competition for scarce resources – food, habitat space, access to mating partners, etc. – is a basic condition of life. Yet, even in primitive societies, this does not imply that human social behavior is limited to genetically coded forms. There are culturally conditioned

---

[3] Inclusive fitness means to account for the genetic commonalities between kin in calculating the fitness value of a particular genetically coded social behavior. Behaving altruistically may lower their chances of reproducing their own genes. On the other hand, depending on the degree of relationship, the reproductive disadvantage may be over-compensated by increased reproduction chances of the same genes in kin who benefit from the social behavior.

and intelligently created forms of behavior. They are the major reason why many primitive (but even more so, the economically highly developed modern) societies are capable of mastering their environment so successfully that the selection pressure on their social and economic behavior has decreased dramatically.

Evidence for this finding is provided by the fading correlation between the amount of resources commanded on the one hand and reproductive success on the other. While the amount of scarce resources an animal can command is positively correlated with its reproductive success, in the developed, human societies average real income increases and population growth are negatively correlated.[4] The fact that such inconsequential reproductive behavior is not wiped out indicates that pressure from natural selection does not suffice any more to cut back on an increasing variety of idiosyncratic behaviors with little or no adaptive value in terms of reproductive success. The question then is how the increasing variety of idiosyncratic behaviors comes about, and what determines which behavior is actually displayed.

As will be explained in the next sections, besides the impact of cognitive reasoning and beliefs, some elementary, innate, behavioral dispositions and adaptation mechanisms do have an influence here, albeit an indirect one. (And, precisely because natural selection is no longer a source of rapid systematic change in the human species, these elementary, innate features are likely to be basically the same as those shaped under selection pressure in the earlier phases of human phylogeny.) The indirect influence affects, it will be argued, the individual's utility or preferences and the way in which they change over time.

20.3   Explaining motivation: utility, preferences, and their inherent dynamics

A person's motivation to act and the reflections about possible actions belong to the inner sphere of that person which cannot be observed in the same way as the action actually taken. This simple fact is the crux of a long philosophical debate. Its repercussions have triggered different responses in economic and psychological theorizing. Starting from Bentham's (1789) sensory utilitarianism – guided by a good psychological intuition but a naive attitude towards measurement – economics has over the past two centuries turned first to a theory of subjective utility (lacking any idea of measurability) and then to subjective preference theory. Initially motivated by the desire to give utility theory a proper mathematical expression (Warke 2000), the conversion into

---

[4] See Maddison (2001, chap. 1), who shows in a cross-country comparison that the more per capita income in real terms increased from 1820 to 1998, the more both birth rates and population growth went down. In pre-industrial societies, in contrast, there is evidence for a positive correlation: see, e.g., Chagnon and Irons (1979).

preference theory followed a different path. Strikingly similar to the positivist attitude underlying behaviorism in psychology, the goal was to eliminate all speculations about unobservable inner states of a person from the foundations of microeconomics (see Samuelson 1947, chaps. I and V).

The few empirical implications of subjective utility theory all rest on the – unknown – shape of a person's utility function (usually defined over quantities of n commodities, $x_1, x_2, \ldots, x_n$). However, if certain conditions are satisfied, such a utility function is logically equivalent to an ordering over alternative bundles of the n commodities. For any two bundles $\mathbf{x} = x_1, x_2, \ldots, x_n$ and $\mathbf{y} = y_1, y_2, \ldots, y_n$ such an ordering implies that either "$\mathbf{x}$ is preferred to $\mathbf{y}$" or "$\mathbf{y}$ is preferred to $\mathbf{x}$" or "$\mathbf{x}$ and $\mathbf{y}$ are equally preferred" (indifference). Which of these preferences a person has was, under controlled conditions, expected to be observable by the quantities a person chooses when prices vary (provided the person acts consistently – a version of the rationality assumption whose validity cannot simultaneously be observed). However, such "revealed preference" experiments were rarely carried out. The theory was factually used as a platform logically to deduce "operational" hypotheses about demand behavior, formulated exclusively in terms of observable prices and quantities. As a consequence, individual utility functions and preference orderings now populate economic textbooks, yet with reference to their subjective nature it is left unexplained what the arguments in the functions stand for, or what it is that people have preferences for.

Psychological theorizing took a different route. The concepts of utility and preferences can hardly be found in the psychological literature. However, with respect to the observability problem, radical behaviorism had a similar positivist stance – with one major difference. While revealed preferences theory was oriented towards deriving abstract logical inferences about demand functions, behavioral psychology focused on explaining observable behavior itself – human and non-human. With a minimalist theory, in hundreds of experiments a narrowly limited number of primary reinforcers were identified – findings that invited reflections about the underlying motivation to act. These reinforcers are shared, with some variance, by all humans and by many other species (Herrnstein 1990). This fact and the physiological mechanisms underlying reinforcement that were later discovered in molecular biology point to a genetic basis. By understanding the physiological foundations, the short-term dynamics of deprivation and satiation and their motivational potential can easily be explained. The behaviorists' genuinely dynamic approach to motivation was complemented by the theory of conditioned reinforcement. That theory postulates a primitive, innate mechanism by which associations are learned between stimuli and by which secondary reinforcers emerge on the basis of conditioning learning.

In economics, Bentham's hedonic interpretation of utility as a sensory perception which is observable and even measurable has recently been rehabilitated (see Kahneman, Wakker and Sarin 1997). However, his question of what generates utility and, thus, motivates people to act still needs to be revived. It is particularly important for evolutionary economics, because without being able to explain what motivates a person to act it is impossible, *a fortiori*, to explain how that motivation changes in the short run, and how it can possibly evolve in systematic ways in the longer run. Contrary to what many economists hold, the subjectivity of individual utility and preferences does not prevent one being specific about their causes and contingencies. In fact, the just-mentioned findings in behavioral psychology are directly relevant here. The innate motivational dispositions and the adaptation mechanism expressed respectively in primary reinforcing events and processes of instrumental conditioning and conditioned reinforcement suggest the following hypothesis: A person derives utility from actions depending on (or prefers them according to) their current potential to induce a rewarding sensory experience either by reducing deprivation with respect to primary reinforcers directly or through conditioned secondary reinforcers.[5]

Thus, at least some of the arguments of a person's utility function (if defined over actions rather than commodities) can be connected with the sensory experiences of reinforcers. First, there are experiences with the limited number of innate primary reinforcers shared, with the usual genetic variance, by all humans. Among them are the removal or reduction of aversive stimuli like pain, fear, etc. Furthermore, in numerous experiments the removal or reduction of deprivation from, among others, air, aqueous solutions, sleeping, food, body heat, sensory arousal of certain kind and strength, social status recognition, sex, care, and affection have been identified as primary reinforcing instances.[6] Following the argument above, actions – usually involving goods and services that are purchased in the markets – that are capable of removing or reducing deprivation in these dimensions thus are what generate utility (or, for that matter, are the objects of preference orderings). Correspondingly, the short-run dynamics of the probabilities for certain actions being chosen reflect the variations in the relative degree of deprivation felt in the respective dimensions.

Based on such innate primary reinforcers, a potentially very long chain of secondary reinforcers emerges over the history of conditioned reinforcement a person goes through. The arguments of the individual utility function therefore represent, second, the varying structure of individually acquired secondary reinforcers. Unlike the widely shared primary reinforcers, this structure is of highly idiosyncratic nature, except perhaps for some cultural commonalities in similarly socialized groups. Given their idiosyncrasy and enormous variety, there would be little sense in trying to produce a list of secondary reinforcers. (It is mainly because of these features that it can rightly be claimed that no

---

[5] As the biologists Pulliam and Dunford (1980, 11–44) have shown, this hypothesis can also be given an interpretation in terms of sensory experiences that are based on hard-wired (genetically coded) neurological processes in higher organisms.

[6] See Millenson (1967, p. 368). The survival value of the primary reinforcers is obvious.

two individual utility functions or preferences are alike.) Furthermore, unlike the primary reinforcers allowing for individual malleability in behavior only through instrumental conditioning, the emergence of a structure of individual secondary reinforcers implies a rich dynamic potential for utility functions and preferences to evolve over both individual lifetimes and cultural epochs.

A recourse to elementary innate behavior dispositions and adaptation mechanisms has been suggested here to provide a behavioral foundation for the concepts of utility, preferences, and their inherent dynamics. This suggestion is not meant to imply that the discussion should be confined to the behavioral level. In the economic context, important motivational influences on human behavior, particularly on intentional choices, are likely to emanate also from the cognitive level. These influences are to be discussed next.

20.4   Acknowledging the role of cognition: attention and unfolding action knowledge

Evolution has endowed humans with an exceptional intelligence. Reflection, intuitive insight, intentionality, and logical inference – unique capacities of our cognitive system – play a constitutive role for many economic actions. This means that, in addition to the elementary, innate behavior dispositions and adaptation mechanisms, a set of further causal factors has to be accounted for. The corresponding hypotheses on cognitive influences have to be merged in a more comprehensive theory of economic behavior and its dynamics.

Subjective perception and interpretation can intervene in stimulus–response reaction patterns. Depending on how perceptions are associated with intentions and other existing memory content to form a more or less reflected action plan, reaction patterns can systematically change. Intentional behavior is selectively controlled for goal achievement, and goals may be adjusted as a result of observing the behavior of others. Success or failure in goal achievement can be reflected in terms of subjective cause-and-effect relationships and, by inference, expectations and/or aspirations can be revised. In any case, in addition to learning in the sense of instrumental conditioning and conditioned reinforcement, cognitive learning through insight and observation of others comes into play in a way that moderates the individual dependence on innate behavior dispositions and adaptation mechanisms (Bandura 1986).

As attribution theory has shown, the intervening cognitive activities are not only rather complex but also somewhat arbitrary with respect to their outcome (see van Raaij 1985). However, whether intervening cognitive activities occur, and which ones these are, hinges on the information input. What information is perceived and processed through personal experience or by observation of, and/or communication with, others is contingent, in turn, on certain constraints in human information processing and, thus, knowledge acquisition. These constraints are also part of the human biological inheritance. Since it may be easier to derive hypotheses on the effects of cognitive intervention on economic behavior from constraints on the information input than from the complex internal cognitive processes, these constraints deserve a closer inspection.

In human perception a limited number of sensory stimuli, such as visual and acoustic signals, can spontaneously be processed in parallel into respective stores and be recognized.[7] Unless attention is quickly paid to any such message it will, however, be lost from memory. If, as often, stimuli are offered in abundance to the sensory system, attention must selectively be allocated to competing processing demands. This means that in the brain's processing capacity there is a bottleneck. Of the information coming in at any given point in time, spontaneous selective attention processes must filter out that information that will be processed further in the working memory. There the selected information is maintained by rehearsal, but the amount of information that can be rehearsed at one point in time is also narrowly limited.

What pieces of incoming information grab attention depends on both their physically based attributes[8] and their meaning-based attributes. Meaning is identified through tracing information from long-term memory (the other source of information entering the working memory). In long-term memory, knowledge is stored that has previously been accumulated. In order for elements of long-term memory to be made available, they have to be activated selectively through cognitive cues contained in messages. Only messages containing cues for which there is an associative basis in long-term memory can have a meaningful interpretation and, by means of this, attract attention. Since only what is gaining attention has a chance of being rehearsed in memory and, thus, of being added to an individual's knowledge, the change of individual knowledge hinges on the already acquired knowledge.

The meaning associated with a particular piece of information often has affective connotations of liking or disliking. These reflect previous rewarding or aversive experiences ultimately based on reinforcing instances as discussed in the previous section. In the terminology chosen here, the affective connotations therefore relate to a person's preferences or utility function. More specifically, this means that the more a person has developed a preference (or an aversion) for a particular item or event, the more affective weight is attributed to its meaning. Accordingly, it is more likely that attention is allocated to incoming information relating to that item or event. Concomitantly, there is also an effect on individual knowledge: if information related to a particular item or event attracts more attention, then that information also tends

---

[7] See, e.g., Anderson (2000, chaps. 3, 6 and 7) for the following.
[8] Sensory arousal elicited by a stimulus in general depends on two attributes of the stimulus: frequency and relative strength (Helson 1964). Applied to the present context of allocating attention to the information carried by a sensory stimulus, these two factors may be identified with the frequency of exposure to that particular information and the intensity with which the stimulus is felt.

to be more frequently attended and rehearsed in thinking and, hence, to be better cognitively represented in action knowledge in the long-term memory. Thus, two mutually reinforcing effects interact. One effect is the affection-driven impact of the current preferences on the selective allocation of attention and the incremental change of knowledge. The other effect is that of selective attention and gradually changing knowledge on the formation of individual preferences. The more something is valued, the more it is also able to attract attention, to be rehearsed, and to be retrieved in long-term memory. Conversely, what is more often and persistently recognized as a positive stimulus, or as being related to one, tends, in turn, to be preferred increasingly (provided that a positively conditioning setting is maintained).

The flip side of the coin in this process with self-augmenting features is the relative neglect of, and the rising ignorance with respect to, other information. The capacity of the working memory required to lay out traces to what has earlier been stored in long-term memory is narrowly confined. For this reason, traces that allow retrieval of a particular piece of information can only be established and maintained at the expense of memory traces to other pieces of information. Therefore, the frequency of practicing particular memory traces and the affective value of the stored information are once more decisive factors – this time, however, with regard to the probability and intensity of recalling information. To put it differently: the less frequently and the less intensively a piece of information has been recalled in the past the more likely it is lost from long-term memory, i.e. from current knowledge.

The implications of these specificities of the human information processing system for economic behavior in general and the transformation processes going on in the economy in particular will be highlighted in the next section. Before that, however, a brief digression may be in order into a problem that is of great importance for the explanatory program of evolutionary economics. The problem – also arising at the cognitive level – is how to explain individual innovativeness, i.e. the creation of new choice alternatives and the motivation to do so. Two different questions are involved: first, how is novelty produced? and second, why? Regarding the first question, the key seems to be the brain's continually ongoing recombination activities of already known cognitive components (Koestler 1964, Campbell 1987). For the processes involved in both the recombination and the attribution of meaning, individual creative skills certainly play a crucial role (Sternberg 1988). How these processes work is, however, still little understood. Moreover, the inquiry into these issues is complicated by intricate epistemological problems. One hypothesis that has been suggested is that the meaning of newly produced recombinations is identified through switches in the underlying interpretative *Gestalt* patterns.[9]

---

[9] See Schlicht (1997); these patterns represent highly idiosyncratic, subjective mental states depending on individual experience and current knowledge. For a reconstruction of the brain's recombinatory activity as an act of "conceptual blending" see Fauconnier and Turner (2002).

The second question – why, and under what conditions, a person is motivated to search for novelty – is epistemologically less problematic and therefore easier to answer. Since neither the outcome of the search endeavor nor the time and effort it will need are known in advance, the search cannot be motivated by the expectation of specific outcomes (as implicitly assumed in optimal search models in economics). Search for novelty is motivated in a different way. In fact, there seem to be different forms of motivation corresponding with different forms of searching.

One form is covered by the "satisficing" hypothesis (Siegel 1957, March and Simon 1958, pp. 47–52). According to this hypothesis, the search motivation is dissatisfaction with the status quo. A person experiences a situation that falls short of the current aspiration level of that person, i.e. the level that reflects a balance of the person's earlier successes and failures. Imagine, to give an example, a producer who has a competitor. If the competitor comes up with an innovative move that causes the producer's revenues to fall whatever feasible reaction she can choose, then such a situation is likely to violate the person's current aspiration level. According to the satisficing hypothesis, a motivation to search for not yet known, better alternatives is triggered, notwithstanding the fact that it is unknown whether the search will indeed lead to better alternatives. The search motivation sooner or later vanishes, however, as the search goes on without generating better options. The person's aspiration level gradually declines and when it eventually converges to the best option presently known, the motivation to search vanishes.

A different motivation to search for novelty, and another form of searching, is highlighted by the taste-for-novelty hypothesis. This hypothesis assumes that humans find the experience of certain kinds of novelty a rewarding experience and deprivation from such sensory arousal an aversive experience (Scitovsky 1976). Hence, the more boring a life becomes, i.e. the more deprivation rises in this dimension, the stronger the motivation either to consume (try) a new source of sensory arousal, if available, or to search actively for, and generate the experience of, novelty. Obviously, the two motivational hypotheses refer to different causal contexts and search contexts so that they may be considered complementary hypotheses. The satisficing hypothesis suggests that search for novelty is typically motivated by, and more frequently triggered in, situations of challenge or crisis (where these may be anticipated crises). The taste-for-novelty hypothesis predicts a short-term fluctuation of the search motivation between deprivation and satiation so that, on average, novelty is sought with a, perhaps rather low but constant, basic rate.

20.5 Pulling things together: the example of consumption evolving

Because of space constraints, what follows from the evolutionary approach to economic behavior laid out in the previous sections can only be discussed here in an exemplary fashion. The case to be chosen is that of the growth and structural change of consumption in the developed countries over the past century, i.e. the explanation of what goes on at the demand side of the economy in the historical transformation process. The underlying facts are as follows: per capita income has risen three to six times in the different countries in real terms (Maddison 2001, chap. 1). Consumer spending has grown by a similar magnitude (Lebergott 1993). The enormous expansion of consumer spending was not equally distributed over all consumption categories. To the contrary, over the century there were massive changes in the compositions of goods and services consumed. As empirical research over the past decades has consistently shown, income elasticities of the demand for the different goods and services not only differ but also change over time, resulting in an unequal growth of consumption expenditures across different consumption categories.[10] Moreover, within each of the consumption categories the quality of existing goods and services has constantly been varied and differentiated. An increasing variety of new goods and services has been introduced to the markets.

How can all these observations be explained? How can consumer spending grow so dramatically with rising income without reaching a level of satiation? What role do satiation phenomena play at least in some consumption categories (as they may indeed be conjectured to express themselves in the differing income elasticities)? It is sometimes argued that vicarious entrepreneurs at the supply side of the markets have found ways to offer new or better products appealing to consumer preferences for which there have previously been no suitable offers. Hence the continuously upheld motivation among the consumers to expand expenditures. However, this argument is difficult to accept or refute as long as it is left unspecified what preferences consumers actually have. The discussion in the previous sections provides a basis for making progress.[11]

To recapitulate, some sources of utility – and the corresponding motivation to act – have been identified above with the removal or reduction of deprivation in physiologically determined activities like breathing air, drinking aqueous solutions, eating food, or pain relief. The motivation to consume the corresponding items – air, water, food, medicine – is easy to understand. It is "consumption" in the literal sense of eating up. A significant feature of that kind of consumption is that it is subject to temporary physical satiation that constrains the amount consumed per unit of time. The motivation for additional consumption vanishes as the satiation level is approached, but it reemerges as the organism's

---

[10] See Stone (1954), Houthakker and Taylor (1966), Deaton and Muellbauer (1980), Lebergott (1993). Let I and x denote income and the amount spent on a consumption good respectively. Assuming that a differentiable function $x = x(I)$ exists, the definition of the income elasticity of demand η for that good is $\eta = (dx/dI) / (x/I)$. The good is said to be income inferior if $\eta < 0$, a "normal" good if $0 < \eta \leq 1$, and income superior if $\eta > 1$. This means that, with a marginal increase in disposable income, the percentage change in spending on that good can be smaller (larger) than the percentage change of income.

[11] For a more detailed discussion see Witt (2001).

metabolism gradually uses up what was consumed. As real income increases, consumption can sooner or later be expanded to the average satiation level. Unless people expand their consumption beyond that level ("consumption" in the sense of purchasing items without "consuming" them in the literal sense any more), the absolute per capita consumption of these inputs per unit of time should therefore be expected to face an upper bound.[12] Yet, this is not what can be observed.

Food is an obvious example and some of its forms are therefore preferred candidates for demonstrating statistically that there are income-inferior goods (see Lebergott 1993, part II). However, the food industry has been battling with the satiation problem for decades and there have been ways of circumventing it so far. Household expenditure surveys show that per capita consumption even of many "normal" goods is continuing to grow in absolute terms. The first reason seems to be that with rising income the kind and quality of the diet changes in the direction of more complex and more expensive ingredients with more refined sensory quality. A second reason is that producers have developed new products by which the sensory perception of a rewarding consumption experience can be enjoyed without rapidly approaching physiological satiation. A prominent case is that of foodstuffs made with artificial sweeteners which allow consumers to increase their intake, and thus their expenditure, to a much higher level than the satiation level for similar products made with sugar (see Ruprecht 2005). A typical example is the introduction of Diet Coke. A similar role is played by spices and, more recently, artificial aromas which can be used as low-calorie substitutes for traditional flavoring ingredients with higher calorific content.

For consumption items other than those directly eaten up, the explanation of the change in consumer behavior is more involved. For example, consumption items such as beds or air conditioning facilities serve as means or "tools" in relation to physiologically determined needs such as getting sleep or maintaining body temperature. A television set, to give another example, is one tool among many other options that serve the rewarding experience of a pleasant sensory arousal through entertainment. (In itself, a television set is fairly useless, if it cannot be turned on to emit the entertaining services in the form of a flow of visual and acoustic information.) Being deprived in the dimension of, say, sleep, body heat, or sensory arousal can thus motivate the expenditure on a consumption item able to provide the proper service like beds, clothes, air conditioning, television sets, etc.

The significant feature here is that not the "tools" purchased, but the services they provide contribute to removing or reducing deprivation. This means that

---

[12] The ambiguity of the term "consumption" reflects the etymology of a word that has been used for an increasingly broader set of phenomena after the organization of the economy evolved from the subsistence economy of self-supporting households to an increasingly differentiated division of labor. The extensive market exchange activities related to the latter imply purchasing acts of the households now usually associated with the term consumption ("consumption expenditures").

a temporary satiation level (defined per unit of time) that stifles the motivation to consume can be reached with respect to the *services*. In using them one may feel warm enough, may have had enough sleep, or enough entertainment. But the motivation to utilize the services of the "tools" one possesses and the motivation to purchase the "tools" in the first place are distinct features. The latter motivation depends on how the instrumental relationship of the tools and their services (means and ends) is perceived and is not necessarily affected by satiation in the services. Other reasons than the relative degree of deprivation in their services may influence the motivation to purchase tools. These reasons are likely to emerge from cognitive reflections (e.g., concerning securing a redundant supply, multiple availability for different purposes or at different places, etc.) and subsequent conditioned reinforcement building up secondary reinforcing instances.

People usually reflect and learn about how to instrumentalize consumption items with tool function – most of them belonging to the category of durables (appliances, equipments, etc.) – before a purchasing decision is made. Often rather elaborate knowledge about the consumption technology is necessary and needs to be built up. This knowledge is obtained not only through personal experimentation, but also through communication and observation and imitation of other consumers. Not least, knowledge of the consumption technology is offered by the producers of consumption items – an important function of their advertising. Given the selective nature of individual information processing discussed in the previous section, attention processes tend to shift from information less frequently and less intensely recognized towards information recognized more often and more intensely. At the same time, the perception and, in the longer run, consumption knowledge of items which continue to attract attention tend to become more detailed (refinement effect). By repeated experience a conditioned reinforcement is likely to build up that creates secondary reinforcement instances. Individual preferences extend to ever more details and attributes – attracting more attention in the same direction.

Because of the limitations of the individual information processing capacity, the already mentioned consequence of this process is specialization in consumption. One person may develop into a true motor sport fan following up, with an increasing preference and growing expertise, the most recent technical achievements of the motor car industry. Another person may develop into a similarly attentive opera fan with highly differentiated perception of, and preferences for, the qualitative differences in the music performance. Some people may develop into knowledgeable motor sport and opera fans simultaneously, but nobody can be a fan with differentiated perceptions of, and preferences for, everything. The upshot of specialization and the simultaneous refinement of perception, knowledge, and preferences is that additional reasons can arise for a consumer to purchase, several times over, consumption items with tool functions. These reasons may override the fact that the items provide one and the same service (or very similar ones) and that, with respect to that service, the satiation level is close to being reached or is already reached. (The extreme case is that of collectibles.)

If there is a satiation level with regard to the services in some deprivation dimension, and if multiple purchases of the same "tool" or similar ones exceed the number technically necessary to furnish the satiation level in the services, this simply results in a decreasing average rate of using the services provided by each single tool. For example, since only one pair of shoes (a "tool" providing pain protection and body warmth as "services") can be worn at the same time, purchasing several pairs of shoes means that on average each single pair of shoes is used less intensely. However, although this may induce some dissonant feeling, seeing things being utilized less intensely is likely not to curb the motivation to consume (purchase) as much as the physiological experience of satiation would do.

Another, but related, cause for expanding consumption irrespective of satiation levels being reached can occur when a consumption good is capable of removing or reducing deprivation in several dimensions simultaneously. Such "combination goods" are often deliberately created by product differentiation and product innovations. If, with rising income, consumption of these goods is growing, satiation levels are usually not reached in all dimensions at the same time. In that case, a sufficient motivation to further expand consumption of the good or service may be upheld in those dimensions not yet satiated. For obtaining additional satisfaction from such "combination goods" in some dimensions, consumption in other dimensions is extended beyond the satiation level. The possibility to create new combinations is strongly supported by the refinement effect just mentioned.

The questions addressed in this section are why and in what way consumer spending has been expanding tremendously in real terms with rising income over the past century and how the unequal growth of consumption expenditures across different consumption categories (the differences in the income elasticities of the goods and services) can be explained. For the consumption categories discussed so far, the answers were based on the assumption that the growth of income and consumption would in principle make a reduction or removal of average deprivation feasible. In some consumption categories, however, the satiation level may not, or not easily, be reached by increasing expenditures.

Consider, for example, the primary reinforcing instance of social status recognition. Consumption items with tool function whose services are able to signal the desired status by distinguishing oneself from others may remove or reduce deprivation in this dimension. Yet, with rising average income, lower income groups may also be able to acquire such consumption items. As a consequence, the status-distinguishing character of the corresponding consumption items is lost and deprivation in this dimension returns. To continue to be able to signal the desired social status differences by one's own consumption, other, and usually more expensive, goods need to be consumed. A level of satiation can, if at all, only be upheld by continuously rising expenditures on status goods (see Hirsch 1978) – an unstable condition like in a weapons race.

Another case in which satiation is difficult to attain and consumption can therefore expand without reducing deprivation significantly is the primary reinforcing instance of sensory arousal. As argued by Scitovsky (1976), the reason is again an instability in the deprivation–satiation mechanism, albeit one that is caused in a different way. This time it arises from a kind of sensory stupefaction effect that calls for ever stronger stimuli to reduce deprivation. With growing consumption, the satiation level is continually rising here. The instability can be conjectured to be visible in modern consumption patterns in the expenditures on entertainment, tourism, and the media that have been growing much faster with rising income than average consumption expenditures and are likely to continue to do so.

20.6 Conclusions

Human economic activity and the human economy have changed dramatically over time. Evolutionary economics has been proposed as a paradigm for analyzing the historical process of change. However, evolutionary economics, as much as economics more generally, requires a foundation in the form of a concise theory of economic behavior. Both the historical changes in economic behavior and the behavioral dispositions on the basis of which they could develop can probably be rationalized, but not explained, by the static (and latently normative) theory of constrained maximization. In this chapter the foundations of an evolutionary approach to economic behavior have been laid out. It has been argued that the historical malleability of economic behavior is based on the interactions between elementary, innate behavior dispositions and adaptation mechanisms on the one hand and the limited, and always selective, cognitive and observational learning that contributes to an ever more extended and differentiated action knowledge. The implications of this interpretation have briefly been outlined in an exemplary fashion for the explanation of the evolution and growth of consumption.

The fact that, as a characteristic of the evolutionary economic transformation process, consumption is continually growing has been attributed to several causes. As a consequence of "nature's parsimony" (as Ricardo put it), i.e. of a minimal real per capita income, humans have throughout their history been confronted by a situation of deprivation with respect to many of their needs. Simply as a reaction to that situation of deprivation, consumption expenditures could therefore be expected to rise from their extremely low value, when per capita income in the developed countries started to rise in the early twentieth century. However, as it turned out, a more detailed investigation of this reaction begs the question of what precisely causes deprivation and whether and when, with further rising income, satiation can remove that consumption motivation.

The hypotheses suggested here to answer the question have emphasized the genetically fixed, physiological, and psychological dimensions of deprivation in which a reduction of deprivation is a rewarding experience. In some of these dimensions it may, for different reasons, be difficult to reach satiation even at very high levels of income. Two examples are often mentioned: social or status recognition, sensory or cognitive arousal. In these few dimensions the simple logic of increasing consumption to reduce deprivation seems to induce a long-lasting, if not unbounded, growth of demand and, hence, a rising share of these consumption categories in overall consumption expenditures. Even though this is a selective effect, it does contribute to consumption further expanding even in the richest countries.

Beyond the motivational mechanism of deprivation and satiation, other parts of the human biological inheritance have been claimed also to play a crucial role for economic behavior and its impact on the economic transformation process. These parts are conditioned learning and the intelligent recognition of means–ends or tool–service relationships from which additional motives to expand consumption emerge. As a result of contingent reinforcement, preferences for goods and services can develop where there have been no such preferences before. With disposable income rising, consumers literally learn to appreciate previously unknown consumption opportunities, to develop refined tastes, and to "specialize" in certain consumption activities.

Furthermore, it has been contended that with rising income the opportunities for purchasing consumption goods with "tool" functions increase, provided the consumers command the corresponding consumption knowledge. The information from which this knowledge arises is not least furnished by commercial advertisements, and its impact is often reinforced by socially contingent opinion formation processes and agenda-setting effects. These are the sources that provide all sorts of plausible reasons for why "tools" should be purchased. At the level of cognitively motivated consumption expenditures they may induce expenses, even when satiation with respect to some of the service dimensions of the tools is already reached. The consequence is a decreasing average rate of using the services of the tools. A special case of this phenomenon is that of "combination goods" nowadays representing a substantial share of the consumer goods.

20.7 References

Anderson, J. R. 2000. *Cognitive Psychology and Its Implications*, 5th edn, New York: Worth.

Bandura, A. 1986. *Social Foundations of Thought and Action – A Social Cognitive Theory*. Englewood Cliffs, NJ: Prentice-Hall.

Bentham, J. 1789. *An Introduction to the Principles of Morals and Legislation*. London: T. Payne.

Campbell, D. T. 1987. "Blind Variation and Selective Retention in Creative Thought as in Other Knowledge Processes," in G. Radnitzky and W. W. Bartley II (eds.), *Evolutionary Epistemology, Theory of Rationality, and the Sociology of Knowledge.* La Salle: Open Court, pp. 91–114.

Caplan, A. L. (ed.) 1978. *The Sociobiology Debate.* New York: Harper.

Chagnon, N. A. and Irons, W. (eds.) 1979. *Evolutionary Biology and Human Social Behavior – An Anthropological Perspective.* North Scituate, RI: Duxbury Press.

Deaton, A. and Muellbauer, J. 1980. *Economics and Consumer Behavior.* Cambridge: Cambridge University Press.

Dugatkin, L. A. 2003. *Principles of Animal Behavior.* New York: Norton.

Fagerberg, J. 2003. "Schumpeter and the Revival of Evolutionary Economics," *Journal of Evolutionary Economics* 13: 125–59.

Fauconnier, G. and Turner, M. 2002. *The Way We Think – Conceptual Blending and the Mind's Hidden Complexities.* New York: Basic Books.

Foster, J. and Metcalfe, J. S. 2001. "Modern Evolutionary Perspectives: An Overview," in J. Foster and J. S. Metcalfe (eds.), *Frontiers of Evolutionary Economics.* Cheltenham: Edward Elgar, pp. 1–16.

Gigerenzer, G. and Goldstein, D. G. 1996. "Reasoning the Fast and Frugal Way: Models of Bounded Rationality," *Psychological Review* 103: 650–69.

Hamilton, W. D. 1964. "The Genetical Evolution of Social Behavior I," *Journal of Theoretical Biology* 7: 1–16.

Helson, H. 1964. *Adaptation Level Theory.* New York: Harper & Row.

Herrnstein, R. J. 1990. "Behavior, Reinforcement, and Utility," *Psychological Sciences* 4: 217–21.

Hirsch, F. 1978. *Social Limits to Growth.* Cambridge, MA: Harvard University Press.

Hodgson, G. M. 2002. "Darwinism in Economics: From Analogy to Ontology," *Journal of Evolutionary Economics* 12: 259–81.

2004. *The Evolution of Institutional Economics.* London: Routledge.

Houthakker, H. S. and Taylor, L. D. 1966. *Consumer Demand in the United States 1929–1970.* Cambridge, MA: Harvard University Press.

Kahneman, D., Wakker, P., and Sarin, R. 1997. "Back to Bentham? Explorations of Experienced Utility," *Quarterly Journal of Economics* 112: 375–405.

Koestler, A. 1964. *The Act of Creation.* London: Penguin Books.

Lebergott, S. 1993. *Pursuing Happiness – American Consumers in the Twentieth Century.* Princeton: Princeton University Press.

Maddison, A. 2001. *The World Economy: A Millennium Perspective.* Paris: OECD.

March, J. G. and Simon, H. A. 1958. *Organizations.* New York: Wiley.

Mayr, E. 1991. *One Long Argument.* Cambridge, MA: Harvard University Press.

Metcalfe, J. S. 1998. *Evolutionary Economics and Creative Destruction.* London: Routledge.

Millenson, J. R. 1967. *Principles of Behavioral Analysis.* New York: Macmillan.

Nelson, R. R. 1995. "Recent Evolutionary Theorizing about Economic Change," *Journal of Economic Literature* 33: 48–90.

Nelson, R. R. and Winter, S. G. 1982. *An Evolutionary Theory of Economic Change.* Cambridge, MA: Harvard University Press.

2002. "Evolutionary Theorizing in Economics," *Journal of Economic Perspectives* 16: 23–46.

Pulliam, H. R. and Dunford, C. 1980. *Programmed to Learn: An Essay on the Evolution of Culture*. New York: Columbia University Press.

Ruprecht, W. 2005. "The Historical Development of the Consumption of Sweeteners – A Learning Approach," *Journal of Evolutionary Economics* 15: 247–72.

Samuelson, P. A. 1947. *Foundations of Economic Analysis*. Cambridge, MA: Harvard University Press.

Schlicht, E. 1997. "Patterned Variation – The Role of Psychological Dispositions in Social and Institutional Evolution," *Journal of Institutional and Theoretical Economics* 153: 722–36.

Schumpeter, J. A. 1934. *Theory of Economic Development*. Cambridge, MA: Harvard University Press.

Scitovsky, T. 1976. *The Joyless Economy*. Oxford: Oxford University Press.

Siegel, S. 1957. "Level of Aspiration and Decision Making," *Psychological Review* 64: 253–62.

Sternberg, R. J. 1988. *The Nature of Creativity*. Cambridge: Cambridge University Press.

Stone, J. R. N. 1954. *Measurement of Consumer Expenditures and Behavior in the United Kingdom*, vol. I. Cambridge: Cambridge University Press.

van Raaij, W. F. 1985. "Attribution of Causality to Economic Actions and Events," *Kyklos* 38: 3–19.

Veblen, T. 1898. "Why Is Economics Not an Evolutionary Science?" *Quarterly Journal of Economics* 12: 373–97.

Vromen, J. J. 2001. "The Human Agent in Evolutionary Economics," in J. Laurent and J. Nightingale (eds.), *Darwinism and Evolutionary Economics*. Cheltenham: Edward Elgar, pp. 184–208.

Warke, T. 2000. "Mathematical Fitness in the Evolution of the Utility Concept from Bentham to Jevons to Marshall," *Journal of History of Economic Thought* 22: 3–23.

Wilson, E. O. 1975. *Sociobiology – The New Synthesis*. Cambridge, MA: Belknap Press.

1998. *Consilience – The Unity of Knowledge*. New York: Knopf.

Witt, U. 1996. "A Darwinian Revolution in Economics?" *Journal of Institutional and Theoretical Economics* 152: 707–15.

2001. "Learning to Consume – A Theory of Wants and the Growth of Demand," *Journal of Evolutionary Economics* 11: 23–36.

2003. *The Evolving Economy*. Cheltenham: Edward Elgar.

2008. "Evolutionary Economics," in S. N. Durlauf and L. E. Blume (eds.), *The New Palgrave Dictionary of Economics*. New York: Palgrave Macmillan, forthcoming.

10

Environmental Innovation and Societal Transitions 1 (2011) 109–114

Contents lists available at ScienceDirect

Environmental Innovation and Societal Transitions

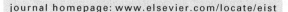

ELSEVIER

journal homepage: www.elsevier.com/locate/eist

The dynamics of consumer behavior and the transition to sustainable consumption patterns

Ulrich Witt

Max Planck Institute of Economics, Kahlaische Str. 10, 07745 Jena, Germany

ARTICLE INFO

Article history:
Received 17 November 2010
Received in revised form 21 February 2011
Accepted 1 March 2011

JEL classification:
A13
B52
D01
D03
D11
Q50
Q56

Keywords:
Consumption
Sustainability
Satiation
Innovation
Welfare

ABSTRACT

Strong growth in disposable income has driven, and is still driving, consumption to unprecedented, but not sustainable levels. To explain the dynamic interplay of needs, need satisfaction, and innovation underlying that growth a behavioral theory of consumption is suggested and discussed with respect to its implications for making a transition to more sustainable patterns of consumer behavior.

© 2011 Elsevier B.V. All rights reserved.

In the developed countries, consumption drives much of the environmental stress, waste, degradation, and resource exhaustion directly or indirectly qua the production of the goods and services demanded. This situation is the result of a century long process fueled by the unprecedented growth of real per capita income. When discussing options for making a transition to consumption patterns with less harmful consequences it seems useful, therefore, to ponder how consumers have come to respond to a situation of relative affluence. Consumption expenditures have followed closely the dramatic increases of per capita income. In the U.S., for example, consumer spending has been rising over just one century in real terms by roughly the factor five (U.S. Bureau of Labor Statistics, Report 991,

---

E-mail address: witt@econ.mpg.de

2210-4224/$ – see front matter © 2011 Elsevier B.V. All rights reserved.
doi:10.1016/j.eist.2011.03.001

2006) – yes, calculated in prices of 2002, the budget an average American could spend in 1901 was only little more than 20% of the budget of 2002! The drastic expansion has not equally taken place in all consumption categories. In some of them income elasticity has been greater than one, in others smaller than one, and in yet others consumption comes close to a state reflecting saturation (see e.g., Lebergott, 1993). To simply assume that consumers are insatiable – as in canonical economics in order to ensure unique solutions for the utility maximization calculus – is therefore not very helpful both for explaining the uneven growth of consumption categories and for inquiring into how a transition to more sustainable consumption patterns can be made.

1. The growth of consumption and its reasons

To explain what is going on it is necessary to account for the highly complex motivations underlying consumer behavior (the revealed, but unexplained preferences of textbook economics). These motivations are likely to change when the ability to spend increases with rising income. As discussed in more detail elsewhere (Witt, 2001), this fundamental conjecture can be substantiated as a dynamics of learning and satiation. For this purpose, a set of hypotheses is required which specify what is left open in canonical economics: the answer to the question where utility comes from. The necessary extension can take recourse to a few general concepts as follows. From behavioral science it is known that, if an organism is deprived of something, a motivation builds up to take an action that is able to (temporarily) reduce deprivation. Let us call that what is deprived a "need".[1] Among these needs are those for water, sleep, food, body heat, shelter, pain relief, physical activity, sex, affection, social recognition and status, sensory and cognitive arousal, and consistency of self-image which are quite universally shared among humans (and not only humans). The partly cognitively mediated satisfaction of these needs is what, in the economic terminology, generates utility.[2]

The crucial insight becoming feasible by this extension is how these needs differ with regard to their satiability when consumption is increased. The intake of food or something to drink, for example, is subject to homoeostatic controls so that normally the motivation for additional consumption vanishes as the satiation level – a certain average quantity per unit of time – is approached. With rising income, it is therefore likely that the growth in the intake of food and drinks is sooner or later stagnating, not necessarily so, however, the corresponding expenditures. The food industry experiences the stagnation (corresponding to an income elasticity smaller than one) as market saturation. And as all businesses in saturated markets facing stiffening price competition and declining profits, suppliers have strong incentives to create extra demand by innovative products.

Since for the entire food industry the satiation level in calories is an increasingly binding constraint, additional expenditures can only be elicited in two ways (ignoring for the moment an increase in waste of food). The producers can either upgrade the quality resulting in a higher price per calorie, provided consumers honor the quality improvement; or they can reduce the satiating content – in this case: of calories – per product. An example of the first innovation strategy is the large scale import of exotic produce from all over the world (inducing major long haul transport activities), finding acceptance among consumers for reasons to be explained shortly. An instance of the second strategy are product innovations that allow to enjoy the rewarding experience of eating something tasty without coming nearer to the physiological satiation level, e.g., food stuffs made with low-calorie, artificial sweeteners. Satiation is postponed and so is market saturation (see Ruprecht, 2005). Diet Coke is a prominent example.

Not all needs are as easily satiated as those for food and drinks, however. It can therefore be expected that, with rising income, consumer expenditures are increasingly shifting in the direction of

---

[1] Since the reduction of deprivation is a reinforcing event in the sense of the theory of instrumental or operant conditioning, the concept of needs, as used here, coincides with what is called primary reinforcers in behavioral science (see e.g., Herrnstein, 1990; Staddon and Cerutti, 2003).

[2] Note that the quantities of water, sleep, food, etc. cannot simply be plugged in for the usual placeholder variables $x_1, \ldots, x_n$ in a static utility function $u = u(x_1, \ldots, x_n)$ since they are consumed on very different time scales with a limited and varying substitutability. The relevant analytic representation would be a program instead of a function, and it is doubtful whether a dynamic optimization of the program in its entirety, if feasible at all, would be relevant for actually observable behavior.

U. Witt / Environmental Innovation and Societal Transitions 1 (2011) 109–114   111

goods that serve the less easily satiable needs. This has been, and will continue to be, reflected in the differences in the income elasticities of the expenditure categories empirically recorded by consumer surveys. Consider, e.g., the need for social recognition and status. Consumption items able to signal the desired status by distinguishing oneself from others can serve the satisfaction of this need. Yet, with rising average income, lower income groups can also acquire such consumption items so that the status-distinguishing character goes lost. To avoid being deprived of one's relative status, other, and usually more expensive, goods need to be consumed. A level of satiation can, if at all, only be upheld by continuously rising the expenditures on status goods – an unstable situation like in an arms race (Hirsch, 1978; Frank, 2007).

Another example in which a lasting satiation is difficult to attain and consumption can therefore expand without average deprivation being reduced significantly is the need for sensory and cognitive arousal. The reason arises here from a kind of stupefaction effect that calls for making ever stronger stimuli available for serving the need (Scitovsky, 1981). With growing income the satiation level is continually rising and so is the corresponding consumption. The instability can be expected to be reflected in the expenditures on entertainment, tourism, particularly long haul and adventure tourism, and the services of mass media – expenditure categories that have been growing much faster with rising income than average consumption expenditures and are likely to continue to do so (see Report 991, 2006 by the U.S. Bureau of Labor Statistics).

If one and the same consumption good appeals to several needs simultaneously, and if the quantities at which the satiation levels of the needs are reached differ, a unique satiation level is not defined – the case of "combination goods". With increasing consumption of such goods the satiation levels of one need after the other are then reached. However, a (successively reduced) motivation to further expand consumption continues to exist up to the satiation level of the least easily satiated need. For producers facing an increasingly saturated market, innovation by means of creating combination goods is therefore an attractive strategy: adding features to their products that appeal to additional needs that are less easily satiable than the ones their products originally serve. Product differentiation strategies aiming in this direction are, for instance, the adding of symbols that can be used to signal status or a particular group identity like in apparel, foot ware, bags, etc. (see Witt, 2010). A further example is the adding of features appealing to sensory and cognitive arousal as in the case of exotic food mentioned above.

An important aspect of any attempt to substantiate the motivational underpinnings of consumer behavior is the question of how preferences (or the ways utility is obtained) are changing over time. Since in the substantiation outlined above the need concept coincides with the notion of reinforcement, an important secondary dynamics of preference change can be traced back to the effects of conditioned reinforcement or conditioning learning on consumer behavior. In this kind of learning the following happens (see Leslie, 1996). Consider the rewarding experience of an action or event reducing deprivation (i.e. satisfying a need as defined above). If this experience coincides repeatedly with actions or events that are initially experienced as neutral an association is learnt by which the originally neutral action eventually triggers a rewarding experience by virtue of the learnt association. A conditioned reinforcers emerges or, to refer to the corresponding consumption motivation, an "acquired want" (unlike the widely inter-personally shared needs that were mentioned, the emerging structure of acquired wants is of a more idiosyncratic nature, though there are also group-specific influences from the particular cultural environment in which conditioning takes place).

Imagine, for example, that it frequently happens that someone takes a meal, when hungry, in a particular setting of scenic architecture, furniture, tableware, table music, etc. Even though such a special environment may initially be a neutral experience, by the association that is learnt, the scenic architecture, furniture, tableware, table music, etc. may become a rewarding experience in its own right – a conditioned reinforcer. Accordingly, enjoying such aesthetic attributes can become an own motivation for consumption, a motivation – this is the clue – that often contributes much more to rising expenditures than the motivation to eat on which it was originally conditioned.

The motivation forces underlying consumer behavior as discussed so far are, of course, often mediated by cognitive deliberation. By cognitive construction of means–ends relationships consumers assess possible actions with respect to their instrumental value for attaining need satisfaction. This assessment can lead to deviations from behavior that reinforcement contingencies alone would pre-

112   *U. Witt / Environmental Innovation and Societal Transitions 1 (2011) 109–114*

dict. This is particularly true where the commodities consumed have "tool" character, i.e. where they provide "services", and where it is these services, not the commodities themselves, that reduce deprivation (e.g., clothes whose service is to contribute to maintain body temperature). The point here is that the motivation to purchase such tools and the motivation to use their services are two different things. Accordingly, satiation occurs, if at all, in the amount of the *services* consumed per unit of time (the service of one dress, say, would suffice to feel warm enough). The number of tools purchased is not subject to direct satiation. A motivation to buy additional ones can therefore still be present when, in terms of their services, a capacity sufficient for satiating the underlying need(s) has already been reached. The reason is that this motivation is cognitively mediated. It depends on how consumers perceive the instrumental relationship between the tools and their services.

If the producers can give reasons that convince consumers of an additional instrumental value of new or differentiated products, a motivation for multiple purchases can be induced where the original service(s) offered by those products would not motivate such purchases. Reasons may, e.g., be convenience or redundancy arguments regarding multiple availabilities for different purposes or at different places, or specialized functionality reasons. Consider the case of foot ware. One pair of shoes (a "tool" providing pain protection and contributing to keeping body temperature as "services") would, in principle, be – and for most of human cultural history has been – sufficient to reach the satiation level with respect to the services. With the introduction of functionally differentiated shoes – serving casual home use, representative purposes, working requirements, leisure activities (walking, hiking, tennis, etc.), and fashion-based status-signaling – sufficiently convincing reasons have been provided for raising multiple purchases of foot ware to ever higher levels. Since only one pair of shoes can be worn at the same time, this means that for each single pair of shoes the average rate of using its services decreases if the utilization period is not proportionately prolonged. Precisely this is, of course, often prevented by changes in fashion (Chai et al., 2007) and aging processes in materials.

Needless to say, multiple purchases mean additional materials, energy, and space being used (up). Furthermore, cognitive activity also implies motivational forces of its own as, for example, consistency of self-image (Dunning, 2007) and the pervasive need for high self-esteem (Gollwitzer and Kirchhof, 1998). These motivations can trigger substantial consumer expenditures and seem to do so the more, the higher per capita income becomes (a striking example is the soaring growth of expenditures on cosmetic surgery). Self-image and self-esteem are both contingent on social norms which are not necessarily stable. If everybody is striving to spend enough to be better than average in satisfying the norm, an inherently unstable winding-up of the norm is set in motion.

2. Implications for societal transition

Since Bentham's inception of utilitarianism, economists have been inspired by the twin idea of explaining economic behavior and assessing its moral legitimacy. Today the latter idea only occurs in the abstract disguise of welfare theory. Once the black box of subjective preferences is opened, however, and the underlying motivational forces are diagnosed as outlined here, welfare theory becomes a debatable basis for assessing what changes in consumption would seem warranted. Welfare economics has no answer to the question of what stage of preference learning should be taken as a basis for assessing whether there are any welfare gains; and it is silent on whether the different motivations underlying consumption can claim different normative legitimacy (see Binder, 2010).

True, the multiplication of per capita disposable income has enabled not only the upper strata of society but also the masses to enjoy what by historical standards is a "good" life. Nonetheless, a judgment on what is a still better life cannot be made independent of the level of income already reached. Once disposable income allows to remove deprivation in the pressing human needs, motivational mechanisms take over in guiding consumer behavior that are less innocent with respect to their environmental impact. What consumers then enjoy as pleasures, to use the utilitarian diction, are largely learnt pleasures, and where the pleasures would, in principle, seem satiable with the income level reached, cognitive motives are usually learnt so as to enjoy ways of further income spending that avoid satiation. Yet, there is a notable asymmetry. Had there been no opportunity to experience all the new consumption possibilities there would have been no opportunity to learn to appreciate them – and no sense of missing something. Once all the experiences have been made, though, foregoing the

U. Witt / Environmental Innovation and Societal Transitions 1 (2011) 109–114   113

learnt pleasures would be felt as a harsh privation. In view of the severe environmental degradation and resource exhaustion caused by modern consumption patterns this asymmetry can be argued to have moral relevance when it comes to assessing what transitions are to be made for reaching more sustainable consumption patterns.

However, one of the puzzling questions in the transition debate is: who has the power and motivation to act to change consumer behavior – the consumers themselves, the producers, the government? It would be an illusion to believe that, in an economy committed to growth, producers could escape from the spiral of saturated markets triggering innovations that aim at creating additional demand that sooner or later is satiated too. It would be illusionary to assume that producers facing increasing saturation in the rich economies would not seek, or even press for, the opportunity to expand into non-saturated markets of the developing economies – advertising and propagating the devastating, resource-intensive consumption patterns there to hundreds of millions of future consumers. And it would be totally illusionary, if not an expression of dual morality (see Chang, 2003), to hope that these new, inexperienced consumers would be the ones who abstain from adopting the advertised life style while consumers in the developed countries seem unable to emancipate themselves from their drifting motivations.

It is difficult to imagine therefore that a transition can come about without regulations and suitable discriminatory taxation being invoked on the innovation and exportation process. Several of the necessary measures have been discussed for quite some while, particularly those focusing on product characteristics and features of the production process. Among them are regulations forcing a "dematerialization" strategy (Schmidt-Bleek, 1994) which to the extent to which the resource savings can be privately internalized, amounts to little more than enforcing corresponding conventions. Stricter regulations here or with respect to energy conversation in, and energy efficiency of, consumer goods and corresponding emission standards need to be supplemented by policies avoiding rebound effects (see van den Bergh, 2011). Also the reduction of incentives for, or even taxation of, mass production in agriculture and food processing, should be mentioned here as measures directly impacting on consumer behavior. If these measures were successfully implemented, the further expansion of demand would develop significantly less environmental harm – provided the costs of these measures in terms of international competitiveness and domestic economic growth still allow any further expansion.

What has much less been discussed are regulations and taxes that try to induce shifts in consumer expenditures themselves, particularly a selective and progressively shaped taxation of consumption. Much environmental harm could be prevented if consumers substituted the consumption of resource-intensive products and services (like those of the tourism industry – one of the fastest growing industries world wide) by less resource-intensive products and services. The latter kind of services like care, personal assistance, the arts, education, research, law enforcement, defense, and others tend to be labor-intensive. Under the influence of rising wages and, hence, rising costs of these services, what actually currently happens is the opposite tendency: substituting away from labor-intensive services. This is equally obvious where the supply of these services is or can privately be organized - as for example in the case of care, personal assistance, the arts, or education - as it is in the cases where the supply is publicly provided - as a public or merit good like research, law enforcement, or defense.

Perhaps surprisingly, a good deal of the transition that seems to be necessary to come closer to sustainable consumption patterns thus requires *reverting* processes that are under way as a result of a declining willingness to pay for the increasing relative costs of labor-intensive services. Ultimately, the substitution is driven by the secularly declining prices of natural resources relative to wages that makes resource-intensive products and services relatively cheaper. But it is precisely this falling price ratio that is not sustainable – calling for correction more generally or, where this is not possible, more specifically by regulations and discriminating taxes on resource-intensive products and services.

The question remains, of course, who is going to act and with what motivation. Where should the majority votes for these measures in democracies come from? All that can probably be hoped for is that a public discourse in the richest economies gains momentum that acknowledges the moral relevance of the notable asymmetric effect which is exerted on our well-being by what we learn to consume. Putting the environmental disturbances of consumption in perspective with the drifting motivations underlying consumption, sovereign voters may show more insight to form the necessary majorities in the political arena where sovereign consumers hesitate to abstain from what they have been conditioned to want. In order to get the public discourse going it is not helpful to treat consumer motivation as a taboo (as some interpretations of consumer sovereignty do; see Norton et al. (1998) for a criticism). Endowed with reason, we are all able to reflect whether certain consumption patterns are worth it, if we become aware of their true costs. Inviting people to reflect on their mind set in this regard is not paternalism.

References

Binder, M., 2010. Elements of an Evolutionary Theory of Welfare. Routledge, London.

Chai, A., Earl, P., Potts, J., 2007. Fashion, growth, and welfare: an evolutionary approach. In: Bianchi, M. (Ed.), The Evolution of Consumption: Theories and Practices, Advances in Austrian Economics, vol. 10. Elsevier, Amsterdam, pp. 231–248.

Chang, H.-J., 2003. Kicking Away the Ladder: Development Strategy in Historical Perspective. Anthem Press, London.

Dunning, D., 2007. Self-image motives and consumer behavior: how sacrosanct self-beliefs sway preferences in the marketplace. Journal of Consumer Psychology 17 (4), 237–249.

Frank, R.H., 2007. Does context matter more for some goods than others? In: Bianchi, M. (Ed.), The Evolution of Consumption: Theories and Practices, Advances in Austrian Economics, vol. 10. Elsevier, Amsterdam, pp. 231–248.

Gollwitzer, P.M., Kirchhof, O., 1998. The willful pursuit of identity. In: Heckhausen, J., Dweck, C.S. (Eds.), Motivation and Self-regulation Across the Life Span. Cambridge University Press, Cambridge.

Herrnstein, R.J., 1990. Behavior, reinforcement and utility. Psychological Science 1, 217–224.

Hirsch, F., 1978. Social Limits to Growth. Harvard University Press, Cambridge, MA.

Lebergott, S., 1993. Pursuing Happiness – American Consumers in the Twentieth Century. Princeton University Press, Princeton.

Leslie, J.C., 1996. Principles of Behavioral Analysis. Harwood Academic Publishers, Amsterdam.

Norton, B., Costanza, R., Bishop, R.C., 1998. The evolution of preferences – why 'sovereign' preferences may not lead to sustainable policies and what to do about it. Ecological Economics 24, 193–211.

Ruprecht, W., 2005. The historical development of the consumption of sweeteners – a learning approach. Journal of Evolutionary Economics 15, 247–272.

Schmidt-Bleek, F., 1994. How to Reach a Sustainable Economy? Wuppertal Papers, 24. Wuppertal Institute for Climate, Environment and Energy, Wuppertal.

Scitovsky, T., 1981. The desire for excitement. Kyklos 34, 3–13.

Staddon, J.E.R., Cerutti, D.T., 2003. Operant conditioning. Annual Review of Psychology 54, 115–144.

van den Bergh, J.C.J.M., 2011. Energy conversation more effective with rebound policy. Environmental and Resource Economics 48 (1), 43–58.

Witt, U., 2001. Learning to consume – a theory of wants and the growth of demand. Journal of Evolutionary Economics 11, 23–36.

Witt, U., 2010. Symbolic consumption and the social construction of product characteristics. Structural Change and Economic Dynamics 21, 17–25.

11

Journal of Institutional Economics (2008), 4: 1, 1–24   Printed in the United Kingdom
© The JOIE Foundation 2008   doi:10.1017/S1744137407000823

Observational learning, group selection, and societal evolution

ULRICH WITT*

Max Planck Institute of Economics, Evolutionary Economics Unit, Germany

Abstract: The core problem of any group selection hypothesis is the possibility that pro-social individual behavior contributing to a selection advantage for the group as a whole is potentially subject to free-riding. If group behavior and, hence, the conditions for group selection change through imitation and migration between groups, as argued in Hayek's theory of societal evolution, the explanation of group selection needs to account for the individuals' cognitively reflected motivation to adopt pro-social behavior in the face of free-riding. To do so a game-theoretic model is suggested that incorporates observational learning as a mechanism of acquiring, and choosing between, strategies.

1. Introduction

What development societies take in historical terms hinges, it may be argued, on their capacities and their incentives to introduce or adopt new technologies, not only in processing economic resources, but also with respect to hygiene, medicine, and warfare. The incentives may be contingent on the particular conditions of the societies' geographic environment – a conjecture, recently popularized by Diamond (1997). But the institutions that societies are able to create also matter for the incentives, and even more so the capacity, to develop, support, and handle innovative technologies. This idea has been shared, despite controversial views in other respects, by such diverse authors as Veblen (1899, 1914) and F. A. Hayek (1967a, 1967b, 1971, 1979, Epilogue; 1988) in his later work. Like Veblen, Hayek developed a Darwinian, naturalistic view on both human institutions and their implications for economic history. Such an approach differs fundamentally from more recent works on competitive economic growth in the very long run in which the idea of competition between human societies is dressed up as a story of optimal choices that societies are supposed to make on the basis of hypothetic aggregate utility functions (cf. Acemoglu, Johnson, and Robinson, 2001; Galor and Moav, 2002).

Unlike Veblen, Hayek tried to cast his conjectures in the form of a more abstract group selection argument, borrowing notions from eugenics

*Correspondence to: Max Planck Institute of Economics, Evolutionary Economics Group, Kahlaische Str. 10, 07745 Jena, Germany. Email: Ulrich.Witt@econ.mpg.de
I am grateful to Luciano Andreozzi, Georg von Wangenheim, the Editor in Chief, and three anonymous referees of this journal for helpful comments.

(Carr-Saunders, 1922) and sociobiology (Wynne-Edwards, 1962) that emerged more recently. In his theory of societal evolution he emphasized the unique human potential for cultural adaptations through collective, 'cultural' learning processes specific to the respective human societies or groups. He claimed that the often unconscious, collective, cultural learning processes form an ontological layer in the development of societies 'between instinct and reason' (Hayek, 1971). With regard to its historical origin and evolutionary pace this layer is situated, Hayek argued, between the layers of intentional human choice on the one hand and natural selection on the other. It is at this layer, he believed, that – as an unintended, collective outcome – 'rules of conduct' (Hayek, 1967a) emerge as basic institutions. Through their impact on incentives and capacities to trade, accumulate, and innovate they should affect population growth and economic prosperity, which, in turn, are the variables driving the group selection process.

However, Hayek's naturalistic group selection approach left many details open. Later commentators therefore argued that there are some vague, incomplete, or even inconsistent features in his view of group selection (Gray, 1984; Vanberg, 1986; Hodgson, 1991; Witt, 1994). Although the debate on Hayek's theory of societal evolution has continued (see Bianchi, 1994; Vanberg, 1997; Caldwell, 2000; Rizzello, 2000), the role of his group selection argument has not been satisfactorily clarified. The core problem of any group selection hypothesis is the possibility that individual behavior contributing to a selection advantage for the group as a whole is potentially subject to free-riding. Such pro-social behavior usually demands individual sacrifices. Benefitting from, but not contributing to, theses sacrifices – i.e. free-riding – is therefore the individually more favorable strategy whenever this is possible.

In a natural selection environment in which both pro-social behavior and free-riding are genetically determined and inheritable, free-riding has a differential reproductive advantage, if there is no way for group members to discriminate against or exclude free-riders. Their propagation in the gene pool of the group threatens to undermine and eventually wipe out the pro-social behavior that established the selection advantage for the group in the first place. It has been argued that the share of carriers of pro-social behavior in the gene pool of a whole population (made up of several groups) may nonetheless increase. The condition for this to happen is that natural selection between groups in the population favors the growth of groups with strong pro-social behavior sufficiently over that of groups of free-riders (cf. e.g. Sober and Wilson, 1998; Field, 2001; Henrich, 2004). Yet, such a process is not sustainable as no group can expand in size indefinitely.

It is highly doubtful, however, whether a natural selection environment is indeed relevant to the discussion of theories about more modern human societies differing in, and competing on the basis of, the institutions that have emerged from their cultural learning processes. In a natural selection environment, the only criterion is differential reproductive success of human groups or societies (whether determined by genetic factors alone or by inherited and acquired, cultural features simultaneously, cf. Boyd and Richerson, 1985; Henrich, 2004). Yet in more recent times, changes in institutions and technology and their demographic and/or economic effects happen at time scales significantly shorter than the several human generations that are necessary for natural selection to develop a shaping effect. Moreover, economic progress seems to have enabled most human societies, except a few, traditional ones at the fringes of the developed world, to reach a state of 'reproductive affluence'. This means that the relationships between group success in terms of (military) power, wealth, or income on the one hand and reproductive success/population growth on the other are no longer as clear as in the natural selection model.

In later formulations of his theory of societal evolution, Hayek (1988) seems to have acknowledged these facts. He argues that in more modern times, the drivers of group selection and differential growth of societies are imitation and migration. Institutions of more successful societies tend to be imitated by less successful ones. In addition, there is a substantial migration from less successful societies to more successful ones, and an assimilation of migrants into successful societies. However, if this is true, the conditions for pro-social behavior need to be explained differently from the genetic and co-evolutionary approach, because both imitation and targeted (not just random) migration rest at least in part on individual, cognitive reflection and decision making that belong to the ontological layer of human reasoning and rational choice.

The present paper tries to make progress with respect to such an explanation. A game-theoretic model is proposed that accounts for the motivations underlying the adoption of pro-social rules of conduct in the presence of a free-riding temptation. The core feature in this model is a mechanism of acquiring attitudes based on observational learning on the one hand and the rational weighing of own strategies against the experience of other players with newly recognized alternatives on the other. Under these conditions, the chances for the emergence and dissemination of socially contingent attitudes ranging from opportunistic free riding to aggressive moralism towards, and punishment of, rule-breaking behavior can be analyzed. Allowing the interaction probabilities to be biased in a way that favors local subgroups interactions, an additional critical mass condition can be derived without invoking the assumption of a genetic disposition for conformism as in Henrich and Boyd (1998). The critical mass condition turns out to be decisive for the emergence and dissemination of pro-social rules of conduct as an institution in groups that gives these groups a competitive advantage in group 'selection'.

The reduction to a game-theoretic framework inevitably has to abstract from the details of the historical record of the competition between societies and to argue on the basis of somewhat artificial, idealizing assumptions. Nonetheless, it may help to clarify some generic condition of how societies are able to create and maintain institutions conducive to societal evolution. The paper proceeds as

4   ULRICH WITT

follows. In Section 2, Hayek's views on societal evolution are briefly summarized. A crucial step in developing the logic of 'group' selection in more detail is the specification of the cultural learning processes allowing for cognitive insight and inference. We borrow here from social cognitive learning theory, which is briefly outlined in Section 3. Section 4 presents a game-theoretic model for the analysis of the evolutionary process. The results derived from the model are discussed in Section 5. They highlight the role of rules of conduct for the differential growth or decline of different groups, the equivalent in the abstract model of different human societies. Although these results are based on several simplifications, they still allow a more detailed appraisal of Hayek's theoretical conjectures. Section 6 offers a brief conclusion.

2. Spontaneous order and societal evolution

When, in the later part of his academic works, Hayek was developing the foundations of his social philosophy, he was increasingly attracted to evolutionary thought and the Darwinian idea of natural selection operating, in the particular form of group selection, on the human society.1 Like his entire social philosophy, his theory of societal evolution is informed by the understanding that the capacity of individual human cognition – despite its uniqueness in nature – is limited. In the domain of societal and economic interactions, the fact that individual knowledge is incomplete, imperfect, and hypothetical in nature has two important implications.

One is that human agents never fully grasp the influence that their own actions have on the scope for, and the limits to, the behavior of other agents. To a certain extent, these effects are transmitted, in an impersonal form, through the price mechanism as is well-known to economists. The other, related, implication is that human agents regularly have difficulties in anticipating the full range of possible behaviors with which they may be confronted by other members of society. The lack of reliable expectations about the outcome of interactions, which might paralyze the willingness to engage in them, is prevented by the emergence of an impersonal system of rules of conduct (Hayek, 1967a). Since the complexity of both the price mechanism and systems of rules of conduct make it extremely difficult for the human mind to comprehend both, they cannot be the result of deliberate design and choice. Rather, these forms of coherent behavior, i.e. the 'spontaneous order', must have emerged from the interactions of all members of society as a largely unintended and unplanned outcome.

The coordination of individual behavior in the economic and political context is thus seen as a phenomenon similar to the inter-individual coordination that turns up in, and is brought about by, language, tradition, morality, custom,

---

1 See Hayek (1967a), (1967b), (1971), the epilogue of the third volume of his *Law, Legislation, and Liberty* (Hayek 1979), and Hayek (1988).

and law.[2] Eager to establish an approach that is built on the 'twin ideas of spontaneous order and evolution', Hayek (1979) distinguishes between three ontological layers at which the development of human society takes place. The first layer is that of biological evolution during human phylogeny. At this level, primitive forms of social behavior, values, and attitudes became genetically fixed as a result of natural selection processes. The criterion that governed that genetic adaptation was fitness for survival under the particular conditions prevailing in the environment. An observable order of social interactions emerged as a result of which sociobiology provides the explanatory model. Once they were genetically established, these attitudes and values have continued to be part of the natural endowment of modern humans, even though biological selection pressure has now been largely relaxed. The second layer of evolution is that of human intelligence and its products, i.e. knowledge and the numerous ways of recording, transmitting, and processing it. The systematic propagation, elaboration, and storing of knowledge, which is independent of the existence of any individual human brain, has made possible an enormously accelerated scientific and technological progress and a mastery of nature as no other species has ever achieved it.

The two layers of evolution mentioned so far – 'instinct and reason' – are widely acknowledged as rather independent, and significantly differing sources of evolution in the human domain. However, Hayek claims – and he considered this the genuine contribution of his own theory – that there is a third, and frequently overlooked, ontological layer of evolution, a layer *between* instinct and reason at which cultural evolution takes place (Hayek, 1971, 1988: chapter 1). From this cultural evolutionary process, the rules of conduct, morals, and traditions emerge that shape human interactions into the orderly forms of civilization.

The cultural evolutionary process goes on, Hayek holds, since the times of the small bands characteristic of the early stages of human phylogeny. In all these times orderly patterns of behavior have been learnt, passed on, and adapted in cultural, not genetic, transmission without much reflection of their meaning. They have been developed into cultural norms without deliberate planning or control. While historical accidents determine what new forms of rule-following behavior arise within the group, which of these survive and are successful is not a matter of chance, but of a selection process. More precisely this is a process of group selection where different rules may allow differential growth of the groups as a result of, e.g., more successful procreation and integration of outsiders. A

---

2 Throughout his writings Hayek has emphasized the long tradition of this interpretation going back to Scottish Enlightenment and writers like Mandeville, Hume, Ferguson, and Adam Smith (cf. Hayek, 1967a and 1967c). The interpretation was given an explicit evolutionary twist by Menger (1963) who argued on the basis of his 'causal-genetic' method that money, language, custom, and law emerge as unintended collective outcomes of social interactions.

growing population fosters specialization and the division of labor, which, in turn, favor groups with the superior rules. By the same logic, groups that do not adopt appropriate rules, whether by inventing or by imitating them, are likely to decline. Through this selection process, the rules of conduct, norms, and morals that eventually prevail are suited for the survival of an increasing number of members of the group.

Hayek thus interprets natural selection as occurring not only between competing species but also between competing groups of humans – and later entire societies – defined by common cultural norms. However, the actual transmission process differs between the case of competing species and the case of competing human societies. At the layer of evolution between instinct and reason Hayek envisages a cultural learning process in which a kind of collective intelligence is accumulated in a population in the form of rules of behavior. Compared to the process of genetic variation that occurs through generational change, rules of conduct and cultural norms can be acquired and transmitted much faster. As the population size has grown significantly in the more recent times, the rules themselves have become more and more differentiated and abstract. They have eventually led to the anonymous extended order of the world-wide interconnected markets that, Hayek (1988: chapter 3) argues, have made civilization and exceptional prosperity possible.

In its somewhat sketchy state, Hayek's theory of societal evolution and spontaneous order leaves several questions open. The selective transmission of group-specific rules of conduct is argued to result from 'cultural learning' and imitation – both seen as largely unconscious processes. But how, precisely, are these supposed to work? To what extent do they interact with genetic fitness and reproductive success (as they are interpreted to do, e.g., in the theory of co-evolution of genes and culture in Boyd and Richerson, 1985)? Similarly, with respect to his group selection hypothesis, it is unclear how that kind of selection is supposed to work. Is it a modified version of 'Social Darwinism' (as Gray, 1984: 140–145 has called it) in which the differential growth of competing groups is to be attributed to comparative advantages in producing descendants or attracting members from competing groups into the own group?[3]

---

3 The sketchy outline also leaves open whether, and to what extent, Hayek's hypotheses about cultural learning and group selection – obviously population bound phenomena – are compatible with the methodological individualism point of view advocated earlier in Hayek (1948), see Vanberg (1986). From that point of view, what would have to be explained is how the individual agents are induced to adopt and adhere to pro-social rules of conduct, despite the free-riding incentives preventing the adoption of such rules. Well-known social dilemmas and rationality traps may be hidden here that Hayek seems to have neglected. In sociobiology, it was precisely because of the problem of explaining altruism in face of these free-riding incentives that the concept of inclusive fitness was developed as a substitute for the older notion of group selection, see Hamilton (1964).

3. Observational learning and the rules of conduct

A way to improve the foundations of a theory of societal evolution based on the notion of collective, cultural learning processes situated 'between instinct and reason' is to elaborate in more detail the process of learning and its social or cultural contingencies. As will be argued in this section, learning has a social dimension and this dimension is decisive for understanding the spontaneous emergence of rules of conduct as a tacitly shared feature within groups of intensely interacting individuals. The point to start from are the limitations of human perception, information processing, and knowledge. Individual decision makers cannot completely grasp the multitude of imaginable series of choices that unfold into the future. Perceptions, and even more so, cognitive reflections are selective. They are based on partial and fallible knowledge of what is relevant for evaluating alternatives. Given that choices can only be made between alternatives that have been recognized, it seems only natural, therefore, to ask to what extent, and in which way, individual choice may be biased by selective knowledge acquisition and recall.

A key role is played here by selective attention processes which, in turn, depend on three features of information offered to the mind.[4] The first is sensory strength and frequency of the stimuli carrying the information. The second feature is whether similarities or an identity with already known elements/patterns can be recognized. (For this purpose relevant patterns stored in the memory must be activated by appropriate cues on an associative basis.) The third feature is the affective or emotional value of recognized similarities/identities in the sense of an association with earlier rewarding, neutral, or aversive experience. The cues instrumental for memorizing patterns and identifying incoming information also occur in larger and more complex systems called frames. These are employed in classificatory and associative activities and allow knowledge to be represented in a meaningful way. The associative capacity of the human mind is able to create longer and longer associative chains with increasingly more complex sets of frames from a limited number of probable genetically coded cues. This development starts in individual socialization, in the learning of language, and in the identification of meaning. As a consequence, the human mind always 'frames' information with already existing interpretation patterns (knowledge representations) even on the level of deliberate reasoning and thus produces mental attitudes of a sometimes fairly rigid nature.

The necessarily selective cognitive development, although entirely internal to the individual and in this sense subjective, is molded in social processes of communication with other agents (Bandura 1986, ch. 2). In the communication process, individuals tend to develop similarities in interpretation patterns and frames. Communication circles have an 'agenda setting' effect, which modifies in

---

4 Cf. Anderson (2000: chapters 3, 6, and 7) for the following.

a self-reinforcing way that is similar for all, the frequency with which particular information is – at the expense of potentially rivaling information – exchanged and attracts attention. In addition, agents who belong to the same social environment are exposed to the same symbolic representation of knowledge, which often suggests similar mental attitudes. They therefore tend to agree more closely about what are rewarding or aversive experiences. Despite the subjectivity of the individuals' unique cognitive history, these common features mean that a tacit, collectively shared, bias can occur within groups of intensely interacting individuals, a bias that influences what actions are selectively perceived, and what are not, as alternatives.

There is thus a socially shaped bias in the individuals' perception of their choice sets. Common beliefs and interpretations emerge tacitly and similarly for the agents in the population. The agents do not normally recognize the fact that, due to their selective information processing, potential choices go unnoticed, because the cognitive system that processes some information cannot at the same time reflect on how that information is processed. As a consequence, the tacit commonalities in perceiving and framing information are neither consciously chosen nor available for deliberate design. Although a precondition of reasoning, they cannot in their entirety themselves be subject to reason. They originate from the innate limitations of the human cognitive system, but, as they develop in a process of social cognitive learning, they are not in themselves genetically determined, that is a matter of instinct. As a basic element of (population-specific) culture they indeed belong to the layer 'between instinct and reason'.

Tacitly socially shared constraints in the perception of alternatives can be expected to result in some similarities of individual choices. There is little motivation to deviate from such similarities as long as the individually experienced consequences of similar behavior do not systematically diverge – which is unlikely to happen given the coherence also of response patterns implied by the similarities in the framing of information and in mental attitudes. For this reason, individual learning from experience should not, in principle, cancel out the effects of tacit cognitive commonalities. In fact, in the form of observational learning, the process of learning from behavioral feed back has itself a social dimension that reinforces, and creates further, cognitive commonalities (cf. Bandura 1986; chapter 2). The actions chosen by the agents and the consequences they experience can usually be observed by others. Those others can thus expand their knowledge about actions and consequences without bearing the risks and costs of experimenting themselves. Inferences with respect to success or failure of certain actions may appear the more meaningful to those agents, the more significant the respective actions of others qualify as models of behavior (which they do when occurring in a sufficiently stereotypical and persistent manner).

Because of its vicarious character, the 'model' of behavior given by some agent(s) and the associated consequences are likely to attract significant attention. Within one and the same population of intensely communicating agents,

Observational learning, group selection, and societal evolution 9

observational learning focuses on much the same 'model' and, therefore, tends to produce correlated results. This, in turn, ensures that such a 'model' becomes an important part of collectively shared knowledge. New and old members of a population – as well as the scientific observer – identify the behavioral regularity and its contingencies and consequences more easily than the underlying cognitive commonalities in the subjective sphere. For this reason, generalizations tend to be made at the phenomenological level: the commonly observed behavioral regularity starts to figure as a 'social model', to use Bandura's terminology, and the more frequently some social model occurs in a population, the more convincingly it may be inferred to be a representation of a 'rule of conduct' in Hayek's terminology.[5]

While tacit, socially shared, cognitive frames are instrumental to the emergence of rules of conduct, the actual variety of subjective knowledge and interpretations may be decisive for understanding the further development of those rules, their perseverance or decline. Variety results, first, from the particularities of the individual learning histories, from ambiguities in associating meaning with one and the same information, or simply from misconceptions. Second, it results from reflection, inventive thinking, and from accidental discovery of choices not perceived earlier, which enable the agents to create novel choices and actions and to widen their knowledge experimentally. At the individual level, subjective variety allows the agents to gradually shift cognitive constraints and to deviate from earlier patterns of behavior, possibly even from established rules of conduct. Variety of behavior within the population thus increases, and rules may be violated. This is very likely to arouse the attention of other group members who directly observe the deviation, and a communication process is likely to be triggered by which the news of novel choices and actions disseminate. Success or failure of the deviating behavior crucially hinges on the reaction of the social environment, i.e. on how, and on how many, group members respond to the deviation. Given the form and intensity of the collective reaction, however, the group members may be induced to start a (re-) appraisal of their own behavior in the light of the innovator's vicarious success or failure. As long as the population members at least roughly agree on what is a success or a failure, the innovator's fate tends to, respectively, induce or inhibit corresponding behavior adjustments by imitation (Bandura, 1986: chapter 7).

The consequences of the innovator's deviation are thus contingent on two different effects. One is the direct effect represented by individual response of those group members being faced with the innovator as their opponent and with

5 Social models and rules of conduct both refer to commonplace patterns of behavior that are generalized beyond the particular historical contingencies of their emergence. They are accepted without ever having been explicitly stated, let alone the actual causation been understood. Once accepted and obeyed to as a rule of conduct, they confirm and reinforce – in their easily grasped form – the cognitive commonalities from which they have originated.

10 ULRICH WITT

her or his deviating behavior – a strategic response that lends itself to a game-theoretic analysis. The other, indirect effect is induced by those group members who do not directly interact with the innovator but, after observing success or failure of her or his innovative strategy in the interaction with others, change their own behavior autonomously. This effect is a matter of observational learning. Both these reactions will be discussed in more detail in the next section. They jointly decide on whether behavioral variety is increasing or decreasing. They may well stabilize the actual degree of variance within narrow bounds. At the same time, both cognitive commonalities and behavioral regularities within the population, i.e. the rules of conduct, may be subject to continuing change.[6]

4. The analytic representation of 'rules of conduct' and 'groups'

When a member of a group is observed to deviate from a rule of conduct (or prevailing social model), the outcome of such a transgression is likely to arouse the attention of other group members. As argued in the preceding section, the outcome is determined by the responses of the members of the population involved in direct interactions with the innovator. It ultimately depends on what the currently prevailing rules of conduct imply as a response to deviant behavior. A dependency like this suggests a game-theoretic analysis. In such an analysis, a rule of conduct can be given the meaning of an equilibrium point of the underlying game. Accordingly, the question of what kind of rule of conduct emerges and persists, or changes, can be reformulated as the question of what solution originates from certain types of games, given the particular behavioral hypotheses about strategy choices and observational learning.

A typical example of a 'rule of conduct' within a group of interacting agents is the 'convention' resulting as equilibrium point in a coordination game (see, e.g., Boyer and Orléan, 1993; Young, 1993) or the non-cooperative solution in a one-shot prisoner's dilemma game. Since the latter, in contrast to the former, has a devastating impact on societal evolution, it represents the case of a destructive rule of conduct that Hayek seems to have neglected – perhaps because he believed that societies unable to prevent the spreading of destructive rules of conduct are bound to decline and eventually disappear. Indeed, if such a rule of conduct becomes endemic in a society whenever social dilemmas occur, this is likely to threaten both the productivity and the competitiveness of that society. Hence, the focus will here be on the generic conditions under which, in social dilemma situations, either pro-social, cooperative 'rules of conduct' or destructive ones

---

6 For distinct populations that do not communicate, or do so only very loosely, it would be surprising to find that the process of change takes the same route. Indeed, the isolation effect means that lack of communication creates conditions that favor the development of different systems of rules of conduct. The immense variety of languages, customs, mores, religious practices, and many other cultural particularities gives strong support to this conjecture.

Observational learning, group selection, and societal evolution   11

will emerge within a society. To make the case as strong as possible, conditions coming close to those in large, anonymous societies will be assumed.

Thus, imagine a large group of players who cannot recognize each others' performance. Let always two players be drawn at random to engage in a one-shot prisoner's dilemma game (pd-game). As is well known, if all players chose their strategies rationally (given the way they selectively perceive their choices), the result would be mutual defection. However, an entirely isolated interaction as in a one-shot pd-game may be a rather rare situation, even in large societies. For pd-games that are sufficiently frequently repeated to be recognized by each player as a series requiring interconnected strategic choices, it is well known from the 'folk theorem' that every solution from continued defection to continued cooperation can result as a solution of the repeated game. Yet, this continued social dilemma may be considered an equally extreme case as the pure one-shot game and, hence, not representative either of the way in which social dilemmas occur in large societies.

A more realistic, intermediate case will therefore be assumed here to explore how pro-social, cooperative rules of conduct for social dilemmas can emerge. This is the case of a singular interaction (still an encounter without recall) in which, however, the spatial proximity or the institutional set-up allow both players to 'get after' their opponent at some cost, if they want to. Getting after the opponent here means taking a singular subsequent action rewarding or punishing the opponent, e.g. by expressing gratitude with a small gift or by beating up someone who has betrayed, or by suing an opponent in court even if there is no chance to recuperate the expenses.[7] Thus, consider a symmetric pd-game with two randomly matched players i and j that is extended into two-stages as follows. In the opening stage, a choice has to be made between the moves c (cooperate) and d (defect) simultaneously. In a second, closing stage, the pay-offs of the choices in the first stage are revealed and the option to react, e.g. by imposing a penalty costly to both players on the opponent is given to both players. To keep things simple, let there be just two simultaneous moves in the second stage, p (punishing the opponent) and a (accepting the outcome of the first stage without taking the response option).[8] By assumption, the interaction between the two players in this particular two-stage game then ends, and the pay-offs for the

7 See the discussion in Congleton and Vanberg (2001) who, however, explore a model with an additional exit option in which the players can recognize their opponents. Note that for ease of exposition, the possibility of further reactions and counter-reactions will be ignored in the present discussion.

8 A response move in the second stage that rewards the opponent would only make sense when the opponent has cooperated at the first stage of the game. If both players have cooperated at the first stage, this case can be neglected, because the reward would only redistribute the cooperation gain between the cooperators without affecting the expected pay-off from mutual cooperation. This is different, if the player using a reward option has been defecting in the first stage. However, since the motivation for such a move is not compatible with the rational choice assumption used here as a bench mark for the conditions most unfavorable to the emergence of a cooperative rule of conduct, this case will also be neglected here.

12   ULRICH WITT

second stage are revealed. Hence, each player has two choices in the opening stage and four contingent choices in the closing stage. The two-stage game is characterized by eight contingent strategies per player and sixteen outcomes or combinations of strategies of both players (see the extensive form of the game in Figure 1).[9]

Let the contingent strategies for player i be denoted by $\{x, y\}$ where $x \in \{c, d\}$ and $y \in \{a|x, p|x\}$. The outcomes accruing to the players from their contingent strategies are determined by summing the pay-offs of the first and second stage of the game. With respect to the first stage, the standard pd-game order relation on the pay-offs is assumed. If T ('temptation') denotes defection while the opponent cooperates, R ('reward') denotes mutual cooperation, P ('punishment') denotes mutual defection, and S ('sucker's pay-off') denotes cooperation while the opponent defects, this means that

$$T > R > P > S. \tag{1}$$

With regard to the second stage pay-offs, it will be assumed that no additional costs arise to any player by choosing move a. However, choosing move p, usually invokes costs on both sides, i.e. on those who take punishing measures and on those being punished. To consider the least favorable case, let the costs C_p incurred by a punishing player be larger than the cost C_o incurred by the punished opponent. Moreover, to push the argument to its limits and to make conditions for the emergence of cooperation as hard as possible, assume that punishment causes such heavy costs that in addition to relation (1) the following holds

$$P > T - C_o \text{ and } S > R - C_p, \text{ where } C_p > C_o.^{10} \tag{2}$$

The game-theoretic setting developed so far is designed to discuss what rule of conduct will emerge in social dilemmas under what conditions. A different, but related, question is whether different rules of conduct affect the survival and growth of the groups that adopt them. To be able to deal with this question the individualistic game-theoretic framework needs to be extended by a proper analytic representation of the concept of 'groups' or 'societies' (the terms used interchangeably here).

In the context of modern human societies, 'group selection', i.e. a differential growth of group size, is more a matter of differences in migration rates between groups or societies than a matter of differential reproductive success. Migration presupposes two things: a spatial dimension in which groups are separated

9 Note, that not all of them are relevant or make sense. Consider a player i who uses move c in the first stage. On the basis of the rational choice assumption invoked here, no opponent j then has a reason to choose move p in the second stage, independent of what j's own move in the first stage has been. The reason is that the option p is costly and therefore dominated by move a. Accordingly, the possibility of 'punishing' cooperation is not considered further.

10 If the additional condition $C_o > T-S$ holds, a complete outcome ranking is induced such that in addition to relation (1) we get $S > T-C_o > P-C_o > P-C_p > S-C_p > P-C_o-C_p$.

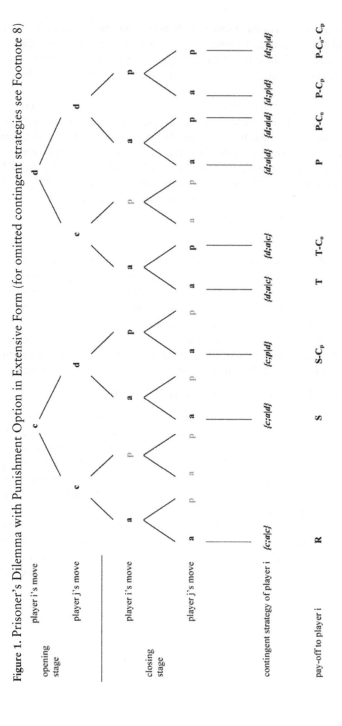

Figure 1. Prisoner's Dilemma with Punishment Option in Extensive Form (for omitted contingent strategies see Footnote 8)

14   ULRICH WITT

from each other and some minimal form of spatial interconnectedness or neighborhood within groups. In an abstract way, these conditions may be captured by assuming that a human population made up of n agents, indexed $i = 1, \ldots, n$, is scattered over a spatial dimension. For expository convenience, let n be a large, but constant, odd number. To simplify the analysis of the diffusion of new strategies, a one-dimensional space is sometimes assumed in game-theoretic models (Boyer and Orléan, 1993; Eshel, Sansone, and Shaked, 1999) so that the interacting agents are represented by n points on a line. Without loss of generality, the line can be arranged into a closed circle so that no bordering cases need to be considered. In this abstract setting, the population on the circle may either be taken to represent a single group, provided it is structured in such a way that proximity between group members matters, or the union of all groups or societies. Both representations will be used further below. For the present let us look into the latter case more closely.

If the spatial distribution of all groups is represented by the circle, each single group in the union corresponds to a closed subset of points on (a segment of) the circle. This means that each agent i has more or less close neighbors to the left and to the right that are either members of her own or other groups. The spatial proximity of any two agents i and j can be expressed by the number of points between them. If each agent belongs to just one group, all groups together form a complete partitioning of the circle. Agents are assumed to interact with each other with a probability that depends on spatial proximity (the very reason why space is accounted for here). To strengthen the argument, suppose that the interaction probability hinges on proximity alone, i.e. not on group membership, and that the agents are unable to discriminate between individuals even within their group (the least favorable assumptions for the emergence of a cooperative rule of conduct). It seems reasonable then that the probability of an agent i being matched with any other agent j in an interaction decreases with the distance between i and j. It may become zero once a critical distance r, $(n-1)/2 \geq r \geq 1$, to the left or to the right of agent i is exceeded. (Interactions of an agent i with other agents have an equal chance of occuring on the left side or the right side of i).

Consider an agent who is h points away from i, either to the left or to the right. The probability $p_{i,h}$ of an interaction of agent i with that agent can then be given as

$$p_{i,h} = \begin{cases} (r - h + 1)/r(r + 1) \text{ for } 1 \leq h \leq r, \\ 0 \text{ for } h > r. \end{cases} \tag{3}$$

On either side of agent i, $\Sigma_h \, p_{i,h} = \frac{1}{2}$. For reasons that will become apparent later (see the appendix) it is useful to define a neighborhood N adjacent to agent i on

Observational learning, group selection, and societal evolution   15

one side by a segment of k points on the circle. By summing over (3) one gets

$$\Phi_k = \sum_{h=1}^{k} p_{i,h} = (2rk - k^2 + k)/(2r(r+1)) \quad \text{for } 1 \leq k \leq r, \tag{4}$$

with $0 < \Phi_k \leq \frac{1}{2}$ for $1 \leq k \leq r$. Φ_k gives the probability for an interaction of agent i within a neighborhood of size k to the right or to the left.

5. The evolution of rules of conduct and the differential growth of groups

On the basis of the assumptions introduced in the previous section, the two core problems of Hayek's theory of societal evolution can now be discussed in more detail. The first problem revolves around the question of what rules of conduct will emerge and survive within groups during societal evolution. More specifically, can pro-social behavior really be expected if societal evolution is faced with social dilemmas? In terms of the two stage pd-game above, this objection translates into the question: are there any cooperative contingent strategies able to emerge and survive and, if so, under what conditions? Obviously, both emergence and survival hinge on the state of the environment, i.e. the initial composition of strategies present in a population. This is called the 'occupancy effect' in evolutionary biology.[11] The effect is of crucial importance also in the context of a socially learned behavior.

As has been explained above, collectively shared cognitive constraints can only give rise to, and observational learning can only operate on, behavioral regularities to the extent to which they can be observed in the population. In the game-theoretic model, this means that, in order to learn about the (dis-)advantage of some so far unknown contingent strategy, there must be an innovator who introduces it into the population in the first place. The comparative (dis-)advantage is then revealed by a difference in the outcomes accruing to the innovator's strategy on the one hand and the (established) strategy of the opponent on the other. Consequently, to assess the prospects for the cooperative rules of conduct to indeed survive and disseminate in the repeated playing of the game, we can explore whether, and in what occupancy setting, these combinations of strategies persist.

---

11 If there are at least two variants of genetically fixed behavior competing with one another for representation in the gene pool of the population, one currently prevailing and one newly entering, the chances the new variant has for invading the population are critically affected by what the prevailing behavior is. The same holds, the other way round, for the chances an initially prevailing variant has for surviving the invasion of the new variant.

16 ULRICH WITT

The criterion that can be used for this assessment is the 'evolutionary stability' of a particular strategy in a game played by the members of a population.[12] An evolutionary stable strategy is a strategy that, if prevailing in a group, cannot be invaded by a deviating strategy s. More precisely, denote two (possibly mixed) strategies by e and s, and their expected pay-off by $E(\pi(l, m))$, where $l, m \in \{e, s\}$. Then, e is an evolutionary stable strategy if and only if either $E(\pi (e, e)) > E(\pi (s, e))$ or $E(\pi (e, e)) = E(\pi (s, e))$ and $E(\pi (e, s)) > E(\pi (s, s))$. Accordingly, consider a single group initially characterized by all players playing one and the same strategy.[13] When, in such a situation, an innovator appears and plays a deviating strategy, several responses are triggered. These responses jointly determine the social learning process and the result in terms of survival or decline of the originally prevailing strategy (i.e. its evolutionary stability).

First, the innovator her/himself learns about the outcome of her/his experiment and reacts to the outcome in her/his future interactions. Since the further development hinges on this reaction, a hypothesis is needed here. A plausible one is the following:

Assumption 1

> *A player following a new strategy continues to do so as long as this does not result in a lower pay-off than the strategy previously prevailing in the group. If a lower pay-off is obtained, the player switches to the strategy previously prevailing after a few trials resulting in a lower average pay-off.*

Second, the innovator's opponent faces a new outcome and may respond to it in future interactions. Third, since the deviation is also likely to attract attention elsewhere in the population, the innovator's experiment becomes an object of observational learning. This means that the pay-off realized with the deviant strategy is also observed by members of the population who have not been directly confronted (and are probably not in close proximity to the innovator). They may rate the vicarious pay-off against that of the currently prevailing strategy. Sooner or later this can induce spontaneous strategy changes (imitation) elsewhere in the population. Again an explicit hypothesis is needed:

Assumption 2

> *Players who either are directly confronted with, or observe from outside, a new strategy introduced to the group adopt it:*
> - *with probability zero, if it yields a pay-off no higher than that of the strategy previously prevailing;*

---

12 See Maynard Smith (1982: 10–20); see also the related criterion of an 'unbeatable strategy' in Eshel, Sansone, and Shaked (1999).

13 If proximity between group members matters for the probability of interactions between them – leaving open whether proximity is defined in social, spatial, or other terms – the circle representation of the previous section can be used to express the internal structure of the group. The probabilities for any members in the group to interact with another member is then given by equations (3) and (4).

Observational learning, group selection, and societal evolution   17

– with a probability ≥ 0 that varies monotonously with a difference ≥ 0 between the pay-off of the new strategy and that of the previously prevailing strategy.

Assumptions 1 and 2 taken together imply a stochastic replication process. Among the realizations it can take over time, those converging to one of the following stable states are of particular interest here. The innovative strategy can:

- invade the population and disseminate without being adopted by the whole population; in the limiting case only the innovator keeps to it ('partial invasion');
- invade and fully disseminate through adoption by the innovator's opponents or through imitation ('complete invasion');
- fail to even gain a foothold, if even the innovator abandons it ('failure').

On the basis of these explications and assumptions and the logic underlying the notion of an evolutionary stable strategy, the question of whether pro-social, cooperative rules of conduct can indeed emerge and survive within groups during societal evolution can be given the following answer:[14]

Proposition 1

A strategy that is newly introduced by an innovator results in partial invasion, complete invasion, or failure as denoted in Table 1, depending on what strategy prevails in the population.

Since a rule of conduct has been above given, the meaning of an equilibrium point of the underlying game, Proposition 1 implies that, if the new strategy fails to invade, the previously prevailing strategy remains the rule of conduct for the social dilemma in the group. Conversely, if the new strategy completely invades, it becomes the new rule of conduct. Table 1 highlights a few remarkable features of the evolutionary process. A first one is the asymmetry between cooperative and defectionist strategies. Consider the 'permissive' cooperative strategy $\{c;$ $a|\ c\}$, $\{c;\ a|\ d\}$ and the 'aggressive' cooperative strategy $\{c;\ a|\ c\}$, $\{c;\ p|\ d\}$. Under the chosen initial conditions neither of them can even gain a foothold, not to speak of successful dissemination, in an all defectionist social environment (the reasons for this difference are discussed in the appendix). Defection as innovation, by contrast, has much better chances of invading an all cooperative group and of driving pro-social, cooperative behavior to extinction. However, this finding – quite destructive for the chances of a pro-social rule of conduct – needs qualifications. It hinges on a special initial condition as will be explained momentarily.

Another remarkable feature is that there are significant differences in terms of evolutionary stability between the permissive cooperative strategy and the aggressive one. Despite the high costs incurred by punishing an opponent when

14 For a sketch of the proof see the appendix.

TABLE 1. Survival and Dissemination of Rivaling Strategies (order numbers refer to the proof)

	new strategy entering the population		
incumbent strategy	defection $\{d; a\,|\,c\}, \{d; a\,|\,d\}$	permissive cooperation $\{c; a\,|\,c\}, \{c; a\,|\,d\}$	aggressive cooperation $\{c; a\,|\,c\}, \{c; p\,|\,d\}$
defection $\{d; a\,|\,c\}, \{d; a\,|\,d\}$	———	failure[3]	failure[5]
permissive cooperation $\{c; a\,|\,c\}, \{c; a\,|\,d\}$	complete invasion[1]	———	partial invasion[6]
aggressive cooperation $\{c; a\,|\,c\}, \{c; p\,|\,d\}$	partial or complete invasion or failure[2]	partial invasion[4]	———

playing the aggressive cooperative strategy, i.e. to cooperate in the first stage and punish opponent after experiencing defection, this strategy is not equally vulnerable to invasion as the permissive cooperative strategy is. In fact, the latter rule of conduct has no chance of surviving. This seems an important finding: cooperation as a rule of conduct in social dilemmas can resist subversive, defectionist deviations provided it comes in an aggressive form.

The question of what rules of conduct will emerge and survive during societal evolution to which Proposition 1 refers is not the only one relevant for Hayek's theory of societal evolution. A second, equally important, element of his theory, to which we now turn, is the hypothesis of a differential growth process during societal evolution which favors groups adopting pro-social behavior as a rule of conduct. To account for this hypothesis requires to distinguish groups which can grow differentially in the first place. In the previous section, it has been suggested that this can be done by representing a group by a closed subset of points (a segment) of a circle where the circle represents the union of two or more groups. As will turn out now, the possibility of forming distinct groups within a population indeed modifies the selection environment significantly by reducing the advantage of defectionist strategies over pro-social, cooperative strategies that are characteristic of the case of undifferentiated populations.

Consider a group formed by players adjacent to each other in a segment of the circle. Let all members of that group simultaneously introduce a strategy that deviates from the strategy played by the rest of all players. If 'group selection' is a process of differential growth of groups, the question arises whether the deviating group is able to profit in terms of its size[15] from its innovation. More specifically, under what conditions is it possible that a group collectively introducing one of the pro-social, cooperative strategies into an otherwise defecting population is

---

15 Since for analytical convenience the entire population size has been assumed to be fixed, differential growth is equivalent to an increase in the size of one group at the expense of the size of the other, i.e. to systematic or targeted migration between groups.

favored by group selection? Under the chosen assumptions, the following answer can be provided:[16]

Proposition 2

> *An aggressive cooperative strategy collectively introduced by a group of players to a defectionist population can result in partial or even complete invasion of the population by this new strategy, if the group size exceeds a critical mass $k^* > (n–1)/2$.*

Proposition 2 implies that group selection can favor a group with pro-social, cooperative behavior in social dilemmas even though that group has to interact with groups with defecting behavior. Hence, a cooperative strategy need not be the rule of conduct from the very beginning in order to be an evolutionary stable strategy. This implication of Proposition 2 seems to support Hayek's optimistic view of societal evolution overcoming the perils of social dilemmas. However, it is bound to two strong conditions being satisfied.

First, pro-social, cooperative behavior must be paired with aggressiveness against attempts to exploit cooperation ('aggressive moralism'). Pro-social behavior must go so far as to be willing to bear the extra costs of punishing a defecting opponent by playing the aggressive strategy $\{c; p| d\}$. Proposition 2 does not hold for the permissive cooperative strategy $\{c; a| d\}$ which fails to be able to invade an otherwise defectionist population, even if introduced by an entire group of agents. Second, the group of aggressive cooperators needs to be large enough so that the relative frequency of being forced to punish and thus to incur the corresponding costs is for each member of the group still bearable. If the group does not make for the majority of the population, the individually born costs of retaliation are too high for the new cooperative strategy to be individually maintained according to Assumption 1. These two contingencies seriously qualify the logical basis for hoping that cooperation can prevail as the rule of conduct for social dilemmas.

6. Conclusions

The theory of societal evolution based by F.A. Hayek in his later work on a group selection argument leaves several important questions open. After identifying the major problems, an attempt has been made in the present paper to dwell on the behavioral foundation of cultural evolution by reference to social cognitive learning theory. On this basis an extended prisoner's dilemma game has been suggested that allows to be more specific with respect to what 'group selection' means and under what conditions it can favor pro-social behavior in social dilemmas. The analysis has shown that groups (which, moreover, need to have a critical size) are essential: unless pro-social, cooperative strategies already

---

16 For a sketch of the proof see the appendix.

20 ULRICH WITT

prevail from the very beginning, they only have a chance to emerge in a non-cooperative world, if collectively adopted by agents belonging to such groups. The cooperative gains such groups can realize may induce migration into those groups and, thus, allow the groups to grow differentially. As was shown, at least in the present model set up, a pro-social, cooperative rule of conduct needs to be paired with a certain 'aggressiveness' in order to be able to survive and grow, more precisely, a willingness to bear the costs of punishing attempts to exploit pro-social behavior.

References

Acemoglu, D., S. Johnson, and J. Robinson (2001), 'The Colonial origins of comparative development: an empirical investigation', *American Economics Review*, **91**: 1369–1401.

Anderson, J. R. (2000), *Cognitive Psychology and its Implications*, 5th edn, New York: Freeman.

Bandura, A. (1986), *Social Foundations of Thought and Action – A Social Cognitive Theory*, Engelwood Cliffs: Prentice-Hall.

Bianchi, M. (1994), 'Hayek's spontaneous order: the "correct" vs. the "corrigible" society', in J. Birner and R. van Zijp (eds), *Hayek, Co-ordination and Evolution*, London: Routledge, pp. 232–251.

Boyd, R. and P. J. Richerson (1985), *Culture and the Evolutionary Process*, Chicago: Chicago University Press.

Boyer, R. and A. Orléan (1993), 'How do conventions evolve?', in U. Witt (ed.), *Evolution in Markets and Institutions*, Wuerzburg: Physica, pp. 17–29.

Caldwell, B. (2000), 'The emergence of Hayek's ideas on cultural evolution', *Review of Austrian Economics*, **13**: 5–22.

Carr-Saunders, A. M. (1922), *The Population Problem: A Study in Human Evolution*, Oxford: Oxford University Press.

Congleton, R. D. and V. Vanberg (2001), 'Help, harm or avoid? On the personal advantage of dispositions to cooperate and punish in multilateral PD games with exit', *Journal of Economic Behavior and Organization*, **44**: 145–167.

Diamond, J. (1997), *Guns, Germs, and Steel – The Fates of Human Societies*, New York: Norton.

Eshel, I., E. Sansone, and A. Shaked (1999), 'The emergence of kinship behavior in strucutred populations of unrelated individuals', *International Journal of Game Theory*, **28**: 447–463.

Field, A. (2001), *Altruistically Inclined? The Behavioral Sciences, Evolutionary Theory, and the Origins of Reciprocity*, Ann Arbor: University of Michigan Press.

Galor, O. and O. Moav (2002), 'Natural selection and the origin of economic growth', *Quarterly Journal of Economics*, **117**: 1133–1191.

Gray, J. (1984), *Hayek on Liberty*, New York: Basil Blackwell.

Hamilton, W. D. (1964), 'The genetical evolution of social behavior I', *Journal of Theoretical Biology*, **7**: 1–16.

Hayek, F. A. (1948), 'Individualism: true and false', in F. A. Hayek, *Individualism and Economic Order*, London: Routledge & Sons, pp. 1–32.

Observational learning, group selection, and societal evolution   21

Hayek, F. A. (1967a), 'Notes on the evolution of systems of rules of conduct', in F. A. Hayek, *Studies in Philosophy, Politics, and Economics*, London: Routledge & Keagan Paul, pp. 66–81.

Hayek, F. A. (1967b), 'Rules, perception and intelligibility', in F. A. Hayek, *Studies in Philosophy, Politics, and Economics*, London: Routledge & Keagan Paul, pp. 43–65.

Hayek, F. A. (1967c), 'Dr. Bernhard Mandeville', *Proceedings of the British Academy*, Vol. 12, London: Oxford University Press.

Hayek, F. A. (1971), 'Nature vs. nurture once again', *Encounter*, **36**: 81–83.

Hayek, F. A. (1979), *Law, Legislation and Liberty. Vol. 3, The Political Order of a Free People*, London: Routledge & Kegan Paul.

Hayek, F. A. (1988), *The Fatal Conceit*, London: Routledge.

Henrich, J. (2004), 'Cultural group selection, coevolutionary processes and large-scale cooperation', *Journal of Economic Behavior and Organization*, **53**: 3–35.

Henrich, J. and R. Boyd (1998), 'The evolution of conformist transmission and the emergence of between-group differences', *Evolution and Human Behavior*, **19**: 215–242.

Hodgson, G.M. (1991), 'Hayek's theory of cultural evolution: an evaluation in the light of Vanberg's critique', *Economics and Philosophy*, **7**: 67–82.

Maynard Smith, J. (1982), *Evolution and the Theory of Games*, Cambridge: Cambridge University Press.

Menger, C. (1963), *Problems of Economics and Sociology*, Urbana: University of Illinois Press 1963 (first published in German 1883).

Rizzello, S. (2000), 'Economic change, subjective perception and institutional evolution', *Metroeconomica*, **51**: 127–150.

Sober, E. and D.S. Wilson (1998), *Unto Others: The Evolution and Psychology of Unselfish Behavior*, Cambridge, MA: Harvard University Press.

Vanberg, V. (1986), 'Spontaneous market order and social rules: a critical examination of F. A.von Hayek's theory of cultural evolution', *Economics and Philosophy*, **2**: 75–100.

Vanberg, V. (1997), 'Institutional evolution through purposeful selection: the constitutional economics of John R. Commons', *Constitutional Political Economy*, **8**: 105–122.

Veblen, T. (1899), *The Theory of the Leisure Class – An Economic Study of Institutions*, New York: MacMillan.

Veblen, T. (1914), *The Instinct of Worksmanship and the State of the Industrial Arts*, New York: MacMillan.

Witt, U. (1994), 'The theory of societal evolution – Hayek's unfinished legacy', in J. Birner and R. Van Zijp (eds), *Hayek, Coordination and Evolution*, London: Routledge, pp. 178–189.

Wynne-Edwards, V.C. (1962), *Animal Dispersion in Relation to Social Behavior*, Edinburgh: Oliver and Boyd.

Young, H. P. (1993), 'The Evolution of Conventions', *Econometrica*, **61**: 57–84.

Appendix

A proof of proposition 1 based on the (static) criterion of evolutionary stability can be sketched as follows (in the sequence of the order numbers in the cells of Table 1):

1 *Defection strategy entering a population playing permissive cooperation strategy:* initially, the innovator obtains $T > R$ with certainty. However, if the

defection strategy disseminates, the frequency of $\{d; a \mid d\}$ being encountered with $\{d; a \mid d\}$ increases and the pay off of defectionist strategy converges to $P < R$. Since returning to the cooperative strategy would entail R when encountering $\{c; a \mid c\}$ and S when playing against $\{d; a \mid c\}$, no player having adopted the defectionist strategy ever switches back to cooperation by Assumption 1. The initially prevailing permissive strategy $\{c; a \mid c\}$, $\{c; a \mid d\}$ obtains R when playing against itself and S against the defection strategy. The defection strategy realizes $P > S$ when playing against itself and $T > R$ against the permissive strategy. This means that $\{c; a \mid c\}$ and $\{c; a \mid d\}$ are dominated under all circumstances. Hence, by Assumption 2, there is a finite waiting time until all players have adopted the defection strategy.

2 *Defection strategy entering a population playing aggressive cooperati'on strategy*: initially, the innovator obtains $T - C_o < R$ by the order relations (1) and (2). If the defection strategy disseminates, a pay off $P > T - C_o$ becomes more frequent. Since returning to cooperation would entail R when playing against the aggressive cooperators and $S - C_p$ when playing against the defectionists, the innovator's future behavior by Assumption 1 hinges on whether defection becomes a frequently played strategy in the population. Consider the initially prevailing aggressive cooperation strategy obtaining R when playing against itself and $S - C_p$ as the innovator's opponent. The player most likely to encounter the innovator and, hence, to switch from cooperation to defection is the innovator's neighbor. Let $E(\pi_c)$ denote the expected outcome of the cooperative strategy and $E(\pi_d)$ the expected outcome of the defectionist strategy. Due to the local structure of interactions reflected by equation (4), the immediate neighbor of the innovating player gets

$$E(\pi_c) = \tfrac{1}{2} R + \Phi_1 (S - C_p) + \left(\tfrac{1}{2} - \Phi_1\right) R.$$

In case of switching, the neighbor gets

$$E(\pi_d) = \tfrac{1}{2}(T - C_o) + \Phi_1 P + \left(\tfrac{1}{2} - \Phi_1\right)(T - C_o).$$

Equating both expected values and solving yields

$$\Phi_1^* = [T - C_o - R]/[T - C_o - R + S - C_p - P] < \tfrac{1}{2},$$

since $0 > T - C_o - R > S - C_p - P$ because of order relations (1) and (2). Hence, it cannot be excluded that the probability Φ_1 happens to satisfy the condition $\Phi_1^* < \Phi_1 \leq \tfrac{1}{2}$. (Note, however, that since $\Phi_1 = 1/(r+1)$, the condition is the less likely satisfied the larger r.) If so, there is a finite waiting time for the neighbor player to switch to defection according to Assumption 2. If the innovator maintains the new strategy for long enough, incurring the opportunity loss $R - (T - C_o)$ in each play, the expected outcome may at best converge to P through the neighbor's switching. Since $R > P > T - C_o$, the innovator may eventually return to the incumbent strategy according to Assumption 1. However, if a neighbor has already switched such a move would amount simply to changing places with the neighbor. While it cannot be excluded that the defection strategy disseminates, if this happens at all, it may therefore be a matter of cyclical convergence. In case $0 < \Phi_1 \leq \Phi_1^*$, by contrast, switching is excluded so that for the corresponding parameter values defection as an innovation cannot survive.

3 *Permissive cooperation strategy entering a population playing defection strategy*: by order relation (1) the innovator is initially certain of obtaining $S < P$. Since returning to defection entails P, by Assumption 1 the innovator returns to defection after playing a limited number of times $\{c;\,a\,|\,d\}$. The prevailing defectionist strategy obtains $P > S$ against itself and $T > S$ as the innovator's opponent, so that, by Assumption 2, no player other than the innovator will ever adopt the cooperative strategy.

4 *Permissive cooperation strategy entering a population playing aggressive cooperation strategy*: when playing against the prevailing strategy, the innovative strategy is indistinguishable. Hence, by Assumptions 1 and 2, none of the players could be induced to adopt the new strategy.

5 *Aggressive cooperation strategy entering a population playing defection strategy*: initially, the innovator realizes $S - C_p < P$. If the defection strategy disseminates, a pay off $R > P$ becomes more frequent. Since returning to defection would entail P when playing against the defectors and $T - C_o$ when playing against aggressive cooperators, the innovator's future behavior according to Assumption 1 hinges on whether aggressive cooperation becomes a frequently played strategy in the population. Consider the initially prevailing defection strategy obtaining P when playing against itself and $T - C_o$ as the innovator's opponent. By switching to the aggressive cooperative strategy $S - C_p$ can be realized against defectionists and $R > T - C_o$ against cooperating players. Again a critical value

$$\Phi_1^{**} = [S - C_p - P]/[S - C_p - P + T - C_o - R] > \tfrac{1}{2}$$

can be derived. This means that no value $\Phi_1 \in (0,\tfrac{1}{2})$ exists such that a switch would be advantageous. Since the innovator is to return to playing defection by Assumption 1, the aggressive cooperation strategy cannot survive.

6 *Aggressive cooperation strategy entering a population playing the permissive cooperation strategy*: when playing against the incumbent strategy, the innovative strategy is indistinguishable. Hence, by Assumptions 1 and 2, none of the players could be induced to adopt the new strategy.

The proof of proposition 2 can be sketched as follows:

Assume all players in a segment of the circle that represents the group with at least two members simultaneously introduce the aggressive cooperative strategy. Accordingly, $n > 2$. Outside the group, defection is the prevailing strategy. A group member's pay-off from an interaction depends on whether it is an in-group or an out-group interaction. The group members at the edge of the segment on the circle profit least from the cooperation gain since, by assumption, they interact equally likely on either side. Cooperative players at the edge are therefore most likely to switch back to defection. The expected outcome of playing the aggressive cooperative strategy for such a player is

$$E(\pi_c) = \tfrac{1}{2}(S - C_p) + \Phi_k R + \left(\tfrac{1}{2} - \Phi_k\right)(S - C_p),$$

given that the innovating group has $k+1$ members.

Should that player switch back to defection, the expected outcome would be

$$E(\pi_d) = \tfrac{1}{2} P + \Phi_k(T - C_o) + \left(\tfrac{1}{2} - \Phi_k\right)P.$$

Equating both values and solving yields

$$\Phi_k^* = [S - C_p - P]/[S - C_p - P + T - C_o - R] > \tfrac{1}{2}.$$

Hence, by equation (4) no number $k \le r$ exists so that $E(\pi_d) \le E(\pi_c)$. By Assumption 2, the cooperative players at the edge of the segment on the circle are to switch back in finite time to defection, while none of their neighbors not belonging to the group is likely to imitate the innovation. If $k > \tfrac{n}{2}$, however, the respective expected outcomes are

$$E(\pi_c) = \tfrac{1}{2} R + \Phi_k(S - C_p) + \left(\tfrac{1}{2} - \Phi_k\right) R \text{ and}$$
$$E(\pi_d) = \tfrac{1}{2}(T - C_o) + \Phi_k P + \left(\tfrac{1}{2} - \Phi_k\right)(T - C_o).$$

In view of order relations (1) and (2), this means that $E(\pi_c) > E(\pi_d)$. A critical number of group members $k^* > (n-1)/2$ exists such that, once k^* has been exceeded, all players initially following the defection strategy will eventually switch to the aggressive cooperation strategy.

Available online at www.sciencedirect.com

SCIENCE @ DIRECT°

Structural Change and Economic Dynamics
16 (2005) 165–179

ELSEVIER

STRUCTURAL
CHANGE AND
ECONOMIC
DYNAMICS

www.elsevier.com/locate/econbase

'Production' in nature and production in the economy—second thoughts about some basic economic concepts

Ulrich Witt[*]

Max-Planck-Institute for Research Into Economic Systems, Kahlaische Strasse 10, D-07745 Jena, Germany

Received 30 September 2002; received in revised form 31 July 2003; accepted 1 November 2003
Available online 8 January 2004

Abstract

If production means generating output by application of specific inputs, then production is a ubiquitous phenomenon in nature. This observation invites a double comparison. First, physical production processes in nature can be compared to those in the economy. The differences highlight cumulative changes in technology which explain how specific modern forms of human production have become feasible through cultural evolution. Second, such a 'naturalistic' perspective on production can be compared to, and sheds new light on, the remarkably different perspective in economics which interprets production not as physical processes, but as a problem of human social interaction and coordination.
© 2003 Elsevier B.V. All rights reserved.

JEL classification: A12; B12; B14; B51; B52; D24; O13; O14

Keywords: Production; Production theory; Factors of production; Technical change; Cultural evolution

1. Introduction

What purpose should production theory serve? Theories, and the heuristic basis on which they rest, are like looking glasses which should help us to better perceive and understand reality. But, like looking glasses, theories offer only partial views. They focus on a fraction of reality, are highly selective and appreciative in recognizing fact and details, and are therefore prone to heuristic biases (Toulmin, 1961). If we want to reflect on these effects of our theories, it is like with looking glasses: we have to put them off, try other ones, and compare both the looking glasses and what they make visible to us. The vehicle which will

[*] Tel.: +49-3641-686801; fax: +49-3641-686868.
E-mail address: ulrich.witt@mpiew-jena.mpg.de (U. Witt).

0954-349X/$ – see front matter © 2003 Elsevier B.V. All rights reserved.
doi:10.1016/j.strueco.2003.11.001

be used here to ease the assessment of possible purposes and potential biases of production theory, is a comparison. It contrasts 'production', as portrayed in economic theory, with a fictitious notion of 'production' as it could be conceived from a biophysical point of view. Such a comparison is not a new idea. It inspired Georgescu-Roegen's biophysical approach to economics (Georgescu-Roegen, 1971), informed Ayres' theory of industrial metabolism (Ayres, 1978), and has been inspiration to the evolutionary approaches in Faber and Proops (1998) and Gowdy (1994), to mention a few prominent examples. Just recently its strength has been reconfirmed in Hall et al. (2001).

In these important contributions, the laws of thermodynamics figure prominently as a starting point for theorizing about production and growth in a way that contrasts with standard interpretations in economics. In the present paper a slightly different, and somewhat less abstract, approach is pursued by starting from some reflections on 'production' as it occurs in *living* systems. This is by no means meant to deny the relevance of the laws of thermodynamics and of the studies just cited, but does imply a shift of emphasis to an evolutionary, or Darwinian, perspective (cf. Witt, 1997, 1999). Such a perspective can be expected to shed some light on what is different in 'production' carried out by homo sapiens on the one hand and all other species on the other hand, and why. More specifically, it suggests to look for possible 'technical' differences on one side and for possible differences in the (social) organization of production in living nature on the other. Particularly important questions turning up here are: what drives human production as compared to production elsewhere in nature? What are the objectives, and what role is played by human culture? Going through these questions should help to better understand the very special character of the looking glasses with which we approach 'production' in economics, looking glasses which seem rather blind with respect to the role of nature (one of the reasons for why notorious difficulties emerge to a dialogue between economists and scientists).

The argumentation proceeds as follows. Section 2 starts by a brief comparative analysis of production in living nature, including the human sphere, from a physical point of view. If we set out to describe the actual 'production techniques' would it make much of a difference how nature 'produces' and how mankind does? Section 3 sketches the historical development of human production which is interpreted before the background of the preceding 'naturalist' analysis as a process of cultural evolution. Section 4 turns to the remarkably different understanding of production theory developed by the classical economists who approached production from a 'cultural' perspective, conceiving it mainly as a social process. They took a prime interest in determining values and distributional shares. The factors of production theory at which the classical writers arrived in their interpretation is then contrasted with what an abstract analysis of the physical processes of production in nature and the human economy would suggest. Section 5 offers a few conclusions.

2. Production as a physical process

Let us define production as the process of 'generating' a specified outcome, i.e. a state or process with certain properties or, in the economic jargon, a certain "output" by means of some "inputs". 'Generating' can mean different things here. In an engineering perspective, it is the process of manipulating the proper means, or "inputs", to accomplish, to a reasonable

U. Witt / Structural Change and Economic Dynamics 16 (2005) 165–179   167

degree, the desired outcome or output. In a scientist's perspective, 'generating' means the causal sequence of events (however it has been brought to happen), e.g., chemical reactions between given substances or mechanical interactions between given masses of certain materials, from which the outcome in question follows. Note that the outcome specified by the economist, the engineer, or the scientist does not necessarily represent all effects of the generation process so that the state or process actually brought about can also have unnoticed or even (temporarily) deliberately ignored properties.[1] The physical process of production as defined above is ubiquitous in living nature. Yet it is rarely subsumed under the abstract label 'production' (and there is, of course, no acting or choosing agent in the background).

Consider, for example, the more or less complex metabolism of living organisms. The outcome of that production process is organized living substance. It is maintained by the process not least through the transformations by which energy is made available for use by the organism from carbohydrates, fats, and proteins which have ultimately arisen from the photosynthesis of radiant energy provided by sun light. The latter, together with minerals, water, oxygen, and possibly some other organic compounds, represent the "inputs" to that production. Similarly, the organisms' anabolism (building up of cells, tissues, organs) and catabolism (breaking down tissue and splitting of larger protoplasmic molecules into smaller ones) are production processes. They form, renew, and repair the biomass of the organism, such as the wickerwork of roots, stems, and foliage of a plant, and jointly determine the organism's growth. All these natural production processes are triggered and controlled by complex cascades of interacting nucleic acids which basically follow genetically coded procedures. Moreover, implicit in these natural production processes the genetic information is over and again reproduced, subject to the shaping forces of natural selection. In a sense, thus, the "technology" on which production in living nature operates is the "knowledge" that has evolved since some billion years and has been accumulated in a coded form in the gene pool of the living organisms.[2]

It is interesting to note that under the influence of natural selection, i.e. driven by competition between the species in a given habitat or ecological system for reproductive success and an expansion of the own niche, production in living nature frequently effects substantial "investments" in biomass which do not directly improve or expand the organisms' metabolism. Rather these investments prevent the chances of the organisms of a given species from suffering in reproductive competition with other species (a phenomenon known as the "red queen effect", see Stenseth and Maynard Smith, 1984). The investment may affect reproductive success directly, particularly in intra-species competition, and more indirectly as in inter-species competition, e.g. in competing for access to sources of free energy required for the metabolic needs and/or in protecting against predators. Particularly instructive examples are those where the competition results in a kind of arms race which leads to "investments" into elaborate structures of non-living substrate built up by, and integrated into, the living organism such as the massive trunks and branches of large trees

---

[1] These "by-effects" of the generation process can be interpreted as cases of unintended joint production, cf. Faber et al. (1998).

[2] Because of its enormous complexity, this "knowledge" is still far from being fully understood and fully accessible to controlled human manipulation. To put it differently, it is far from being integrated into human knowledge, but chemistry and the biosciences have been eager and progressively successful over the past two hundred years to gain insights into it.

or the shells in snails and turtles.[3] Despite the fact that, because of the red queen effect, such investments do not necessarily lead to an expansion of the outcome of the production process, they indicate that there is also "roundabout production" in nature—albeit with no intention behind it, since it is an adaptation phenomenon brought about by natural selection.

While plants have basically a stationary position in their habitat, animals show some additional physical production activities related to their mobility. These activities rest on an anatomic apparatus which enables animals to carry out physical work (force × displacement). This capacity results, in turn, from the organisms' metabolism, anabolism, and catabolism and the "inputs" corresponding to those processes. The outcome are more complex forms of behavior enabling the animal to escape from, and/or combat with, predators, to conquer and defend a habitat, to engage in territorial feeding and mating strategies, and many other forms of social behavior. Carnivores are enabled, moreover, to hunting—often in socially organized ways. Again driven by natural selection there are forms of "investments" into "roundabout production" which, because of the animals' motility, can be separate from the organism. These investments occur in the context of only a few core activities: in food acquisition (as, e.g., the spider's cobweb or the dam construction by beavers); in food storing (as, e.g., the bees' honeycombs); in creating shelter and raring offspring (as, e.g., territaries or the nests of birds). Such investments usually require anatomic provisions for fine-tuned motor skills. In some cases they presuppose in addition the socially coordinated behavior of several individuals of the species as in the case of the beavers and the termites. Sometimes special anabolic organs have even evolved in support of these investments such as the spider' spinneret.

As with plants, the "technology" on which the production of more or less complex forms of behavior in the animal kingdom rest—including the "investments" to which that behavior can lead—is mostly based on genetically coded knowledge (instinct) that has been, and still is, shaped by natural selection. Adaptations in those kinds of behavior are therefore a matter of several generations, the time span during which new genetic dispositions and traits (new genetic knowledge) can selectively disseminate and become effective. But there are also some more rapid forms of behavior adaptations within the sometimes fairly broad limits left by what an animal is physically capable of doing. These adaptations are shown by the single organism, i.e. occur within one generation, as a result of reinforcement learning—of which the organism is capable thanks to the innate layout of its nervous system (cf., e.g., Pulliam and Dunford, 1980). Within very narrow limits, higher developed animals are also able to learn from observation of what their own kind are doing (imitation), speeding up the dissemination of better adapted behavior over what is feasible to mere reinforcement learning. However, in all these forms of adapting behavior and, hence, the corresponding production, the underlying "technology" basically remains the one determined by the inherited behavioral repertoire.

It is only among the most advanced mammals that the intellectual capacity and the capacity of the anatomic apparatus to do fine-tuned physical work jointly allow those animals to

---

[3] On the level of intra-species competition for reproductive success a similar arms race phenomenon can emerge from sexual selection which sometimes leads to resource intensive, if not even dysfunctional, gender specific investments such as the peacock's fan or excessive horns in some male cavicornia (see Wilson, 1975; chapter 5).

invent or discover and use primitive tools which they create from suitable materials. Tools are defined as equipments which, as an *outcome of an intelligent act*, are created by, but not physically integrated into, an organism. (Note that the outcome of an intelligent act points to a production process of a particular quality not previously encountered in nature.) The intelligent act at the origin of tools is what makes the difference to "investments" made by animal as discussed before which are guided by instinct. The creation of tools is an invest-ment based on intention rather than instinct — where intention presupposes understanding and insight into how means and ends relate, i.e. the pursuit of a more or less consciously perceived purpose. Tool creation is therefore a qualitatively distinct, and very rare, form of production in nature and a first instance of "round-about" production which is not based on genetic but on phenotypic knowledge.

An important class of production processes in nature are symbiotic forms of production. In these processes exemplars of different species rely in different forms on each other, or the organisms of one species rely in a one-sided beneficial way on those of another species. Symbiotic interactions thus not only include mutualism, i.e. a situation in which both parties involved benefit from each other, which is often associated with symbiosis in a narrower sense. (A frequent case of mutualism is the one where one species provides some form of protection and the other species provides food.) Inter-species interactions in production also include commensalism and parasitism in which the benefits are one-sided. In some cases the symbiotic relationship goes so far that one species systematically manipulates the produc-tion processes in the other species. The organisms of the one species may then almost appear as having tool like character for the other species. However, tools have just been defined as the outcome of an intelligent act of production, and symbiotic interactions in production in nature, even the manipulative ones, are based on instinct, i.e. the various species' geneti-cally fixed behavioral repertoire. Therefore, it is only in humans and in rather recent times that, with the introduction of agriculture and animal husbandry, organisms of other species involved in symbiotic production processes have indeed obtained tool-like character.

Before those times, in the human hunter and gatherer economy, anthropological evidence suggests that physical production is (except for the tools used in hunting) basically identical with the production processes of the advanced mammals. If a scientific observer from a different stellar system would have studied production and technology in the early times of man, (s)he would not have seen much reason to speak of (human) economic production. What has changed since then so that we see a need today to consider economic production as a topic of its own? An answer to this question can be attempted at two different levels. One relates to objective changes in the physical production conditions, the other relating to how we (as humans) have come to perceive and frame our production activities, a point referring back to the problem of our theoretical 'looking glasses'. We will address these two different level in turn in the next two sections.

3. Reconstructing human physical production as a process of cultural evolution

What has objectively changed since the days of our early ancestors in the physical pro-duction processes of the human kind is initially, it will be claimed here, a matter of de-gree rather than of principle: the extent of tool use and tool making and of symbiotic manipulation of other species. Both correspond with, and are contingent on, a growing intentionality and a refined motorial skill in applying man's physical working capacity—labor—and a growing amount of 'cultural', i.e. not genetically coded knowledge that can be made available for pursuing human intentions. Indeed, cultural knowledge, intention, and their mutual inter-dependency can be considered the hallmark of the economy of the human species—and of its inherently evolutionary character which in rather recent times has led to the emergence of techniques of physical production which have no precedent in living nature. One of the reasons for why the exceptional development of human production could be brought about is a unique historical contingency: man found ways to fuel his expanding production by increasingly tapping sources of free energy not otherwise used in nature, more recently (and, of course only temporarily) the relatively abundant fossil energy deposits.

The divergence of human forms of production from the natural patterns is a long and slow historical process. The anthropological record of that development, which is basically one of human artefacts as the only remnants of the production processes of those times, documents over hundreds of thousands of years extremely simple tools such as wedges, clubs, spears, arrows, bows—all conceived as crude supplements to man's anatomic apparatus of force exertion. Their making by hand with considerable mechanical skills is a transformation of materials found in nature like stone, bone, wood, and antler. They have presumably been used with equal mechanical skills for processing/transforming materials in relation to hunting and feeding purposes or directly for hunting applications. Even though early man may have invented or discovered such primitive tools by accident or in a playful rather than purpose seeking act, it is most likely that once their tool character had been understood they were associated with, and applied in, purposeful action.

With the introduction of agriculture—mankind's first technological revolution—some 10–15,000 years ago the manipulation of organisms of other species in symbiotic production forms began to be systematically cultivated. The preparation of arable land by means of primitive tools like sticks and stone plows and the cropping of millet, wheat, barley, rice, etc. clearly resulted from a combination of skillful physical work, learning and the improvement of the respective technical (cultural) knowledge, and its intentional use. It meant an enlargement of the ecological niche of both the human and the symbiotic species—at the expense, of course, of other species in the habitat. In terms of the quantitative outcome of the human production of food (protein, fat, carbohydrates, vitamins, and digestible minerals) the result was a great leap forward compared to the inherited food production techniques of hunting and gathering which kept in place and were used in parallel. The outcome of the food production process was significantly enhanced by the invention of pottery at about the same time, i.e. of new tools which facilitated and improved food storage and preparation.

Pottery production is again a transformation with considerable mechanical skills of materials found in nature, mainly clay. This time, however, a new element was added to the production process, namely the systematic application of heat, i.e. free energy. As is well known, this addendum is a prerequisite for the metallurgical technology which was discovered or invented some 9000 years ago. First it was copper and later copper and tin, materials found in nature, which were transformed (melted and purified) by use of heat from ordinary wood fire and then cast and hammered into form. Bronze, the alloy of cop-

U. Witt / Structural Change and Economic Dynamics 16 (2005) 165–179   171

per and tin, is good for almost everything pottery is good for. In addition it is good for many other applications like tools for cutting and ploughing which were thus improved over those feasible on the basis of stone or bone. Not least, bronze allowed to improve some specific tools of the human species, namely weapons, both for hunting and for warfare, and armaments.

The increasing domestication and breeding of animals like cattle, goats, sheep, pigs, and horses since the agricultural revolution—technically an intensification and extension of natural symbiotic production forms again due to an interaction between intention and growing cultural knowledge—improved the outcome of human production processes further. A first effect was an increase in the availability of food, particularly in the supply of proteins and fat. A second, and technologically more significant, effect was the tapping of a first non-anthropogenic source of kinetic energy. Where previously motorial work on simple mechanical devices adapted to the human anatomy had been done by the human muscle power, it could be carried out by trained and supervised muscle power of ox, horse, or donkey: drawing the plow, carrying loads, trashing and milling corn. With the invention of the wheel, a mechanical device of power transmission became feasible which transcended those inspired by the human anatomy. Opportunities for designing new tools were opened up which helped to further substitute human muscle power, and which helped to expand symbiotic production beyond the naturally available habitats, e.g. by allowing to erect and operate irrigation systems.

The further development of tools within the mechanical paradigm of levers and wheels based on stone, wood, and the metallurgic technology, which strongly improved further with the invention of iron-working techniques about 3000 years ago, is well documented in Usher (1954). The development of the mechanical paradigm was significantly enhanced when devices were found to tap wind power and water power as new sources of free energy. It literally boosted with the introduction of the steam engine, first fired by wood then by coal (cf. von Tunzelmann, 1978). Indeed, it were the discoveries and inventions which allowed to exploit fossil energy sources, coal and later oil and gas, that have been driving the industrialization process to unprecedented forms since the industrial revolution (Landes, 1969; Rosenberg, 1982)—both the steam engine and the later invented combustion engine based on construction and operation principles with no equivalent in nature. Furthermore, once non-anthropogenic free energy could be accessed in its fossil deposited form, it could be dissipated on large scale basis for heating purposes in the nineteenth century. As a result, the chemical processing technology, which had had its forerunners in the alchemists at the beginning of the modern times, could develop into a powerful, independent paradigm of transforming materials (cf. Murmann and Homburg, 2001).

The mechanical paradigm experienced another great boost in the last 100 years with the invention of electricity generating and transmitting facilities and electricity powered appliances. Its major advantage was in making energy instantaneously and in exact dosage available for kinetic use on a variable scale basis which allowed an unprecedented decentralization, modularization, and miniaturization of all mechanical devices. In fact, once electric power and the media to transmit it were available, an additional application independent of the mechanical paradigm was discovered in signal generation, transmission, and storage—the information technology which, it is commonly believed, is just now in its heyday. In the most recent extension of technological (cultural) knowledge and tool use human intentionality pushes the symbiotic production forms to an unprecedented level of manipulation of living nature in what is called biotechnology (cf. McKelvey, 1996).

With respect to the rich details of all these developments one may refer to an extensive research spanning from innovation studies like those just cited with a background in economic history to the history of technology proper (cf., e.g., Cardwell, 1994). The economic precondition, concomitants, and consequences of the history of technical progress have been discussed with great care from different points of view, e.g., in Rosenberg and Birdzell (1986) and Mokyr (1990). Unlike these historical works, but not in conflict with their results, we have tried here to highlight how and where human production slowly evolved beyond the technological principles that had evolved earlier in natural history. This has happened as a result of the interplay between intentionality and cultural knowledge which is not only the hallmark of the human economy, but also characteristic of the modalities of the new form of evolution that has occurred on our planet, namely the evolution of human culture.

Together with the available resource endowment, the cultural knowledge actually used at a given point in time constrains the realization of human intentions. An important part of the explanation for why the above outlined development has been possible therefore rests in the question of how the growing and improved cultural knowledge has become available. Of course, human inventiveness and the intentional search and pursuit of problem solutions once problems had been recognized play a decisive role here as has always been emphasized in innovation research. However, this alone does not explain the very slow start of the deviation of human production from production in living nature and its enormous acceleration over just the past few centuries. There have also been changes in the production and transmission of cultural knowledge which, it may be claimed, systematically affected the pace of cultural evolution. Again, a comparison with nature, this time the case of genetically coded knowledge, is instructive.

Both cultural and genetically coded knowledge are incorporated or 'stored' in organisms, though in very different ways. In the one case it is represented in the habits, beliefs, experiences, in short: the stored content of memory (as far as it can be retrieved). In the other case, it is stored in the genetic code expressed in DNA and RNA strings contained in the organisms' cells. Due to the finite life time of the organisms, both kinds of knowledge must be transmitted between the generations in order not to be lost. Corresponding to the different ways in which the two kinds of knowledge are stored in the organisms, the transmission process is fundamentally different.[4] Genetically coded knowledge is automatically passed on exclusively between successive generations of organisms in biological reproduction which implies a process of (potentially recombinatory) copying of genetic information contained in the successive organisms' germ cells. Cultural knowledge is passed on both between organisms of the same generation as well as between generations through operant conditioning (or habit formation), observational or social learning (imitation), and—where the intellectual capacity of the organism allows this—conscious instruction by some medium. Different elements of cultural knowledge draw on different forms of learning: habits,

---

[4] For sake of simplicity possible interactions between the transmission of the two kinds of knowledge, which may have been influential in early phases of human phylogeny, are ignored here. For a discussion of the co-evolutionary process they may imply cf. Boyd and Richerson (1985).

U. Witt / Structural Change and Economic Dynamics 16 (2005) 165–179   173

social rules of conduct, and to a lesser extent skills are predominantly transmitted by operant conditioning and imitation, technological and abstract knowledge by observational learning and instruction.

The use of tools and their making is the part of the cultural knowledge of a species that interests us here most. Field studies in primates have shown that in the rare cases where tools are used, they are discovered by individuals by trial and error. Once adopted as a regular practice, tool use is transmitted between the members of a band by imitation. Imitation may even become ritualized as part of the play and inauguration procedures during socialization of the next generation. Nonetheless, the complexity of tool use as a cultural practice is constrained by what can be acquired by mere observation. It is with the command of language that the transmission of knowledge on more complex tools and their use and making becomes feasible or is at least facilitated. More complex tools usually emerge from intentional search for improvements on techniques and tools carried out by some individuals. Oral communication paired with demonstration, i.e. instruction, and observational learning jointly establish an effective way of passing on improved techniques between their inventors and other individuals, particularly individuals of the next generation. Potentially there is a knowledge cumulating effect here, provided instructors are present for long enough to both improve their experience and skills and to pass them on to other individuals. Life expectancy is therefore a significant variable in the effectiveness of the oral transmission of cultural knowledge, and the slow increase of average life expectancy as a result of the improving human production methods therefore meant a self-reinforcing effect for further enhancing cultural evolution.

With the early high cultures pictographic writing systems emerged which, however, had little to do with the transmission or dissemination of cultural knowledge. This changed only with the development of true alphabetic writing some 4000 years ago. Written documents were used, e.g., by the Greek scholars to disseminate and exchange the fruits of their studies. Most of the texts produced till the Middle Ages, of course, served religious and theological purposes, with a minor part for philosophy and law. Both writing and reading were very serious human production processes, reserved to a small elite. Only with the invention of the printing press in the 15th century and the subsequently developing broader literacy in Europe, writings in science and technology gained more influence and started to trigger a significant effect on the transmission of cultural knowledge, speeding up the transmission and improving the quality of the content. With writing, cultural knowledge can be codified and stored and the personal contingencies of oral instruction thus be substantially reduced. With the printing press, the audience that can be instructed or informed can be multiplied. Since reading is a parallel process, information could much quicker be diffused than by spoken word (at least until the radio was invented). At the same time, competition between ideas, opinions, theories and practices suggested to the readers increased vigorously. While under oral transmission the best knowledge that could be obtained was the best the individual teacher was able to offer, with the new competition the best knowledge could, in principle, be the best transmitted by all teachers.

Codification of cultural knowledge, particularly technological knowledge (relating to tool making and tool use), a rapidly rising rate of literacy, and the spread of formal education thus seem to be major ingredients to the success story told by the economic historians about human production over the past two centuries. The organization and institutionalization of (re-)search for new knowledge in science is another ingredient. The consequence has been a soaring growth of mostly (but not only) useful knowledge which, because of the limited capacity of the individual mind, required specialization and the division of knowledge. There is no doubt that the (re-)production of the respective body of knowledge in the mind of every new user and every new generation of users is itself a substantial part of modern human production which has no equivalent in living nature. It is epitomized by the library reading room occupied with silent, hard working students—a picture that may well be taken to suggest that there are upper bounds to the amount of problem solving knowledge that can be processed by a finite human population.

The codification of knowledge by means of written documents has most recently been topped by an automatization of information processing, independent from the human brain, on the basis of electronic signal processing technologies. However, the reproduction of individual knowledge in command of this new technology in each new generation of students still has to rely on the old, inherited information processing technology of the human brain. As long as intelligence cannot be shifted to machinery, this is likely to be a hard constraint. Should ways be been found sometime to create a truly intelligent machinery, cultural evolution will have reached a stage in which humans are no longer in control of its outcome. The future fate of human production, indeed of the human species in general, may then hinge on whether the finite human problem solving capacity will be able to force the new intelligent beings into symbiotic forms of production of knowledge under human guidance or vice versa (cf. Wadman, 2001).

4. Production as a social affair and the theory of the "factors of production"

Unlike industrial engineers and management scientists engaged in production engineering who have developed elaborate descriptions and technical notions of production, economists have rarely considered the physical conditions of production processes in any detail, not to speak of any comparisons with production processes in living nature. The reason is that, since the classical writers, economists have approached production as a problem of human social interactions and their coordination—the orderly division of labor among men—and the resulting distribution of wealth and income. Accordingly, economists have come to perceive and frame production activities as a matter of choice and within the framework of a "science of value" (as economics is, often implicitly, defined to the present day). The relationship between such an approach and the analysis of physical production processes is, of course, at best an indirect one. An attempt to draw inferences from the one sphere to the other one can therefore be expected to be faced with lots of complications as, for example, the debate on various versions of abstract "corn models" (cf. Skourtos, 1998) and on all substance theories of value have indeed shown.

Asking what physical preparations people actually make to obtain outputs with certain characteristics (and why), and asking for the values that can be imputed both to the activities and the outcomes are thus different pairs of shoes. With their moral and political ambitions, the latter question has been more appealing to the classical economists than the former. Quesnay and the physiocratic school are a good example. Perhaps more than any other school later, these early classical writers in France had a concrete understanding of the fact that the symbiotic forms of production in agriculture allow, at the expense of some human labor, to grow and reap fruits which themselves are not 'produced' by labor but by nature. Yet, their theoretical concern was to establish a theory of value based on the exchange of the products which would explain *whose property* contributes how much to the overall expansion of wealth (or creation of income) in the economy and what distribution of income therefore results. Obviously, property is a category of human social (or, in the terminology of the previous section: cultural) affairs, since it regulates the entitlement rights between human individuals with respect to some object. In an age-old tradition recorded in anthropology, entitlement rights to the fruits of nature are associated with the possession of the land on which they grow, a notion probably reaching back in human phylogeny to the territorial claims of our ancestors in habitat. The advanced institutions of France under Louis XV, however, distinguished already between possession of land (by the tenant) and property in land (by the feudal proprietors). Accordingly, Quesnay was eager to show that it was not the tenant's property in circulating and fixed capital that deserved the *produit net* accruing from nature's contribution, but the feudal Lord's property in land to which is was paid as the rent.

In later schools, the role of land—and even more so that of nature—moved to the background or disappeared completely (cf. Weissmahr, 1992). But the major interest continued to be in the theory of value explaining whose property contributes to wealth creation in the economy how, and how much of income should therefore be distributed to the respective property owner. Instead of feudal Lords, their property in land, and their entitlement to earn the rent, the dynamism and rising importance of industry (and the antifeudal resentments of the disciples of economics) suggested to preferably consider, on the one hand, capitalists as the owners of capital and the profits that accrued to them as their distributive share. On the other hand, concern was with workers who (for physical reasons) were obviously necessary to run the production in the factories, who were considered to own their labor force, and who were seen to obtain wages in return for selling their labor force. A focus like this appeared particularly promising as the dynamism of industry was rightly connected with the observation that, with every new industry and its expansion, ever more capital was accumulated by capitalists who were eager to make profit, an interdependency that could easily be anticipated to have major implications for the distribution of wealth and income in society.

On the other side, it was clear from classical times on that very heterogeneous things can be employed as capital. The term "capital" actually stands for all sorts of means (except land and labor) provided they are used in, and can themselves be produced and accumulated for, production. Capital therefore be treated as a homogeneous quantity only in a trivial way in regard to its abstract means character or, non-trivially, on the basis of some properly constructed value measure. In order to be able to consistently impute distributional shares of income and wealth to the proprietors of the means or "factors" of production such a value measure would, of course, be required to cover all economic quantities including the amount of labor, wages, and the final products. Confusion and controversy between monetary and real value concepts, between equilibrium (or long run) values and disequilibrium prices of current transactions, and eventually between objective or substantive and subjective value measures, were preprogrammed and, indeed, characterize the history of economic thought (cf., e.g., Kurz and Salvadori, 1995). The debate on whether and, if so, how a proper and coherent evaluation of both products and means can be constructed shall, however, not be addressed here.[5] The question rather is what insights beyond value theory an analysis of the physical production processes can provide. In what light do basic concepts of production theory, such as the factors of production, appear once value considerations are abandoned?

As physical, chemical, and biological engineering teach, the non-trivial challenges in production lie in the details of the used materials, the variety of processing steps and their timing, including the application of heat, pressure, and kinetic energy for mechanical treatments, the quality and reliability of the equipment, etc. To abstract from the details and circumstances of the transformations taking place in physical production processes is therefore not without problems. This holds equally for the analysis of production processes in living nature. On the other hand, without a substantial increase in the level of abstraction any comparison to the highly abstract concepts and assumptions in the economic theory of production is difficult to achieve. To outline how the dilemma may be resolved let us focus on what would be the natural equivalents to the abstract core notion of the factors of production in economics. These are usually defined as inputs to production. For the present purpose it is useful to distinguish, as is done in the classical literature, between two kinds: a given (non-produced) input of an invariable, measurable quality and an input that is itself produced.

In the production processes in living nature two given factors of production can then trivially be identified: free energy and matter or materials, i.e. substances of a certain chemical or molecular composition. All living organisms including humans absorb and dissipate free energy to maintain their life functions which consist basically in processing and transforming materials. The non-trivial point is to identify the produced input or production factor(s). As has been explained in the previous sections, a central role is played in production in living nature by genetically coded knowledge. The latter triggers and controls the various reductions and transformations and their order in time. Moreover, genetically coded knowledge has the unique feature of containing the program for replicating itself, in fact, of replicating multiple copies of itself. In order to do this, however, the genetic information needs to be expressed and carried on in living organisms which have been 'produced' according to the genetic program from, and make a living by means of, dissipating free energy and transforming materials.

The particular, 'produced' input or factor(s) of production, if this language is to be used here, are thus the mutually dependent elements of genetic knowledge and its organismic expression. With the programmed multiple (and potentially recombinatory) reproduction of genetic knowledge in several organisms who share genes, production processes in living nature cause two effects at the same time. They create the variety on the basis of which natural selection can bring about adaptations of the genetically coded knowledge to changing environmental conditions. And they tend to generate a self-augmenting growth

---

[5] The debate has sometimes been considered indicative of the anthropocentric framing of the problems related to production in economics. With the accumulation of undesired and harmful side-effects of human production in the natural environment which are not adequately represented by the value measures in economics, opposition to the anthropocentric interpretation of production and productive forces has risen and, in more recent times, motivated the ecological economics movement (cf. Constanza, 1989; Daly and Cobb, 1989; Norgaard, 1994). Yet, as Constanza et al. (1997) shows, even that movement seems to be attracted to valuation problems, only in a more encompassing interpretation that tries to extend (anthropocentric) value measures to natural stocks and services.

of the population of the species (as long as, for whatever reasons, the death rate in the population is not driven up to or above the birth rate).

In comparison to these 'factors of production' in nature there is very little of a common basis with the factors of production land, capital, and labor traditionally considered in economics for reasons mentioned above. Indeed, it seems difficult to even break down land, capital, and labor analytically to the categories free energy, materials, and knowledge and its mediation. Following the foundations that have been laid with the comparison between physical production in living nature and in human production in the previous sections an attempt can instead be made to identify the differences between these two forms of production in terms of the 'factors of production' in nature. Free energy and materials clearly continue to be given inputs. Since, however, humans cannot generate genetically coded knowledge, the latter together with its organismic expression, are also given factors of production which can only marginally be manipulated (e.g. by breeding and, most recently increasingly so, in biotechnology).

A produced input is obviously human cultural, particularly technological, knowledge. It is decisive to understand that, as in the case of the natural equivalent, knowledge needs to be expressed or mediated in order to have an impact on the human production process. Knowledge as such can neither transform materials, let free energy work, or crop the produce. In the early human phylogeny the mediation of human knowledge into the production process was confined to man's anatomic apparatus. Culturally acquired knowledge in gathering, hunting, preparing food, and making first artefacts basically came down to learned manual skills. Such skills still play an economically significant role in mediating human knowledge. Only with the creation of the first tools, ways were found for an extra-somatic mediation of learned knowledge (albeit, as has been explained, for a very long time heavily relying on the human anatomy). These tools are produced according to the tool maker's knowledge from dissipating free energy and transforming materials either by hand and/or by means of other tools. The produced input or factors of production are thus, strange as it may appear, similar to the case of the produced inputs in natural production processes, the mutually dependent elements of cultural knowledge and its expression in tools and machinery.[6]

There are, however, significant differences between nature's and man's case. First, the mutual dependency between genetically coded knowledge and its organismic expression is, due to the reproduction mechanism, a hardwired recursiveness. Lacking that, the mutual dependency between cultural knowledge and tools or machinery is much weaker. Neither is cultural knowledge that has been created automatically expressed in tools, nor do tools actively express knowledge. Each of the two elements can simply be left idle by man who, by his activity, has to connect them. Second, lacking the multiple copying feature of the genetic program, human cultural knowledge tends to create both variety and self-augmenting effects differently. A greater rate of variety production is potentially implied by intentionality in searching for problem solutions which, moreover, is not bound to the pace of generational change. An autocatalylic effect in human production processes is due to the fact that cultural knowledge allows tool making and usually multiple tool use. Everything else unchanged,

---

[6] Note that, according to the classification just given, the human anatomy is a given input to human production processes.

multiple use of tools usually reduces the time necessary for carrying out production of the same output. The spare time can be used for producing even more tools or for intentionally trying to enhance the very knowledge of making and using tools.

5. Conclusions

"Production" means the generation of some result or output by the application of specific inputs. In this sense, production has been shown in this paper to be a ubiquitous phenomenon in nature, way beyond and, of course, preceding human productive activity. This simple fact has invited to reflect about similarities and differences in the two spheres of production. Two kinds of problems are involved, and often difficult to separate, in such a comparison. One relates to the questions of what is being produced, in what quantities, and for what purposes. In the human sphere, the answers to these questions depend on human intentions as they emerge together with the social organization of production from cultural evolution. This is why economics is traditionally concerned with problems of value and distribution of wealth and income. Elsewhere in nature production serves a (non-intentional) functionality for survival and reproductive success. The other kind of problems relates to the questions of how the observed result or output is being produced, by what means. This is the physical side of production which can, of course, be made subject of a reasonable comparison only at a rather abstract level. A discussion of the concept of the factors of production has been given from such a perspective. It has been shown that, once the orientation towards value assessment and imputation of distributional shares is skipped, some systematic differences between production processes in nature and in the human economy can better be grasped.

References

Ayres, R.U., 1978. Resources, Environment, and Economics. Wiley, New York.

Boyd, R., Richerson, P.J., 1985. Culture and the Evolutionary Process. Chicago University Press, Chicago.

Cardwell, D., 1994. The Fontana History of Technology. Fontana Press, London.

Constanza, R., 1989. What is ecological economics? Ecological Economics 1, 1–8.

Constanza, R., d'Arge, R., de Groot, R., Farber, S., Grasso, W., Hannon, B., Limburg, K., Naeem, S., O'Neill, R.V., Paruelo, J., Raskin, R.G., Sutton, P., van den Belt, M., 1997. The value of the world's ecosystem services and natural capital. Nature 387, 253–260.

Daly, H.E., Cobb Jr., J.B., 1989. For the Common Good. Green Print, London.

Faber, M., Proops, J.L.R., 1998. Evolution, Time, Production and the Environment, third ed. Springer, Berlin.

Faber, M., Proops, J.L.R., Baumgaertner, S., 1998. All production is joint production—a thermodynamic analysis. In: Faucheux, S., Gowdy, J., Nicolai, I. (Eds.), Sustainability and Firms. Edward Elgar, Cheltenham, pp. 131–158.

Georgescu-Roegen, N., 1971. The Entropy Law and the Economic Process. Harvard University Press, Cambridge, MA.

Gowdy, J., 1994. Coevolutionary Economics. Kluwer Academic Publishers, Boston.

Hall, C., Lindenberger, D., Kümmel, R., Kroeger, T., Eichhorn, W., 2001. The need to reintegrate the natural sciences with economics. Bioscience 51, 663–673.

Kurz, H.D., Salvadori, N., 1995. Theory of Production: A Long Period Analysis. Cambridge University Press, Cambridge.

Landes, D.S., 1969. The Unbound Prometheus—Technological Change and Industrial Development in Western Europe From 1750 to the Present. Cambridge University Press, Cambridge.

McKelvey, M., 1996. Evolutionary Innovations: The Business of Biotechnology. Oxford University Press, Oxford.

Mokyr, J., 1990. The Lever of Riches—Technological Creativity and Economic Progress. Oxford University Press, Oxford.

Murmann, J.P., Homburg, E., 2001. Comparing evolutionary dynamics across different national settings: the case of the synthetic dye industry, 1857–1914. Journal of Evolutionary Economics 11, 177–205.

Norgaard, R.B., 1994. Development Betrayed: The End of Progress and a Coevolutionary Revisioning of the Future. New York.

Pulliam, H.R., Dunford, C., 1980. Programmed to Learn: An Essay on the Evolution of Culture. Columbia University Press, New York.

Rosenberg, N., 1982. Inside the Black Box: Technology and Economics. Cambridge University Press, Cambridge.

Rosenberg, N., Birdzell Jr., L.E., 1986. How the West Grew Rich: The Economic Transformation of the Industrial World. Basic Books, New York.

Skourtos, M.S., 1998. Corn model. In: Kurz, H.D., Salvadori, N. (Eds.), The Elgar Companion to Classical Economics, vol. I. Edward Elgar, Cheltenham, pp. 194–196.

Stenseth, N.C., Maynard Smith, J., 1984. Coevolution in ecosystems: red queen evolution or stasis? Evolution 38, 870–880.

Toulmin, S., 1961. Foresight and Understanding—An Inquiry into the Aims of Science. Hutchison, London.

von Tunzelmann, G.N., 1978. Steam Power and British Industrialization to 1860. Oxford University Press, Oxford.

Usher, A.P., 1954. A History of Mechanical Inventions. Harvard University Press, Cambridge, MA.

Wadman, W.M., 2001. Technological change, human capital and extinction. Papers on Economics and Evolution #0112. Max Planck Institute for Research into Economic Systems, Jena, Germany.

Weissmahr, J.A., 1992. The factors of production of evolutionary economics. In: Witt, U. (Ed.), Explaining Process and Change—Approaches to Evolutionary Economics. Michigan University Press, Ann Arbor, pp. 67–79.

Wilson, E.O., 1975. Sociobiology—The New Synthesis. Belknap Press, Cambridge, MA.

Witt, U., 1997. Self-organization and economics—what is new? Structural Change and Economic Dynamics 8, 489–507.

Witt, U., 1999. Bioeconomics as economics from a Darwinian perspective. Journal of Bioeconomics 1, 19–34.

[13]

J Evol Econ (2008) 18:249–260
DOI 10.1007/s00191-007-0078-0

REGULAR ARTICLE

Output dynamics, flow equilibria and structural change—A prolegomenon to evolutionary macroeconomics

Ulrich Witt · Thomas Brenner

Published online: 9 January 2008
© Springer-Verlag 2007

Abstract In an evolutionary approach to macroeconomics, the market disequilibrium dynamics resulting from structural change need to be properly represented at the aggregate level. As suggested by the late F.A. Hayek, a suitable equilibrium concept required to this end as a frame of reference, is that of a flow equilibrium. The paper explores the corresponding flow dynamics that draw attention to variables not usually considered in macroeconomic theorizing. Using statistical estimates for these new variables for the West German manufacturing sector during the German unification process allows some important new insights on the relationships between structural change and macroeconomic performance.

Keywords Macroeconomics · Structural change · Disequilibrium dynamics · Flow equilibrium · Business cycle

JEL classification B 52 · D 50 · E 00 · E 11 · E 32

1 Introduction

The contours of an evolutionary approach to macroeconomic theory are still far from being clear. An early inquiry by Foster (1987) develops an evolutionary perspective on macroeconomic issues in comparison to Keynesian and post-Keynesian positions. This work was later extended to an econometric approach focusing on the impact of logistic diffusion processes on macroeconomic time series (Foster 1992, Foster and Wild 1999). Another strand of thought is informed by the seminal work of Nelson and Winter (1982, Chap. 4) on innovation driven structural change in industries. The macroeconomic implications of their approach are discussed in terms of disequilibrium growth processes accompanied by productivity changes at the aggregate level, GNP

U. Witt (✉) · T. Brenner
Max Planck Institute of Economics, Kahlaische Str. 10, 07745 Jena, Germany
e-mail: Ulrich.Witt@econ.mpg.de

growth rate variations, and a catching up and falling behind in international competitiveness (Silverberg and Verspagen 1995, Fagerberg et al. 1997, Fagerberg and Verspagen 2002, Los and Verspagen 2006, Metcalfe et al. 2006).

The agenda of the latter contributions partly overlaps with that of macroeconomic "out-of-equilibrium" models that draw much of their inspiration from the neo-Austrian theory of production and growth (Amendola and Gaffard 1998, 2003, Amendola et al. 2005). However, the former literature focuses on how the evolutionary process of structural change results in disequilibria, breaks, and fluctuations reflected in growth accounting at the regional, national, and international levels. The latter writings, in contrast, emphasize how the results of the restructuring of the productive capacity hinge on whether or not inter-temporal complementarities can be upheld in the process of innovation-driven growth. This is the problem of coordination in the economy. It relates to the influence of expectations held by the agents, to the intra-temporal and inter-temporal working of the price mechanism, to the time structure of the flows of goods and services arising from capital accumulation, and to the impact of monetary and fiscal policies.

In the "out-of-equilibrium" approach to evolutionary macroeconomics, a vision of the coordination of aggregate economic activity lives on as it can be found already in Hayek (1941) before the advent of Keynesian macroeconomics, and in Hicks (1973) afterwards. In this vision, the incessant structural change in the economy is seen as an expectation-driven venturing into future production and trade opportunities offered by new technologies. It induces restructurings and disruptions and, hence, a disequilibrium state of the economy. However, as the disequilibrium state is seen as one that elicits coordinating forces, false expectations, prices, and production engagements should sooner or later be corrected. If there were no further profitable restructuring opportunities emerging, aggregate economic activity should therefore be expected to return to an equilibrium state—albeit one that may vary with the technological conditions and the policy regimes chosen.

The association of technological change, capital accumulation, and the restructuring of production with a disequilibrium state of affairs indeed seems uncontroversial in all approaches to evolutionary macroeconomics. Not so, however, the question of what concept of equilibrium, if any, is relevant as a standard of reference. This is an old question that not only concerns definitions, but also, and more fundamentally, the way in which the evolutionary transformation process in the economy can be approached from a macroeconomic point of view. In macroeconomic theorizing, the frame of reference for defining disequilibria is usually the notion of a market equilibrium, i.e. of equality of supply and demand. As will be argued in this paper, on closer inspection of the time structure of aggregate economic activity, a different equilibrium notion shows up. This notion draws attention to dynamic macroeconomic features that, despite the ongoing structural change in the economy, are remarkably robust over time and may therefore play the role of invariance in evolutionary macroeconomics.

The paper proceeds as follows. Section 2 discusses the alternative notions of equilibria relevant for the macroeconomic level. Drawing on a metaphor introduced by Hayek (1981), the notion of an equilibrium in the flow of goods and services over time is contrasted with that of an equilibrium in the aggregate markets for goods and services at a certain point in time, and it is argued that the former fits an evolutionary perspective better. In Section 3 the corresponding macro flow dynamics are explored and are shown to transcend the usual focus on market equilibria. The critical role of

🍎 Springer

a velocity variable for the flow equilibrium is pointed out—a variable that is usually not even considered in macroeconomic models. Section 4 looks into the empirical evidence for flow equilibria at the macroeconomic level. Time series data for West Germany are used to estimate the velocity variable whose behavior over time allows to infer whether or not the conditions for a flow equilibrium are met for the time period under consideration. Section 5 offers conclusions.

2 What notion of equilibrium?

The very notion of a *dis*-equilibrium can be claimed to make sense only with reference to a state of equilibrium. This does not necessarily mean, however, that equilibrium states are indeed relevant for the trajectories of macroeconomic variables. A trajectory in which no equilibrium point or orbit occurs is sufficiently characterized as a disequilibrium (or "out-of-equilibrium," Amendola and Gaffard 1998) process.[1] Furthermore, in the cases in which an equilibrium concept is, in fact, relevant, it does not necessarily have to refer to equilibria in markets, as is usually the case in macroeconomic theories. Most of these focus on (simultaneous) equilibria in the aggregate markets for goods, money, and the factors of production (or on equilibrium growth paths characterized by equal growth rates for all relevant variables). If supply were indeed equal to demand in all markets, this would be a state of perfect market coordination. While such a state is a precondition for an efficient resource allocation at the disaggregate level and, ultimately, for the concept of a general equilibrium in the economy, it is unlikely to occur in reality.

This is true, in particular, in the presence of structural change. Characteristic of competitive, capitalist economies and their growth, structural change necessarily implies disruptions for many market participants and elements of de-coordination or "creative destruction," as Schumpeter (1942) put it. Though perfect market coordination cannot be expected to prevail under such conditions, a considerable degree of coordination of production and exchange can still be observed. The idea of market coordination therefore seems to call here for a conceptualization that is not confined to market equilibrium states. An equilibrium notion corresponding to such a broader view of the coordinating problem has been suggested by Hayek (1981). This contrasts remarkably with Hayek's earlier contributions to business cycle theory, monetary issues, and the time structure of investment and capital accumulation that had gained him a reputation as a leading economic theorist and that are all firmly molded in a market equilibrium analysis. For understanding the broader notion of equilibrium, it is worth noting the reasons that induced Hayek to dismiss the narrower one.

By the end of the 1940s, Hayek had for several reasons turned his back on issues related to aggregate economic activity (McCormick 1992) and started working on social philosophy instead. The outgrowth of this work was his evolutionary theory of the spontaneously emerging "extended order of the markets" (Hayek 1988). The theory holds that individual knowledge is incomplete and hypothetical. As a

---

[1] This is, e.g., the case for chaotic time series. See the discussion in Baumol and Benhabib (1989) and Ruelle (1991).

 Springer

consequence, there is room for experimentation, discoveries, and surprises in the economy (Hayek 1978). However, through their learning via market interactions, agents are able to realize ordered forms of production and trade. In Hayek's reflections on what "the twin idea of a spontaneous order and societal evolution" implies for the cultural, legal, and political basis of market economies, the 'macroeconomic' topics that interested him earlier no longer played a particular role. If this had not been the case, the strong equilibrium focus of the earlier writings would have been difficult to reconcile with the evolutionary views he was about to elaborate.

Hayek (1981) addressed this problem in a rather late and little noticed lecture.[2] To solve it he introduced the metaphor of a river system by which he intended to capture crucial features of the flow of goods and services in an economy: "... conceive of the whole process of production as a continuous stream or flow which at its mouth yields a continuous output, emerging after having passed through various transformations since the first resources had been applied. At any one moment a great number of such streams, or rather complex ramified river systems, will be proceeding concurrently, each a little more advanced than the next one. The finished products of all these streams will emerge at more or less distant future dates" (ibid. p.3). In view of the complex time structure of the flows alluded to in the metaphor, it is by no means clear what role an equilibrium concept can play.

Accordingly, Hayek writes: "It is very tempting to describe as an 'equilibrium' an ideal state of affairs in which the intentions of all participants precisely match and where each will find a partner willing to enter into the intended transaction. But for all capitalistic production there must exist a considerable interval of time between the beginning of a process and its various later stages which makes the achievement of such an equilibrium impossible.... Even an apparent momentary state of balance in which everybody succeeds in selling or buying what he intended, may be *inherently* unrepeatable, irrespective of any change in the internal data, because some of the constituents of the stream will be the results of past conditions which have changed long ago" (ibid. p.8).

Obviously, using the metaphor of the flow for the evolving aggregate economic process, the price system and, even more so, the notion of a market equilibrium lose much of their significance for understanding how, and to what extent, economic activities are coordinated. There is no basis for assuming a uniform price for the goods and services. But, even in the presence of massive structural change, agents can be assumed to be aware of the fact that the prices they can charge for their offers have an upper bound where demand becomes zero. Moreover, there is a lower bound where the unit costs of making an offer—usually hinging on earlier investment decisions—can no longer be covered. Search activities and competition tend to bring down over time the upper bound and learning and technological progress the lower bound.

---

[2] The lecture was given in 1981 at the London School of Economics;"...to the day exactly 50 years after I delivered from the same platform the first of four lectures that led to my appointment to a professorship at this school", Hayek starts. Time and location signal that Hayek himself considered the lecture an occasion on which to present second thoughts about his earlier views. The English manuscript of the lecture was never published. It has, however, been translated and published in German (Hayek 1984). The authors are grateful to Dr. Claudia Loy, who translated the manuscript, for making available a copy of her private exemplar, cited here as Hayek (1981).

🕿 Springer

As long as the agents' margin between the upper and lower bounds does not persistently turn negative, and as long as agents adjust prices and quantities properly, they can stay in business. Losses and overdrawing of budgets alert them of the need to review their costs and prices, to engage in developing improved products and to invest in new technologies. Agents who nonetheless fail to uphold and profit from a non-negative margin are forced out of business and their resources are laid idle. In this sense, there are indeed coordinating incentives mediated by the price mechanism that keep up a *viable* degree of coordination in the economy. It is less than perfect because of losses and failures, mis-allocations and idle resources that may occur and because of profit opportunities and windfall gains. Even if all businesses could survive under the viable degree of coordination in the markets, the state of a general equilibrium (corresponding to a unique equilibrium price vector) would therefore not be attained.

What follows for the macroeconomic variables from these dynamic features of a less than perfect market coordination process—and what follows for the equilibrium notion? Amendola and Gaffard (1998, Chap.1) rightly make the following point. If the extent of coordination is no more than a viable one as just described, both the inter-temporal and the intra-temporal complementarity of aggregate variables is no longer guaranteed. This concerns consumption, saving, and investment on the one hand, and employment opportunities, factor supply, and factor income on the other. Deviations from the complementarity conditions upstream are likely to affect the flow of goods and services coming out of the production process downstream, both in its growth potential over time and in its business cycle patterns. This is the immediate consequence of giving up the fiction of perfect coordination. A challenge that remains is to demonstrate that, despite its fluctuations over time, the observable stream of goods and services and the corresponding macroeconomic variables still express a significant degree of coordination. Hayek's metaphor suggests a way to demonstrate this — and, by the same token, puts forth a different equilibrium notion.

In spite of the fluctuations in aggregate output and the likely lack of inter-temporal complementarities in producing it, one form of complementarity may still be sustained in the processing of goods and services. This is, to stick to Hayek's metaphor, the balance between the influx upstream and the outflow at the mouth of the stream. The condition relevant for this kind of intra-temporal and inter-temporal complementarity can be stated by means of the concept of a flow equilibrium.

Definition A flow equilibrium results if influx and outflow in a flow system over a given period of time are balanced in such a way that a constant relation between the system's capacity and its throughput is stabilized (steady flow).

Obviously, this is an inherently dynamic equilibrium concept which, when applied to the flow of goods and services, implies a much weaker condition for the extent of coordination in the economy than the concept of a general equilibrium in all markets does. If the concept of a flow equilibrium is used to test empirically the presence of a viable coordination in aggregate economic time series, two problems arise. The first is to find adequate economic variables by which influx and outflow can be measured. The second problem is to determine theoretically by what kind of economic processes the influx is translated into an outflow. These two problems will be discussed in the next section.

 Springer

3 Macro flow dynamics and the neglected velocity variable

The extent of intra-temporal and inter-temporal coordination in the flow of goods and services can best be grasped when attention is redirected from market exchange activities to the time structure of the production process on which the timing of the market transactions rests. Imagine the production sector of the economy as a huge system of servicing channels in which arriving orders (and—as will be tacitly assumed—future offers planned by the producers) are processed by passing through various processing steps and/or processing units. Accordingly, the orders received in a given period of time t, $r(t)$, can be taken to represent the influx variable in the flow interpretation. The outflow variable is the output produced in a period t, $q(t)$, that results from the earlier orders. The time lag between an influx turning into an outflow hinges on the kind of the goods and services, the technology by which they are produced, and other, usually industry-specific, features. Foremost, however, it depends on the average number of processing units required to be passed through under the given organizational and technical conditions and the potentially varying, average speed $v(t)$ with which the processing advances under the given capacity constraints per unit of time.

The average number of processing units and the other industry specific features can be treated as technological parameters that are independent of the production capacity. In contrast, the time that is needed on average for processing orders in the economy is a variable that depends on the ratio between the total orders in process in a given period of time t, $R(t)$, and the production capacity available at that time. $R(t)$ is defined more precisely as the sum of $r(t)$ and the orders received previous to t that have not yet been worked off, i.e.

$$R(t) = r(t) + \sum_{n=1}^{t-1} r(n) - q(n). \tag{1}$$

A straight forward hypothesis can be stated as follows.

Assumption 1 The average order processing speed $v(t)$ is constant as long as there is no bottleneck in the processing (production) capacity of the economy. Once $R(t)$ exceeds the existing processing capacity at a critical value R^*, however, $v(t)$ starts to decrease.

Note that the reaction of the processing speed to the servicing or production capacity becoming jammed is a technical feature that cannot be influenced by price adjustments. Prices may, of course, vary when the orders in process grow and may thus affect the order activities. But even this is not self-evident as is sometimes presupposed within a market equilibrium framework.

If economic agents have incomplete, fallible knowledge, it is quite natural for them to fail to foresee, or to account for, the actual volume of demand in the future when they make their necessarily speculative investment and saving decisions on the basis of the price information available today. The consequence is a lack of inter-temporal complementary of accumulation, production, and consumption activities. At the end of the pipe, this may result in a change in spot prices that can clear the markets, but it cannot prevent the failure to achieve inter-temporal market equilibria. Moreover, even market clearing spot prices do not ensure an intra-temporal complementarity between orders given on the one side and the existing production capacity on the other. It is because of this fact that the average processing speed in the economy varies in the asymmetric way stated in Assumption 1.

A similar asymmetry holds with respect to the conditions of a flow equilibrium. A lasting slump in the order volume (the influx), which results in excess capacity, leads to a lasting reduction in deliveries (the outflow) later. However, because of the steady throughput after the reduction, the economy is still in a flow equilibrium, albeit at a lower throughput level. In contrast, a lasting order volume in excess of R^* tends to pile up over time. This is an unsteady flow condition. By Assumption 1, $v(t)$ is constant in the first case and decreases in the second case. Hence it follows from the above definition of a flow equilibrium and by Assumption 1 that

Proposition 1 A constant processing speed $v(t)$ is a necessary condition for a flow equilibrium in the economic production system.

The simple logic of the flow metaphor thus suggests a functional relationship between aggregate output $q(t)$ per period of time t as the dependent variable and a few independent variables not usually considered in macroeconomic theorizing. The average order processing speed $v(t)$, for instance, is neglected even in dynamic macroeconomic models, although it represents a constitutive aspect of the time dependence of the aggregate production process. Another variable to which attention is drawn is the capacity of the economy's servicing or production system, a variable that is difficult to measure. However, using the flow analogy, a way can be found to relate it to the orders in process, $R(t)$, a variable that can more easily be measured.

In certain fluid systems, the throughput, measured by the number of particles leaving a certain segment of the flow per period of time, can be approximated by the density of the particles in the flow segment times their average flow velocity (see e.g. Helbig 1995). Here, the density indirectly reflects a capacity measure. Analogously, one can assume for the flow representation of macroeconomic dynamics:

Assumption 2 $q(t)$ results from the orders in process $R(t)$ in a given period of time t multiplied by the average speed $v(t)$ with which they are processed.[3]

Thus, we can write

$$q(t) = v(t) \times R(t) \tag{2}$$

As long as $v(t)$=const., $q(t)$ varies proportionally with $R(t)$ and, by Proposition 1, the condition for a flow equilibrium is satisfied. Given the functional relationship stated in Assumption 2 a further proposition can be deduced.

Proposition 2 For $R(t)>R^*$, $q(t)$ increases less than proportionally with $R(t)$, implying that Eq. 2 becomes non-linear.

---

[3] The dimensions are output in money value per period, orders in money value per number of processing units, and number of processing units passed per period, respectively. The average processing speed $v(t)$ is treated as a constant in t. Note that $R(t)$ captures all orders currently in the system, independently of how far they have gotten in their processing.

🕏 Springer

Proposition 2 follows directly from Assumption 1 stating that $v(t)$ decreases with growing $R(t)>R^*$.

This result points to a macroeconomic dynamic in which even the weak condition of a flow equilibrium is violated. To put it differently, the less than perfect degree of coordination no longer ensures a steady macro flow in the economy. The consequence of the lacking inter-temporal and intra-temporal complementarities are, in this case, the market shortages that are induced by a booming order activity. Increasingly growing order backlogs lead to bottlenecks at some places that begin to induce delays at other places. Firms start to have troubles with finishing projects and delivering on time. Tight schedules prevailing everywhere, substitutes may not quickly be available. The average processing speed can thus be significantly reduced until an expansion of the production capacity (resulting from revised investment decisions becoming effective) eventually allows a reduction of order backlogs. Lost time can be made up so that the average processing speed goes up again.

Once more an asymmetry turns up here, though one with more dramatic macroeconomic implications. As has been shown elsewhere (Witt and Sun 2002), once the critical range $R(t)>R^*$ is reached—i.e. for a non-linear specification of Eq. 2—under certain conditions, shortage induced cyclical variations of $q(t)$ can occur. Note that this is not possible as long as $R(t) \leq R^*$—i.e. for a linear specification of Eq. 2. (Cyclical variations in output, if they occur in that range, can of course have other causes.) An intra-temporal lack of complementarity between aggregate output and income, resulting in an effective demand failure that figures so prominently in Keynesian macroeconomics (see Leijonhufvud 1981), would be tantamount to a slump in the order volume and a later reduction in output. It would not, however, affect the processing speed and, hence, the flow equilibrium.

It is not clear, though, whether a situation with resources laid idle—unemployment of labor and capital—would indeed persist for long in the presence of an incessant process of structural change. Under such conditions, an inter-temporal complementarity between consumption expenditures and accumulation rates that would preserve a situation of effective demand failure is not very likely. One reason is that the two variables vary at different, and not perfectly coordinated, time scales. A further reason is that investment decisions in the past can affect not only the production capacity but also the order volume today in a way that is largely independent of the current income. To put it in Hayek's metaphorical terms: "... the volume of the stream will tend to swell or shrink in some degree because final demand, and demand for primary factors, will change at different rates, and at times even in opposite directions. The conventional picture on which the whole of Keynesian analysis is based which represents the connection between final demand and employment as analogous to the relation between the suction applied at one end of the pipe and its intake at the other end, is thus very misleading. Between the two lies an elastic or variable reservoir" (Hayek 1981, p. 4).

4 Macroeconomic dynamics and the flow equilibrium: an empirical investigation

To assess the empirical relevance of the analytical tools presented in the previous section, an attempt can be made to estimate the variation of the average order

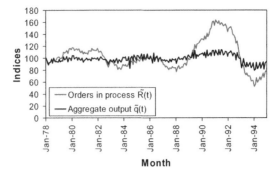

Fig. 1 Monthly variations of aggregate output and orders in process (West German Manufacturing Sector). *source:* German Federal Statistical Office and own calculations

processing speed on the basis of the time series of the macroeconomic variables in Eq. 2. If, in estimating the parameters of Eq. 2 for a time series over an extended period, a linear specification turns out to be statistically significant, the average processing speed is a constant. By Proposition 1 this would imply an economic situation during the chosen period of time which is characterized by a flow equilibrium. If, in contrast, the estimation supports a non-linear specification of Eq. 2, then, by Proposition 2, the $q(t)/R(t)$ ratio and, hence, $v(t)$ decrease for growing $R(t)$ values. In this case the flow equilibrium condition would not be satisfied.

In order to carry out this test, we use the monthly turnover data published by the German Federal Statistical Office for the West German manufacturing sector as the basis for measuring aggregate output. The time period chosen is January 1978 to December 1994. The orders in process as defined in Eq. 1 above are measured on the basis of the monthly data for the index of the orders $r^\sim$ (t) received by the manufacturing sector per month. This index time series has been compiled for West Germany by the German Federal Statistical Office only for the years 1978 to 1994. For measuring aggregate output over the same period of time, the monthly data for the index of aggregate output $q^\sim$ (t) of the West German manufacturing sector are used as published by the German Federal Statistical Office.[4] The indices have been transformed to eliminate seasonal variations and to remove the exponential trend from each of the time series. Finally, both indices have been normalized to a value $q^\sim$ $(t=$January 1978$)=R^\sim$ $(t=$January 1978$)=100$.

The time series of the index values $q^\sim$ (t) and $R^\sim$ (t) thus calculated are displayed in Fig. 1. The soaring growth of $R^\sim$ (t) in the period 1989–1991 reflects the effect of the German unification. The West German economy was not prepared for this extraordinary expansion in orders, as the modest increase in $q^\sim$ (t) over this period of time shows. The production capacity could simply not be adjusted rapidly enough. The equally dramatic subsequent decline of $R^\sim$ (t) indicates that the order expansion was indeed a singular event that did not create a lasting rise of the output level.

---

[4] Since both $r^\sim$ (t) and $q^\sim$ (t) are in index form, identical value for the two variables do not necessarily imply that the underlying absolute money values are identical. For the period 1978 to 1984, the German Federal Statistical Office has also calculated on a monthly basis an index for the money value of the stock of orders corresponding to $R(t)-r(t)$. This time series has been used here for calibrating $r^\sim$ (t) by means of the corresponding $q^\sim$ (t)-values.

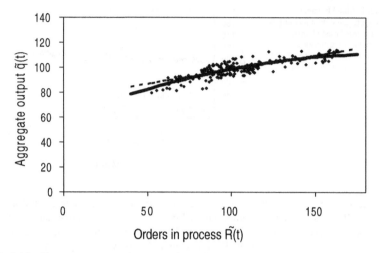

Fig. 2 Monthly aggregate output values regressed on orders in process

The question of whether or not the average processing speed in the West German economy was constant over the period 1978–1994 and, thus, whether or not the condition for a flow equilibrium was satisfied, can be answered by using the empirical data to estimate the relationship between $q^\sim(t)$ and $R^\sim(t)$. We test the quadratic form

$$q^\sim(t) = \alpha + \beta R^\sim(t) + \gamma[R^\sim(t)]^2 \tag{3}$$

that can be derived from Eq. 2.[5] Figure 2 presents the scatter diagram in which the $q^\sim$-values for each month are depicted against the corresponding $R^\sim$-values. Applying a standard OLS regression on Eq. 3, it turns out that the coefficient γ for the quadratic term is highly significant (see Table 1). The hypothesis that the average processing speed is constant in $R^\sim(t)$, i.e. the hypothesis of a linear relationship, can therefore be rejected.

The empirical findings for the manufacturing sector in West Germany provide evidence for the fact that, during the period 1978–1994, the economy was not in a flow equilibrium. Increases in the orders in process jammed the manufacturing sector, causing statistically significant delays in the average order processing speed. The singular order boom accompanying the German unification certainly contributed to this result, but may not have been the only reason.

At a deeper level, this finding points to the limitations of the price mechanism for coordinating the economic activities both inter-temporally and intra-temporally. It is not able to prevent or immediately control strong variations in orders received over time, so that the production capacity of the economy, determined by earlier

---

[5] Since the indices $q^\sim(t)$ and $R^\sim(t)$ are scalar transformations of the absolute values, their ratio is equivalent to $q(t)/R(t)=v(t)$ in Eq. 1.

Table 1. Regression results for Eq. 3	Parameters	Estimates	Significance
	α	59.970	0.000
	β	0.516	0.000
	γ	−0.001297	0.000
$R^2 = 0.686$			

accumulation and investment decisions, can become strained or even exhausted. The missing coordinating power casts doubts on the usefulness of the strong reliance in macroeconomic theorizing on the concept of market equilibria, as these may not be as significant for the dynamics of macroeconomic variables, as is often implicitly assumed. Moreover, the evidence found for the violation of the flow equilibrium condition raises additional questions regarding the explanation of the cyclical variations in growth of aggregate output in the manufacturing sector as shown in Fig. 1. For a non-linear shape of the graph of Eq. 2 it has been proved by Witt and Sun (2002) that endogenously emerging cyclical variations in aggregate output are possible. With the statistically significant quadratic term in Eq. 3 one cannot exclude the possibility that the order processing dynamics also contributes to business cycle fluctuations in the economy.

5 Conclusions

A problem to be tackled by an evolutionary approach to macroeconomics is to represent the disequilibrium dynamics in the markets resulting from the incessant structural change at the aggregate level. To this end, some notion of an equilibrium must be chosen as a frame of reference. In this paper, the concept of a flow equilibrium has been proposed as a solution to the problem. This concept only requires a balance in the flow of goods and services over time, but not necessarily an equilibrium in the aggregate markets at every point in time. Hence, it is a concept that fits the conditions of a less than perfect inter-temporal and intra-temporal coordination of the economy via the markets, as it is needed to account for the impact of structural change and adjustments. The concept has been illustrated by means of a metaphor suggested by the late F.A. Hayek. His motivation for using the metaphor highlights a development in his own work away from narrow market equilibrium notions to a broader, evolutionary view.

The macro flow dynamics corresponding to the notion of a flow equilibrium have been theoretically outlined. As it turned out, an approach like this draws attention to variables not usually considered in macroeconomic theorizing. These variables relate to the volume of orders, the order processing (production) capacity, and the order processing speed. In a flow perspective, these are decisive for the output dynamics. By a simple specification of the relationships between them, it has been possible to derive two core hypotheses. One concerns the necessary condition for a flow equilibrium, the other focuses on the critical behavior of the velocity variable.

Finally, the paper explored the empirical evidence for flow equilibria occurring at the macroeconomic level. On the basis of time series data for the West German manufacturing sector 1978 – 1994, the velocity variable has been estimated. It has been shown that the condition for a flow equilibrium was not satisfied for the time period under consideration. From earlier work (Witt and Sun 2002) it is known that, in this case, cyclical variations of aggregate output can occur. The empirical findings therefore also provide evidence for the possibility that flow equilibria play an important role for the relationships between structural change and business cycle phenomena.

References

Amendola M, Gaffard J-L (1998) Out of equilibrium. Clarendon, Oxford

Amendola M, Gaffard J-L (2003) Persistent unemployment and co-ordination issues: an evolutionary perspective. J Evol Econ 13:1–27

Amendola M, Gaffard J-L, Saraceno F (2005) Technical progress, accumulation of capital and financial constraints: is the productivity paradox really a paradox. Struct Chang Econ Dyn 16:243–261

Baumol WJ, Benhabib J (1989) Chaos: significance, mechanisms, and economic applications. J Econ Perspect 3:77–105

Fagerberg J, Verspagen B (2002) Technology-gaps, innovation-diffusion and transformation: an evolutionary interpretation. Res Policy 31:1291–1304

Fagerberg J, Verspagen B, Caniels M (1997) Technology growth and unemployment across European regions. Reg Stud 31:457–466

Foster J (1987) Evolutionary macroeconomics. Allen & Unwin, London

Foster J (1992) The determination of the sterling M 3, 1963–88: an evolutionary macroeconomic approach. Econ J 02:481–496

Foster J, Wild Ph (1999) Econometric modelling in the presence of evolutionary change. Camb J Econ 23:749–770

Hayek FA (1941) The pure theory of capital. Routledge, London

Hayek FA (1978) Competition as a discovery procedure. In: Hayek FA (ed) New studies in philosophy, politics, economics and the history of ideas. Routledge, London, pp 179–190

Hayek FA (1981) The flow of goods and services. Lecture at L.S.E., January 27, 1981

Hayek FA (1984) Der Strom der Güter und Leistungen. Walter-Eucken-Institut, Vorträge und Aufsätze No. 63, Tübingen: Mohr-Siebeck

Hayek FA (1988) In: Bartely WW III (ed) The fatal conceit: the errors of socialism. Routledge, London

Helbig D (1995) Improved fluid-dynamic model for vehicular traffic. Phys Rev, E 51:3164–3169

Hicks JR (1973) Capital and time. Clarendon, Oxford

Leijonhufvud A (1981) Information and coordination—essays in macroeconomic theory. Oxford University Press, Oxford

Los B, Verspagen B (2006) The evolution of productivity gaps and specialization patterns. Metroeconomica 57:464–493

McCormick BJ (1992) Hayek and the Keynesian avalanche. Harvester Wheatsheaf, New York

Metcalfe JS, Foster J, Ramlogan R (2006) Adaptive economic growth. Camb J Econ 30:7–32

Nelson RR, Winter SG (1982) An evolutionary theory of economic change. Harvard University Press, Cambridge, Mass

Ruelle D (1991) Chaotic evolution and strange attractors. Cambridge University Press, Cambridge

Schumpeter JA (1942) Capitalism, socialism and democracy. Harper, New York

Silverberg G, Verspagen B (1995) Long term cyclical variations of catching up and falling behind—an evolutionary model. J Evol Econ 5:209–227

Witt U, Sun G-Z (2002) Myopic behavior and cycles in aggregate output. Jahrbuecher fuer Nationaloekonomie und Statistik 222:366–376

[14]

J Evol Econ (2003) 13: 77–94

Journal of **Evolutionary**

Economics

© Springer-Verlag 2003

Economic policy making
in evolutionary perspective[*]

Ulrich Witt

Max-Planck-Institute for Research into Economic Systems, 07745 Jena, Germany
(e-mail: witt@mpiew-jena.mpg.de)

Abstract. Economic policy making is discussed from three different angles: the
political economy of actual policy making ("what policy does do"), the analysis
of policy instruments for given ends ("what policy could do"), and the debate on
policy goals and their legitimization ("what policy ought to do"). Center stage in
the evolutionary perspective is new, positive and normative knowledge which is
unfolding during the policy making process and in its aftermath. It is argued that
this implies regularities and constraints which extend and modify the comparative-
static interpretations of public choice theory, economic policy making theory, and
social philosophy.

Key words: Evolutionary economics – Economic policy making – Policy advice
– Policy goals – Public choice theory – Regulation

JEL Classification: A11, B41, D72, D78, E61, L50

1 Introduction

Evolutionary economics has been able to establish itself as a distinct research
program which can claim to offer new insights in many fields of economics (cf., e.g.,
Nelson, 1995; Witt, 2001a; Cantner and Hanusch, 2002). However, what has so far
only rarely been addressed as an own object of theoretical reflections in evolutionary
economics is the theory of economic policy making. In part this neglect may be
due to a rather controversial assessment of the effectiveness of policy interventions
(cf., e.g., such diverse statements as those in Hayek, 1978a; Gerybadze, 1992;

---

[*] The author should like to thank three anonymous referees of this journal and the editor for helpful
comments on an earlier version of the paper.

Metcalfe, 1994; Pelikan, 2003). Yet policy interventions are so pervasive in all modern economies that they cannot be ignored. In order to come to terms with this fact and to develop a foundation for an evolutionary theory of economic policy making, it is useful to distinguish between three different angles from which policy making can be scientifically approached. The first is the explanatory approach to the political economy of actual policy making epitomized by the question "what does economic policy making do?" The second angle is that of theoretical reflections on instrumental policy options characterized by the question "what could economic policy making do?" The third angle is that of a normative debate on political goals and their legitimization expressed by the question "what ought economic policy making do?"

Each of the questions alludes to a different level of the theory of economic policy making. Each of the different levels represents an own field of vast research: political economy and public choice, applied, or instrumental, economic theorizing, and normative social philosophy. What new insights can an evolutionary perspective contribute to the ongoing research in those fields? Where and why can it be expected to make a difference compared to established views? The present paper tries to outline an answer to these questions. As will turn out, the evolutionary approach is *not* likely to imply an entirely new political economy, nor is it likely to furnish the policy maker with *specific* new instruments or normative foundations. Instead, it will be claimed that what is really different is the framing of the policy problems. In an evolutionary perspective, during the process of policy making, and in its aftermath, the positive and normative knowledge that informs the actions of the agents involved can change through experience and induced inventive learning. Accordingly, at each of the different levels of the theory of economic policy making the time horizon in tracking causes and effects and in assessing means-ends relationships needs to be extended to account for the repercussions of the changes induced in the agents' knowledge constraints.

To substantiate these claims the paper offers a discussion of some insights that can be derived from approaching each of the three different levels from an evolutionary perspective. Section 2 inquires into economic policy making from the angle of public choice theory or, more generally, political economy. Section 3 then turns to instrumental policy analysis – the hypothetical or practical application of economic theory to achieve given ends – which economists engage in when they derive "policy implications" from their theoretical reflections. It is explained, with the use of an example, why the evolutionary approach appraises the effects of particular policy measures quite differently from the way they are assessed by the usual comparative-static instrumental policy analysis. In Sect. 4 the normative foundations of economic policy making are briefly considered. The argumentation here quickly crosses the borderline between economics and moral philosophy and leads to some philosophical reflections on the implications of evolutionary thought more generally. In each of the sections the focus is on the process of learning about facts on the one hand and values or goals on the other. Since each of the parties involved in, and affected by, policy making is exposed to experience and may have incentives to search for novel action, the analysis must consider the changing knowledge of both the policy maker(s) and of the agent(s) affected by the policy measures implemented. Section 5 offers the conclusions.

2 Explaining the process of policy making

A first way of dealing with economic policy making involves the question of *what economic policy making actually does*. This means that the approach of the theory of economic policy making is descriptive and explanatory. The intention of research done here is to record the actual activities of policy makers and to explain why and how they are carried out. Since Schumpeter's theory of democracy (Schumpeter, 1942, ch. 22) a huge body of theory focusing on public choices that are being made has emerged (cf. Mueller, 1993, for a survey). It offers explanations for a wide range of policy related phenomena including democratic voting and government behavior. As is well known, the paradigmatic assumption here is that self-interest governs political behavior (and, hence, policy making) no less than it is supposed to govern economic behavior. A government's policy making is thus connected to a political process in which separate, vested interests are pursued inside and outside government under given constitutional and judicial constraints. Not surprisingly, the self-interest assumption induces a rather critical attitude towards instrumental (or "technocratic") views of the role of government as they underlie many interventionist policy recommendations.[1] Setting the wide-spread preoccupation with market failure in perspective, public choice theory argues about "policy failure". The latter is attributed to the fact that in politics separate interests are pursued and that defects in the constitutional set-up, in voting rules, judicial practices, etc. cause outcomes which often enough turn out to even run counter the goals actually pursued.

What new insights can be gained here by adopting an evolutionary perspective? There seems to be no reason to question or even reject public choice theory's realism with respect to the existence of separate interests in politics and their implications. To the contrary, an evolutionary approach suggests enhancing realism by adding the dimension of historical time to the picture, a dimension that allows the consequences of changing knowledge constraints to be accounted for. Most of public choice theory still centers around the equilibrium-oriented, comparative-static methodology and, correspondingly, assumes perfect or almost perfect information. But this assumption is a fiction. Voters, interest group members, and a policy makers – as much as everyone else – have bounded rationality. Because they lack perfect knowledge these agents are likely to try to improve their knowledge. But since their learning takes time, bounded rationality transcends the boundaries of a static representation of choice problems, be they private or public.

---

[1] Since the times of mercantilism such views have been influential, if not dominant, in the theories of economic policy making and public finance. In fact, even today, economists adopting the instrumental approach – to be discussed in the next section – often implicitly assume that policy makers do not pursue any interests of their own. They are supposed to intervene where markets fail to achieve certain goals or the hypothesized social optimum spontaneously. In some thought experiments, policy maker have even been portrayed as benevolent dictators.

The implications of bounded rationality and social cognitive learning

At any time, agents involved in the making of economic policy – just like agents being affected by political action – have limited factual knowledge of the means at their disposal, of means-ends relationships, and of possible effects they will have to face. They also hold incomplete views of the values, ends, and interests they believe in and find desirable. This is the result of their constrained attention and information processing capacity. It forces them to be highly selective in their learning. Some information receives attention and has a chance of affecting their current beliefs while other information is ignored or neglected. But precisely because in the past attention has been directed to only some information, it may also be possible to discover hitherto ignored information and to change perceptions and beliefs over time, sometimes even dramatically. Attention may be shifted. Likewise, certain values, norms, and ends receive the individuals' attention and may arouse their (com-) passion while other normative standards are ignored or neglected. With attention being shifted over time, normative perceptions and frames may be revalued.[2]

Both, selective attention processes and the information on which learning focuses are in many respects socially contingent – an often neglected concomitant of bounded rationality. Individual knowledge is acquired not least through communication with, and observations of, the social environment (for a survey, cf. Bandura, 1986). Newly emerging information, be it about problems, actions, values, goals, instruments, or constraints, can disseminate throughout a community or polity if it attracts sufficient attention. This may happen by way of a decentralized, direct face-to-face communication within the community or through a more centralized information dissemination by some mass media. As a result, normative and factual information is often processed in parallel by the members of a population. A characteristic feature of such parallel communication processes is that they are subject to "agenda-setting" effects (Schnabl, 1991), indicating that societal communication is highly selective too. The agenda-setting effect means that, at a given time, in social communication only a few of a vast number of potentially positively or negatively valued topics are actually processed while the rest is ignored.

This is important for understanding the conditions under which a public opinion is formed and under which collective action can be organized. As explained elsewhere (Witt, 1996a), in order for some policy item to attract sufficient public attention in a self-amplifying process, a "critical mass" of people communicating that policy item within their individual networks must be reached.[3] Since the less public attention and support they attract, the less influence separate interests usually have on actual policy making, there is a strong incentive for all interest groups to participate in the communication and agenda setting process. Not surprisingly, the communication and agenda setting process is subject to highly competitive

---

[2] An obvious implication of potentially shifting attention processes is a "path-dependency" (David, 1993) in the evolving values, norms, and ends.

[3] As a result of the selective channeling of public attention, beliefs, convictions, and ideologies are socially shared and become a characteristic of groups, communities, and polities. But the prevalence of some belief, conviction, or ideology over other ones is potentially fragile. Prevalence may rapidly break down once a critical mass of community members openly converts to rivaling notions (cf. Kuran, 1997).

influences from interest groups. The consequences of selective communication, social-cognitive learning, and shifting constraints at the levels of both factual and normative knowledge can thus be expected to play a central role in an evolutionary approach to explaining the actual political process.

Policy making as a collective learning process

Let us turn to the policy maker(s) and the actual policy making process first. Here it is often difficult to disentangle the processes of learning about facts from those of learning about values or goals, but the selectiveness of problem perceptions and agenda effects are clearly present in both cases. This has been highlighted in an exemplary case study by Hutter (1986) for the political process that led to the (by international comparison rather belated) adoption of patent law in Italy in the 1960s. Social networks – Hutter calls them "conversation circles" – had previously been established between interest groups, politicians, and lawyers. These are shown to have crucially affected the outcome of public opinion formation and, ultimately, of the political and legislative measures taken. Hutter's case is one of selectively shifting factual and normative knowledge constraints on the part of policy makers and interest groups affected by the policy outcome (the patent regulation). The interactive learning and adaptation process made a compromise between divergent separate interests feasible. It may be inferred that, had different networks been formed earlier, communication might have pushed opinion formation and policy making in a different direction – an obvious instance of "path-dependency".

Similarly, in an empirical study of the evolution of regulatory policy in Switzerland Meier and Mettler (1988) were able to demonstrate the significance of the interactions between problem perception, growing knowledge, and the pursuit of separate interests on the part of the involved legislative bodies, interest groups, and the media for the actual shaping of policies.[4] Olson (1965) is right in that separate political interests do need to materialize in some form of collective action. However, before it comes to organizing collective action, the separate interests must be articulated in the first place. This implies an often complex process of collective attribution of meaning to political issues, because agents affected by a certain economic or social problem do not necessarily, or easily, agree on what their true interests are and whether and how they can be pursued. As Meier and Durrer (1992) argue, emotional affection – fears and disappointments – play an important role at this level. They are a strong *agens movens* in successfully organizing collective action capable of attracting public attention. Moreover, they also play a crucial role in the later process of actual policy making which usually involves complicated, multi-stage negotiations with other interest groups, legislative representatives, and bureaucrats. The success of separate interests in remaining on the public agenda, in resisting reinterpretations and revaluations, and eventually in effecting favorable policy interventions is correlated with the emotional potential these interests can arouse.

---

[4] For an English summary of the "cognitive evolutionary model of economic policy making" developed by Meier and his school, cf. Slembeck (1997).

As these examples show, in actual policy making, learning by the policy maker(s) about facts and learning about values or goals are usually interactive processes. The same holds for the agents or interest groups who are, or expect to be, affected by concrete policy measures. Indeed, the very essence of reaching compromises among and between policy making bodies and interest groups is often a mutual recognition of the likely effects (i.e. of facts) and of the intensity and legitimacy of the interests behind the pursuit of certain goals (i.e. of values or norms).Learning on both levels can lead to at least a certain degree of acceptance of a proposed policy measure and its intended impact. Persuasion is, after all, an important element in the political learning process. Again, the social-cognitive underpinnings of the communication process with which persuasion can be attempted imply a critical mass phenomenon. Once it has been possible to convince a critical mass of voters of some policy it is usually much easier to persuade even more people.

Political entrepreneurship and the role of the political economist

It is important to note that, wherever social-cognitive learning implies critical mass phenomena, the actual bringing together of the critical mass amounts to organizing a collective action. Accordingly, it may be claimed that two features need to be recognized in an evolutionary perspective on the process of actual policy making. One feature is the diverse processes of factual and normative learning, both by policy makers and those affected, which intervene in economic policy making. The other feature is the crucial role of those agents who engage in organizing the collective actions that lead to learning about, and adoption and/or support of, certain political values, goals, and measures. In democratic institutional settings, a form in which such "agents of collective action" appear is political entrepreneurship. Political actors compete for a majority of votes in elections for government office and, ultimately, for being able to engage in concrete policy making. This competition may be seen as forcing onto the political actors a "vicarious" attitude of trying to anticipate and serve the preferences and intentions of the electorate – the analog to the vicarious role entrepreneurs adopt in serving their customers in the markets (cf., e.g., Schumpeter, 1942, ch. 22; Wohlgemuth, 2003). In view of this analogy, and given the pivotal role attributed to entrepreneurs in Schumpeterian innovation economics, political entrepreneurship may also be considered to figure prominently in the evolutionary approach to economic policy making. Indeed, political entrepreneurs seem to be an integral part of the democratic process. They participate in advocating and gaining support for new policies and other policy innovations and act as mediators of those innovations by channeling them through the various voting procedures.

A question different from that of seeing through political innovations in the democratic process is where the ideas about policy innovations originate from. Opinions, public beliefs, and ideologies that shape the (self-) perception of the political actors do not fall from heaven, nor are they usually created by political entrepreneurs. They rather emanate from the societal communication, learning, and opinion formation processes in which the ideas of agitators, preachers, prophets, philosophers, and many others – among them, not least, political economists – are influential. Take a political economist who is arguing, pleading, or even crusading, for some policy concept or plan. It is remarkable how many economists find it worthwhile to offer their political concepts or proposals concerning the solution of certain economic problems and/or advance of the common good. Yet they have given little, if any, thought to the question of how their proposals can develop an impact on actual policy making.

In the explanatory approach to economic policy making some hypotheses should be included which allow to reflect the political economist's role (cf. Witt, 1992). In a world of perfectly informed policy makers who are determined to follow their own private interests, as often assumed in static public choice theory, the role would be difficult to explain. Not so, however, in the evolutionary perspective in which bounded rationality, social-cognitive learning, and competitive opinion formation processes are acknowledged as the framing conditions of policy making. These conditions leave the room which political economists and many others try to use for their persuasive activities. The latter usually start within some sub-cultural, e.g. academic or political, circles. Within comparatively small groups like these, it is easier to attract attention, to convince people, and to gain their support. Since the members of such circles also simultaneously participate in wider communication networks, the political economist's ideas are likely to be diffused further, the more persuaded and, perhaps, emotionally affected people are. The ideas may be taken up by political entrepreneurs as a basis for their own activities. Diffusion processes like these of course involve a vast number of historical contingencies. It is therefore difficult to predict what their outcome will be. However, already a vague chance of eventually influencing public opinion and policy making seems to suffice to motivate many political economists to engage in pleading and crusading for their concepts and proposals.

3 Instrumental policy analysis

A second approach to the theory of economic policy making is instrumental policy analysis. It is epitomized by the question of *what economic policy making could (try to) do.* In this approach, economic theory is hypothetically or practically applied to solve policy problems. This is a widely pursued practice also in evolutionary economics. The intention is to offer advice to the policy maker, much as engineers offer technological advice to clients who wish, say, to erect a building. Unlike in the approach to economic policy making discussed in the previous section, here the policy makers' goals are usually taken as given. The motives and interests why these goals are pursued are not made an object of analysis. What does the evolutionary perspective contribute to this second approach? Does it propose specific new instruments, say for monetary policy, fiscal policy, or competition policy? Does it imply a different attitude towards policy making – e.g. a skeptical one as argued by some authors who have been mentioned in the introduction? Does it lead to significantly different policy conclusions and, if so, by what standards could these be considered improvements? For some of these questions, no answer is currently available simply because no corresponding evolutionary theories exist.[5] For other questions, an answer would require going into the details of (existing) specific evolutionary theories and deriving and evaluating their policy implications. Since this is not possible here, a more general assessment must suffice.

Like in the previous section, the basic premises of the evolutionary perspective provide the point of departure: the hypothesis of bounded rationality and its corollary, the hypothesis that, due to learning, the knowledge constraints of both policy makers and the agents affected by the policy can systematically change in the process of policy making. In the evolutionary perspective, instrumental policy analysis therefore faces two problems which will be discussed in turn. First, how can the consequences of changing knowledge constraints be accounted for in the analysis of policy measures? Second, and more specifically, given that the means-ends dichotomy informs the entire policy analysis approach, does that dichotomy have to be modified in the presence of learning about facts and values or goals?

Accounting for induced learning in economic policy analysis

Instrumental policy analysis presupposes that the theories applied have predictive power. However, the predictive power of a theory used in instrumental policy analysis is flawed *per se*, if the theory fails to account for potential repercussions which a policy measure can have because of the learning it induces. Such repercussions are likely to occur when people are affected by a policy measure in a way that changes their incentives. For instance, depending on the kind of policy measure, incentives to search for novel actions may be weakened or strengthened. Often policy measures may elicit search for new ways of acting because people are unfavorably affected by the measures and seek to neutralize or avoid that effect. Indeed, historically, on many occasions people have been induced to search for a "creative response" (Schumpeter, 1947), and policy measures imposed on them have figured prominently among the causes. A theory which incompletely reflects the reactions of the agents affected by the policy measure cannot inform the policy maker about the full range of consequences of that policy measure. In some cases the repercussions may directly contravene the specific policy making goal(s). In other cases no such directly impairing effect may occur, but other goal(s) may be affected adversely.

To give an example of a policy measure that affects the incentives for learning and behavior adaptation consider a text book case of a market interventions, the subsidy payment on unit costs in some industry. The comparative-static, price-theoretic analysis suggests that the subsidy will shift the industry supply curve so that, in a new market equilibrium, a larger quantity is produced and is sold at a lower price. No further learning and behavior adaptation is assumed. Yet that is likely to occur, and even though it does not necessarily undermine the specific

---

[5] There is no evolutionary monetary or fiscal theory, to take that example, that would allow the instrumental policy implications to be discussed. Nor is it entirely clear – even after almost 50 years of debate on "Schumpeterian competition" – what an evolutionary approach to competition theory implies with regard to possible policy instruments (cf., e.g. Kerber, 2003).

policy goal immediately and directly, detrimental effects are likely to crop up in the longer run. In order to theoretically keep track of the repercussions, the particular circumstances in which the policy measure is implemented have to be considered more closely. In the case of the subsidy payment they can be sketched as follows. The typical market situation in which interest groups pressure for subsidies and policy makers are inclined to grant them is one in which there is a tendency for politically significant producers to be driven out of the market. The causes usually are inflexible cost structures and/or competitive pressure on the prices. A situation like that regularly occurs at a stage of an industry's life cycle when an industry's overall market volume stagnates or shrinks.[6]

If the industry were left alone, that stage of the industry life cycle would create strong incentives for the resource owners in the industry to reorient, diversify, innovate, or search for relocating their resources. If the subsidy is granted, however, competitive pressure on the resource owners is reduced. By the same token the incentive to search for innovations or new business opportunities outside the market is weakened or eliminated. The aim pursued with the subsidy payment – to keep these resources in business – is attained (at the taxpayer's expense), at least temporarily. However, many of the cost reducing process innovations, many product innovations which increase the overall market volume, and many relocations of resources that might otherwise have been elicited do not occur. Since industries not enjoying subsidy payments continue to search for innovations, they tend to increasingly drain resources with innovative potential, like creative and entrepreneurial labor force or venture capital, from the subsidized industries. As a consequence, a division of labor emerges in the longer run through which some industries enhance their innovative capacity while other industries increasingly lose it. The competitive situation of the subsidized industry keeps on worsening. Due to the induced detrimental behavior adaptation, the policy of subsidy payments sooner or later turns out not to be sustainable.

It is not difficult to also find examples of policy measures which induce learning, because they create incentives to search for a creative response. And these examples again show what difference it makes, whether induced learning is, or is not, accounted for in the instrumental policy analysis. Consider the effects of a quantity tax on some particular item. All that the comparative static analysis predicts here is that the tax will shift the industry supply curve so that, in a new market equilibrium, a smaller quantity is sold at a higher price and a deadweight loss due to taxation will have to be incurred. However, if induced (inventive) learning is considered, a whole bundle of tax evasion activities can be expected to be tried which can cause many more reactions than just shifting the industry supply and demand curves further. If the tax is motivated by the desire to raise tax revenues, this will surely be counteracted by some of the effects of induced learning. If the tax is motivated by the policy maker's desire to curb the consumption of some item (like, e.g., alcohol), the consumers' induced substitution of the taxed item may lead

---

[6] Cf., e.g., Klepper (1996). It is also a significant concomitant of trade liberalization, or "globalization", which allows low cost producers from abroad to enter domestic markets in which high cost producers used to operate without such competition.

to an increase consumption of items even less desired by the policy maker (like, e.g., self-produced, unsafe alcohol or designer drugs).

Procedural devices to mitigate policy making limitations

A desideratum in an evolutionary approach to instrumental policy analysis thus is to go sufficiently deeply into the particular, historical circumstances under which a policy measure shall be implemented in order to be able (i) to assess how and how likely the measure affects the incentives to learn and search and (ii) to anticipate potential longer term consequences of the changes in incentives and possible creative responses. From an evolutionary point of view it needs to be admitted, however, that in the case of induced learning and creative responses it will often be impossible to predict the outcome and, hence, the consequences for, or the repercussions on, the chosen policy measures. Due to the epistemological boundaries implied by the very nature of novelty, instrumental policy analysis reaches its logical limitations here. For this reason, the notion that a policy maker could "engineer" some desirable state of affairs in the economy by choosing from a "tool box" of policy measures[7] is questionable, if not illusionary. The induced inventive learning challenges the effectiveness of instrumental policy analysis and sets narrow limits to it.[8]

Nevertheless, for more modest policy goals, the theory may suffice to design policy measures that avoid creating incentives for inventive learning. An example are technology policy measures like policy moderated coordination and standardization efforts (Gerybadze, 1992) or measures enhancing the diffusion of innovations (Foray and Llerena, 1996; Metcalfe and Georghiou, 1997). Thus, even though "engineering" visions of instrumental policy analysis seem mistaken, an evolutionary perspective on economic policy making does not imply a verdict against *any* kind of instrumental policy analysis. Moreover, from an evolutionary point of view, special procedural devices for policy making can be identified which seem particularly well attuned to the possibility of induced learning on the part of the agents affected by policy measures. These procedures and methods amount to a political trial and error process which enables the policy maker to learn, too, and to readjust to the responses that were triggered earlier in the process.

The basic idea was launched already by Popper (1960, ch. 24) with his notion of "piecemeal policy". It has been expressed more recently in more detail by Metcalfe (1994) and his conception of "adaptive policy making", which explicitly wants to account for the fact that there is no omniscient policy maker. The inbuilt readjustment procedures may avoid, or at least reduce, unintended and undesirable effects of policy measures. However, the flexibility which can be gained by such

[7] This notion was, for a while, successfully propagated, particularly in the context of macroeconomic policy making, for instance by Theil (1961) and Tinbergen (1964).

[8] In a similar vein, Hayek (1978a) has castigated the "pretence of knowledge" underlying the idea that, by a proper choice of policy measures, policy making could "fix" specific states or outcomes of the markets in an interventionist manner, cf. the discussion in Streit (1998). This "Hayekian impossibility theorem", as Wegner (1997) has called it, is sometimes misread as a dismissive attitude towards policy making *in toto* which, as Wegner demonstrated, it is not.

procedural devices designed to cope with the above mentioned policy making limitations raises a new question. When it has been claimed above that, by the policy
maker's learning, both her/his factual and normative knowledge may change, then
it may now be asked whether and how the relationships between the two sets of
knowledge are affected. The question relates to the second problem to be addressed
in this section, the distinction between means and ends which is characteristic for
instrumental policy analysis.

The means-ends-dichotomy in procedural policy making devices

Does the means-ends dichotomy have to be modified in an evolutionary perspective?
To recall, the distinction between means and ends was invented to keep separate two
logically different kinds of statements. These are, on the one side, factual statements
concerning the effects of instruments and, on the other side, normative statements
about the legitimacy or desirability of goals and their underlying values and norms.
The former statements express the effects of a policy measure, e.g., in terms of a
properly defined ordinal or cardinal measuring scale. These statements may be true
or false. Hence, the criterion for assessing them is their empirical validity which
can be verified inter-personally. For normative statements, by contrast, no such
inter-personal validity can be established. True or false is not a relevant criterion
for them.

Now consider an adaptive or piecemeal policy making procedure in which a
certain measure is implemented to set the course for a certain goal. The policy
maker gathers information to learn about the consequences, i.e. finds out what the
pursuit of the particular goal means in terms of the changes factually triggered.
Hence, means and ends become better understood by the policy maker and the
public, both as a matter of fact and of, e.g., emotional experience. For example,
if the proclaimed goal is a "more just" income distribution, it is only with the
experience made with some concrete redistributive policy measure that the policy
maker finds out what kind of "justice" actually results (which is a factual question)
and whether its observed consequences are indeed considered to be worthwhile
(which is a normative question). It may turn out that other goals are also being
affected by a chosen policy, and these unforeseen, additional effects need to be
evaluated. The experience made will most probably be one of trade-offs which
may induce revisions and revaluations at the level of the goals. A prominent case
are inconsistencies or conflicts between the attainment of short run goals and the
attainment of long run goals which are discovered only later.[9]

The discovery of normative conflicts between goals almost surely feeds back
to the assessment of the instruments. Does this imply that the boundaries between
means and ends are blurred? As far as the *logical* distinction between the factual
and the normative level is concerned, this not the case. The implications of the
feedback on the level of the means can still be discussed in a descriptive language.
In an evolutionary perspective on policy making, including the procedural devices

---

[9] Cf. Pelikan (2003). The subsidy policy discussed above is an example.

to mitigate policy limitations, the means-ends dichotomy can therefore be maintained.[10] What may have to be revised, however, is the common belief that, because of the logical distinction, there is always also a *factual* separability between the scientific discussion on instrumental policy advice and the political debate on the normative assessment of goals. The feedback relationship between the factual and the normative level which the procedural devices for policy making imply tends to undermine the separation. The economist as a scientific advisor will factually find it difficult to confine her-/himself to the instrumental level, receiving the goals to be pursued from some politically legitimized decision maker.

The reason is the scientific advisor's and the policy maker's selectiveness in perceiving and tracking those feedbacks – a consequence of their bounded rationality. This may mean that the economist as scientific advisor can keep track of, and selectively draw attention to, some goal conflicts emerging from the use of instruments, while not alerting the policy maker or the public of others. The basis for selectively tracking some goals while neglecting others are implicit value judgements. With his/her value judgements the scientific advisor may thus influence the selective perception of goals and goal conflicts on the public agenda. If so, the advisor's involvement in policy making is factually going far beyond the commonly endorsed division of tasks between the politically legitimized process of determining the goals on the one hand and scientific economic policy engineering on the basis of the given goals on the other hand.

From an evolutionary point of view, the adequate interpretation of the division of tasks between science and politics, and hence of instrumental policy analysis, is therefore a quite different one. In line with the political economist's role discussed in the previous section, instrumental policy analysis should be understood as a part of a collective learning process in which policy makers, interest groups, the public, and economists as interpreters and advisors are involved. Whoever wants to influence this collective learning process needs to attract the public's attention (that follows agenda setting effects) to the particular goal conflicts (s)he is interested in. No wonder, this is what interest groups and also various, sometimes self-appointed, economic advisors try to achieve. Conversely, it may be concluded that, to keep potential manipulation in check, plurality in the debate on short-term and long-term means-ends-relationships is indispensable. Theoretically, all claims relating to the effects of policy measures on policy goals can be contested scientifically. Practically, however, scientific contestability depends on the plurality of contributions both allowed and made available in the public discourse. As should have become apparent, the evolutionary approach to economics may well be considered an im-

---

[10] Objections were made early on to the possibility of making a neat distinction between means at the factual level and ends at the normative level. Myrdal (1933) claimed that the distinction is invalid because policy instruments may have an intrinsic normative value, e.g. because their implementation may be a goal in its own right. However, policy instruments with such an intrinsic value may be treated as instruments which can serve at least two (potentially conflicting) goals. This means that in such a case the instrument's effects (or goal attainment) has to be measured on a multi-dimensional scale. Even with this complication, the corresponding statements are still either true or false. In contrast, the question of how much one of the relevant goals should be valued in comparison to other ones, and thus the desirable proportions for the attainment of the goals, are a normative issue. Hence, the argument does not contradict the logical distinction between the two levels.

portant prerequisite for, and a source of concepts and hypotheses suggested to, such a discourse.

4 Reappraising the normative foundations

A third angle from which economic policy making can be approached scientifically is focusing on the question of *what policy making ought to do*. This is the level of the theory of economic policy making at which the ends or goals are discussed on the basis of normative judgements. Can the pursuit of some particular goal be legitimized and, if so, how? Which goals are compatible with one another and which ones are conflicting? This is, perhaps, the most controversial of the three approaches to the theory of economic policy making, yet it directly relates to the origins of economic theorizing in moral philosophy. What new insights can an evolutionary perspective contribute at this level, i.e. to the normative foundations of economic policy making? An exhaustive discussion is hardly possible here. However, the range of problems likely to be encountered in future research can perhaps be highlighted by elaborating on two points. The first relates to normative judgements evolutionary economics implicitly subscribes to when it is applied to policy advice – which, up to now, has happened mostly in connection with questions of R&D, technological progress, innovations, and growth. The second point relates to a more general problem. In the evolutionary perspective, the basis for normative judgements may change: ends and results of policy making are assessed in a way which itself evolves. What does this imply for the normative foundations of economic policy making?

Judgements on the outcome of evolution

It has to be admitted that moral philosophy has up to now not been a central concern in evolutionary economics.[11] The moral connotations even of a phenomenon as central to the evolutionary approach as the secular innovativeness of modern times are therefore still unclear. An implicit presumption in evolutionary economics and its policy making applications is that innovativeness – if it does not just invalidate policy efforts in the form of "creative responses" as discussed above – is, by and large, beneficial and therefore ought to be encouraged. However, on a closer look, this judgement is not so easy to justify. There is no guarantee that evolution, whether in nature or in the economy, will be beneficial in any particular sense. For good reasons, innovations – the trying out of new paths – have, in many traditional societies, and for most of mankind's history, been regarded as dangerous and, with few exceptions, unwelcome. It is only in modern industrial societies that this attitude has changed dramatically, and that the individuals have been freed from the previously prevailing rigid institutional constraints on their innovativeness. When measured in terms of per capita real income, which in these societies has been

---

[11] An exception is Hayek's theory of societal evolution (Hayek, 1988). However, for reasons discussed elsewhere (Witt, 1995), this theory has not been very widely adopted in evolutionary economics.

in soaring to an unprecedented extent, the consequences have up to now been extremely beneficial.

In the light of this past experience, economic policy making today encourages innovations *grosso modo*. Yet innovations can also have unpleasant consequences. For example, at least some members of society for at least some period in their life have to bear the consequences of the inevitable "pecuniary" externalities of innovations. They usually come in the form of devaluations of investments which people have made before the innovations occurred. This may often mean harsh losses of wealth and sometimes true hardship. Furthermore, there is always potential danger lurking in everything that has not previously been secured by experience. In this case, it is the danger of possible damages and social costs that may accrue to society from technological externalities of an innovation which neither the innovator nor society have anticipated.

An attempt to balance favorable and unfavorable consequences of innovations is confronted with all the problems of interpersonal comparisons well known in economics and, on top of this, with severe epistemological problems. While hardship and danger are unavoidable if innovativeness is to be encouraged, a faster pace of innovations is not sufficient to guarantee the material growth and increasing prosperity, even of the poor, which have been experienced in the past. The rising standard of living of the masses proclaimed by Schumpeter (1942, chs. 7 and 8) is a historical fact. But it would be a naive extrapolation to take it for granted also as a concomitant of future innovativeness. First, because the future balance of benefits and (social) costs of innovativeness cannot be anticipated. Second, because the personal distribution of any net benefits of innovativeness in the future is indeterminate. As has been explained elsewhere (Witt, 1996b), in view of these imponderables, quite elaborate theoretical constructions are necessary to derive a legitimization for normative judgements supporting a positive attitude towards innovations. Even these conditions presume the standard utilitarian framework of unchanging individual preferences, i.e. of unchanging constraints on normative knowledge. In the evolutionary perspective, that assumption is, of course, untenable.

Implications of co-evolving preferences for the common good

Since the days of Mandeville, economists have traditionally been concerned with the problem of the "common good", taking it as the criterion for determining what institutions, states of society, and what policy actions should be considered desirable. Although other foundations, e.g. relating to natural rights, would be possible, economists have always favored utilitarian interpretations of the common good. Modern utilitarians subscribe to what might be called a radical preference subjectivism.[12] On that basis, it is difficult to imagine that new factual knowledge that becomes available, and which people become used to, will not affect their preferences. If preferences are affected, however, this means that possibilities of action

---

[12] On its basis, the common good problem appears as a problem of aggregating autonomous, individual preferences in a properly chosen (set of) variable(s) and of identifying maxima, or at least relative improvements, in that variable(s), if alternative states or policy action are compared. Such a comparative statics exercise is manageable as long as individual preferences do not change.

(or, to put it that way, economic constraints) and preferences co-evolve – people face different states of their preferences, or different utility functions, at different points in time. Such a situation induces well-known utilitarian puzzles (see Sen, 1977; Elster, 1982). Not surprisingly, normative judgements on economic policy making in the presence of changing individual preferences have not yet been investigated.

In order to make progress with a non-standard utilitarian framework in which the basis for normative judgement itself evolves, a theory about how preferences are formed, and how, and under what conditions, they change over time would be necessary.[13] On the basis of such a theory it might be possible to assess the implications for the development over time of the well being of individuals and, hence, the common good. Again, an important part of such a theory is likely to be the explanation of the role of social interactions and agenda setting effects. We do not only cultivate our own tastes over a lifetime. We also try to educate those of others in a way we would (currently) prefer. The outcome of that complex social interaction process is highly unclear. The very possibility of such effects, together with the general malleability of individual preferences, suffices, however, to infer that, with respect to the normative level of argument, a strong relativism will result. Radical preference subjectivism and its more practical relatives, consumer sovereignty or, for that matter, voter sovereignty, may therefore no longer provide the relevant normative measuring rod. But a debate on what may instead be a proper frame of orientation for normative judgements about human choices is only just about to begin (cf. e.g. Binmore, 1998).

Perhaps, some form of a more objective utilitarian approach may re-emerge like that prevailing before the subjectivist revolution in economics at the end of the eighteenth century.[14] In such an approach, the likely future outcomes of economic evolution under different policy measures, including possible regulation of inno-vativeness, would not be assessed exclusively according to the current state of our preferences. Neither would be the efforts and costs of obtaining those outcomes. Educated guesses would rather have to be made about how we would assess the likely outcomes in the light of the probable future state of preferences. If there is then reason to believe that we may not feel happier after becoming used to the future achievements than we feel right now (after we have become used to our present achievements), the present efforts and costs to be expended may strike a different balance with the future outcomes. This is particularly true where policy measures cannot prevent onerous, unequally born, pecuniary and/or technological external-ities resulting from current innovative endeavors to improve well being. As may be guessed, to enter such reflections may entail a fresh look, from an evolutionary point of view, at a normative issue currently traded high in the economic policy making debate: the problem of sustainability (cf. Witt, 2000).

---

[13] Cf. Witt (2001b); it would seem a desideratum in evolutionary economics anyway.
[14] Cf. Warke (2000) for a characterization of that approach.

5 Conclusions

In this paper it has been argued that an evolutionary perspective on economic policy making has, first of all, to recognize the significance of the changing knowledge which the actors in the political arena have about desiderata and about the ways of achieving them. The crucial role of knowledge and, connected with this, the communication of new knowledge for economic policy making are the result of the narrow constraints on individual information processing capacity. Markets can account for these constraints by allowing decentralization and competitive special-ization in information generation and processing (Hayek, 1978b). Political action, in contrast, requires the formation of some collective decisions, particularly in democracies. The need to obtain political support and/or a majority of votes in elections sets natural limits to decentralization and specialization in the process-ing of political information. Accordingly, the societal communication and agenda setting process can deal selectively with only a few of an incalculable number of potentially positively or negatively valued topics and tends to ignore the rest. Since the less public attention and support they attract, the less influence separate inter-ests usually have on actual policy making, there is a strong incentive for all interest groups to participate in the communication and agenda setting process. Not sur-prisingly, the communication and agenda setting process is, and has always been, highly competitive.

The implications of changing knowledge constraints for the theory of economic policy making were discussed at three levels. The first level was that of the political economy of actual policy making ("what policy making does do"). The percep-tion of their political desiderata by the actors in the political arena and the ways these can be achieved change as a matter of experience. This kind of change may shape policy making in the longer run more significantly than the current short-run constellations of interests and power on which established theories of political econ-omy focus. The second level at which systematic changes in factual and normative knowledge are pivotal is that of instrumental policy analysis ("what policy making could do"). Assume that the implementation of some particular policy measures can induce systematic searching and learning efforts so that the agents intentionally or unintentionally affected by the measures may eventually come up with innova-tive (and, hence, non-anticipatable) responses. Then, the efficacy and suitability of particular policy measures may well appear quite different from the way they do when assessed on the basis of a standard comparative-static equilibrium analysis. The same holds true, of course, for the effects of systematic learning on the part of the policy maker(s). Finally, some implications at the normative level of economic policy committed to the idea of a 'good society' ("what policy making ought to do") were highlighted. An evolutionary perspective does not itself imply any normative conclusions. But the insight that factual and normative knowledge may change is likely to have an effect both on the possibilities of making normative judgements and on their content. The actual experience of some norms may affect norm pref-erences and value judgements. The insight that subjectively held norms and values are the result of earlier learning usually leads to a strong norm-relativism.

As it has turned out, to adopt an evolutionary perspective does not result in a wholesale rejection of what public choice theory, political economy, theoretical politics, and social philosophy have to say on economic policy making. However, those theories have to be extended and modified to account for the possibility of changing knowledge constraints. Correspondingly, the evolutionary perspective can also be expected to make a difference for the content of economic policy advice due to the fact that emphasis is shifted, problems are framed differently, new questions are raised, and the attitude towards, and the style of, policy making is changed. This will have to be proved, of course, in concrete and detailed policy analyses, something that could not be offered here in the limited space available.

References

Bandura A (1986) Social foundations of thought and action – a social cognitive theory. Prentice-Hall, Englewood Cliffs

Binmore K (1998) Just playing – game theory and the social contract II. MIT Press, Cambridge, MA

Cantner U, Hanusch H (2002) Evolutionary economics, its basic concepts and methods. In: Lim H, Park U K, Harcourt G C (eds) Editing economics – Essays in honor of Mark Perlman, pp 182–207. Routledge, London

David P A (1993) Path-dependence and predictability in dynamical systems with local network externalities: a paradigm for historical economics. In: Foray D G, Freeman C (eds) Technology and the wealth of nations, pp 208–231. Pinter, London

Elster J (1982) Sour grapes – utilitarianism and the genesis of wants. In: Sen A, Williams B (eds) Utilitarianism and beyond, pp 219–238. Cambridge University Press, Cambridge

Foray D, Llerena P (1996) Information structure and coordination in technology policy. Journal of Evolutionary Economics 6: 157–173

Gerybadze A (1992) The implementation of industrial policy in an evolutionary perspective. In: Witt U (ed) Explaining process and change – approaches to evolutionary economics, pp 151–173. Michigan University Press, Ann Arbor, MI

Hayek F A (1978a) The pretence of knowledge. In: Hayek F A, New studies in philosophy, politics, and economics, and the history of ideas, pp 23–34. Routledge & Kegan Paul, London

Hayek F A (1978b) Competition as a discovery procedure. In: Hayek F A, New studies in philosophy, politics, and economics, and the history of ideas, pp 179–190. Routledge & Kegan Paul, London

Hayek, F A (1988) The fatal conceit. Routledge, London

Hutter M (1986) Transaction costs and communication: a theory of institutional change applied to the case of patent law. In: von der Schulenburg J M, Skogh G (eds) Law and economics and the economics of legal regulations, pp 113–129. Kluwer, Dordrecht

Kerber W (2003) An international multi-level system of competition laws: federalism in antitrust. In: Drexl J (ed) The future of transnational antitrust – from comparative to common competition law. Kluwer, Boston (forthcoming)

Klepper S (1996) Entry, exit, growth and innovation over the product life cycle. American Economic Review 86: 560–581

Kuran T (1997) Private truths, public lies – the social consequences of preference falsification. Harvard University Press, Cambridge, MA

Meier A, Mettler D (1988) Wirtschaftspolitik: Kampf um Einfluß und Sinngebung. Paul Haupt, Bern

Meier A, Durrer K (1992) Ein kognitiv-evolutionäres Modell des wirtschaftspolitischen Prozesses. In: Witt U (ed.) Studien zur Evolutorischen Ökonomik II, pp 229–254. Duncker und Humblot, Berlin

Metcalfe J S (1994) Evolutionary economics and technology policy. Economic Journal 104: 931–944

Metcalfe J S, Georghiou L (1997) Equilibrium and evolutionary foundations of technology policy. University of Manchester, CRIC Discussion Paper, No. 3

Mueller D C (1993) The public choice approach to politics. Edward Elgar, Aldershot

Myrdal G (1933) Das Zweck-Mittel-Denken in der Nationaloekonomie. Zeitschrift fuer National-oekonomie 4: 305–329

Nelson R R (1995) Recent evolutionary theorizing about economic change. Journal of Economic Literature 33: 48–90

Olson M (1965) The logic of collective action. Harvard University Press, Harvard

Pelikan P (2003) Why economic policies need comprehensive evolutionary analysis. In: Pelikan P, Wegner G (eds) The evolutionary analysis of economic policy. Edward Elgar, Aldershot (forthcoming)

Popper K R (1960) The poverty of historicism. 2nd edn. Routledge and Kegan Paul, London

Schnabl H (1991) Agenda-diffusion and innovation. A simulation model. Journal of Evolutionary Economics 1: 65–85

Schumpeter J A (1942) Capitalism, socialism, and democracy. Harper & Brothers, New York

Schumpeter J A (1947) The creative response in economic history. Journal of Economic History 7: 149–159

Sen A (1977) Rational fools: a critique of the behavioral foundations of economic theory. Philosophy and Public Affairs 6: 317–144

Slembeck T (1997) The formation of economic policy: a cognitive-evolutionary approach to policy making. Constitutional Political Economy 8: 225–254

Streit M E (1998) Constitutional ignorance, spontaneous order and rule orientation: Hayekian paradigms from a policy perspective. In: Frowen S F (ed) Hayek: Economist and social philosopher – a critical retrospect, pp 37–58. MacMillan, London

Theil H (1961) Economic forecasts and policy. 2nd edn. North-Holland, Amsterdam

Tinbergen J (1964) Economic policy: principles and design. North-Holland, Amsterdam

Warke T (2000) A reconstruction of classical utilitarianism. Journal of Bentham Studies 3: unpaged (http://www.ucl.ac.uk/Bentham.Project)

Wegner G (1997) Economic policy from an evolutionary perspective. Journal of Theoretical and Institutional Economics 153: 485–509

Witt U (1992) The endogenous public choice theorist. Public Choice 73: 117–129

Witt U (1995) Schumpeter vs. Hayek: two approaches to evolutionary economics. In: Meijer G (ed) New perspectives on Austrian economics, pp 81–101. Routledge, London

Witt U (1996a) The political economy of mass media societies. Papers on Economics and Evolution, Max Planck Institute Jena, No. 9601

Witt U (1996b) Innovations, externalities and the problem of economic progress. Public Choice 89: 113–130

Witt U (2000) Genes, culture, and utility. Papers on Economics and Evolution, Max Planck Institute Jena, No. 0009

Witt U (2001a) Evolutionary economics: an interpretative survey. In: Dopfer K (ed) Evolutionary economics – program and scope, pp 45–88. Kluwer, Boston

Witt U (2001b) Learning to consume – a theory of wants and the growth of demand. Journal of Evolutionary Economics 11: 23–36

Wohlgemuth M (2003) Democracy as an evolutionary method. In: Pelikan P, Wegner G (eds) The evolutionary analysis of economic policy. Edward Elgar, Aldershot (forthcoming)

Printed and bound by CPI Group (UK) Ltd, Croydon, CR0 4YY

23/04/2025

14660978-0001